A Mother's Love

The Story of a Widow and Her Seven Children

A Mother's Love
The Story of a Widow and Her Seven Children

Scandinavia Publishing House
Drejervej 15,3 DK-Copenhagen NV
Denmark
www.scanpublishing.dk
info@scanpublishing.dk

A book by Yan Ling Ling
English translation by Yan Ling Ling
Edited by Josie Freer and Anne Katherine Clark
Graphic Design by Gao Hanyu
All rights reserved

ISBN: 9788771320237
Printed in China

A Mother's Love

The Story of a Widow and Her Seven Children

by Yan Ling Ling

SCANDINAVIA

CONTENTS

Foreword 7

The story of the Yan family in the newspaper 10

Yan Zi Zhen and Yong Chang Xiang trading company (1903—1956) 20

Yan Ze Gao and Chang Ming textile mill (1935—1955) 36

The career of San Sao, the widow in the Yan family (1955—1979) 168

The story on An Ning lane (1955—1970) 284

Painful memories (1970-1982) 352

Mama's final years (1978—1979) 508

Postscript 534

FOREWORD

I first met Ling Ling in 2007 when my wife and I visited a Danish
friend living in Kunming, China. We were invited to the home of Ling
Ling and her husband for a delicious Chinese meal. Ling Ling showed
us her old family photos and told us about the book she was writing
about her family's history and in particular about her mother's short but
extraordinary life.

Ling Ling shared how her mother became a widow when she was only
38 years old with 7 children ages two to sixteen. Ling Ling was only four
years old at that time. They were growing up under Mao's communist
regime and endured great suffering during the Cultural Revolution. I felt
this was an amazing and enlightening story, and I was very eager to read
this book.

In October 2009, I heard from Ling Ling that she had finished writing
her book and that the book had been published by China International
Culture Publishing (HK) in Hong Kong. She sent me a copy of the
book in Chinese. Although I was not able to read it, I looked through
all the old pictures and read the English outline of each chapter. I
was in awe of this family's history told by such engaging true stories.

I felt that it would be a very interesting book for others to read and gain a deeper understanding about Chinese landlords, rich peasants, counterrevolutionaries, evildoers, and rightists and their families during Mao's regime.

I decided to publish this book in English, so I asked Ling Ling to translate it, which took about a year. When I read through her book for the first time, I was overwhelmed by all the suffering she and her family went through, and I was touched by her mother's great love.

Ling Ling's mother was a Buddhist and probably never had a chance to hear the Gospel before she passed away, but thank God that Ling Ling met some Christians who led her to faith in Christ. When Ling Ling entered the local church in 1993 for the first time, she was touched by hearing the people singing "What a friend I have in Jesus" and hearing the words about Jesus who would carry all her burdens and sorrows. She told me that since then her life has totally changed and has become full of meaning. She is now living in God's grace.

I have been inspired and awed by reading this book about Ling Ling's family, and it is my hope that it will be of great value for many people around the world.

Copenhagen, November 2012.

Jorgen Vium Olesen.

THE STORY OF THE YAN FAMILY
IN THE NEWSPAPER

洲严氏家族

造商业传奇

大片古建筑群十分
家大院,"严家大
去的。这个大院
元 1907 年),一进
照壁"、"四合五天
庭,三层楼、西
究,结构严谨,光
抗震能力极强,虽
门窗活动自如。
的大门是原第
有"司马第"三
根据当时清政
严子珍的几个
了一幢西式楼,
院占地面积约
长。
院西边距离 20
。走进严家大
的一砖一瓦
奢华与富有。
究竟是个什
里究竟发生
我们必须得
对准这幢房

本姓名如今
到杨家后,
突然病故,
结据。"穷
的他已经十
做起了生
拿不出
本生意是
店铺,
没有水

10

1、严子珍后人收藏的老照片(翻
2、严家的祖居地
3、本报记

On the April 22, 2006, a report entitled "The Business Legend of the Yan Family" was published in the *New Life* newspaper in Kunming. Accompanied by wonderful pictures, it was an in-depth account of the well-known figure Yan Zi Zhen and the fascinating story of his famous trade company, Yong Chang Xiang, which he founded in 1903 and managed until 1945.

The writer, Mr. Xiaguang Long, said that in order to write the article, he used several historical documents such as *The Annals of Xizhou Town, The Annals of Dali Count, The History of the Ancient Civilization of Dali,* and *The Foundation and Work of the Xizhou Business Society.* He also visited Mr. Zhang Ci Lu, the vice-chairman of the Culture Research Institute of the Dali Nationality College, and Mr. Zhang Tian Lun, the oldest living person in Xizhou town. These two sources both verified the accuracy of Mr. Xiaguang Long's research and provided first-hand information about the history of the Yan family.

Yan Zi Zhen, who created this successful business, was the first generation of the Yan family. My brothers and sisters and I are the fourth generation of this large family. We were all very interested in the article and read it carefully. To be honest, even though we are descendants of Yan Zi Zhen, much of the information in the article we had never heard before, and we were amazed by what we read.

This remarkable story took place in the undeveloped little town of Xizhou in Dali County in Yunnan Province about 100 years ago. That part of the story we already knew, but we wondered how our Yan family ancestors, who were from the indigenous Bai people group, could have had such advanced business ideas, practices, and philosophies that are still valued today. How did they develop these ideas and create this prosperous business which, at the time, monopolized the market? After building such a successful business empire, what became of the famous Yan family? How did the strongest business family in the commercial circles of Yunnan province with such a long and prosperous business history suddenly disappear from public life?

The answers to these questions interested me greatly as I know they did many others who read the article. As a member of the Yan family, I decided to write down the story of my father's own small family.

I wanted to paint a picture of what happened to the third and fourth generations of the Yan family during the turbulent time that became a huge turning point in our country and to tell people the historical truth about how the capitalist class was destroyed when Mao Ze Dong ruled the country. I knew that such an account would be meaningful for future generations to learn the truth of the past.

For a brief introduction to the Yan family and as background information for

The street view in Xizhou town, Dali.

The first yard in Yan's House.

my book, the following article which
was published in the newspaper has
been included. It tells what kind of business the Yan family in Xizhou,
Dali of Yunnan Province had and how it made them famous. Below is an
edited version of the article's contents:

> "Yong Chang Xiang was a large enterprise established by
> the Yan family, led by Yan Zi Zhen, and assisted by his sons,
> nephews, and cousins. This large business group engaged in
> agricultural, industrial, and commercial trade.
>
> The company first established a tea factory in Xia Guan town
> in 1908 where they created a new product "Tuo Cha" (a bowl-
> shaped compressed mass of tea leaves) which became well known
> both at home and abroad. The factory was well known and
> respected in business circles.

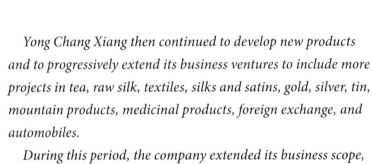

Yong Chang Xiang then continued to develop new products and to progressively extend its business ventures to include more projects in tea, raw silk, textiles, silks and satins, gold, silver, tin, mountain products, medicinal products, foreign exchange, and automobiles.

During this period, the company extended its business scope, and in addition to the old shop in Xiaguan, the family set up new branches in Dali, Kunming, Lijiang, Weixi and Xufu of Sichuan province.

Later, their business expanded abroad into the Southeast Asian market and was based in Burma. The period of 1917-1937 had the greatest development for the Yong Chang Xiang Trade Company. In 1943 the whole family's capital investment was more than 200,000,000 silver ingots. In today's currency that would be 3 billion RMB.

They were at the forefront in a very competitive market, and the Yan family was famous in Xizhou's business circles and known as the most successful and largest business group in Yunnan province. Those from the Yan family of Dali were legendary people in the history of business in China during the first half of the 20th century."

As the writer looked back at the foundation and operation of this family business, he summarized their success in this way:

"Even now the local people in Xizhou have a sense of pride and honor when they talk about the legend of the Yan family's business and their honesty, dependability, and faithfulness. It seems that the foundation of the Yan's business success was their management skills, their ability to seize opportunities, their

training of staff, and their skill in harnessing the abilities of their staff. The Yan family trained many people with special skills to become managers, accountants, consultants and specialists who could speak English, as well as the languages of Burma, India, and the indigenous languages.

The Yan family established a professional management and operations system which reflected their high reputation and famous brand. They paid close attention to business ethics and had their own "10 Rules" which all staff were required to obey. These regulations still have practical and relevant significance today.

But my research has found that nobody from the Yan family is doing business now, which is truly a great pity."

At the end of the article, the writer wrote with great feeling:

"After all this prosperity, only the Yan family's house still stands. The building of this house was started in 1907 and finished in 1910 by its owner Yan Zi Zhen. The property has three sides with a screen wall at the front facing the gate, a compound with houses built around five courtyards, a three storey house with a loft, and a western style building in the back yard. The Yan's house used special building materials and was built with a tightly knit structure; all the rooms in each yard were able to get plenty of sunlight and were very bright. With carved beams and painted rafters, it is elegant in its simplicity. When you enter the Yan's house, you feel as though you are leaping through space and time; those old bricks and tiles speak of how luxurious and rich this family was in the past. Everyone who visits here comments on what an amazing family this was and

全国重点文物保护单位

喜洲白族古建筑群

（严家院）

中华人民共和国国务院

二〇〇一年六月二十五日 公布

云南省人民政府 立

The monument set before the Yan's House.

how prosperous they were! And one might wonder what kind of
legendary story took place on this property."

Now, that classical and wonderful building of the Yan's 100 year old
house, which is still standing very quietly in the Xizhou town of Dali,
Yunnan, is the only proof of the brilliant and glorious life of this family.
In 2001, the building was registered and recognized with a memorial
stone as part of "The National Major Protection of Historical Relics Unit"
by the Yunnan provincial government and has now become a museum
for people to visit. (In Xizhou town there are some other beautiful
buildings which were built by the Yan family's other relatives. They also
have the characteristic style of the houses of the Bai nationality and have
been completely preserved serving as historical relics for people to visit
in the town.) These old buildings speak without words and tell of the
prosperity and the changing fortunes this family has experienced.

For many years due to the unique events which took place, the people of China felt ashamed to talk about business. This was because after the People's Republic of China was established, people who were successful in business and had become rich in the past were looked upon as the "exploiting class," of which the new state power wanted to "overthrow" and "put down." This capitalist class became the enemy of the proletariat. Many of them were not annihilated immediately, but they spent years struggling and slowly deteriorating in a steadily worsening condition.

Because the Yan family had been very successful in business for more than 50 years and because they were people of great renown, they were naturally classified as part of the capitalist class. They became targets of the proletariat dictatorship and every member of the Yan family had heavy losses inflicted on them by the political movement after the liberation and during the Cultural Revolution. All the members of the Yan family were continually wounded by the political events of that time, wounds which were not given an opportunity to heal before the next event opened up their scars and wounded them again.

Even the new generation who was born after the liberation, which includes me, had never experienced anything of this capitalist lifestyle and would be called "the black puppy of the capitalist" just because of our bloodlines. We would have to accept our fate and be rejected by society for thirty years.

From 1949 to 1979, the Chinese people had to live under the divisive and absurd slogan: "We would rather have the grass of socialism than to have the plant of capitalism." For thirty long years, China was a country that was closed to the outside world and all the people lived ignorant, backward lives, starved of resources, and with no freedom. It was not until that "great person" passed away that the political situation of the nation would be changed completely.

Our new system of government is in step with the times but will not discuss the question - is our country "socialist" or "capitalist"? Everyone can see that there are many new capitalist companies in China today (although they are called private enterprises). They have sprung up just like the bamboo shoots that appear after a spring rain all over our vast land. Their number is well into the thousands. They are creating great wealth and causing the Chinese economy to expand very rapidly. As a result China now stands as one of the strongest countries in the world and has caused people around the world to look at China with new eyes.

The same land and the same people – so what has made the life of the Chinese so dramatically different?

Over the past thirty years, some of the truth of Chinese history has come to light, and we have finally seen conditions gradually return to their original state, one by one. As was written in that published article, it is time to "set wrong things right," and now it is time for me to finally document the true story of the Yan family.

YAN ZI ZHEN AND YONG CHANG XIANG TRADING COMPANY (1903–1956)

Yan Zi Zhen (1871—1941).

In looking at the rise and fall of the Yan family, we must start with the story of Yan Zi Zhen, who was the founder of the Yan family dynasty.

Yan Zi Zhen's ancestors were all from the Xizhou town of Dali, the area of the Bai people group. His forefathers were government officials, as well as landlords, in the prefecture and county for many years.

By the time Yan Zi Zhen was born in 1871, some of the family's fortunes had declined, and his father Yan Chen Yuan was now in business. He ran a small shop called Yong Xin Xiang, which sold daily commodities in Xia Guan town. Yan Zi Zhen grew up to become a handsome young man, who was known for his intelligence and wisdom. At the age of 13, after 6 years of study in a private school, he started to work in the family shop learning the business from his father. He was a very diligent worker, but after a short time, he realized that the money his father was making in the business was only enough to support the basic needs of the family. This depressed him, so he decided to do some business independently of his father.

Yan Zi Zhen proved to be a clever businessman. He borrowed 500 grams of silver from one of his mother's relatives, bought a donkey, and became a traveling salesman, selling local fabrics at the markets around Xizhou. As sales expanded, he bought a mule and a horse and began to sell a variety of goods such as tea and foreign voile to places as far away as Baoshan and Huili in Sichuan province. He would then bring back tobacco, raw silk, and other special local products and sell them in Xiaguan.

During the ensuing years he educated himself, and his business continued to expand. His father was very impressed with Yan Zi Zhen's business success and decided to put his son in charge of the Yong Xin Xiang shop. So at the young age of 19, Yan Zi Zhen had inherited capital of about 25,000 grams in silver from his father.

Through the business, Yan Zi Zhen met another businessman named Peng Yong Chang from Jiangxi Province. Peng had been doing the same business as Yan for years. His train of horses carried china and other commodities between Jiangxi and Sichuan provinces and into Yunnan. Peng had a very successful business and had made his mark in the trade circles of Yunnan and Sichuan provinces.

Yan and Peng met in Huili in Sichuan and soon developed a mutual trust, becoming very good friends. Later, Yan Zi Zhen met another businessman Yang Hong Chun from the northern village of Xizhou only 3 km from Yan's home. They also developed a close friendship and business relationship. The products Yang sold and the channel he used were different from Yan's. He bought mountain and medicinal products from Lijiang and Weixi and sold them in Xiaguan and Kunming. Among them, these three businessmen dominated the market in the provision of raw materials for the handicraft industry, as well as most of the consumables needed by the general population and the local traders. Trade was brisk for all three men, and their businesses were well matched.

In 1903 they agreed to form a partnership in order to expand the scope and the scale of their business. They decided to use Yan Zi Zhen's trade mark as the company name in this joint-venture. Because Peng brought more capital into the new firm than the other two men, he was highly esteemed. To show their respect, Yan and Yang agreed to use one of Peng's names in the business name. Now their trade mark became "Yong Chang Xiang" (Yong Chang was Peng's second name), making it clear that he was the major partner in the company.

The Yong Chang Xiang Trading Company was first founded in Xiaguan in the Dali prefecture and soon had expanded to seven branches located in Dali, Kunming, Lijiang, Weixi in Yunnan province, Yibing in Sichuan province, and two branches in Huili.

Peng, Yan, and Yang became famous in business circles at that time. Once they had formed the partnership, the business soon gained momentum and experienced great financial growth. They used the business networks they had already built, and their company immediately occupied half the market share in Yunnan and Sichuan. Records show that from the beginning of the establishment of Yong Chang Xiang Company, Peng, Yan, and Yang put in place strict and detailed rules and regulations including policies for operation management and profit distribution which all three strictly adhered to. This provided a strong foundation for expanding the business year after year.

Peng Yong Chang, Yan Zi Zhen, and Yang Hong Chun operated and worked together in the company for 14 years. During this time, their excellent management skills caused their capital investment to increase fourfold with all three men becoming wealthier and more influential.

In 1907 Yan Zi Zhen used a huge sum of money to build the Yan family's house - a large and luxurious building. This house gives us some idea of how rich they were at that time.

During this period, twelve new partners became shareholders of Yong Chang Xiang as the company grew both in manpower and wealth. All these new partners were Bai people from Xizhou and Dali and were relatives of Yan Zi Zhen and Yang Hong Chun. Eventually, Yan Zi Zhen's eldest son married Yang Hong Chun's eldest daughter.

The organizational structure in the company began to change and Yan Zi Zhen gradually took on more of a key role. Peng Yong Chang and Yang Hong Chun took advantage of this opportunity and decided to withdraw amicably from the company, returning all of their capital stock. Now all the financial authority was held by the Yan family, and Yan Zi Zhen became the senior leader of Yong Chang Xiang Company, managing the company on his own. This gave him an opportunity to show his exceptional business talent on an even bigger stage.

During the 24 years from 1917 to his death in 1941, Yan Zi Zhen used his unique management style to lead his sons, nephews, and cousins and to lift the position of Yong Chang Xiang Company to its peak. He expanded trade both inside and outside China and so created an amazing business legend.

As mentioned in the newspaper article, 1937 was the greatest and most successful period for the Yan family business. In Xizhou town, people who owned their own houses were usually bureaucrats who had secured an official position and become wealthy. The Yan family had also become famous and wealthy but had then enabled many of the local people to prosper.

By 1930 there were more than 100 families who had been able to build their own houses because they worked for the Yong Chang Xiang Company. Yan Zi Zhen wanted to invest his growing wealth, and nothing gave him more pleasure than to build new properties. The new Yan family house took three years to construct and was built on 3,066 square meters in the centre of the town. It was finished in 1910. Today, it is called Yan's House. He and his family moved into this Bai style house - a three-sided house separated by a wall. In 1918 he built another home. It had a large entrance gate which opened up to four enclosed yards each of which had living areas on two levels above three sides of the yard. This was also built in the traditional Bai style. A few years later, he built another grand villa named "Hai Xin Kiosk" by the Er Hai Lake. These beautiful buildings were designed with intricate detail and constructed with great care using the geomantic lines and patterns of classical Chinese architecture. For the past 100 years, these houses have attracted a great number of visitors; students of architecture, as well as specialists in culture and history, have gone there to observe and study them.

It is amazing that Yan Zi Zhen was able to build so many wonderful buildings in one small town 100 years ago. By 1937 the first road from Kunming to Xiaguan was completed, but many of the materials used for constructing these exquisite buildings were purchased in Shanghai. Without the huge financial investment of the Yan family, this would have been impossible.

So what was the secret of Yan Zi Zhen's business success? What were the business principles that enabled him to accumulate such wealth over many years?

Let's read through the "10 Rules" that Yan Zi Zhen developed and on which he based the operation of Yong Chang Xiang Company from the time he took over its management.

All management and staff must abide by these rules. For those who disobey, if it is a major infringement, they must leave the company. For a smaller infringement, the circumstances will be taken into consideration when a decision is made about the penalty.

Employees must not engage in malpractice for selfish ends, practice corruption, or do business without keeping strict accounts.

Employees must not engage in any wrongdoing such as leaving their wives and marrying concubines, smoking opium, gambling, visiting prostitutes, being idle and other malpractices.

Employees must not divulge market information, financial data, plans or any other secret company information to the public.

Employees must not consort with personnel who are idle, abusive, dishonest or unprincipled in their behavior. Do not make friends with such people. Do not allow a dishonest, abusive, or unauthorized person to live in the dormitory.

All employees must protect the company's reputation and treat customers politely. Never use fake products instead of genuine goods, and never use substandard products instead of high quality goods. Do not give short measures.

No one must be absent without approved leave or absent from work without a reason; in special cases an explanation must be given and approval sought from management.

All employees must work hard in their line of duty and responsibility. Anyone who makes exceptional profits for the company will be rewarded and will receive a percentage of shares from the income.

All employees who work diligently and provide accurate market information will be rewarded.

All employees who work in the finance department, and whose work is completed in an accurate and timely manner, enabling the business operations to balance and make a profit for the company, will be rewarded as a top priority.

These rules are an indication of the type of management and administration Yan Zi Zhen had put in place in the company. They included rewards and punishments for the employees, paid great attention to business ethics, and gave consideration to the benefit of both staff and clients. All was in line with good business practices. In addition, Yan Zi Zhen placed importance on issues such as the marriage relationship, not allowing men to leave their wives to marry a concubine. Smoking opium, gambling, visiting prostitutes, and being lazy were also classified as misconduct.

These comprehensive rules and regulations indicated the high standards Yan had. As a result he created a resilient and growing company which occupied a huge space in the market. During Yan's lifetime he never entered the rice and salt business because these products had great fluctuations in price and were basic to people's daily lives including the poor. Because he knew that doing this kind of business would mean profiting from the poor people, his conscience would not allow him to earn even one cent in this way. For the same reason, he chose not to touch the pawnshop business either.

He also knew how to choose the right person for the right job. Yan had two well known sayings about his way of making use of human resources. The first one was: "Even my own flesh and blood will be assessed on their skills and talents; family will not automatically be given a high position." The second one was: "The worth of a person is not determined by his strengths but by his morals."

Yan also taught his employees to remember the following business principles: "Don't buy goods when they are going up in price, and don't sell goods when they go down. Focus on what you are doing; always keep the quality high; one day this will benefit you."

So it is clear that Yan Zi Zhen had a great business mind and that he was a man who showed originality and had a bold vision. He was very different from many businessmen who believe the sayings of "There is no businessman who can do business without fraud" and "No evil

- no business." As a result he was able to survive in business for many years and never see a loss. It caused him to become a famous high-level business legend.

There is a brief introduction of Yan Zi Zhen on the gate of the Yan House, which is now a museum for the public to visit. Today's government evaluated Yan Zi Zhen's life as follows:

> "Yan had extensive social interaction skills, no matter whether people were high-ranking officers and noble lords or common people of low position. He treated them all in the same way, with sincerity, granting them whatever they requested. Yan Zi Zhen's service is deserving of outstanding honor and recognition and must be commended in the highest possible way."

From this it is evident that Yan Zi Zhen was not only talented in business but also had a very good relationship with all kinds of people. He had a humble attitude and his high moral standards enabled his business to make steady progress.

During its time, the Yong Chang Xiang Trading Company worked with more than 10 products; but there were two main products that they dealt with for more than 50 years - raw silk and tea. Early in 1908, Yan Zi Zhen saw the big opportunities in the tea market. He researched and developed a new and special tea product "Tuo Cha," which is a compressed mass of tea leaves in the shape of a bowl. This new tea product resolved the problem of how to keep the quality of tea in good condition during the production process. Yan Zi Zhen was very enthusiastic about the tea because when he was 13 years old he had begun his business experience by dealing with tea products.

The name "Tuo Cha" indicated its shape. It was as big as a moon cake, and at the bottom there was a little bulge with a hole like a copper catch on the top. In Sichuan and Yunnan provinces, people use the word "tuo" for things that look like a cake. Therefore, when this kind of tea appeared in the market, it was given the name "Tuo Cha" ("Cha" is tea).

The tea cake weighed 125g and used high quality tea leaves. The best grade of tea leaves would be chosen, then mashed and braised, and finally shaped into a tight ball. It would take one or two months to transport the tea products by a team of horses over the mountains and the rivers. "Tuo Cha" resolved the difficult problem of the tea becoming mildewed and going bad. What set this new tea product apart were its color, fragrance, and taste, which were all much stronger than ordinary tea. It met the requirements of the people who lived on the tableland in Sichuan, Yunnan, and Tibet. When it came on the market it immediately sold very well and became a very competitive product. After Yong Chang Xiang set up the tea factory in Xiaguan, Yan Zi Zhen bought a 667 hectare tea garden in Feng Qing for himself. This then formed a complete distribution channel including production, supply, and sales. During that period there were many companies who saw the opportunity of Tuo Cha and invested in this type of business competing with one another; but none of them succeeded and eventually exited the market. Tuo Cha, trade marked by the Xiaguan Yong Chang Xiang Company, was produced for about 40 years in the upper Yangtze River.

Raw silk, the other main product of Yong Chang Xiang, was even bigger than the tea business because this product was not only sold inside China but also across the border in Burma and other countries. It became an important pathway for international trade as the Bai people moved in and out of Burma to do business with the Yong Chang Xiang Company. Raw silk is traditionally used by the Burmese. The traditional pinafores they wear are made from raw silk, so there was a huge demand for this product. With this business opportunity, there were many business people who wanted to take the market share, but finally it was

Yan Zi Zhen and "Yong Chang Xiang" partners.

Yong Chang Xiang which monopolized the market. Why? First, Yan Zi Zhen had a good business reputation, so he made friends easily and had many people willing to help him. Second, Yan Zi Zhen had a superior product. According to historical records, Yong Chang Xiang spent about 20 years researching the needs and quality requirements of the raw silk market in Burma. Finally, his company developed a reliable product and brand name, a soft plain-weave silk fabric trade-marked "Double Silk." Its price was higher than other products by about 20% to 30%, but the company's quality and credit rating guaranteed that there supply would always meet the demand. Yong Chang Xiang made a fortune from this business, and the export of raw silk became the main pillar of the company's development.

From the internal accounts book which the Yong Chang Xiang leadership authorized at the end of 1948, there were five major businesses listed and audited with the products put in order as "Tea, Gold, Voile, Tin and Silk." We can see that before the new China was established the Yong Chang Xiang Company was involved in a wide range of enterprises and became very successful.

My great grandfather Yan Zi An was Yan Zi Zhen's older brother. Yan Zi An's first son was Yan Zhi Cheng and was 11 years younger than Yan Zi Zhen. In the Yan family, the Chinese character Cheng is the last name of all of the sons and cousins in that same generation. So, they were called "the Cheng generation" of the Yan family.

In the early days when Yan Zi Zhen founded the Yong Chang Xiang Company with Peng and Yang, my great grandfather Yan Zi An had invested some money into the partnership, so it was only natural that his son Yan Zhi Cheng became involved in the Yong Chang Xiang business.

Before working for the company, he followed in his father's footsteps and did some business of his own as a young man. He was 30 years old when he joined the company and took to it "like a duck to water." He worked diligently, demonstrating obvious administration skills and devising good business strategies. He offered advice that often helped the company to gain more business opportunities.

The three major shareholders valued his expertise and for a time appointed him as the chief sales representative of the Yong Chang Xiang Company. After Peng and Yang withdrew from the company, he became Yan Zi Zhen's right-hand man and the Managing Director of Yong Chang Xiang. Together with Yan Zi Zhen he managed the business of the Yong Chang Xiang Company for more than 20 years and became its biggest shareholder, owning a 20% share of the total capital in Yong Chang Xiang. When Yan Zi Zhen died in 1941, his oldest son Yan Xie Cheng took over the whole business of Yong Chang Xiang and my grandfather left Yong Chang Xiang in order to support my father Yan Ze Gao as he broke new ground and developed our own family business the Chang Ming Textile Mill.

Just like Yan Zi Zhen, my grandfather only had a few years of education in a private school in Dali, having lived in the countryside like most of the common people. As his business skills grew and his career developed at Yong Chang Xiang, my grandfather was mentored by Yan Zi Zhen who had built the family fortune and taught him by example, as well as by verbal instruction.

The destiny of this whole generation had been completely turned around. Yan Zi Zhen used the business principles and practices that he had developed to thoroughly train and instruct his son, his nephews and his cousins who were part of Yong Chang Xiang, training each of them to become excellent in business. During the prosperous years of Yong Chang Xiang, all of these men were at the prime of their lives.

Over a period of nearly 20 years, they took high management positions in the company, each having to deal with a variety of tasks in different business areas as Yong Chang Xiang expanded its business scope into many and varied areas. This enabled them to practice all kinds of business skills and made them very capable. Their involvement in the business changed their thinking and their lives and brought them great affluence. While they were building their careers, each of these men were married and purchased large pieces of fertile land in Xizhou and Dali. Here they built luxury houses with large, beautiful gardens, enjoying an extravagant life. So the Yan family became a group with a powerful influence in the community.

The Chinese character "Ze" is the middle name of all the brothers, sisters and cousins of my father's generation, so they are called the "Ze generation". They were born while their family was achieving great success and gaining recognition, and this enabled them to grow up in an abundant environment.

The "Ze generation" was able to receive a new modern education, and most of them were sent to study abroad. Having had this experience, they came home no longer satisfied with the old management style of their elders. Using the money the previous generations had accumulated, they began to carve out their own business in Yunnan's capital city Kunming and also in other large cities, some overseas. This younger generation of the Yan family was able to expand the business even more, and so it grew with tremendous momentum.

The newspaper article I mentioned earlier introduced Yan Zi Zhen and the Yong Chang Xiang Company that he founded. It referred to the fact that the Yan family was involved in agriculture, industry and trade, becoming involved in most of the main business areas in Yunnan. The total capital at that time would have been equal to 3 billion RMB in today's economy. However this amount would have been far greater if all the businesses and assets which the third generation of the Yan family had accumulated before 1949 had been taken into account. This third generation became great entrepreneurs, developing even more creative business ideas and quickly moving ahead in their field.

This is how the young Bai boy, Yan Zi Zhen, pioneered the way for his family to do business in the future generations, and as a result, he is remembered as a legend.

But the path of most of the members of the "Cheng" and "Ze" generations of the Yan family, especially the "Ze generation," was not to be as smooth as it had been for the older generation. In fact it was amazing how short lived the success of these hapless people would be because they ran headlong into "the red storm," which shocked the whole world when it swept across mainland China in 1949.

This "political cleansing" was as devastating as a force 10 tornado, bringing great misfortune to the men folk of the Yan family who had never before been in any political danger. For years they had lived quiet lives, far removed from the common masses and hating any kind of violence. One by one they were devastated, many of their lives were destroyed; some were imprisoned; some were killed, but those who lived often had their personalities distorted by their suffering. The wealth and honor which they and their forebears had spent years and years building up was completely gone. The people were alive but dead inside, their lights had gone out. They lived in fear and terror until 1956 by which time the Yong Chang Xiang Company had finished its splendid 53 year journey and had completely withdrawn from the stage of Chinese history. None of the other industries and commercial operations that the Yan family had pioneered was fortunate enough to escape destruction. They were all surrendered and closed down. The family submissively handed over their factories and houses to the new masters of the republic. "Once the tree falls, the monkeys scatter," so the Yan family ceased all its public activities in business circles in Yunnan from that time on.

It was very sad indeed! But some of the people survived these terrible circumstances; several families were left with only widows and a large number of fatherless children. These high class ladies, who had previously had a good life and enjoyed high positions and lived at ease and in comfort in society, now had lost the support of a husband, and their status had immediately changed to the poorest and lowest position in this new society. The children, who had lost their wealth and their fathers, were now regarded as straw to be carelessly trampled on. How were they able to stay alive and eke out a humble and bare existence during that long period, the red years of Mao Ze Dong's rule?

I was born in 1951, and I am one member of the fourth generation of the Yan family. I was only 4 years old when I too became fatherless when my mother was widowed. My father passed away after he had suffered terrible injustice. When I began to think back to the past and to put together the story of our family, an immense feeling of great sorrow immediately engulfed my soul. There were too many heart-felt memories which sprung up in my mind. I could almost not bear to look back. I often found myself thinking over and over again that maybe we children should not have been born because our existence meant that there would be one more tragic mother in the world. These mothers were not culpable in this situation, as their children were also blameless. Just thinking of how they survived in this "new society" and the pain and hardship they suffered still fills my heart with deep, uncontrollable sorrow even though several decades have now passed.

At the same time, I have always felt very fortunate to have had a mother who made our lives very different from the lives of other people. In our life's journey, we experienced very sweet and pleasant emotions because of the beauty our mother brought into our lives, and she was also the protection which sheltered us and brought us through those deadly times. When my father left this world, he left my mother with seven children, ages 2 – 16. I can't imagine what would have happened to us if we had not had our mother!

I know I can't possibly write about the experiences of the whole Yan family during the "red storm" as well as the story of all "the leftover tribe" whose children and widows survived without a husband and father in their family. How did they live under the powerful dictatorship of the proletariat during the 30 years to follow? If I wrote about this, it would be another Yan family legend because it was extremely tragic and violent. What I have written down in the following chapters is only the story of my father Yan Ze Gao's own small family.

And the main character of my book is not just any person named Yan but an ordinary woman. She was the wife of the first master and became the young mistress of the house - "the San Sao (third sister-in-law) of the Yan family," this common but great mother of mine.

YAN ZE GAO AND
CHANG MING
TEXTILE MILL
(1935–1955)

My mother Su Ruo Bi was born on January 1st, 1917, into an old and well-known Chinese doctor's family in Kunming. She was the eldest daughter and had two younger brothers. But one brother died at the age of seven, and another brother was killed by a bomb when the Japanese air force attacked Kunming in 1938. Her mother died of an illness when she was only eight years old and her father died of heart disease in 1930. My Mama lost both her parents by the time she was only thirteen years old. Luckily, her grandmother, who loved her

Mama (on the left) and her classmate.

dearly, was still living and in good health, so from that time on she lived with her.

Although the conditions my Mama grew up with were very difficult, she still had the opportunity to receive an education and was able to finish middle school. Between 1920 and 1930, very few Chinese women had the opportunity to go to school, but my Mama was able to complete nine years of formal education in the capital city of Kunming. This gave her an important advantage and influenced her personality, her spiritual life, and her world view.

The family my Mama grew up in was not rich, but the whole household was cultured, and the home was filled with harmony and kindness. When my Mama was a young school girl, people were very fond of her because of her cleverness and quick wit. Then, because of the great upheaval in her family and the destructive events which took place in China, she was forced to give up her studies and live with her grandmother. She and her grandmother took care of each other and learned to depend on each other. Her grandmother was a very diligent, active person who was always busy even though her feet had been bound and were only 10 cm long. Year after year she taught my Mama many skills and together they did handicraft work from home in order to make a living. In this way my Mama started to work from home during her childhood and was able to make money to support herself. Since her grandmother was getting older and older and needed to be looked after, my Mama did most of the housework and learned how to do many crafts such as embroidering, knitting sweaters, and using a sewing machine. She was very accomplished in all that she did, very fast and neat.

Mama was not tall, and her appearance was not exceptionally beautiful, but she was a calm and elegant person with a smile on her face and kindness and sincerity in her actions. Because of her adverse circumstances, she had become mature for her age, and because of the difficulties she had faced, she had developed a personality which exhibited an air of contentment in all circumstances. She was self-controlled and was called "a very sensible girl" by the adults. She grew up to become a woman who had eyes filled with kindness and humility. She always made an effort to show understanding and empathy for people and was willing to suffer loss, trying to be satisfied with what she had. Before doing anything or speaking she would carefully watch what other people were doing and saying. She was willing to go without and never wanted to trouble other people. These characteristics had already developed when she was only in her teens.

When she was 20 years old, she married my Dad. On that day, this intelligent woman who had such a depth of heart literally sparkled as she was filled with longing for a new life. There is one picture which has been preserved taken on the second day of Dad's and Mama's wedding. This photograph shows the peace and contentment she must have felt that day. She wore a traditional Chinese dress called a "cheongsam" made of white silk, and she carried an exquisite handbag and a parasol under her arm. She is standing beside my Dad and smiling sweetly, looking so elegant. Her husband, our father, was a tall, very handsome man with the noblest face, a real gentleman. He wore a trim western style black suit and a white shirt with a gray and red colored necktie. He had a white wide-brimmed hat in his hand, which was very popular then. By

all appearances it seems the hat was taken off just for the picture. In this photograph Dad and Mama look mature, magnanimous, and very stylish.

On the back of this photo, Dad wrote in French: "The second day of our wedding, this photo was taken as a memento in Yuan Tong Hill, Kunming."

Every time when I look at this picture I always feel grateful. These are the two people who would give life to us seven children, bringing us into the world one by one.

Mama and Dad's wedding picture.

As a couple, our parents went hand in hand to the marriage palace in March 1937. At that time they truly were the sweethearts most admired by all the people because they seemed so well matched, two people in harmony with one another and filled with joy.

Our Dad's name was Yan Ze Gao, and he was born on the 12th of April, 1908, into an old and well-known Bai family in Xizhou, Dali in Yunnan Province. He had one younger brother and one sister. He was the first son of Yan Zhi Cheng who was one of the partners of Yong Chang Xiang Company, the biggest company in Dali at that time.

Dad was born in a small town, Xizhou, located by Er Hai Lake in Dali which is famous for its scenic beauty. Dali is an old town with a long and interesting history and considerable culture. Si Fang Street runs through the center of the town and then divides into seven streets branching off in all directions. The streets, which are very clean and tidy, have large numbers of shops. The most notable scenic attraction is the melting snow which causes crystal clear water to rush down from Cang Shan Mountain down both sides of the street all year round. The famous writer Lao She who has been to many countries and visited Xizhou in 1942 was amazed by what he saw there and wrote:

> "Xizhou is a miracle. I can't remember where I have seen such an honorable town in the many and varied places I have visited overseas. When I entered that town, I felt I was in Cambridge, England. Living water flowed everywhere down the sides of the street....the imposing dwellings and spacious courtyards are like palaces with their carved beams and painted rafters. There are also many memorial temples there, looking splendid in green and gold. ...."

The words Mr. Lao She used to describe Xizhou paint a very accurate picture. But Mr. Lao She may not know that the honor and magnificence of Xizhou is closely related to one family named Yan, and my Dad was born into this well-off family in this place with all its advantages.

After working in the Yong Chang Xiang Company, my grandfather had accumulated enormous wealth, so this native-born Bai man purchased a big piece of fertile land in Xizhou, just as others who had made money from doing business had done, and built his own luxury manor there. Something he did differently though is that he put very high expectations on his eldest son, encouraging him to leave Dali, establish his own industry, and fulfill his goals and dreams in the big city. In order to do this, my Dad only studied for six years at the primary school in Dali and then was sent off to Kunming where he completed middle and high school. My grandfather then decided to send my Dad to Shanghai to receive his higher education. He chose a private university, Zhen Dan University, which had been started by the French and where they taught in French.

By the beginning of 1930, Yong Chang Xiang had developed into its peak period. Besides tea, they had started dealing in raw silk, fabrics, mountain products and Chinese herbs, etc. They had set up new branches in many cities and had established the Southeast Asian market base with Burma as the center, as well as made preparations to expand their business into England and the U.S. As one of the managers of the expanded business, my grandfather often communicated with other well-known business people from Tianjing and Shanghai in China as well as people from abroad.

All this experience widened his field of vision. When he saw the national industries and commercial activities so full of vitality in those big coastal cities, he was inspired and even began to look down on the methods Yong Chang Xiang had been using. He really hoped his son would aspire to become like the business men he had met in those cities and would expand his own business to the same level of industry. When he found out that the textile industry was very popular in the big cities of China, although it was virtually non-existent in Kunming, he hoped he could encourage his son to work more energetically in this field. So my visionary grandfather made his decision and moved the whole family to Kunming.

He collected and read many newspapers and magazines from inside and outside China and finally realized that France was the most developed capitalist country in the world. In order to achieve his dream he understood that his son would first have to learn French, and then he could learn the technology of the advanced French textile industry. He set his mind to this and started to move his son forward one step at a time.

In 1927 when my Dad was 19 years old, he was sent by my grandfather to France for two years. He traveled across the high seas and stayed in Lyon to study French. He came home in 1929 and immediately entered the chemistry department of Zhen Dan University in Shanghai. After four years he finished his studies there and then continued to study in Wu Han University specializing in textile printing and dyeing. For more than 10 years he was continuously developing and being built up by the best aspects of both Chinese and foreign culture. He concentrated his attention on the best weaving, printing and dyeing techniques at that time. After all of those years of study and practical work, he became a professional person with great ability who was both proficient in French and a master of the textile industry.

During most of this period, my grandfather and his son only saw each other once a year when my Dad would come home for vacation, but they also kept in contact with each other by writing letters. Grandfather devoted all of his effort to building up his son, not wasting any of his

finances, and the son would
send his school results home
to show how hard he was
studying.

When he came back home
from France, his speech and
behavior were very cultured.
He now only wore western-
style clothes; he combed his
hair neatly, and his leather
shoes were spotless. When he
walked down the streets of
Dali, he seemed dazzling in
people's eyes. He looked so
different than the neighbors'

Dad studied at Lyon University in France.

sons with his stylish clothes and his French manner of conversation.
This young man, who had always been very handsome, now looked even
more like a gentleman. My grandfather was very pleased with his son's
maturity. My Dad was a person with a really nice demeanor. In a picture
taken at Lyon University in which he wears a white suit, he could almost
be mistaken for the famous American movie star Gregory Peck.

In 1934 as Dad was finishing his studies, his younger brother Yan Ze
Wen was accepted by the Finance Department of the Central University
in Nanjing. That summer, my grandfather went to Shanghai and looked
around the Yangzi River with his two sons. When I looked at the old
pictures which were taken of the three of them nearby those sites of
historic interest and in various scenic places, a sigh of emotion arose
spontaneously from my heart. In the pictures, my grandfather still has
on the traditional long Chinese gown, but his two sons are in western
dress and leather shoes, holding in their hands the wide-brimmed hats

which were so popular then. They look so elegant and accomplished and in the prime of their lives. There is no sign that these two smart looking brothers with their free and relaxed in manner are Bai people from a remote small town, Xizhou, in Dali of Yunnan Province.

Looking at the appearance of these two generations it is obvious that they had been through huge changes during the past twenty years. They certainly have an inherent quality which makes them look very distinguished with an impressive presence. Their confident expressions indicate that these three men will be instrumental in continuing the grand tradition of the Yan family business, bringing even more honor to their ancestors. On this trip, my grandfather, who is now a very experienced business man, takes the opportunity to show his two sons the Yong Chang Xiang branch office which at that time was thriving in the Yangzi river area. When the two brothers and their father entered each of the ornately decorated gates, they were warmly welcomed by the

Grandfather and his two sons.

grand old man of Yong Chang Xiang. They were inspired as they listened to the reports of the success of the business in this location. Their minds were full of excitement and they were anxious to start putting their energies into the same kind of meaningful work as soon as possible.

By July 1934, my Dad had completed 20 years of study, achieving excellent results in every subject before returning to Kunming. Now that his son was back at home, with very specialized knowledge acquired during his years of study, my grandfather was very excited and said, "This is very good, my son has met all my expectations and now that he is prepared, I can hand over the ancestral property to him!"

He couldn't wait and asked his son to start researching which materials and all related details needed for setting up a textile mill. They spent many hours a day working at their desks and also visiting similar factories of which there were only a few in Kunming at that time, reviewing their advantages and disadvantages.

Of course during this time my grandfather took my Dad, who was just a fledgling in the business world, and introduced him to the grand old men in the business circles of Kunming and recommended him to all his colleagues at Yong Chang Xiang. When all Yan's relatives saw Yan Zhi Cheng's new protégé standing before them, having achieved such a level of high education and having such an impressive presence, they all commended him. I had heard that there was one person who particularly liked my Dad and had a high appraisal of him, Yan Zi Zhen. Although Yan Zi Zhen had been very fortunate in creating great wealth and was always prosperous, he had kept his hands clean throughout his life. He never visited prostitutes and never gambled; he was an honest and decent man. When he saw his gentle grand-nephew, he was frank in his praise of him, "You are a credit to our Yan family!" he said, and as Yan Zi Zhen watched my Dad grow up, he observed some important qualities in him, such as his lack of bad habits and his willingness to study hard. So he recognized that this was young man had great value. After my Dad had made contact with all these business men, he became especially friendly with Ke Cheng, the third son of Yan Zi Zhen who had just finished his MBA at Harvard University and had returned home. Although they were from two different generations, they were close in age. Due to their similar backgrounds, having both studied abroad, they were both very

*Dad and the "Yong Chang Xiang" staff
in Shanghai branch.*

Grandfather led two sons to meet "Yong Chang Xiang" partners of Shanghai branch.

different, not only from the rest of the Yan family but also from others
who had lived in Yunnan all their lives. Neither of them liked some of the
bad practices which were often enjoyed by rich families, such as playing
Mahjong and smoking opium. Instead, they liked to spend time together
drinking coffee, playing tennis, and listening to western music, and they
soon became very close friends. Naturally, they no longer approved of
the way their elders did business. In their minds there were some new
ideas they thought would be more in tune with the trends of the outside
world. Not only could they see beyond the politics and worldly interests
of the family, but even their clothing set them apart. They would often
communicate with each other in a foreign language, imparting a fresh
and modern atmosphere into a family which had never experienced this
before.

Everyone was waiting in anticipation to see what would happen and
what kind of specialized skills this new generation would bring to the
Yan family.

In the spring of 1935 after 6 months of preparation, my grandfather and my Dad chose the site of their factory in Ni Jia Wang, a place not far from Kunming city. They bought the land for building and started construction. Dad agreed with his father's decision to order complete sets of weaving machines and equipment from Germany. A few months later the freight finally arrived in Kunming and included: 16 electric locomotives, 1 wheel vehicle, 24 handcars, and 12 spinning wheels. The father and his son worked together each day to install the equipment. No matter how large or small the job, they did all the work themselves. They left home early in the morning and worked hard all day until the evening, often streaming with sweat. At the end of the day they ate their dinner and drank cup after cup. The father and his son caroused and worked together cheerfully, full of confidence about the future of their textile mill. They named the factory "Chang Ming Textile Mill," the character "Chang" came from the name of "Yong Chang Xiang." On the one hand, they hoped to benefit from the association with that company's continuous good fortune. On the other hand they hoped that when people saw the sign they would recognize that this factory was linked with Yong Chang Xiang and would know it was the property of the Yan family.

For the next 6 months, they were busy setting up business systems for the factory and in the August of the same year, this modern and advanced corporation had finished testing the machinery, done all the preparatory work, and stepped onto the commercial stage in Kunming. It was not a big factory when it started, but in Kunming where industry and commerce, especially the textile industry, was undeveloped, this news had huge repercussions and attracted the attention of many business people. Because of my grandfather's position in Yunnan's business circles, the celebrations for the opening lasted for 3 days.

My grandfather was a very enlightened man, and he trusted his son completely, deciding to give him authority to manage all the affairs of the factory. Naturally, what he hoped in his heart was that having been tempered by the difficulties and dangers he had battled in the world around him, the factory his son would run would be as successful as Yong Chang Xiang had been in my grandfather's own generation. So, before the formal authorization, he thought the most important thing he should deliver to his son was the management concept of Yong Chang Xiang. He believed that passing on this business philosophy and theory was the best gift he could give to his offspring and far exceeded all wealth. One morning he wrote down the "ten rules" which he remembered fluently on one piece of rice paper. After eating dinner in the evening, he brought the paper out and solemnly handed it to his son.

My Dad didn't want to waste the usual tea and chatting time after the meal which the whole family always enjoyed. A few minutes later he was back in his study, rolled out the paper and started reading the ten rules which my grandfather had carefully written and signed.

Although my Dad had known from his childhood that the whole Yan family had been involved with the business of the Yong Chang Xiang Company, he had studied away from home for so long that he had never read through these business rules before, and this was the first time for him to set his eyes on them. After reading it word for word, he was deeply impressed by the contents. This was the secret which caused the Yan family to prosper in business and to continue for so many years without fail.

Suddenly he felt he had a grave responsibility on his shoulders, and he understood that my grandfather had presented him with something very important and what its purpose was. Dad had studied abroad for years and was westernized externally; but in his heart he was a person who obeyed the Confucian way, respecting and reverencing his father.

Now he wanted to present a satisfactory management strategy to his father, so he spread out some paper, took a pen in his hand, and started to plan immediately. That evening the lights in his room stayed on as he went without sleep for most of the night. Two days later he presented a thick pile of paper containing "The First Draft for Factory Organization and Management" to my grandfather. My grandfather was delighted to read it, even though the draft was not perfect, it was precise and thoughtful. Together they made some changes, and then both approved it. Grandfather wrote the document on two pieces of rice paper, framed them and hung them on the wall of the factory director's office. Everything was ready; he patted Dad's shoulder and only said this one thing to his son, "Ok, the factory is now handed over to you; do a good job!"

From them on he did not touch any of the factory's affairs but went back to Yong Chang Xiang to continue his duty there. Occasionally, people would see his figure appear in the factory, wearing a long gown, holding a pipe with his kind smile; he would just go into the workshop to see how the modern machines operated.

In this enlightened way, my grandfather left my Dad a large space in which to exhibit his capacity. Dad, together with one shareholder, managed all the affairs of the factory, including manufacturing and distribution, when he had not yet reached the age of 30.

On the first day they had 10 machines operating together, on one side cotton yarns would twine and become a piece as the machines made the noise "Kua, Kua, Kua," and on the other side there were bolts of cloth already falling onto the ground. Both father and son were so happy. They picked up a piece of cloth, looking and looking at it and talking about it with great excitement. But they knew that this was just the first step, if the products sold and made a good profit, this would mean real success for the factory. This worsted textile had a market in Kunming. At first the fabric manufactured in the factory was wholesaled to some small clothing shops in order to test the market. But within 6 months, one special tartan product would be warmly received by the people, both because it had never been seen in Kunming before and because of its perfect texture. My Dad made a determined decision and chose the most bustling street, Zheng Yi Road, to immediately set up his own shop, right beside the shop where Yong Chang Xiang sold tea and silk. He hung up red lanterns on both sides and the shop was open for business. The saying "win the victory in the first battle," sums up the opening day as all the fabrics sold very well bringing great excitement to the whole family.

Dad was a dependable person with a humble attitude although not a great talker. He would just smile and continue to manage the factory and shop with a steady hand. He took great care in all his business dealings both in the factory and the shop.

In the first year, he put his whole heart into his career and never had any free time. He knew this factory had been built on the assets of the older generation and had been established to fulfill the greatest desire of my grandfather. Dad was a dutiful son, and people acknowledged that he told himself every day, "For the family's glory, I must succeed and I can't fail! I must keep trying harder and harder!" So he forgot all about entertainment and leisure and completely threw himself into the affairs of the factory.

Everything with the corporation was going smoothly. There is one old picture that shows how Dad worked in his laboratory. He is wearing a long white coat, concentrating his attention on the chemical analysis which he did as part of the fabric's printing and dying process. At that time, his factory was a picture of prosperity. Although he was young, he was steady and mature and was soon regarded as a professional entrepreneur by the business community.

This new enterprise gave him a stage to show off his ambitions. He applied all of the advanced techniques which he had learned at university and abroad to the production of printing and dyeing. At that time there were many kinds of fabrics that looked very good, but when they were washed, the color always faded. This was a big problem that had not been resolved for years. Dad focused his energies on this and began to look into the production of a cloth which was a mixture of cotton and wool. Eventually, after much research, a finely grained and non-fade fabric was launched onto the market. It went beyond all expectations, and all the fabric was sold out within a week. The factory had to work overtime to produce enough to meet the demand of the market. Every day many people came to buy this new fabric from the shop in Zheng Yi Road. At first, people could be seen on the streets of Kunming carrying pieces of fabric in a wrapper imprinted with the "Ming Da Chang" trade mark. Later those fabrics became garments worn by the citizens of Kunming, especially young women who loved beauty. The fabric my Dad had developed was made of a combination of cotton and wool in a small lattice pattern which used a thick thread, with an alternating fine thread. It was a little thicker than the usual cloth, and had a "woolen cloth" feel. It resonated with the fashion trends of the day and became a very popular fabric that year. Within a year Dad had made his business so profitable, the whole family rejoiced.

Dad was an impressive figure with his much loved career and uninhibited progress. Two years later my grandfather urged him to consider marriage, and when he felt ready to have his own family, he met my Mama.

Dad and Mama's marriage was not arranged by anybody but was based on their love for each other and their desire to benefit the another.

The happiest time mama ever had.

At that time this was considered a novelty. There was an aunt who introduced them to each other, and after seeing each other only once, they fell in love at first sight. They both realized that they would bring out the best in each other and very soon began to discuss their wedding plans.

One thing worth mentioning here is that from the first day Mama met the Yan family she was approved of by all the elders. They used three words to praise Mama: virtuous, capable, and warmhearted. They all thought Dad had found a wife who was very suitable for the Yan family as well as for himself and his career.

Dad was an introverted person whose behavior was always charming but sometimes overcautious. Mama was extroverted and frank, and they complemented each other perfectly. Later, many relatives and friends told us that our Dad liked to play tennis and piano and that he spoke French fluently. Although he lived in a rich family from the day he was born, he didn't have any of the bad habits trendy people often have. He treated others with sincerity and handled his business affairs seriously. He was a good man who paid attention to self-cultivation and good morals. As the first son of the family, he clearly knew what role his wife would have to take, and he knew he must choose carefully. His personality and his position in the family meant he must choose a wife with both talent and virtue. Mama's good qualities touched Dad deeply. After dating her a few times and spending time talking to her, he made his decision that this woman was his partner for life. When he heard about the sad life experiences of Mama's childhood, sympathy rose up within him. One day he told Mama with deep love, "All these things are in the past; in the future I guarantee you will not have to bear hardships anymore." Mama was moved by these words, and her eyes brimmed with tears.

Mama and her friends at a spring outing.

Meeting a person who treasured her so much, Mama felt that god had blessed her. Meeting a man like Dad who had studied abroad, was cultured, and had his own business was the dream and desire of every modern woman. But she herself had only received a few years of primary education, and she felt her background may be too common and she must only dream about having a husband like my Dad. But now this wonderful dream had become a reality. She was filled with deep gratitude. Afterwards, Mama often talked about her good fortune saying, "Meeting your Dad was the greatest reward of my whole life." Therefore, we know that from the beginning of their relationship, Mama not only had great love for Dad but was also full of adoration and deep respect for him.

Dad loved my Mama with a passion after they were married. Those days were the happiest times in her life, and Mama was intoxicated with joy. Years later as we were growing up, whenever she told us of her memories about their times as newlyweds, her eyes would shine. She could not refrain from showing her excitement, her whole body and mind filled with happiness and satisfaction.

She would often recall the period of time both before and after her marriage and would say that the spiritual and material comforts my Dad gave her were things she had never experienced in her 20 years. She would say how she had missed out on the life of an undergraduate, something she always longed for and was unable to experience. When she revealed it to my Dad he told her, "Don't worry; you can still dress like one of the female students."

One day he actually made to order the outfit of a girl student's modern clothing and wrapped it in colored paper giving it to Mama with both hands. He said to Mama mysteriously, "You wear this clothing tomorrow and show it to me." Mama naturally didn't imagine this type of clothing was in the parcel, and when she opened it and saw it, she was moved, and her eyes filled with tears. Her husband treasured her so much; it made Mama feel as though she were living in a dream. "Oh, your Dad treated me so kindly," were the words my Mama spoke to us thousands of times in later years.

Mama had loved literature and liked to read since she was a child. But by the time she was in her teens, the family circumstances had become so poor, she had no opportunity to read books to her heart's content. But now this all changed because my Dad would often take her to the bookstore and let her select any books she liked. Whenever she would bring her books home, she would lie down on the sofa, and Dad would give her a cup of tea, allowing her to immerse herself in a sea of books, enjoying the pleasure of reading as much as she liked. What unforgettable times - and Mama said that she really felt overwhelmed by such unexpected favor. During that time Dad bought her the first edition bound book "Dream of the Red Chamber" which she treasured and took great care of because it was so precious to her.

Mama loved to sing Beijing opera, so Dad asked a specialist Mr. Xu Min Chu who was a master in Yunnan theatrical circles to teach her.

While she continued to train in the basic skills, Dad had discussions with the teacher and asked him to rehearse several different plays from a list of Qing Yi arias of the Beijing opera that especially showcased Mama's voice. Later, because he wanted to make Mama feel happy, Dad decided to organize a party for theatre fans one evening a week in their home, inviting

Mama was singing Beijing Opera.

all of the relatives and friends who were fond of Beijing opera to come. By doing this, he enabled Mama to go on stage and sing a few parts of the opera while also being able to enjoy herself by acting out roles in the plays. Dad even purchased many genuine theatrical costumes for Mama so she would really feel authentic while she was performing. In the mornings, when Dad kissed her and went off to the factory, Mama would always put on the stage costumes one by one and look at herself in the mirror, swinging her sleeves while she sang and danced.

At that time, Mama was only a 20 year-old girl and found it hard to avoid having some vanity. She told us a story once about one day when some wives of big business men came to the party to show off their singing voices. She knew that each of them had made some particularly beautiful stage costumes. After trying on her new dress, Mama acted like a spoiled child in front of Dad, demanding that she wanted a diamond ring added onto the neckline of the stage costume. She believed that if this was done her appearance on the stage would be very spectacular and out of the ordinary. Dad laughed and agreed with her immediately. Holding Mama's hand he went to the shop and bought a big diamond ring for her, putting it on the neckline himself when Mama wore the dress. That evening, Mama was as dazzlingly and brilliant as she had expected. As soon as she entered the stage, she received an immediate standing ovation. Mama said this was the most extravagant thing she had ever had in her whole life.

In order to memorialize Dad's favor as well the happy years they had together, Mama preserved the theatrical costume and the diamond ring in the bottom of a big suitcase in her home, treasuring them for many years. Years later, the diamond ring was torn from the clothing and taken away by the workers who came to search our house and confiscate our property during the "Three –anti/five –anti campaigns movement" when Mao had just started to rule the mainland of China. Mama watched hopelessly as they did what they liked, not daring to utter a word. But the clothing she managed to save until 1966 when the Cultural Revolution started. In that year, all the things from the past were regarded as "Four Old Things" which the red guards sought out from each family and threw into the fires. Mama knew there was no escape for this theatrical costume; she did not want anyone else to destroy this clothing which had so much meaning for her, so one evening as she was crying she put the clothing into the fire and burned it herself.

The whole family went sight-seeing in Daguan Park in 1937.

When they married, Dad and Mama lived together with their parents and Dad's brother and sister. The house was located in Si Ma Di Lane of Kunming. When my grandfather brought my grandmother,

The whole family in their garden in 1938.

with her bound feet, here was the first time they left Xi Zhou of Dali. They came to Kunming and moved into this lovely house he had purchased. The house was in the Chinese style of "Si He Yuan" and had two floors. There were two very comfortable courtyards. The courtyard in the front was quite big; the floor of the whole yard was paved with one meter thick flagstones. On the first floor a big living room faced the gate, and there were two small hallways on either side. There was a complete set of old-style sandal wood furniture and calligraphy and paintings from famous Chinese artists on the walls. On the second floor there were six bedrooms. Behind this yard was a big garden with fruit trees, bamboo, and a rockery, as well as a stone table and stone chairs. There were flowers always blooming like a piece of brocade and it became a nice place for grandfather and grandmother to enjoy the flowers and birds, for the family to meet relatives and friends, and for all to drink tea and chat.

Because there was such a big yard in this house, there were always parties during the years after Dad and Mama married. They also had western concerts but not as often. Usually there were parties for Beijing opera theater fans, the operas Mama liked. On the day of the party, the inside and outside of the house was always decorated with lanterns and streamers, which shone brilliantly all through the night. Normally, from the afternoon onward the guests would come to the house in an endless stream. They were invited to eat a feast together first; then the party would start, and they would play Beijing opera. Dinner was often eaten in the big yard where four or five tables were put together with the guests eating amidst cheerful and humorous conversation. After the meal when melon seeds and sweets were put on the table and each guest had a cup of hot tea in front of them, there would be a lively start to the singing and performing. At that moment, an impassioned tone would be made by Jing Hu with the deafening sound of gongs and drums followed by the beautiful melodies and dramatic arias sounding out one after another, and the guests chimed in at the chorus. Such was the continuous sound coming from the yard. There were often many people standing around outside the house listening in or tapping their toes and watching the excitement. With crowds bustling with activity around the house, this family really made a wonderful scene.

Due to my grandfather's position and my father's reputation in

business circles, the theater parties became bigger and bigger and a social meeting place for the reputable business people and government officials in Kunming. There were many people from high society; even the Yunnan governor

In the big yard of Si Ma Di Lane in Kunming.

Mr. Long Yun had been there with his wife. Mama was slender and graceful in stature; she was very beautiful when she wore her theatrical costumes and make up. Because she was trained by a specialist, her singing and recitation skills, her movements and form were even more precise. Often, just as she would open her mouth to sing, immediate loud and warm applause and cheering would ring out. During that period, Mama really felt her deepest desires were satisfied. She did something she loved the most. This was the first time she had presented herself so conspicuously to the public. Her capacity and her serious attitude meant that she only needed to display a small part of her skill in order to capture her audience. Dad felt he had won a great reputation among his relatives and friends. Mama felt very happy to see her husband so delighted. Each time after her program, she would change out of her theatrical costumes and meticulously get dressed, presenting herself at her husband's side and sitting beside him gently like a bird resting on a tree. Usually, the performance would last until 10 o'clock in the evening, and when it was finished, the hospitable host would always offer some refreshments to the guests. Popular Kunming snacks, cakes, and sweets would be put on the table one by one as all the guests once again broke into a jolly and cheerful time of conversation. When they had finished eating and talking, all the guests would finally leave around midnight. The courtyard would then slowly calm down.

After the guests had left to go home, the master of the house would go to bed to rest. Mama always took off her high-heeled shoes, tied on an apron, and started to help the servants clean up the mess late into the night before going to sleep. Normally, she should not do these things because she was the young mistress of the house. But she said this was what came naturally to her, as she had never been served by others during the years of her childhood right through to becoming an adult. So, she really was not used to living a life high above the masses. She said that if she made the servants do everything, she would feel sorry for them. Her mother-in-law was a hardworking Bai woman from the countryside who had never received any education and never travelled in her life. As she observed her daughter-in-law, she recognized that her son had found the right wife.

Mama said that although she loved to perform on stage at the theater parties, she only did this during the first and second year after the parties began. Later, when she realized what role she would have as a daughter-in-law married to the eldest son in a big family and what kind of the skills she needed to cultivate, she decided not to come out on the stage to perform anymore and was willing instead to be a hero behind the curtain. She always had her hands full with the parties in her home, so as she listened to others singing, she filled her eyes and ears with the pleasure of the performance of the Beijing opera. She forced herself not to be affected by the situation because she found out that it was not easy to arrange a party and to manage the entertainment and the reception for so many people. As the daughter-in-law married to the eldest son, her duty was not to seek her own ease and comfort but to take care of and manage the whole event. So, it was only a short time that Mama enjoyed the fun of performing before she started to learn how to become a good hostess.

During this time, a noble woman called "Widow Liu" influenced her very much. In 1927, the headquarters of Yong Chang Xiang had moved to Kunming, and Yan Zi Zhen had built several high-quality houses with red walls and green tiles in Jing Ding Lane of Jin Bi Road in Kunming. In this kind of compound with its connecting courtyards, it was difficult to avoid some social interaction. And Yan Zi Zhen was a businessman who always placed great importance on relationships with the people. After living in Kunming for a few years, he decided to have a dinner party in his house once a week. He invited important people from the business circles of Kunming to come and meet and eat, making friendly contacts with them in this way. The Yan family had wealth which gave them a louder voice than others, and with Yong Chang Xiang's well-known reputation, the "Friday dinner party" grew bigger and bigger as the years went by. Often, some of the outstanding figures from the business circles of Yunnan would come without invitation, as well as some prominent figures from political and financial circles. Celebrities from the literary and art circles in Yunnan also presented themselves at the party at times. One day, after their marriage, Dad took Mama to attend the party. They got there a little early before the guests had arrived. While Mama was sitting and drinking tea, she noticed a graceful middle-aged lady leading a group of servants to set up the hall and tables for the party. The lady looked elegant and poised, moving steadily and with agility as she arranged the affairs. Finally, when the hall and tables were finished, everything looked wonderful - modern and with stylish good taste. These things caused Mama to greatly admire this lady. When the dinner party started, she noticed this lady and the eldest child of Yan Zi Zhen moving and interacting with different guests continuously. She charmed each of the wives of the big businessmen, and they lit up with pleasure at her warm hospitality. After the dinner, some servant girls in uniforms appeared, each holding a rosewood tray inlaid with spiral shells, which they offered to the guests in turn. There was a wineglass filled with clean water, a pretty enamel mug and a piece of white towel on the tray. They would squat down before the guests letting them gargle and wipe their faces. After this, when some guests had started playing Ma Jiang and some started chatting, cups of hot tea and some special local products from Xi Zhou such as candied fruit, sesame candy, and dried plums were put on the table right away. Dad and Yan Ke Cheng, who was such a trendy person, were invited to sit in the kiosk of the house and offered coffee and sweet food. At about 10:30, all the people again ate some special food; that evening they ate edible bird's nest cooked with crystal sugar and gruel. This was served in small amounts and was very popular at that time in rich families. Something which surprised Mama was the type of dishes each person held in their hands. The bowls and spoons were so exquisite that Mama thought they really were the most beautiful dishes she had ever seen. Of course, such a display of wealth and extravagance also showed off the success and good taste of the master of this house. Mama realized all these details must have been arranged by this lady.

After the party as she left Jing Ding Lane, Mama started to inquire about this lady. Dad told her that her name was Liu Shu Qing and that she was the wife of a big warlord. She was a person who had special life experiences because she had travelled with her husband extensively and had even been to Hong Kong and Tokyo many times. Unfortunately, her husband passed away suddenly after an illness, and she became a widow when she was younger than 40 years old. After she had dealt with her husband's funeral arrangements, she sold off their house and property in Sichuan and moved with her daughter to Kunming. She was unwilling to stay out of the limelight and used the legacy her husband had left to build a very modern cinema located in the busiest section of town, Nan Ping Street. She also became the hostess of the top-level social scene in Kunming at that time. As one of society's celebrities, she was invited to the Yan family's dinner party. But the feasts in the Yan house had no modern taste, and she secretly scoffed at the whole thing. Back then, the Yan family had only just moved to Kunming a short time before, and some of the customs of the local rich people still influenced them; the wives had come from the small town Xi Zhou, and some were still practicing foot-binding. Among them there was no one like her with her experience of society, as well as her intelligence and capability. So, the social activities in their house were often a little petty and penny-pinching. This enthusiastic and capable woman contacted Yong Chang Xiang and gradually made his acquaintance. From then on, if there was a big activity or some VIPs came to visit, Yan Zi Zhen would always send a person to pick her up, and she would help Yong Chang Xiang take care of all the preparations. She managed each affair so well that she lifted the level of social interaction of the Yan family to a new and high standard.

"Oh, so this is how it should be done," thought Mama; she had already set this lady up as an example for herself. After she married, when Mama often went to these dinner parties, she would consciously connect with this lady and they soon became good friends. She followed this lady and carefully learned from her, putting into practice in her home everything she learned. After only a few years, her craftsmanship already far exceeded that of Widow Liu. At the Yong Chang Xiang dinner parties, people often saw Mama and this lady's figure both working together. But Mama arranged all the affairs of Yan Zhi Cheng's family in Si Ma Di Lane by herself. She took care of many aspects, such as arranging the daily activities of the family, preparing three meals a day, setting up the hall, dealing with the public as well as knowing how to relate to people in different positions in the family hierarchy. Mama steeled herself through practical work and mastered all the skills needed to get along with people; she had the style of a great master.

From the beginning, Mama realized that knowing how to fit in with her mother-in-law, brother-in-law, and sister-in-law would take a lot of learning. And without any friction, she lived in peace with each of them. She said, "It is easy; you just have to surrender yourself. If you are willing to give and not think about repayment, you will easily get along with anyone." No matter who she met, the principle she followed was to greet them with a smile, listening more than speaking.

In her interaction with the wives of the wealthy, Mama also had successful harmony. Her magic weapon was that she was neither arrogant nor inferior but behaved as a decent equal -whether they were the wife of the rich and powerful or the small business owner. In this way she earned their respect.

Mama was a typical traditional and kind Chinese woman. As her children were born one by one and as her husband's business enlarged, she was instantly content to focus her whole life on supporting her husband and taking care of the children.

In a resume she wrote years later, she stated, "After I married I was at home as a house wife; I took charge of all the children and the housework, as well as arranging the supplies and food for the factory."

She was a person who naturally loved her family and her husband. She fell into her new roles very easily. In all the things she had to deal with, she did not just order others about but took care of every single thing personally.

Eventually, my grandfather hired a chef to do the cooking, a tailor to make clothing, several servants with the responsibility for all the sundries in the family, and each child also had a nurse to look after them. But Mama participated in everything because she was not used to giving orders. She always kept herself busy, got up on time, and was the last one to go to bed each day. She never seemed to indulge in leisure or laziness and didn't stir up discord, which were often the flaws of rich wives.

The first Spring Festival after her marriage, Mama decided that she would cook the New Year's Eve dinner for the whole family by herself when she was only 20 years old. Grandfather's ancestry was from the Bai people, and he had lived in Dali all his life, so his favorite meals were those with the hometown flavor. Although he had now settled in Kunming for years, the Chinese New Year's Eve dinner had to have some traditional Bai dishes. Mama knew this, so she secretly practiced and practiced cooking the Bai food. That evening, she made several perfect special Bai flavored dishes and put them on the table. When she took a sparkling crystal clear cooked but now frozen fish and turned it over and displayed it on an orchid diskette, my grandfather nodded and began to commend it. He picked up some to taste and was full of praise right away. After this, all the people started to taste the stir-fried Er Kuai, the food every family would eat on New Year's Eve. Mama cooked it with a Bai flavor. When everybody had eaten just a little bit they immediately said this dish exceeded what their chefs cooked at home. It had a good balance of sour and sweet and was very delicious. They started to taste other dishes—crisp meats stewed with lotus root, chicken brine, and so on. With the sound of praise, Dad went to the kitchen to see Mama because she was still busy making something else.

He put his hand on Mama's shoulder and gave her a soulful kiss, saying to her, "Everybody liked the dishes you made."

Mama spoke to him proudly, "The best is yet to come."

"Eh? What surprise do you have planned?"

"Please go back to the table; I will show you."

Dad joyfully left his wife and returned to the banquet. For a while, nothing happened; but then he saw Mama come out carrying a tray with a steaming hot rice cake. When she put this rice cake on the center of the table, all the people marveled and gasped, "Oh, it is too beautiful, it is too pretty."

Grandfather said, "We should display it in our living room; it is a pity to eat it." And everyone broke into laughter.

Grinding rice into rice powder in a stone mortar and pestle and then steaming a rice cake to eat during the Chinese New year is customary for the Bai people. From ancient times families have eaten this every year. The rice cake this year was made by the same method as before; what was different was that Mama showed some originality. She put three colored layers into the main part of the rice cake which used to be about 10 cm tall and all white. On the bottom she used the original color—white; then, she put in a layer of pink mixed with some red color and another layer of brown in which she had used some brown sugar mixture. She spread the white rice powder quite thickly, the brown rice powder was spread in a very thin layer, she then added the pink color, and then another layer in white. So, when this rice cake came out of the tray it looked so unlike any from other years. The top of the rice cake would usually be dusted with some walnut, peanut and brown sugar, but Mama had now added some candied fruit inlaid with red and green colors. Therefore, when this rice cake was presented to the people, it was certainly very pleasing to the eye. All the people stood up and enjoyed this cake for a long time before it was cut to eat. Once each person had a piece of rice cake on a plate in front of them, Mama carried in a bowl with some honey and put it on the table, saying, "Dip it in a little honey to eat it; the taste will be better, try!" Oh, she just had so many creative ideas. Everyone thought the dinner on New Year's Eve that year was one of the most special meals they ever had, and they all felt fully satisfied.

That day, both the old and the young members of the Yan family got to know Mama. Everyone could see what potential would open up from this little woman. Dad could see that Mama would bring to this big family the happiness they had never had.

He spoke to Mama in the evening, "Wherever you are, there is laughter. I am very joyful!" He absolutely enjoyed and appreciated his wife.

As each child was born one by one, Mama looked after them carefully. She also managed all the behind the scenes affairs of the whole family. There was nothing Dad needed to be concerned about. After work, Dad was still like a boy and kept many of his personal interests. He continued to play tennis, take photographs, and develop the film in a dark room for long periods of time, going on outings with friends and so on.

Mama and Dad have been loving each other very much at all times.

Dad said, "Your Mama always takes care of what kind of clothes I should wear to each place, matching the color of my necktie as well the right shoes. I don't need to think about anything."

He said too, "Your Mama also takes care of all the needs of our big family. She arranges for the butler to go and buy what we need, so I don't need to think about that either." She kept the records of the family expenses in an account book, managing the finances in a methodical way. Even my grandfather often commended Mama to other people:

"We all can set our minds at rest, living with her, everything is just fine."

More than 10 years had passed. Mama had now gained outstanding abilities in all kinds of skills. Whether it was taking care of the children, cutting out a set of garments, arranging the family's affairs, cooking a special meal for a banquet, pickling vegetables in the local Bai flavor, or managing the factory's logistics or performing some program for the public; even the way she got along with people, she did everything very well. Everybody recognized that she was a capable person who, as the saying goes "Can go up to the hall and can also go down to the kitchen."

Some capable people can sometimes have a nasty temper, but not Mama. She always had a smile on her face for everyone and was very easy to approach. Therefore, in the whole of the big Yan family, no matter whether they were old or young, no matter how high or low their position, everyone liked and admired her.

Of the "Ze generation" of the Yan family, my father is the third, so, he was called "San Ge" (San in Chinese is three, Ge in Chinese is brother), and Mama is called "San Sao" (Sao in Chinese is oldest brother's wife) by everybody. "San Sao" of the Yan family was a famous name among the relatives and friends, as well as in the business circles of Kunming. When Yong Chang Xiang had some important activities, Yan Zi Zhen always entreated people to "go, go and call Ze Gao's wife to come and help."

"Ask San Sao, ask San Sao!" whenever the relatives or friends needed any help, the first person they thought of was always Mama.

Many people told us later that Mama was the kind of person who always observed her duty, was easily content with her lot, showed kindness, and took charge of a situation whenever something happened. This could not be said of many people.

Because she played such an unusual role standing behind Dad and supporting him in everything, both their family and career prospered day by day. In 1945, Dad's career was like the sun at high noon. Demand for the products his factory produced always exceeded supply. Because of his excellent achievements in the textile industry, he was chosen to be the chairman of the Textile Association by the people in the business circles in Kunming.

Social activities and parties were still often held in their home. But Mama had changed her role a long time ago, she had already moved from the front of the stage to behind the curtain. This change was quite easy

Mama and her first baby.

Mama pregnant with her third child.

and natural for her, and she didn't express even a tiny bit of her displeasure about this. During this period of time, Dad's guests were often unwilling to eat the meals their own chef had cooked, preferring to visit our place and eating Mama's special dishes. When guests were coming, Mama would dress neatly, her hair hackled with a comb and as clean as a whistle. She would welcome the guests by taking them to their seats and serving them their favorite tea; then while Dad talked with them, Mama would leave and go to the kitchen. She put an apron around her waist and started to prepare food for them. The guests were always full of praise for the great variety of meals she made. This really showed proper respect for Dad's feelings. While they were eating, Mama would hold her youngest baby in her arms and bring the other children in to come and meet and greet the guests. The children were always commended and admired by the guests; this gave her so much joy, and under the guests' admiring gaze, she could not refrain from kissing her children one by one and happily telling the guests, "I love those babies so much; I do love them."

After the children had greeted the guests politely, they would go back to their room. Mama would then sit beside Dad quietly and talk with the guests for a while. This was now her time to have social interaction with the wives of the guests. She always behaved decently and evoked an overflowing feeling of tenderness around the dining table. After the meal she would often sit with the guests and chat with them. Sometimes she would put up a table and play Mahjong with them. No matter whether she lost or won, Mama laughed constantly. Chinese people always say, "At the Mahjong table, the character trait of a person is seen." Mama never failed to show her passion and magnanimity at the Mahjong table. She would win positive comments from Dad's friends and their wives, and Dad lived in an atmosphere of harmony with no pressure in his home.

Every family member experienced the blessing of Mama's good care every day. Each morning, Mama was always the first person to appear in the yard even though she had given birth to four babies in succession. She loved beauty, loved being clean and tidy, and as was her nature, never lacked vigor. No matter what day it was, whenever people saw her, she had always paid attention to her appearance and was never slovenly as some women could be after they had given birth to a baby. No, she was a person who always took great care of her appearance no matter where she was; she was always pure and fresh like a spring breeze. She always washed her hair with a special lotion made from the Chinese honey locust fruit, ensuring her hair was always smooth and shiny. Her trimmed eyebrows looked like crescent moons. Mama didn't like to wear brightly colored clothes; all of her cheongsams were of a quiet color and at the most, they had some small flower patterns. Before she wore any of her cheongsams, they were ironed perfectly with absolutely no creases. She herself would choose a special and exquisite white handkerchief to wear as an accessory. This handkerchief had plum blossom embroidery in various colors in one corner. Depending on what color she would be dressing in that day, this small handkerchief would be either inserted under the armpit in the sleeve of the cheongsam or held in her hand. People could see that the color of the blossom always matched the color of the clothes she wore that day. Mama also loved fresh flowers. When there were no fresh flowers in the garden at home, the place she preferred to go was the flower market in Kunming. She would bring the flowers home, and then take the big vases into the center of the yard where she would arrange the flowers in different ways, carrying them into the living room, Dad's study, and her bedroom. These were the things she loved to do so much. When there were flowers in the garden, she had to go there once a day after she had washed and dressed in the early morning. With a smile she would cut a few fresh flowers and some of the green leaves, and then arrange them in vases. She always enjoyed doing this very much and was never bored with it. Each time she had put the flowers into vases, she would stand back critically, looking at them and rearranging them until she thought their design was pleasing to the eye.

Every morning she would go to the kitchen to help the chef put the breakfast on the table, organize Dad's and the children's meals, and see them out. Then she would have a cup of tea and read the newspaper and rest a while. Mama was a typical good wife and loving mother.

During the 17 years Dad and Mama lived together, they were always an affectionate couple. Mama said, "There has never been a cross word between the two of us; we could always settle things easily by discussing everything."

They had a sweet life. They brought 8 children into the world. I was the seventh of them. The third child died from an unfortunate illness at the young age of 14, but the rest of my brothers and sisters are alive up to the present time.

Our Dad and Mama loved each of their children very much. Six of the children were born before the "liberation" (before Mao's Times), and besides the love they received from our parents, they also experienced a rich life, full of all the pleasures of material abundance which their prosperous family circumstances brought them. Of all the children, the ones who obtained the most long-lasting favor were, of course, my eldest and second sister. From the pictures of their birthdays each year, which show them dressed and primped from head to toe, we can see and feel what a deep love they had from our parents.

At that time, my eldest and second sisters were so happy and looked like angels. They wore the same styled skirts, long white socks, and leather shoes. When they started to go to primary school, in order for them to go there and get back home safely, Dad bought a western-style vehicle with two wheels, which was very popular at that time, just to send them and pick them up.

Every morning, the carter Zhang would pull the cart with the two girls to the school, and while he walked, a small bell on the front of the cart would ring in the wind. The clear and melodious tinkle of bells became a most wonderful memory from the days of their childhood. After class they would go back home in the afternoon, and when the cart turned into the alleyway, from a distance, they would see the familiar figures of either Dad or Mama already waiting for them by the gate. They would lift them down from the cart, and holding one hand they would walk into the house.

Dad had studied abroad, and so he especially advocated western education. The school he chose for my eldest and second sister was a private school the church had launched in Kunming. He hoped his children would benefit from this modern and new type of education, even from childhood. The tuition fee for this kind of school was quite high, but it gave them a chance to experience many new things, such as piano, painting and a strict fostering of the good behavior and morals of the students. Dad believed these were the most important things for a child.

The two older sisters once had a happy childhood.

Mama told us that the names Dad gave to the first four children were full of meaning. The eldest sister was named: Zu Yin, the second sister: Zu Hui, the third one: Zu Chang, the fourth one: Zu Ming. The last name in Chinese characters is "Yin Hui Chang Ming" - the implied meaning is - "In a place that is protected by the shade, the family will have a prosperous and bright future." Just from these words, we can imagine the wonderful wishes and high expectations our parents had placed on their children!

In 1946, Dad and Mama had their fifth child, a boy. This was their first boy and also the first boy in the whole family, so it was a time of great happiness for the family. Dad and Mama were overjoyed. Ge Ge's (eldest brother in Chinese) name was different from the four sisters. He was called "Mao Qi"; these two Chinese characters were given by a fortune teller at my grandfather's special request. The two Chinese characters

Mama and Dad were happy to have their first boy.

had a special meaning. "Mao" meant grand and abundance. "Qi" meant blessing and luck. The monthly birthday party for Ge Ge was very grand as all the relatives, friends, and VIPs of the business circles of Kunming were invited to come. That day Wang Tian Chuan, the boss of the "Tong Qing Feng" gold shop, wanted to accept Ge Ge as his godson. That day he changed Ge Ge's name into "Mao Gong Wei Ye, Shou Kao Wei Qi" which meant Mao Qi is a person who will do great things and he will live a long life. He engraved those 8 Chinese characters on an exquisite plaque and brought it when he came to celebrate. Grandfather held his first grand-son and was radiant with joy, continuing to tell the guests the same words over and over again, "This grand-child is just like me. He has a blessed face. It is so wonderful, our family now has everything! Good, good, very good!" As people looked at this vigorous and energetic plump boy, they thought this family really prospered in every way, both their careers and family numbers were flourishing.

Mama had given birth to four daughters in succession. She didn't come under blame or censure from this enlightened family. But, she still hoped anxiously for a boy. Now her wishes had finally come true. She was so happy; she had a smile on her face every day. Because he was the eldest son of the Yan family, he knew when this boy came into the world what that meant for him as well as for the whole family. During those days, Dad felt as though he was soaring on wings with all the complimentary words he received. His prudent character was changing, and on many days, he would whistle with joy. After work he hurried home, entered the gate, and ran straight to the small bed of his son. Whether the baby was sleeping or awake, he would always pick up the baby in his arms, singing and humming with the pleasure of his son. Mama's enjoyment was even greater than Dad's, she protectively watched the baby all the time. She would hold him in her arms, looking at him with deep love for long periods of time; however, she felt that to love him was not enough.

It could be said that when this boy came into the world, Dad and Mama placed especially great expectations on him. Therefore, they chose a special wet nurse for him. They served her first-rate food every day, and let her have her fill of milk so she could breastfeed Ge Ge. When Ge Ge was just three years old, they hired a special teacher to give him some initial education, teaching him to play music, play chess, read and draw - the 4 skills which Chinese think are important for a child's intellectual development. They tried to teach them all. Even though he came into the family a little later, Dad and Mama, like all ordinary Chinese people, loved this boy in a partial way. They nursed this young sapling and hoped Ge Ge would lead great ventures when he grew up, bringing honor to the Yan's ancestors.

During this period, Dad's career also went smoothly. The fabric his factory made still sold well. The shop in Zheng Yi Road had been enlarged; but the place was always packed with customers. So, they had to open a new shop on Jin Bi Road. This was just when the family had their boy, so wasn't it so gratifying? For a long time, the house was full of guests and the scene of bustling excitement.

One day, a grand piano Dad had ordered was sent by the shop to the yard, it replaced the old style organ which had been in the home. After setting it up in the right place, he was so delighted with it that he sat at the piano and played with high spirits. After awhile, to everybody's surprise, he sang a song along with the music. It was a piece from an American film which was very popular then:

> "One day when we were young,
> Wonderful morning in May,
> You told me you love me ... remember,
> One day when we were young,
> You told me you love me!"

His full-bodied baritone resounded around the yard. His four daughters all ran up to him and embraced him. Mama held Ge Ge and leaned against the entrance to the living room also listening to her husband singing and playing.

"Oh, that was really the best time god gave to us!" In Mama's later years she often recalled that time by saying those words.

From then on, Dad prescribed that each child had to learn to play the piano. Dad hired special teachers to teach each child with a time-sharing arrangement. My eldest sister was 8 years old; she was the best one amongst the five children. The sweet basic pieces she played, one after another, always reverberated in the yard. Her practice time was arranged to be from 5-6 o'clock in the afternoon after her classes, and Dad could often hear the music when he had just turned into the lane on his way home. As soon as he heard the music, he would jump out of his car right away, even forgetting to lock it, and run straight in to my eldest sister and the piano. Sometimes a common scene would be the father and his daughter using four hands together to play one piano music piece. Mama had the meal ready, but nobody went in to eat. Everyone enjoyed their playing, and it was only after Dad had enjoyed himself to the full that everyone would start to eat dinner.

In 1947, Dad bought a new house and courtyard for his own small family in Shi Qiao Pu in Kunming. The small family moved out of the old house in Si Ma Di lane and now lived separately in this house.

This house was a Chinese and Western-style mixture with two floors; the floors were paved with marble stone. Based on the record of contract on the title deed, there were a total of 33 rooms included, and the purchase price was 4.5 billion in the old currency (equivalent to 45 million RMB). Dad and Mama were very happy with this new house, because it had established western-style sanitation, a toilet and bathroom. The best thing was that each child now had their own room. Dad hung a distich on the wall of the living room; this distich was written by a famous calligraphist in Yunnan at that time, Mr. Cheng

Rong Chang. It read: "The stream flows into the rice field, sounding far and near, the best weather for flowers is a fine drizzle." He loved a quiet, elegant and peaceful atmosphere. Mama planted many flowers around the yard, filling the yard with colors and atmosphere right away. Not much later, they felt there were too many empty rooms, so they rented one side with 8 rooms to Mr. Li Qin Nian's family. He was a technician at the Hong Da cigarette factory. They were from Shanghai and had two girls the same ages as my eldest and second sisters. When they moved in, both families hit it off and lived together in harmony. Dad and Mama, who had just had a boy and were still intoxicated with the spirit of happiness, believed that they would have more children. Living in such circumstances, their kids would have a much more healthy and joyous life.

At that time, there was a maidservant, a man helper and a driver who assisted Mama to take care of all the affairs of the family.

Not long after they moved into this new house, Dad discovered that the lane which ran by the house, which was about 100 meters long and was not a cement road, was very muddy when it rained and muddied their shoes. He spent a lot of money to rebuild it and paved the lane with big flagstones. The neighbor said they benefited from their association with our family, after we moved into this lane, it changed completely.

Dad went to work the same way every day no matter if it was raining or shining; he always wore western dress and leather shoes. When he came back home at nightfall, he would sometimes buy a bag of snacks or fried chestnuts to bring home to the kids. Mama dressed in a close-fitting cheongsam, her delicate and exquisite figure was always bustling about with something in the home. Though she had given birth to five kids, Mama never gained weight; she kept her slender figure having many ways to retain her stature and keep slim. In addition, she was very neat, keeping the courtyard clean, the home clean, the children clean, and herself clean. She always worked hard with nimble agility every day from morning to night and never had time to be inactive. This was also the reason she did not put on extra weight.

Mama was a person who paid attention to detail, presenting herself to other people in a way that they took special notice. She looked down on women who became slovenly after having babies. Another thing which differentiated Mama from most other middle-aged women was that she loved to laugh. The tiring work of taking care of the children never made her annoyed and unhappy. She always had a pleasant smile on her face. Even if she had to spend all her time only with the children, she would always have been joyful. As Mama laughed heartily, her teeth were spotless and flawless. And the sound of her laughter, which could be heard from far away, had a strong appeal to people. It can be said that our Mama was a person who was a natural mother.

When she had servants working in the home, Mama would only ask them to help her to go out and do some shopping or to do some heavy manual labor. Each meal, especially the dishes for dinner when the whole family would eat with their Dad each evening, would without fail be cooked by her. If her husband and children were pleasant and healthy, it was her greatest joy. Sometimes, she asked the driver to take her to the factory to help Dad arrange or deal with some of the behind-the-scenes affairs for the factory. For instance, when the Chinese New Year or Moon Festival or other traditional festivals came, she had to go to the kitchen at the factory to prepare a nice dinner. She always cooked some dishes she was good at for them and she and Dad would eat together with all the staff. After finishing those things at the factory, they would talk and laugh on their way back home. At the end of year, when it was time to give a bonus to the employees, Mama would go to the bank first to change the paper currency into brand-new notes and put it into a red bag according to the employees' level. Then she wrote down the name on each bag and passed them to Dad to deal out the next day. In any case, there was no need to ask as Mama would keep in order all the things she ought to do and would do them reliably. Once in a while she would go to watch the performance of the Beijing Opera with Dad in the evening; this was the thing which gave her the most happiness in her life. After putting on her dress and make up, Mama was as elegant and tasteful as ever. As she stood with her husband who had a successful business and looked even more honest and sincere, pride and satisfaction would rise up in her mind. She always said, "We had such a nice life then."

In their own courtyard of Shi Qiao Pu, they welcomed their sixth baby. She was a girl again, but she was a very beautiful girl. Dad gave her the name "Zu Fang" (Fang in Chinese means fragrant), because she really looked like a flower, sweet and touching. A family with six children was not a small family; the noise filled every corner of the rooms. Each evening when Dad came back home after work, it was a very jolly time for this family. Often, there was not just one kid sitting on Dad's knee but two sitting on both his knees. As he looked at those chirpy kids around him who were all healthy and happy, Dad enjoyed the time very much. He would ask the eldest sister to play music on the piano, and ask the second sister to recite a section of a Tang poem, then he would sing a children's song with the rest of the younger kids. The house was full of happy songs and laughter all the time. Later at night, after the kids had gone to sleep, Dad and Mama would go together to their room, and before going to bed, he would tell Mama again and again, "It is so wonderful god has given us these children; I do love them very much. I don't know how to give more of my love to them. I am sure I will give them the happiest life in the world."

Mama would ask him in return, "You mean you will give them a better life than now?"

"Yes! The world is so big. The good life far exceeds what we have now; you just don't know," he answered Mama affirmatively. So yes, the life that for Mama was already extremely good and very satisfactory, for Dad was regarded as nothing. His vision was quite large. In his mind he had planned the future for each child many times. He hoped that all of his children would go to receive higher education abroad; he thought that his first daughter should study medicine; the second daughter should study literature. He and his wife were both fond of drama and music; he hoped that among all of the children one would be engaged in art. His son—this plump baby, would be going into business of course as he was the person to inherit the family's property.

"My son should go to study in France, and I will accompany him. I will take him to visit Lyons University where I studied." His thoughts had already gone this far. Often when these thoughts delighted him, he even got out of bed and put on a night-suit and would run to the small beds where the kids were sleeping, quietly filling his heart with the sight of them.

From some people's point of view, our Dad did not seem like a total business man. As his children were born one after the other, he spent more and more time with his kids. He loved each of his children deeply. He paid attention to their school work and their behavior as well as taking care of how they dressed. Each year when new clothes were needed for them, he always took Mama to the most expensive and fashionable children's clothes shop to buy what they needed. Because Ge Ge was the only boy in the family, his dress and hairstyle were Dad's responsibility too. The small western-style clothes were made for Ge Ge in a shop located in Hu Guo Road, a shop run by a Vietnamese man who had been making clothes for him for many years. The boy's hair was always cut at the "Ming Xing Barbershop" by a famous barber who came from Yang Zhou. After Ge Ge had his hair cut, mid-split and waxed, he looked like no other child. If those children needed to participate in some formal activities, they always attracted people's attention. They were not only healthy and well dressed but looked very handsome. This could have been because of their bloodline; my Dad was of full blood Bai nationality descent, and Mama's original family home was in Nanjing which is located south of the Yangtze River. This marriage meant that their children looked a little different from others.

During the years, Dad and Mama were very happy, enjoying the sense of warmth their family brought them every day.

Dad's brother Yan Ze Wen was five years younger. He had been cultivated as a finance professional by my grandfather. When he had just finished school, he found a good job in the Kunming Communication Bank. Soon after that he married Miss Yin Gui Zhen who was the daughter of an illustrious family in Dali. His wife, Si Shen (Si in Chinese is four, Shen is aunt-in-law, the wife of my father's younger brother), was a university graduate, she was very beautiful and in pursuit of modern fashion. Dad's younger sister Yan Zhu Ying had grown up and was now studying English in college. She was the kind of person who not only looked dignified but also had a very haughty character. When Dad brought his family out of Si Ma Di Lane, and they began to reside in their own modern house, living by themselves, they still kept a very close relationship with his brother and sister. Unusually, Mama stayed involved with her sister-in-law who had just come into the Yan house, and they all grew up with my father's sister in harmony just as before. After she had been busy taking care of the affairs of her small family, she would spruce up and take with her some sweets which her brother-in-law's wife liked or some small gifts she had especially bought for her, and so Mama often went to visit her sister-in-law. She guided this lady who was not named Yan, and slowly helped her learn about all the things of the Yan family; gradually they became like full sisters. They built up a good friendship with each other. She found out that San Sao was warmhearted and capable and genuinely got along with her. She trusted Mama very much. Whenever they met together, they always seemed to talk for a long time, seemingly with no end. Even decades later, they have kept a very deep relationship right into their old age. To learn how to treat Dad's sister whom now was an undergraduate, Mama first grew to know her personality, and then looked after her like one of her own children. She always chose to buy the most expensive and best things for her, things for which she would hate to part with money for if she were to buy them for herself. From this, Dad's whole family saw Mama's excellent character. Although Dad's sister was supercilious, she could not find any fault with Mama, so there was never any conflict between them over the years.

On the desk in front of me, there is an old picture which was taken in about 1940 when the whole family was on an outing. I have carefully looked at the expression of each person in the photo. From the expression in Mama's eyes I get the feeling that she must have faced humiliation in order to carry out this important mission; because she was a diligent person with remarkable endurance and for the sake of family harmony, she was willing to put up with anything. At that time she was only 30 years old. Her dress

Yan family had a prosperous business and harmonious atmosphere in 1940s.

was common to all the people; she had not even the slightest hint of arrogance but was restrained and self-disciplined. Maybe she knew this was her duty and the position she must take in this big family. Only by humbling herself, could she fulfill the role which formed a connecting link between the preceding and the following generations. Even though she was the wife of the eldest son in this family, she didn't show any feeling that she occupied a commanding or elevated position. In this picture, Mama is standing beside her sister-in-law who is wearing a western-style long overcoat, in the same picture, is Dad's younger sister who has a modern hairstyle and is dressed in a fashionable outfit. Comparing the three women in this picture, we can see our Mama is so mature and knows her place.

Certainly, it is not easy to play a nice role of the wife of the eldest son in an old style family. In 1947, grandfather and grandmother passed away from illness. Dad and Mama took on the responsibility of looking after their younger brother and sister. They would often go on outings together. One car would be driven by a hired driver; another car was always driven by Dad who also took the photos. The old pictures which we still have now show us what a joyful and peaceful time this family experienced. Each of them was always well dressed and wreathed in smiles. This cannot be separated from the key role our Mama played.

Later, Dad's younger sister graduated from college. After falling passionately in love, she declared that she would marry a classmate named Yang. This young man had just finished school and was from a common family, but to help their younger sister, Dad and Mama held a luxurious wedding for them which made a great stir in Kunming at the time. The conduct of her older brother and his wife touched the younger sister who had lost both her parents. It was also praised by all the relatives and friends. Our Si Shen still talks about it in her later years

Sixth anniversary for Chang Ming Textile Mill.

saying, "Nobody can do things like San Sao, what she contributed to the marriage of her sister-in-law was worth two full truckloads."

This was Mama, who always had cardinal principles in mind, and took the overall situation into account. Wherever she was, she was harmonious. In regards to family relationships, she loved to say, "The family's happiness is worth a thousand pieces of gold, if the family lives in harmony, all their affairs will prosper." So, because of her, the one big family and the one small family she held together could live peacefully and amicably for years and years.

When the camera had just come onto the scene, Dad liked it from the beginning, and soon he was simply bewitched by photography. He always took photos and developed them himself. Then he bought albums and edited and organized them, writing some memorable words under the pictures. Because of his work, many portraits of their real life have been left to us.

Meanwhile from 1937-1945, the whole of China suffered from 8 years of the War of Resistance against Japan. Kunming as the more distant area was comparatively stable. When many big cities were occupied by the enemy, great numbers of politicians and intellectuals moved into Kunming. The necessities of their lives, including a large requirement for textiles, brought a good development opportunity to Dad's corporation. His factory and shop prospered, and everything went smoothly. There didn't appear to be any problems.

Grandfather died a natural death while the family's financial situation was very comfortable. On his deathbed, he spoke final words for Dad. First, he hoped he could be buried in his hometown in Dali on the Ji Zu Mountain. Second, he demanded Dad not forget to repay society and to be willing to take care of the community's public welfare even as he has an abundant life. And he asked that much of his heritage be given to the temple on Ji Zu Mountain. Dad went to the Ji Zu Mountain and did what his father told him. Because the fund my grandfather donated to the temple was so large, the temple set up an inscription in memory of him. This inscription still stands on the lofty Ji Zu Mountain.

After this, Dad and Mama followed grandfather's wishes and willingly donated to help others. They contributed a large sum of money to repair the famous Golden Temple in Kunming. As one of its great benefactors, my father's name was engraved on the monument of the Golden Temple.

Now we also know that the Yan family's eagerness to contribute to public welfare did not begin with my grandfather but started with an elder of my grandfather. In a brief introduction of the family history which was put on the "Yan Family House" at Xi Zhou in Dali, the following words were written - "Attaching importance to education and warmheartedly contributing to common welfare have been the

Yan family's ancestral instructions from generation to generation."
According to the official records, the Yan family did many large-scale
social and public welfare projects during those times of prosperity, such
as contributing to and setting up hospitals, schools, and libraries.

In 1946, the anti-Japanese War had finished, and the whole nation
was festive. When Dad was the chairman of the textile association of
Kunming, in order to celebrate the Chinese victory, he initiated the
raising of funds from the members of the association and built a new
school outside the city gate, so that the poor children who lived there
could have easy access to study. The new school was named "Bu Xin
School." (Bu in Chinese is fabric, Xin in Chinese is new.) At the school's
opening ceremony, Mama went onto the stage and sang a segment of
the Beijing opera from "The Story of the White Snake." That day, her

Dad was elected as the chairman of the textile association of Kunming.

five children sat there watching her on the stage singing. What an honor my Mama had! This primary school was built completely in the Bai nationality style; the auditorium on the campus later became the place for members of the association to have meetings and parties. My older brother and sisters went there many times with Dad and Mama to share their stationary and other writing materials with the children. There is a steel foundation still standing at this school today, with the main donors' names engraved on it. Our father Yan Ze Gao's name is there.

This all paints a true historical picture of this older generation. This account and its facts prove that they were filled with honesty and kindness.

The following few years during the time of the Kuomintang and Communist Party was a crucial period of life-and-death struggle between Jiang Jie Shi and Mao Ze Dong. During many years of continual fighting, it became clear to both parties that they were as incompatible as fire and water. It was impossible for them to unite and come into power to manage the country. Whoever would be in control of the power of the nation would determine the perspective and future for hundreds of millions of people in China. At that time, the people's eyes were blurred by the strong political public opinion which both the KMT and the Communist Party expressed. Who was right and who was wrong, nobody could clearly say.

Dad was just 40 years old and about to step into middle age. He had never paid any attention to politics; he wore business suits and went to his workplace each day just as before and dealt with the affairs of his factory. After he arrived back home, he was surrounded by his wife and children, and he felt very satisfied. Sometimes at the weekend, he would meet some of his friends and relatives; he still spent some time on photography, played tennis, and lived a carefree and leisurely life.

In the summer of 1949, Mao Ze Dong and his army thoroughly defeated Jiang Jie Shi and occupied most of the regions and cities of China. Jiang Jie Shi was foul-mouthed and cursed, "The Communists are just thieves and robbers; the communist party is the party that just wants to take all the people's property, and the communist party is the party which takes the women to be their wives. Mao Ze Dong will come to a bad end and will die without a burial place." And he fled to Taiwan in despair.

Government officials at all the levels of the Kuomintang also took their families away from mainland. My dad knew several officials through the tennis club who worked for the Kunming and Yunnan provincial government, and they left too. Before they left, they told Dad, "The situation now seems fraught with grim possibilities, it is better you think about your opportunity for freedom while there is still time."

Dad just laughed them out of court. He thought, "Whoever comes into power, people still need to eat and dress. We are law-abiding and pay our taxes, the enterprise we are working with benefits society and the people; any government should welcome us and treat us well."

On October first, Mao Ze Dong stood on the gate tower of Tian An Men and officially declared to the world in his very strong Hunan accent, "The People's Republic of China has come into existence." A new state power had now been established in the eastern world.

In the beginning, the red storm did not sweep across the whole nation right away. While the great political changes started to happen in many of the big cities of China, in the frontiers and small cities like Kunming which were far away from Beijing, the people's lives and work stayed the same as before.

Compared with many of the other cities, the Kunming people's lives were always deemed to be like the weather here, it was not very hot, also not very cold. They were living in a state of aimlessness and leisure. Just like most of the Kunming people, Dad and Mama were disinterested in politics. They also didn't pay attention to how this new state power would influence their lives. They were living in their own bourgeois life filled with sentiment.

After about a year of the news paper and radio emphasizing again and again that the guiding principle for the party in power was "to destroy the feudalistic exploitative system, to destroy the private ownership of capitalism, and to establish the publicly-owned system of the socialism," some of the people from the business circles of Kunming started to talk about it and to worry about their situation. But they half believed and half doubted the communist party's publicity, and were full of the idea of leaving things to change.

Dad held a meeting for the members of the association, and when they were talking about how to face to the changes of the new state power, those outstanding people from the business circles were drinking fragrant tea and talking as cheerfully and humorously as before. One of the entrepreneurs joked and he said loudly, "They cannot go as far as they say; my property, my factory, how can they be destroyed by all their words, it is impossible."

They were laughing and joking, and their demeanor showed that they never saw it as a big event that the red power was now at the point of entering the political stage.

They knew there were so many middle and small-sized enterprises like theirs. If those enterprises would be overthrown, or destroyed, the life line of the state economy would become critical. How could the new state power run the country? No one party would take such rash and arbitrary action, doing whatever they wished. The shouting and whooping they used now were just the customary tactics all new governments used for their public voice.

"This is just the communist party's way of voicing their political opinion; they will not be able to do anything toward us," the members said, and they considered themselves above politics and worldly interests, but they were presumptuous. Whenever they met together, they usually just encouraged each other. Many of them said that the factories and the enterprises they owned were built up from nothing. They had worked hard for generations and generations, working laboriously day after day. Never once did they think that they would be divided off as an exploiting class. They paid their taxes on time and supported the common welfare; they are the people who have contributed to society. The new government should only affirm their achievements not strike them down. Some people even said that no matter what kind of society they had, private property would always be protected; this was not something the government would steal or rob to get. So, there was nothing else they could be afraid of. What they should do is just continue to do what they liked. Only as a safeguard, they decided to withdraw some cash from their bank deposits and merely keep it safe at home. But those were just a few people who were quite sensitive. They had learned and heard from the newspaper and radio about the guiding principles this new political power would be enforcing, and they felt it was against the grain of the life they had been used to. Later, they sensed something happening in Beijing and Shanghai and other such big cities. They found out from the big capitalists and their corporations that there had been some misfortunes and changes. Now they didn't believe the evolution of the situation would be as easy as some had imagined. "Go while the going is good," they said and started to take into account that maybe the best and most secure way for them would be to take their whole family and leave the mainland. There were some close friends of Dad who came to our home almost every day; they brought the newspaper to analyze the situation, talking and talking the whole evening. They discussed it with Dad and believed that under the protection of Kunming not having been declared "liberated" yet as it was still not controlled completely by the communist party, the best thing to do now would be to sell off the family's property quickly and fly the whole family to Hong Kong or Taiwan for refuge. Dad, wearing a white shirt covered with a black waistcoat and holding a favorite cigar in his hand, listened and smiled as they talked. He didn't agree with them; he thought their evaluation of the situation was too harsh. He told them, "I would rather wait for a period of time to see how things go. But only two weeks later, these two good friends of his had bought air tickets and left with the family. Dad went to the airport to send them off. When he was back home, he continued smoking, and for the first time began to think deeply about the fate of his own family. He didn't know what course he should take. He had never encountered such huge changes, and he also had never made such an important decision in his life before.

Many evenings in succession, he talked it over and over with Mama; the light in their room was on until daybreak. Mama was the kind of person who longed for her family; for her, it was difficult to move to another place, abandoning all the things she had there. She only knew a little bit about other countries, and she did not even have much knowledge about Taiwan and Hong Kong. She was not at all willing to leave Kunming to go to any of the other places to live. She held her youngest baby in her arms and talked to Dad, "Our family is not as easy to move as other families; we have six children, we are used to living in Kunming, and I don't want to go to any other place." Dad was a person who regarded Mama's ideas. His gentle and kind character also made it hard for him to decide to hand over this factory, which was a result of two generations' painstaking efforts, to others so easily and just go away.

The western education he had received made him believe doggedly that no matter which political power had control in the country, progress and development always needed industry and commerce. He felt confident with his professional knowledge, and he thought he was law-abiding and was a cautious and conscientious person. There was not any reason he would be excluded by the new nation. Just like many of the patriotic intelligentsia, Dad was full of trust in the new political power. He said, "I know this new society will bring some new changes; for the Chinese, I think it is a good thing."

The circle of my Dad's life had been just his factory and his family for years. He didn't know anything about the Communist Party or about Mao Ze Dong. Now he saw there were more and more people wearing the green army uniform on the street, and he learned about some new policies from the newspaper. Day by day he found that the articles in the newspaper had totally changed their tone, so he decided that he should get to know more about this new ruling party. He purposely went to the bookshop. He brought back a brochure which published Mao Ze Dong's new article "The Theory of the New Democracy." He read it carefully many times and tried to figure out the major principles in this book that said:

> "The political aim of the Communist party of China is to overthrow the onslaught of imperialism and feudalism. To establish a democratic republic state under the leadership of the proletariat with other revolutionary political parties united under dictatorship. The new democracy toward a transition to socialism needs quite a long historical period. During this period, we will protect the national industries and commerce and develop capitalism."

Though he was puzzled and could not see the evolution of this situation now, he trusted these black words written on white paper. He thought that the party now leading such a big country could not be doing anything indiscriminate. He would just go to work on time as normal and thought it would be fine to keep a normal attitude and wait for this transformation.

During this period, many of their friends and relatives had left their native land and moved to Hong Kong, Taiwan, and even to other countries, but the final decision Dad and Mama made was not to go anywhere and just stay in Kunming. They would just meet these monumental changes as they happened, and maybe something good would happen with them, so they consoled each other day by day.

Kunming was declared liberated in October 1950. Dad and Mama stood together with many of the Kunming people on both sides of Jin Bi Road holding small red flags in their hands to welcome a large body of the marching liberation army into the city. The first time they saw these new power holders close up, they looked affable and not fearsome at all. They were dressed simply and had radiant smiles. One day a month later, Dad received a call from the city business association telling him that there were some army representatives coming to visit his factory. Immediately, Dad arranged for people to clean the factory inside and out; he prepared some sweets to be put on the table of the meeting room, and then he led all of his staff out to line up on both sides of the gate. They beat drums and struck gongs to welcome the guests as they entered the factory. The army representatives walked through the factory and inspected the workshop and the office; they didn't drink and didn't touch the sweets. When they were leaving, one man who looked like an officer in appearance shook Dad's hand firmly and said, "We don't know anything about business; you are the specialist in this field. We will learn from you in the future."

Dad was touched and smiled as he said to the man, "You flatter me, you flatter me." So Dad had an extremely good impression of this leader of the communist party. That afternoon he strode through the gate of the house almost at a run and immediately told Mama the words the officer had spoken to him. Their hearts had been filled with anxiety and fear for a long time, and now they suddenly settled down. "Oh, society has changed but we still can live our lives as before," they said and both suddenly laughed heartily like two children. At the dinner table that evening, all the people listened with excitement to Dad as he described the whole process of what had happened in the factory.

After the army representatives had visited the factory, Dad and Mama felt relaxed, and before long Mama was pregnant again; the baby in her womb was me. I am the one with the greatest age difference between myself and my older brothers and sisters. I am 4 years younger than my sister who was born in 1947. This gives an indication that during this period of historic transformation when the new state power replaced the old; Dad and Mama had been living in fear and trembling waiting to see what would happen. During the first half year of the new political power being set up in Kunming, there were no changes anywhere in the city. The people's lives went on as before. Dad and Mama and their family lived in their small courtyard. Mama looked after the house which was spotless, not soiled by even a speck of dust filled with the delicate fragrance of flowers and plants. They were still full of joy as before.

At the beginning of 1951, the War of Resistance to US Aggression and to aid Korea broke out. The central government which had just been set up met with financial difficulty, so the government encouraged people to donate and to support this "just war." Mama who was heavily pregnant at that time participated in activities organized by the women of the business circles in Kunming for the collection of donations. She worked with all her energy. She and many of the wives of famous business

Mama was elected as the member of the executive committee of the women congress for resistance to US aggression and to aid Korea in Kunming.

men held collection boxes and stood on the street every day. They held up a large scroll proclaiming the great importance of supporting this war to the public with a stern voice and countenance. In the evening, they counted the money they had collected carefully and with great excitement. They were delighted as they registered, checked in, and handed in the money to the government office. They were so excited and never felt tired. Although this was the first time they had done such things, taking a position which connected each of them to the great change of socialism in the new China, they felt greatly honored.

Despite their excitement, they thought what they did was not enough. Each of them should make their own specific contribution. They went home to discuss this with their husbands and each of them also contributed money to support the nation in their own name. To do this, some ladies received money from their husbands and immediately ran to the relevant department of the government to send it off; some ladies sold their treasures and cheerfully delivered the money. Mama said that she received enthusiastic support from Dad for this; she donated a large sum of money. Looking at the numbers, her contribution was amongst the top amounts. The fund into which the women of the business circle donated was very large and was sufficient to buy a plane to assist on the battlefront of Korea. In order to commend the enthusiastic actions of these women, the Kunming city government held a meeting on the 7th of July. The leaders of the new political power interviewed these women. That day, based on the number of contributions, some of the bigger donors were elected as members of the executive committee to sit on the stage; Mama was one of them. After the meeting, all the members of the executive committee had their photo taken as a souvenir. In this photo, Mama is wearing a cheongsam in a deep blue color; her hair was combed beautifully as usual, and she had coiled her hair into a knot at the back of her neck. She was standing on the inside of the second row smiling and looking very proud.

It could be said that I participated in all these activities together with Mama, because I was in her womb and a few months later would be born. Before, when Mama was pregnant, she always received Dad's favor and had a lot of time to relax and rest. Now Mama could not be in Dad's care as she went out and ceaselessly attended many activities; she was doing something she had never done before in her life. She said the women of the business circle discussed how they would set up a women's federation and would contribute their strength and talent to the community, not just serve their own families. When she got home each day, she gave information to Dad and her children at great length; she was too excited to remember she was a pregnant woman. All the family members were inspired by her passion and happiness; the time went faster and more joyfully than in former years. She made new style Lenin uniforms for the children and asked them to wear them. She encouraged her two daughters who were now studying in the middle school to take part in the propaganda activities which the school organized to promote the new society and the new life. Only one word "new" encompassed her and the family.

Everything to do with the factory and the home was just as before. Dad and Mama were waiting for their seventh child to come.

Mama said that at that time, they were impacted by and experienced a series of novel things. Just going out into the street, the first thing they noticed was that people's dress and hairstyles had changed. Many of the women voluntary no longer wore their cheongsams, their hair was not permed; they cut their hair very short just above their ears. For the first time, they put on the coat and pants worn by the women soldiers who had just entered the city. Some women were more open; they even started to try wearing the one-piece dress made from a cotton print called "Bu La Ji." (It was in the Russian tone.) This was learned from Russia which was the first socialist country in the world; the Russian women all wore this "Bu La Ji," so the new style of Chinese women wanted to follow this latest fashion. Where the family lived was not far away from Jin Bi Road, an area where there had previously been some brothels and opium houses. Now, what people saw every day were the five star flags fluttering in the wind on the gate of Jin Ma. Those brothels and opium houses which before had created a foul atmosphere now had been closed down by force. There were big and small five star flags and red slogans everywhere, and the deafening sound of gongs and drums. This new world was now indeed full of novelty and celebration dazzling people.

August 15th on the Chinese calendar is the Moon Festival in China. Mama prepared a sumptuous dinner for the family, and when they had finished eating, she was busy cooking chestnuts and green soy beans. At about 9 o'clock, all the food was ready to eat. On one round table with a fine table cloth, Mama displayed a range of moon festival foodstuffs. There were five types of moon cakes, each one she had cut into four small pieces and put them on a big plate. Mama steamed the moon cake which was stuffed with ham. This was her special creative way to eat this cake. After heating it up, this moon cake was very limp and soft, and the smell would overflow the whole room. On the table, there were red watermelons and white pears, sunflower seeds and peanuts, too. When Mama called the people to sit together around the table, she announced grinning, "Now, let us have our moon festival. This is the first moon festival after the liberation; it is meaningful. Let us celebrate it. Ok, let's eat the moon cake."

The six children started eating wild with joy. Mama picked up one piece of ham moon cake and put it on a nice porcelain tray and gave it to Dad. Looking at her husband and her children, she began to soliloquize, "I am so glad. This moon festival is very interesting. After eating, let us go out together; we will go out on the street to look at the moon; there must be many people there."

"Yes, this moon festival is special, there must be something happening on the street; we should all go to take a look," Dad agreed with Mama. After eating it was nearly 10 o'clock. Mama held Ge Ge and the sixth sister one on each hand, and the other four kids walked close to Dad; under the light of the moon the family went through the lane and walked together toward the main street. Ten minutes later, when they had just walked to the crossroads, Mama suddenly stood still and said to Dad in a low voice, "Oh, I am afraid I will be having the baby soon. I don't think I can go anywhere."

Dad told the first and second daughter to take care of the younger brother and sisters and to come back home early. He and Mama returned home quickly. As Mama was in the throes of labor, they took some things they needed and quickly drove to the hospital. At 6 minutes past 12 o'clock, I, the seventh of their children, came into the world safe and sound.

When Dad held me in his arms, I opened both my big eyes, keeping a close watch on him.

"What a clever girl!" Dad said to Mama happily, "This girl should not follow in the family name at all; it is a new society. Let's give her a new name; call her Ling Ling - that will be fine." Mama naturally agreed with Dad. She took me from Dad's arms and hugged me firmly to her bosom.

"Oh, our little daughter, you have come to pursue this new era, Ling Ling, my little dear." She kissed me on my cheek again and again and then lay down to rest. And so my name is very special and different from my other brothers and sisters. I was also the first child among the seven children to grow up drinking Mama's milk. Mama said that among all the outdated, irrational customs which the communist party wanted to annul from the old society was that of having a wet nurse, so rich people were not allowed to hire a wet nurse. She and Dad thought this was fair and reasonable. They were certain they wanted to respond to this call, so Mama started to feed me with her milk and from then on I slept beside her on one bed. That year Mama was 34 years old. She thought I would be her last child. She carried me in her arms at all times of the day; she would say to whoever happened to come her way, "Our Ling Ling is the only baby I will look after and nurse myself as she grows. Look, how lovely she is."

As the saying goes, "The emperor loves the first son, but the common people love their youngest child." It was the same in our family and went even further than that. I was loved in a special way by Mama and Dad. I was not only their favorite, but I was also like a toy to be played with in turn by my other five sisters. They combed my hair in funny ways and taught me to say this and to do that; I would repeat the words of others like a parrot and always continually made all of them laugh. Maybe for that reason, I have a personality which is always cheerful, and I have loved laughing from the time I was young.

These were the sweetest times I have ever had in my whole life. I came into this world while Dad and Mama's dream had not yet been disillusioned. Mama said my eyes were very big and very bright from when I was born, and I always gazed around and around, interested in everything and continually exploring.

As I grew up day after day, what did I see with my big eyes?

In the early part of 1952, when I was just six months old, political movements called "The three-anti and five-anti campaigns" were suddenly rolled out across the whole nation. "The three-anti campaign" was set up to challenge corruption, fight against waste and fight against bureaucracy in the government offices of the state run economic departments, organizations, and enterprises. "The five-anti campaign" was set up to challenge and fight against bribery, tax dodging and tax evasion, stealing and deception involving state assets, shoddy work and the use of inferior materials, theft of state economic information by private corporations in industry, and commerce in the large and middle-sized cities. Why did the communist party initiate these nationwide political movements? It was because Mao Ze Dong who considered himself ignorant of economic matters had found out that the capitalist class was now secretly conducting an internal measurement of their strength against him. The newspaper said:

> "The illegal capitalist class is corrupting the cadres of the state
> by every possible means, to cut down the ground of socialism,
> attempting to dispute the leadership of the state run socialist
> economy and trying to cripple the national economy. There
> are some leaders who have just come to power, especially those

leaders who are in major positions controlling wealth, they
cannot withstand the test of an attack by a "sugar-coated bullet",
and they have become corrupt and have degenerated."

The newspaper also soon reported some startling news. Liu Qing Shan who had the official post of the communist party secretary of Tianjing and Zhang Zi Shan who had the official post of commissioner of Tianjing area were typical examples of corruption. Even though they had been part of the old cadre of the communist party and had been involved in the revolution for many years, in February these two "big bad wolves" were publicly executed by the central committee. Pictures of them tied up and sent under escort to the execution ground were published in all the nation's newspapers. The death penalty had been put into effect, and its deterrent force was tremendous. On the one hand the central communist party called on all embezzlers to surrender and confess their crimes, and on the other hand they mobilized the masses to impeach and expose others, and so a powerful and dynamic political movement was unveiled across the whole nation without warning, in the twinkling of an eye. As the revolution started in real earnest, Dad and many other people from the business arena were inevitably involved. Throughout their lifetime, they had never heard of or experienced such a political movement, and they were momentarily struck dumb with fear. In their life's journey, this was the first time they had encountered the political cleansing of a proletarian dictatorship.

Now army representatives had entered and garrisoned themselves in the factories, eating and living there. They convened the working class congress and proclaimed that the time had come for the working class to become the masters of their own destiny. At the same time, they mobilized them to boldly expose all the illegal acts of the capitalists who had exploited them for years. As the targets of the revolution in this movement, the enterprisers were not given the right to participate in the movement along with the working class. They were taken to a gathering at a place called Gan Tou Cun located at the foot of the Western Hills. Here they received training in how to abide by the law and waited to be impeached by the masses. They still received good food and lived in a nice hotel every day, were able to listen to some reports, read the newspaper, and had access to documents and decisions made by the communist party about this movement; but from the attitude of the army representatives and the way the government officers treated them and from the phrasing in the newspaper and the documents, they knew their own position had quietly changed in this society. They had been the managers, standing high above the masses for years, now they were to be impeached and have their "problems" exposed by others one after another. Naturally, they could not all adjust to this new situation they now found themselves in, so some of them were very low-spirited. Whenever they attended the meetings or were in group discussions, nothing could be seen in the meeting place but smoke. Almost every one of them would hold a cigarette in their hands and smoke continuously. They sat there absent-mindedly. Deep in thought they were considering their own destiny, imagining what would happen to them later. At this time, many of them had already conformed to the mainstream, taking off their trim western-style clothes and putting on the gray and blue "Mao Suits" for the first time. Some people wore hats as well; these were the same hats the PLA men wore when they entered the city; everyone had one on their head. Dressed like this, they looked crestfallen and nondescript. An ominous foreboding enveloped them; they felt that a great misfortune was coming.

As expected, when they came back to Kunming just few days later, they found out right away that the slogans and watchwords in every street were filled with murderous expressions; the atmosphere was totally different than before. Dad didn't attend the meeting the army representatives held with his workers, so he didn't know what they said at that meeting. Mama told him what the speaker had said and what was written in the newspaper in those days in Kunming, when he entered his factory. But he still could not bear to face the scene he saw: the gate of his factory was now controlled by some workers who wore red armbands with "worker pickets" characters written on them. When they saw their boss walk into the factory, they didn't smile as they would have in the past but now looked triumphant. When he stepped into his office, he noticed there was one more desk there where two workers with the same red armbands on their arms were seated. They saw him come in but gave him no greeting, not even a nod.

What had happened? This was a sight never seen before, and it made him very uncomfortable.

But worse was still to come. Soon, he was told that he had been impeached and that the workers of his factory had exposed many problems. Those "problems" revealed by the army representative who interviewed him startled Dad and he said, "Tax dodging and tax evasion for a long period of time;, the total amount is over million Yuan." This accusation Dad would not accept at all. He requested that the finance director come and clarify this with him face to face. However, he was told that those numbers had come out when he was impeached by the workers who were assisted by the finance department.

"Oh, this is terrible! I myself hired those workers and trained them to become skilled workers; some were even promoted to become administrators. We worked together and ate together for more than ten years, why now would they change their faces and frame a case against me?" Dad could not believe what he heard. He talked to the army representatives to prove that they were incorrect. But the army representatives were not the same people as one year ago; their faces showed they now gloated over another's misfortune. Because they had "arrested a tiger," it meant they had finally completed their task. During that period of time, the newspapers were cheering on each province to compete to "catch a tiger," and the way to find a tiger was to get them to confess and then impeach them. All the government officers and army cadres used a whole bag of tricks like inquisition by torture to extort a confession; one after one "tigers" were ferreted out in this way. That day, when Dad talked to them, their usual attitude was expressed in the callous words of one sentence, "We are the army of the laboring people; we only trust the working class. As far as your affairs are concerned, you should know how to deal with them!"

"What do you mean? What things should I know?!" Dad walked back home dejected; he didn't know how to take the next step; he really had no idea. He was gripped by fear. At that time, the countrywide "three-anti/five-anti campaigns" were an echo of "the land reform movement" which had reached its climax in the countryside and was advancing at an amazing pace, and soon it came into a period where it was white-hot. In this land reform movement in the countryside, the farmers who had not owned land before were now suddenly given land by the communist party who had seized it from the landlords and rich peasants. Because of their simple thinking, they were deeply grateful to the communist party who had enabled them "to free themselves to be the masters." These illiterate and unenlightened people found it easy to automatically follow the policies of their benefactors. And those who were suddenly classified as landlords and rich peasants lost their land. Most of them could not understand and could not accept their economic status and refused to give up the management of their land. It was clear that the land and house they owned was the result of a whole family having worked laboriously to save money in order to buy a little piece after a little piece over many years and generations. How was it now said to have been "exploited"? They would either go to the village office and abuse them or stupidly rope off their land and not allow anyone to touch it. This was action the communist party was waiting for; they wanted the people to react first. Now they had a reason to incriminate them. If it was thought that some people's attitude was not as "good" as they expected, a label of "counter-revolutionary" was immediately put on their heads. Then they held some meetings to mobilize the farmers who were now designated as the poor and lower-middle peasants and had become the group they relied on; their emotions had been stirred up with hatred and instigated so they were immediately ready to play the game. Under the direction of the Tu Gai Gang Bu of the communist party (the Tu Gai Gang Bu – were the land reform cadres who were sent to the countryside to help conduct this movement), they used pieces of bamboo and a board to make signs which had a pointed end and big signboard. They brought ropes and ran into the houses of those counterrevolution landlords, trussing them up with no excuse. They hung the big signs they had prepared over their chests, with the characters "to beat down reactionary landlord XXX" written in black oil paint and inserted the label with the pointed end on their backs. Then in their faces they painted a red X on their name on the sign. After that they escorted them, parading them through the streets and ridiculing them by beating drums and striking gongs. Alas! Those people who had formerly had dignity in the village, didn't even know what they had done wrong. After the indignant masses had struck and kicked them on their way through the streets, some of the older ones could not bear this mental and physical suffering and only a few days later lost their lives. Under the eyes of the leaders of "land reform working team" there were some who, at the meeting which was held to criticize and denounce them, were beaten with the shoulder pole and died. There were a few who were given the name of "flagrant," which meant they were guilty of the most heinous crimes. They were judged by the government with enforced spectator participation in mass trials and then escorted to the execution ground to be publicly shot. After the "land reform movement," there was another movement which followed called "The Campaign to Suppress Counter-revolutionaries." Mao Ze Dong was very clear about the necessity of killing some people as a deterrent force to any opposition to the new power. Of course, these people whose class status was now designated as "the enemy of the new nation" had their land and houses confiscated and given to the public. Even death would not expiate all their crimes, so their family members, if they were still alive, would now be doomed to live a life of suffering like hell on earth.

The luxurious house which Yan Zi Zhen had spent a huge amount of money building and which was later called "Yan's House" was at that time forcibly occupied by the "stand up farmers"; all the later generations of the Yan family were driven from their houses and became destitute and homeless. Suddenly the Yan relatives living in Xi Zhou at that time were all declared to be "despotic landlords and illegal capitalists." Their land and property instantly disappeared into thin air. With such a hat on their heads, their peaceful lives were totally over. They had to accept being bound and criticized and denounced every day, they never knew what would happen next. In every city across the whole country, the progression of the "three-anti/five-anti campaigns" created a situation which became tense and confused. Some capitalists were deemed to be illegal and reactionary capitalists; they were arrested and waited for punishment. Their corporations and property were entirely confiscated, now belonging to the state. According to the policy published in the newspaper, they would be sentenced to death as "counter-revolutionaries" and had to accept their fate of execution by public shooting.

"Yong Chang Xiang" was the big company founded by Yan Zi Zhen, and after 50 years of successful operation, the second son of Yan Zi Zhen was named as one of "the flagitious local tyrant landlords" and tied up and shot in full view of Xi Zhou town. When this shocking news came, all the staff knew that they could not escape this calamity; each person was like a bird startled by the mere twang of a bow-string. They all realized that despite the cohesive and painstaking effort of many generations of the Yan family, which had caused them to thrive and prosper for half a century, "Yong Chang Xiang" from this moment on would no longer be "forever, flourishing, lucky." Its fate could only be - sudden destruction. (Note: the meaning of Yong in Chinese is permanent; the meaning of Chang in Chinese is flourishing; the meaning of Xiang in Chinese is auspicious.)

As these unexpected events happened, Dad heard with his own ears and saw with his own eyes how people with the same status as himself had suddenly encountered misfortune and had difficulty saving even their lives. Dad became more and more anxious and frail as the more he thought about the situation, the more afraid he became. Once he had been designated as an illegal capitalist, he could no longer protect the property which had been held for generations from harm. What would his end be? He could scarcely bear to think about it. He suffered a disastrous decline. Although in his heart he resented the "problems" for which he had been impeached and exposed, after a cycle of being abducted and bullied by the army representatives and the "working pickets," he had to "confess" that he had engaged in some tax evasion from the liberation until now, and he was willing to mortgage his property to repay this debt. Even after this, he still could not avoid their investigations. Many times he was asked to stand on the stage to receive their disapproval; they criticized and rudely rebuked him. This was the first time in his life that he had lost his dignity; the pain of being rebuked and having insults hurled at him made Dad feel extremely discouraged. His bright eyes had lost their former radiant look. During this time, the only thing which could comfort him was to go back home to see no one other than Mama; telling her his inner feelings would calm his temper a little bit.

Mama said no one could imagine that the situation would change like this. They were living in a state of stress which they had never experienced before. They didn't know what would happen next; they adopted a fatalistic mentality, leaving things to chance. They hoped it was just a short-lived movement, and that after the government had checked them out, there would be no big problem. In a few months it would be over. They thought maybe their life would have some changes; they might lose some money, but if they could save their lives, it would be enough. Experiencing such a violent shake up really alarmed and bewildered them. In the evening, there were some bold relatives and friends who still came to our home covertly. They liked to talk and analyze the situation together. But they were already dressing sloppily as a result of this hard reality. Just from their appearance it was clear they were in dire straits. Laden with anxiety they would say to each other:

"How much have you confessed?"

"Oh, I am almost becoming crazy."

"The communist party doing things this way is too ruthless; it is clear they want to steal our property; when they bring charges against you, they ask you to pay them for no purpose."

"We are finished, finished; we are completely doomed. I have nothing but fear; we will be reduced to poverty and ruin!"

Each time, after these comments and all the pessimistic talk, they would part, their faces full of confusion, walking back home stealthily along the wall like thieves. Each of them had become aware that the most severe test of their lives had crept up on them quietly. They never imagined that in the days to come, this "violent action by one class to overthrow another class," would bring such a great change and how it would impact their lives!

In March, the first part of the movement was over. The central communist party announced five principles on how to treat the illegals: (i)to treat with leniency for the past; to treat with severity for the future; (ii) to show leniency to the majority, to show severity to the few; (iii) to treat with leniency those who confess, to treat with severity those who resist; (iv) to show leniency to industry, to show severity to trade (v) to show leniency to general business, to treat with severity all speculative business.

When the newspaper published this policy, it caused all the private entrepreneurs who were now being examined to relax a little. Up until now, the number of those who were impeached and exposed comprised the majority of the people as there were huge numbers of industry and commercial enterprises who were involved at different levels of "the five illegal actions," so the percentage of the population that was affected reached 80%. Reputedly, in many parts of the whole country, this was not based on substantial evidence but based on the status of each administrative unit and how much property they had, which determined the number of "tigers." And they set up the "beat the tiger team" to catch these "tigers." They developed tactics to beat these "tigers," such as not allowing the "tiger" to sleep, forcing the "tiger" to stand for long periods of time, or making the "tiger" spend time in introspection on bended knees and using other tricks to obtain forced confessions to give the accusers credibility. So, this is how they had acquired such a brilliant military victory. The central party suspected this huge number may have been the result of excessive and extreme methods. The punishments measured out were milder in the countryside. During the following few months, all the private enterprises received their final assessment from this movement. They were divided into five kinds of corporations - those who were abiding by the law, those who were essentially abiding by the law, those who were abiding by the law half the time, those who seriously broke the law, and those who completely broke the law. In October the three-anti/five-anti campaign movement was over. The party media "People's Daily" published an editorial, which said:

> "The three-anti/five-anti campaign movement is the movement to beat off the bourgeoisie offensive towards the working class from both the government offices and the private corporations and to establish the leadership position of the working class and state operations. It has built up the workers' supervision in the private corporations and put into practice democratic reform. The owners of industry and commercial enterprises have generally accepted this universal legal re-education."

Yes, all the owners of industry and commercial enterprises like my dad in 1952 had accepted the most unforgettable lesson in "re-education of the socialist legal system" of their lives. They had voluntarily and wholly paid the amount of money for falsely accused tax evasion which the government demanded. After going through this movement, the Communist Party had taken a huge amount of money from them, and from then on they responded to every request of the Communist Party with reverence and respect. So the communist party had achieved its purpose. Following this, the central party called on the representatives of the working class to democratically manage the corporations together with the owners; this was the trend of the times and the sign of a progressive society, so they nearly all accepted this unconditionally. It had been a terrifying time for about a year, and now as long as they could live at peace with each other and there were no more political movements, they were happy to do whatever they were asked. So almost everyone declared voluntarily that they would welcome the representatives of the working class to come and supervise the corporations. They were trapped by the schemes of the Communist Party. The first step the Communist Party wanted to take was to establish the leadership position of the working class and the state operation of private corporations. Logically, wouldn't this be an undoubted success?

Dad's "Chang Ming Textile Mill" was then divided down the middle as the law required when the announcement came out. Although this was unexpected, Dad and Mama still accepted it and submitted to this humiliation. The amount of money the government had identified as "tax evasion," they paid at once. They consoled each other saying that later they would be able to work with the working class.

"Speak and act discreetly!" Mama said before Dad went to work. Mama was not as relaxed as she would normally be; she always left these words with Dad. They hoped that they would be able to hold onto a peaceful life.

But this peaceful time only lasted a few months. At the beginning of 1953, another movement called "The State-private Joint Operation" was launched throughout the whole country on a grand scale. By this time, the owners of enterprises, like my dad, were horrified to hear the word "movement" and now this movement was facing them again, and they had nowhere to escape. The working class was by now already participating in all of the management of the corporations; their position was almost parallel to the owners'. Was it not enough? What was the real meaning of "joint operation"? Amongst them all, no one knew what tricks the Communist Party would play with this movement.

Even though they were unwilling to cooperate with the workers in managing the factories, they had to accept this; they didn't have any other way to go. Since this was the requirement of the new times, Dad persuaded himself to accept the facts and went to the factory to take part in the movement. He listened to the radio and read the newspaper;

however, he still held out a gleam of hope with this "joint operation." He hoped that if the Communist Party called it a "joint operation," the owner of a private corporation would still have a position and some of the ownership. From his knowledge of Marxism-Leninism, private ownership could not be annihilated immediately, and in Mao's work he read, "The new democracy toward a transition to socialism needs quite a long historical period." He thought this meant that it would be impossible for there to be an immediate transition from democracy to socialism. For him he thought the most important thing was: no matter how the times were changing, a human being must have human rights and must have dignity and live equally with others; otherwise, there would be no meaning at all.

But he was wrong. This time he, a gentle and weak intellectual, would be doomed to suffer a crushing defeat because Mao Ze Dong, this son of a farmer of Xiang Tan in Hunan, had now already stepped powerfully on to the international communist stage. "China has Mao Ze Dong" (these were words from the most famous song in China called "The East is Red," a song written to worship him). He was the person who had changed China and the destiny of the Chinese people; because of him, the land of China had experienced an earth shattering change, so Chinese history could be written only by him. The destiny of the Chinese people was now held completely in his hands. In order to know which course they would follow, all the people had to listen to him. Mao Ze Dong praised himself as the representative character who would work for the welfare of the toiling masses around the world, as well as serving the people. But on the first day that he entered Beijing city, he chose the Zhong Nan Hai in the Forbidden City, which is the most beautiful palace in Beijing and the palace where many emperors from different dynasties had lived, as his place of residence to start his life as the "red emperor" there. He never worshipped or had blind faith in all things foreign, but he had an ardent love and zeal for Chinese traditional culture. He was highly admired for his high hopes and great ambition to dominate the world just like the monarchs in the feudal society. At the beginning of 1949, while he hadn't ascended to the throne of absolute ruler in China, he wrote a poem named "Snow-to the tune of Spring Beaming in Garden." In this poem, he expressed his bold ambition to exercise authority as a king in a great country:

> "... With so much beauty is the land endowed,
> So many heroes thus in homage bowed,
> The first king of Qin and the seventh king of Han,
> Neither was a true literary man;
> The first king of Song and the second king of Tang,
> Neither was noted for poetry or song,
> Even the Proud Son of Haven, for a time,
> Called Genghis Khan, in his prime,
> Knew only how to shoot an eagle, over his tent with a bow so bent...
> Alas, all no longer remain!
> For truly great men,
> One should look within this age's ken."

(Mao added a note to this poem that "truly great men" refers to the proletariat.)

In this poem, he was full of disdain and mocked the monarchs of historical China. The old time was over. Today, in 1950 in the 20th century in China where a quarter of the world's population lived, everyone should take notice of him. In the song "The East is Red," which all the men and women, both old and young in China knew and sang every day, Mao was praised as a great savior; he accepted this with pleasure, and felt very satisfied. He was the person who had caused this great event in the land, which would shock the country and the whole world. And his ambition was not only to stir up trouble in China. He said he would also "lead the Chinese people to go on to liberate the other two-thirds of the people in the world who are living in an abyss of suffering and to raise the great flag of communism all over the world." Those words were written in the text books at school and in the newspapers because he wanted all the people to know his mission. This was the great thing he wanted to do in the world.

When the Communist Party of China led by Mao Ze Dong decided to develop Marxism, they wanted to do some pioneering work which was unprecedented on the stage of international history. From the theory of Marxism, I learned that the basic principle was to destroy all private ownership and to take away all the rights of the exploiting class. But Marx and Engels also thought that the proletariat should not use acts of violence but use the policies of redemption to acquire and nationalize the property of the capitalists. That would be the cheapest way for the proletariat. The strategy of "redemption" which Marx developed for dealing with the capitalist class, Lenin had tried to put into practice after his success in the October Revolution, but he was unable to see it through. Now, Mao Ze Dong believed it was the time for him to fulfill this prophecy of Marx himself. Because he was clear about the powerful people's democratic dictatorship and the strong worker –peasant alliance which he had struck up, he had now formed a tremendous political force. Under this powerful force, the capitalist did not dare and also was not able to revolt against the government. Their only option was to cooperate with the Communist Party. Yes, there was only one choice for them in 1953.

At that time, the Chinese Communist Party (CCP) had no stock in any of the private corporations. Mao Ze Dong created a "peace reform guideline," which was a "use, restrict, transform" policy toward capitalist industry and commerce. The CCP first became a shareholder in every private corporation, then progressively "bought out" everyone else, moving from an elementary form of state capitalism to a high form of state capitalism and finally transforming into state run socialism. What Mao was doing at that time violated the political promises he had written in his works before the liberation when he declared he would implement the new democracy and protect the national bourgeoisie over a long period of time in China. Nobody could believe how in such a short time, he was so quick to take action, carrying through the socialist revolution and destroying the capitalist economy. The government sent the cadres (the state representatives) of the party membership to each private enterprise to take charge of the management of the corporation. The six word policy he constituted "to redeem in a peaceful way" was indeed a great strategic policy. It was so astute and can be described in one phrase "to kill people without spilling blood." Because the policy of "redemption" was what the communist party talked about, it in fact now already existed in word only. Mao Ze Dong always said laughingly that the purpose for this policy to be put into practice would be to finally achieve "the death of the class system, the pleasure of the individual." This "cheapest thing" which Marx had mentioned would now be taken over by the CCP and be easy to accomplish because at that moment the entrance door of China had already closed. To beat the dog inside the gate, those capitalists who saw themselves to be above politics and worldly considerations actually had no way out now. They had no other choice but to link up with socialism. "A wise man submits to fate" in order to protect their own lives and property. Within a very short time, people from the industry and commerce circles throughout the nation started to cooperate with the Communist Party one by one initially; soon state and private joint - operated enterprises were all over China. The

Communist Party used this sentence in the party newspaper to describe the status then:

"To have all the owners of industry and commerce accept the transformation so happily and in such a peaceful manner is unprecedented."

The capitalists as a class would certainly soon be destroyed. Were the capitalists as the representative characters of this class really willing to "accept the transformation so happily"? What kind of people would they be forced to become?

"The Campaign to Suppress Counter-revolutionaries" had just finished in the countryside and the cities across the nation. People had seen with their own eyes that those who were unwilling to receive this socialist rebuilding program or who didn't appear happy to hand over their property were weeded out from the earth by just one bullet. In order to save his life, the last emperor Pu Yi was receiving re-education in the prison at Fushon. Hundreds of thousands of people who had been designated by the Communist Party as their opponents and social enemies of the proletariat were also starting to receive their re-education with fear and trepidation. What kinds of processes and methods could Mao Ze Dong use to transform a person? Can one person really be reformed into another person? I don't know what kind of cruel and inhuman treatment my dear dad experienced or what kind of grim attack he was suffering. I only saw with my wide-open eyes that he often would not eat or drink for the whole day, and he was suffering from insomnia. Within only a few months, he had become pessimistic and seemed as though he was in a trance. From his appearance, he had certainly already changed into a completely different person.

Often, when Dad came home, I would stretch out my hands and want him to carry me as before, but I would no longer see the kind smile on his face I used to see. He was laden with anxiety, his brow was knit, and his eyes were dull. He picked me up in his arms in a stupefied state; he didn't want to play with me, would not kiss me as before, and after only a very short time, he laid me back on the floor. He could not cover up his inner suffering, and often, he would close the door and stay in his room alone.

He didn't know when the harassment of the "use, restrict, transform" policy would be finished. How low would his status and position in his own factory fall? The issue of the tax evasion was brought up again during this campaign. They now said that the crime he had perpetrated meant they would take the whole factory to meet his obligations; it was not enough that he had refunded the money. To submissively give away his own property, which his forefathers and he had worked so hard to earn, in such an inglorious way was just too much. Again and again, his heart revolted, and he struggled along. He was not reconciled to it, and he was not averse to it. So this caused the cooperate partners to reach an impasse. He was now considered to be an "incorrigibly obstinate and difficult person to rebuild." But, how can an arm move the thigh? He would be defeated, and that would become clear very soon.

One day, he was told officially: The authorities cannot wait any more for him, a person who was ignorant of the times according to the current policy. So now they had decided that the ownership of this factory would be taken over by the state; the name of the factory was changed to the "Kunming Da Hua State Run Weaving Factory." They would keep him as an employee in this "Joint state-private operations factory." But now he had no more power in this factory. The administration and management functions were taken over by the party branch and labor union which were formed from the army and worker representatives. They asked him to go home to wait for the notification of his punishment.

That day, unable to fight with his fate, Dad dragged his exhausted feet back home. He entered the room without saying a word, went straight to his bed, and sat on it staring blankly. Mama realized something bad must have happened in the factory. She didn't ask, just handed Dad a cup of tea. She held me in her arms and sat beside him.

After a few days had passed, Dad hadn't received any message from the factory, and his heart was full of fear and trembling. For so many years he had gone to his factory almost every day, and now he was not used to doing nothing and just staying home. So one morning he went to the office where he had gone every day before.

But while he was just sitting at his desk, he reached out his hand to open the drawer to get something. A worker representative who was already sitting at another table in his office spoke to him suddenly, "Put it down! You have no permission from the army representative; you can touch nothing." Formerly a common young worker, he now spoke in such a conceited tone. Dad didn't know how to reply, so he had no choice but to sit there. A few hours later, Dad was asked to go to attend a meeting. When he walked into the meeting place, he was called to stand on the stage. He wasn't sure what was going to happen; he just listened to the army representative speaking plausibly and at length, "According to the government policy, our factory has finished the transformation into a joint state-private operation. From now, the new leadership will manage all the affairs of the factory. In order to save the primary owner Yan Ze Gao, the government decided to give him a chance to begin his life anew. Now let me declare that Yan Ze Gao, this representative figure of the exploiting class, from today, his identity has changed to become a target of the revolution. He needs to receive the labor reformation; his job would be to fire up the boiler in our factory's boiler room every day. We hope that this process of labor reform will help him to transition in his role, changing from the exploiting class into a laborer to support his own living. As employees, we all have the right to supervise him."

"I am afraid I cannot to do this physical labor well; maybe I can assist with some technical work," Dad really was a bookworm, and he still dared to "haggle over the price" at that moment, but while he had just started to speak, he was immediately completely rejected.

The officer said, "What are you now, why do you still not know? Let me tell you, you are now equal to a dog, you are only a stray dog, a stray dog, understand?" The army and worker representatives pointed in his face and spoke to him laughing wildly, "You must receive this labor reform to begin your life anew. This is the one and only way for you at present. You need to wake up, you are nothing, and you also have nothing. Yan Ze Gao, this is the last chance for you!"

The workers who were sitting below the stage, that proletariat whose status had now changed, clearly knew they were the people with the Communist Party behind them and supporting them, and they learned how to adapt themselves to the circumstances. One person began to loudly shout out slogans, and they all shook their fists and chimed in with the others shouting at the top of their voices:

"Treat with leniency those who confess, punish severely those who dispute!"

"Long live the dictatorship of the proletariat!"

"If the bourgeoisie will not surrender, let them die out!"

"Get out, get out of here!" at the sound of their angry rebukes, under the watch of all the staff, both Dad's arms were lifted up towards his back and his head was pressed over his heels by two workers. This terrible way they treated him was called "jet-propelled," it was the popular method used to fight against "the enemy of the proletariat" back then. He lost his balance; he was sent away under escort from the stage and walked to the back of the room. This was the most unbearable humiliation he had ever had in his life. When he was thrown down on the ground, he didn't have the courage to raise his head and look at anyone. His face became pale, his head was almost drawn back to his chest, and he staggered out of the factory gate.

What he experienced during that year made him understand what was meant by the revolution, and how it touched your soul. How it was pressed hard into you step by step; for him it was more and more difficult to endure. First, it had caused him to lose his scholarly dignity which he had had for more than 40 years. Losing money now was the trend of the times; there was no choice than to accept it. But, to be treated like he was today in such a way, standing on the stage to having abuse hurled directly to his head and face and then being physically injured…the unfounded defamation and humiliation, all this treatment of him, made him feel too ashamed to show his face. At that moment, he could do nothing but go home immediately to hide.

Along the street, the five-starred flags and Chairman Mao's huge portrait could be seen everywhere; long narrow pieces of the red cloth with slogans written on them hung on the buildings, and the people all wore green army uniforms. There were some people who looked respectable, but now their dress and appearance were strange. While they were walking, their expressions looked as though they were on tenterhooks. He met an acquaintance, and he just thought to nod a greeting, but the person looked like he had met a ghost and immediately jumped aside. On his way home, he saw in the doorways of the shops and factories that there were many people in uniform waving little red flags. They were either surrounding the shopkeepers or owners of the factory to repudiate them or beating drums and striking gongs and doing the Yang Ge (a popular rural folk dance). They were celebrating "the working class standing up to be the master." Dad knew clearly that these people had the same status as he did now and were making an impact in varying degrees. The world he had been used to had already officially changed.

"Oh, there is no escape for our family right now!" Dad was disheartened as he spoke to himself.

How about tomorrow? He simply could not pour out what had happened in the factory to Mama. Dad was a person who was very concerned about face-saving. That day when he was back home, he just sat in his bedroom and smoked one cigarette after another without saying a word. He was thinking about how to face tomorrow. If he accepted the job and went to fire up the boiler, maybe there was a gleam of hope; it might be possible for him to connect himself to another job later. He needed to be able to earn some wages; this big family needed money to support it every day. But, when he thought of doing such a lowly job, he was really absolutely unwilling. This was physical labor he had never done before, and it was dirty and exhausting. He would have to do this in his own factory and in front of all his former subordinates.

"Why are they treating me in this way? Is this the only outlet for me?" He couldn't work out the answer. If he didn't go to the factory tomorrow, what would happen next? What about the family's life? The situation now had taken a sudden turn and rapidly became worse as their bank account was frozen, there was only a small amount of cash at home, and it was like water in a jar, it would soon be used up. He considered those things silently. After smoking many cigarettes, he still didn't know what he should do. Mama observed this; she knew at once that Dad had met some trouble he could not resolve. But with Mama's personality, she would never urge her husband to make decisions or talk to him too much while he was embarrassed. She respected her husband at all times and always let him decide things by himself, especially the affairs of the factory. So, what Mama did that day was to tell my two older sisters to take all of the younger siblings and go out in order to keep the home quiet. This only left her to stay home with her husband. Mama sat on the sofa at the bedside window; she didn't speak a word either; she was knitting a sweater by hand. When she saw the water in the teacup in front of Dad was dry, she stood up and put some warm water in it. She was just like a gentle butterfly flashing before Dad's eyes at intervals. Dad was very touched by Mama's behavior.

"My family needs me; I cannot fall down." Before he went to bed Dad spoke to Mama, "Can you help me prepare a set of clothing for doing labor? They asked me to go to work in the workshop tomorrow." Mama knew the knot in Dad's heart had untied, and she rushed to prepare the clothing for her husband. She certainly didn't know what kind of job her husband was going to do. She picked out a set of clothes which looked a little old; she ironed them as she was used to doing, hung them up, then went to bed.

The second evening when Dad came home and Mama moved towards him to take his bag, she saw the collar and wristbands of the shirt Dad was wearing had become black and his hair was full of cinders; there were dark marks on his face and neck. She looked straight into Dad's eyes and saw from the expression in her husband's eyes that he was in dire straits. The smile on Mama's face immediately turned to horror. Right then, she awoke to the fact that her husband's status and position had completely changed. That evening Dad told Mama what great changes had happened in his factory. Mama finally knew that all the property they had once owned was now gone and they had nothing. Mama said that her first reaction then was not to brood about the pain of losing their belongings. Wealth was just an external thing; the thing she worried about most was Dad. The idea came to her immediately that she could do that job instead of Dad. It was very clear to her that if her husband, who had worked hard and been so successful throughout his whole life, had to take such a job now it would be too hard for him, both emotionally and physically.

Each day before this, Dad would go to work dressed in western clothes. Now, he was pitch-black all over from shoveling coal in the boiler room. He had gone from being an owner and manager of the factory to now suddenly being a person with no identity and position with everyone shouting at him and giving him orders. Of course, he could not adapt to all the changes of this role. He talked with Mama, "It is too difficult for me. First of all, I have to become a compliant person—without the ability to say no and just doing whatever I am asked even though it is unreasonable, but I have never done anything to lose face in my life." Mama knew it was not easy for Dad to learn these things because she knew what kind of person her husband was. Dad was over 40 years old by then, but sometimes he would still blush with shame when he spoke. After one week of working in the boiler room, he lowered his head one day and said to Mama, "I cannot bear to be so depressed; I really don't want to go to the factory any more. If they want to snatch it, just let them take it. Each day I am there seems like a year!"

What was actually happening in this world? Mama visited some rich ladies she had known before in private, only a few of the wives of the big owners looked the same as they had before. That was because their husbands were wise and submitted to reality. When they saw the situation not going well, they immediately agreed to the joint state-private operation without any conditions and handed over their entire property to the communist party. By doing it this way, they obtained the glorious title of the commission of C.P.P.C.C. (the Chinese People's political Consultative Conference) and kept a kind of position in the factory. Those wives believed that they, though not living as elegantly as before, would still have social status; they would soon adjust to their new life. Most of the wives of the middle-sized and smaller business owners were heavyhearted, and it showed on their faces. Their husbands were neither drifting with the tide nor did they willingly and happily hand over the property which had always belonged to them. They had never experienced such a strong storm; now, just like their husbands, they were scared and didn't know what course to take. They were exactly the same as our family.

Mama found out this information and went back home. She was aware in any case that this high pressure time, this world-shaking transformation, could never be avoided by her or Dad. She started to consider her own family; one day if Dad really stayed home, what would we live on?

Since her marriage until now, she had been a housewife for years. The year before when she had a large of sum money, she took part in social activities, and she dreamt that she would be able to participate in more social activities in the future. Now the dream was over, and she knew that a person like her would never be welcomed by society. If her husband now did something wrong, she was afraid that the children would suffer misfortune too. She had no means of making a living to support the family. Our family depended on a man, so she decided that she would have a talk with Dad. At that moment, nothing could be done but to endure.

She analyzed the situation with Dad gently and softly. Dad accepted Mama's advice and still went to the factory, though he didn't like and it no longer belonged to him, to do a hard demeaning job in the following few days. In order to make Dad look more like a laborer, Mama quickly made a "Mao suit" for Dad, which was the gray clothing many people wore on the street now. But when Dad looked at himself in the mirror, he felt ashamed. Throughout his life he never wore any other clothing except western-style clothes and long gowns; he immediately took off the clothing and threw it aside.

"No, I will definitely not wear this kind of clothing. When I put this on, I will look more and more like a ghost, not like a man." So when he went to the boiler room to work, he still wore his suits. It made him look like a crane standing among the chickens while he worked in the boiler room; it also showed how very ignorant of the times he was. The army representative didn't like him any more.

"Hum! I will see how many days you can be proud," they often shook their heads, crying out to Dad in bewilderment. The labor reform kept going on in this way. "When will this transformation campaign be over? What about the next step? What kind of coercive methods will they treat me with? With such a small payment they give to me each month, how can I support the family in the future? What will happen tomorrow?" he thought. Each day, while he sat in a lonely corner and ate the food Mama prepared for him, he was puzzled by those questions. He felt vexed. He stayed there but was absent-minded and had a mournful countenance. Frightened and tired by the heavy physical labor, Dad finally went down with an illness. For several days he didn't go to the factory; he stayed home depressed. Mama said this was the most difficult year for Dad she had seen since they married. But all the things he could not endure had just started.

As the revolutionary campaign to beat down the bourgeois went deeper into the whole nation, the proletariat occupied everything, and their violent actions became more and more fierce. One day at nightfall, a gang of workers wearing "the worker pickets" armbands suddenly rushed into our house. They started searching each room and confiscated our property. With talk which was interspersed with curses, they said, "Yan Ze Gao dares to absent himself from the factory to receive labor reform; it must be because he has hidden some wealth at home. That's why he can live a parasitic life, lead an idle life. He will not be allowed to live in this way."

They searched and checked everywhere for almost one hour. They even put their hands in the tea caddy to agitate it, so as not to let slip any treasures which may be concealed there. Finally, they put together all the things they thought were the most costly into a bed sheet, wrapped them up, then put them into a truck and swaggered off. This was the first time Dad and Mama had faced and suffered such a catastrophe. They were frightened and in a state of utter shock. They stood to one side blankly, and after those people had gone, they cried on each other's shoulder. My sixth sister and I were playing on the floor when the gang came in; we were already frightened by their surly attitude. We were too scared to cry out loud while they ransacked the boxes and chests. Now this was the first time we had ever seen Dad and Mama crying bitterly and holding on to each other. We were frightened and cried out involuntarily. Our older sisters and brother come back home after class, one after another, and they were shocked by the blow of the great confusing scene which met their eyes and they burst into tears. That day, the whole courtyard of our house was immersed with terror and sorrow and for the first time had no life or joy about it.

But the adversity did not stop there. One morning some people wearing the uniforms of the court suddenly came into our house and took Dad away. After waiting for a long time and when he didn't come back, Mama carried me on her back and went to the intermediate people's court to ask about him. On the way home she could not stop crying loudly and without restraint. She had been told that in this movement of "joint state-private operations," Yan Ze Gao had not taken positive, concerted action with the government, and his attitude was not good. They had decided to check up on his crime of "tax evasion" again. As a result they figured out that the sum of money was huge, the taxation he had paid for it before was not enough to pay the debt. At present, Yan Ze Gao had received a formal complaint from the factory. If he could not pay the remaining sum within a limited time, he would be condemned and sent to prison.

"This is too terrible; it is obvious that what they are doing is taking possession of other people's property as their own under the cover of pretense. It had not even been two years since the start of the liberation; even if we had dared to evade taxes, we could not have evaded so much. If our whole factory compensated for it, we still could not pay it off!?" Mama cried and could not sleep for the whole night. To be able in a moment to frame a case against somebody which can condemn the person to death, what's to be done, what's to be done? As she thought it over and over she became more and more afraid. Right now getting Dad out of that dreadful place was the most important thing; Mama thought that only by selling our house would they have enough money to pay off what they wanted. In the morning of the second day, she lifted her spirits and went to the house of detention in the court again; she wanted to discuss her thoughts with Dad. She couldn't believe her eyes; she saw Dad crouched in a corner sitting on the floor with his hair disheveled. It was his first time to be taken to such a place, and he was already scared out of his wits. Mama called out to him at a distance from the window, he was too ashamed to face his wife and did not so much as raise his eyes to look at Mama. He had not eaten anything for two days, he looked ghostly pale, and his hands shook. Mama wanted to console him, but she couldn't say any words without bursting into tears. Finally, she held back her tears and sorrow to speak to Dad, "I will do everything possible to repay the debt and to get you out. You need to eat something; you must pull yourself together."

Mama left her husband with a lowered head and cried all the way home again. The children were too young to discuss this with them. She took the title deed for our house property and went back to the court where she met with the judge and told him decidedly, "We will pay the debt with our house property, you can auction it. I beg you to get Yan Ze Gao out as soon as possible." One week later, our nice house with its two floors and 33 rooms was bought at a very low price by the Yunnan provincial postal service bureau. This house we had only lived in for 6 years. By paying off the big sum of the money which the court requested, Dad was released and went home.

In the one week the purchaser gave us to move out, Mama thought the good life of our family was over; we should use the rest of the surplus money to rent a shabby house to live in now. But Dad didn't agree with her. For more than 40 years from when he was born until now, he hadn't had a day of hardship which kept him from facing reality even now. He was not open to living in a simple place, not at all. Mama didn't want to give any pressure to Dad. She only wanted her husband to recover as soon as possible. So, she found another house in Shu Lin Street, the space was much smaller than our house but was nice, and we moved into it. After a few days, Dad gradually got his health and emotional strength back, but from then on he would not even go out of the gate. Many times Mama tried patiently to talk Dad into getting the meager wage from the factory at the end of month. He reluctantly went back to do that hard job in the boiler room again. When he came home in the evenings, he often would not to speak a word; he silently sat in his room. Sometimes, he stood and looked out the window where he saw the world had completely changed and become so different from before. He did nothing but shook his head frequently saying to himself, "No, it is impossible for me to be in harmony with this community. They are a gang of bandits, a motley crowd. I cannot associate with those evil people and live together with them no matter what happens."

Mama thought, "When the situation becomes critical, one has to do things according to the trend." In order to make a living, there is no choice but to force oneself to accept the facts. She was patiently waiting for Dad to change. And she took care of all the affairs of the family by herself. A few days later, they heard the bad news that all the relatives in Xi Zhou had been driven out of their houses and deprived of everything. After moving out of their luxury houses, some couldn't find a place to live; they had to live in the pigsty of the farmers. "Now, it is our turn."

Dad felt the end of the world was coming. He walked around in his bedroom with a melancholy look and smoked ceaselessly. He did not speak a word for several days. However each morning Mama got up on time and prepared breakfast for Dad and the four children before they went to school. After they had eaten and gone out, Mama started to look after the other kids helping them to take a shower and to eat. At about 9 o'clock, she put on an apron and started to clean up the rooms. Once each room was bright and clean, she was able to have a rest. She would have a cup of tea and sit at the table to relax. Then she would have her breakfast and read some newspapers. This was her habit for many years. Now that the helpers and servants had already been dismissed, she still enjoyed doing all of those things herself. But in those days, while she was doing the house work, her thoughts were far away and her heart was heavy.

"What about the next step, where will our home be later?" she could scarcely continue to think. Sometimes she purposely took her mind off things and sat on the floor playing with us three kids. But, her face had no smile, her eyes always full of tears.

"Why is Mama crying again?" my instinct told me that Mama had met something bad once more.

"Waaaaaaaaa..." in a tearful voice, I often burst into tears in an instant. Why is Mama grieved? I really didn't like to see Mama crying. I only wanted to see the happy appearance she used to have every day! Therefore, from then on, whenever I saw Mama, my big eyes would always gaze at her face first. If I saw there was a teardrop in Mama's eyes,

No. 7 of An Ning Lane.

I would throw myself into Mama's arms and cry loudly with fear. So, later for many years, Mama often said, "Ling Ling was a kid growing up in my tears."

Yes, from when I was under the age of two years old, during my growing up years, the life I experienced was always accompanied by Mama's tears. The happiness and joy were far away from me; my big eyes were full of sorrow.

As our cash became less and less, Mama felt that to cut down on expenses we should move out of this nice house as soon as possible. With no time to hesitate, she took off her cheongsam for the first time and exchanged it for a set of dui jin shan in blue (a kind of Chinese style jacket with buttons down the front) which she made herself. She carried me on her back and started to inquire about the new houses all round. A few days later, she finally found one small yard in An Ning Lane. It was an old house located in another narrow and crossing lane. There were two yards linked together, the house owner lived in the backyard, the front yard was now for lease. The rental price was 1/4 of the nice house where we lived, and we had no choice at all, so Mama rented it. This small yard we were going to move into, had about a 30 square meter big room on the east and west on both sides and one yard in the middle about 6, or 7 square meters big. On the east there was only one room, and on the west there were two rooms and a little kitchen behind. She knew the conditions here were not really good, but one family could live there, and it was not far from the city center. The most important reason Mama chose this place, she said, was because of the name of the lane. (An Ning, the meaning in Chinese is peaceful.) During the past two years, the whole family had been living in stress; the name of this small lane gave her a lot of comfort, and she hoped that moving into this lane would bring our family peace and safety. Mama relaxed for a while. The second day, she talked with Dad and explained the situation to him, and she brought Dad to see the new house. On the way, Dad walked with his head lowered just as before and felt embarrassed. He followed Mama into the most secluded, lonely and jumbled lane he had ever been in before. Naturally, he was not satisfied with this house at all. But at that moment, he had lost his right to argue about it. Cowardly and unable to earn the whole family's living, his wife had organized things after busily rushing about. He thought he had no alternative but to reluctantly agree. Although he nodded his head to say, "All right, let's move in here." in his mind the thought was that it was only a temporary place for us to live.

In May 1953, Mama hired 4 carriages to carry all of the furniture, each person also brought up some things in their hands, and we made a move again. We left the nice house in Shu Lin Street and moved into the small yard where nobody realized that was the place we would spend the whole of our life. What words can be used to describe a person who is scared out of his wits? Those words now describe how my Dad looked that day.

That day, I had been carried on Mama's back for a long time. She was busy with many different things; her back was drenched. I was tied up on her back and very uncomfortable; I would sleep for a while and wake up for a while. My small face became redder and redder, and I felt very oppressed. From the morning, when everyone started to pack and move things out, Dad did not look like himself; he was extremely sad and insecure. On the way from Shu Lin Street to An Ning lane, he led Liu Jie and Wu Ge along by the hand; one was five years old and the other one was six. He followed the whole moving procession and walked slowly and very passively at the rear. For him, such a great change coming to pass was still like a dream. From now on had we really left all of the life we had before? He was certainly too scared to think deeply about it. Arriving at the gate of the yard in An Ning lane, all the things were unloaded from the carriage and were all piled up everywhere in the yard. Some things had to be put outside the gate. On both sides, the rooms were too small to fit the furniture. Mama decided to use one side room to stack the furniture. In another side room, Mama soon made three beds,

The small room where we grew up.

and immediately, the room was completely full. From that evening, the whole family of 9 people crowded in and slept together in this gloomy room.

After being in a rush and a muddle all day long, things still had not settled down, and dusk was coming. Mama lit the stove near the doorway and started to cook dinner there for the family. The small room immediately filled with smoke. Dad had never experienced the life of the urban poor, not even for one day, and now he was personally confronted with it, and it made him feel very uncomfortable. He became restless and fidgety. After unwrapping me from Mama's back, he carried me in his arms as he moved around the yard. He shook his head continuously. Little Wu Ge and Liu Jie, who didn't know why they had to move to such a place, were crying loudly and noisily; they were shouting in confusion that they wanted to be back in the nice house. As he thought about how the whole family would tolerate living in such a place from now on, Dad could not suppress his feelings, covering his face with both hands he wept, "Oh, my god! How could things have become like this! What a downhill slide we are on!"

Mama said this society had forced her man into a position where he could do nothing but cry, so how could she possibly censure him? No, she didn't speak a word; she only shed tears. That day, on the first evening in An Ning lane, everyone tossed and turned in their beds, unable to sleep. My older brother and sister and I could not adapt to the new environment. One by one we all cried in fear throughout the whole night. The other four children, who were in school, realized that it was a disgrace for them to be born into a family such as ours. Now having moved to a place like this they felt they were being punished. Before they had only had a vague idea of what was happening to them, but now they were full of doubts and suspicions, They all wept quietly and thought deeply about their fate and their sad future. All these great changes had happened in the space of three years. It was totally unexpected, and it had never occurred to Dad and Mama that these things could happen. They were psychologically unprepared. They had not wanted to accept their circumstances but had to face the facts; they had thought it through again and again but could not avoid it. They felt very low as they were forced into this situation, thinking about the children, thinking about the family, at that moment, they could say nothing. They held each other's hands, tears covered their faces.

At that time our relatives and friends all managed to stay alive by making great sacrifices; not daring to contact each other. Living in such a place and having lost all reputation, they no longer needed to save face. For the first time Dad took off his suit and pulled a long gown out of the chest and put it on. It was no longer necessary to pay attention to appearances; he wasn't even inclined to shave each day. When half a year had passed, he wore his hair and beard long and untidily on his face. He had changed into a completely different person, having fallen into completely passive and negative thinking.

The family's standard of living gradually declined as they joined the crowded poor masses in that noisy lane. When he needed to go to the toilet, Dad discovered that there was only one public toilet in the whole lane where 10 people would have to squat face to face.

"Oh, it is too terrible!" Dad said the first time he saw this and was overwhelmed and fled away. He could not adapt to such a life, so he used the spittoon as a toilet at home for a long time.

All the kids were huddled together in one small dark and moist room day and night. The floor in this dilapidated house was not smooth but was full of bumps and hollows that the two little kids often slipped over. The ground in the yard was clay, and when it rained, there was mud everywhere. The children were not used to living in such a place, one was crying, another was shouting ......

How have we been degraded like this? What mistakes did we make? Why have we fallen into such a low place? This outcome could never have been imagined. Dad felt his ability to endure had reached its limit. He could no longer rationalize why these things had happened; all he could do was sigh deeply and continually ask, "Oh, why? Why do we have to live like this?!"

Now he seldom walked out of the gate of No.7 An Ning Lane; he didn't go to the job they asked him to do in the boiler room at the factory either.

"Just let them do what they like; it doesn't matter to me at all," he said to Mama.

So he had a very bad relationship with the new hierarchy at the factory. They said that he kept contravening the labor reforms of the new society, and their controlling punishment and their attitude towards him became more and more severe. Three months later they stopped paying him his basic living allowance. Mama went to the factory one day hoping to talk with the leader of the factory to plead for mercy for Dad and to ask them to give Dad another job. They told Mama ferociously, "He is a parasite! We gave him a chance to change into a person who could work to support himself, but he didn't appreciate the opportunity. I tell you now, our society doesn't need a man like him, and his end will be a road to destruction!"

"But we are a big family, how can we support ourselves and live?" Mama asked them tearfully.

"How? You want to know how? You stood so high above the masses for so many years; now it is your turn to taste the hard life. How should you live? You need to think about your situation and accept the facts. It is not our problem! Ha, Ha, Ha!"

This was the answer Mama got from them. That day I was also being carried on Mama's back. I opened my eyes at the sound of roaring machinery. Alarmed, I shied away from the gaze of the people in the factory. And then still on Mama's back, I heard her weeping as she went home; I cried together with Mama the whole way.

On the way home, Mama remembered what it had been like when she would visit the factory with the kids in the past. Back then when she and Dad were there, holding the children's hands; no matter where they were they would receive a kind welcome and be highly esteemed. But now in the same place, with the same people, how had she become a beggar? We didn't do anything wrong? Everything we had before was now gone. But for now she forced herself to keep her resentment to herself; she knew clearly that for the rest of their lives, she and the whole family would only be able to scrape together a very low existence in this society.

"How pitiful my seven children are! What future will they have?" As she thought about this question she used her hand to pat me on her back because I had already been hungry and cold for a long time. Mama walked home streaming with sweat. When she passed the food market in Wei Yuan Street which was not far from home, she stopped and bought some vegetables to carry home. As she drew closer to the gate of the house, she fished out a handkerchief and wiped her eyes and tidied her hair, and then she strode home.

She didn't tell Dad any of the offensive language she had heard in the factory; she lifted me down from her back and handed me over to Dad, mixed some rice flour so Dad could feed me, and started to cook without saying any word. Because the children who were in school were home now, she took care of the whole family and prepared their dinner, and then she presented a cigarette and a cup of tea to Dad as was her custom. Holding me in her arms, she quietly sat down beside him. Dad was a very sensitive person, Mama had told him that she was going to the factory this afternoon, but she had said nothing when she got home, so he knew immediately that Mama had something on her mind. He wanted to ask about it, but right now all the kids were doing their homework together in this small room, and he found it difficult to bring the matter up. He looked into Mama's eyes questioningly. Mama understood what he meant and stood up saying, "Let's go for a walk."

Mama carried me and together with Dad went out of the gate. Walking down An Ning lane, they came to Jin Ri Park near Nan Ping Street. Just as they sat down on a bench, without Dad having to ask, Mama could not suppress her feelings and started crying aloud. Dad held her to his chest, his eyes also full of tears. In between them I looked at them uncertainly. I saw they were both crying, and I felt very scared. "Wa!" I cried with them. Mama straightened her body and started to soothe me, "It's all right, Dad and Mama will not cry, little darling. Be good. Don't cry."

With Dad's right arm around Mama's shoulder, they started to talk. When I saw they had calmed down, I stopped crying. They talked there for a long time. Dad had broken off his relationship with the factory, and they were discussing how they could maintain the life of the whole family in the future. They tried to find a solution, but after thinking it over and over, they still could not find an way. At present, the only thing they could do was to sell off some of their valuables to tide them over this difficult time. At about 11 o'clock, they carried me already sleeping back to the house. In the dim light, they saw the six children crowded together sleeping on two beds. Dad went to their beds and fixed their quilts. For some reason he was suddenly in very low spirits.

"Oh, why do we have to suffer such a punishment? I still cannot understand it. With our children having to live this way; it would be better if we all died!" He shook his head and sighed deeply.

"Ah, why has your mood changed again? Sleep, sleep, now. It is not only our family living in this way." Mama drew Dad to the bed as she comforted Dad gently.

During the initial time while these great changes were happening, as we lived in this simple and crude little room, the whole family was forced to silently adapt to all these things. They had no alternative but to waste away their forlorn and hopeless lives. Their source of income for the support of the family at that time was a bit of money Mama had from selling off some of her jewelry. They had no idea how they would spend the rest of their lives; they could only just manage that day then think about the next day.

But then something totally unexpected happened. Mama found out that she was pregnant again. She had conceived Dad's eighth child. That day after the old Chinese doctor had diagnosed her by taking her pulse and telling Mama this undeniable news, Mama's tears immediately began to flow, and she cried all the way home. When she got home, the handkerchief with the plum embroidery she held in her hand was dripping wet. Dad was also startled by this news; he was too scared to speak.

Before, Dad and Mama had been wild with joy at each of their pregnancies and at the thought of having a new baby. But this time, they were shocked and had a worried frown. Mama was very anxious about it and wept for many days. Now that our whole family had become stuck in this deep mud and one more child was coming, how could they survive?

However, this was their own flesh and blood, so what could they do? Dad and Mama made a decision that they would give birth to this baby. This was the first time that Mama had become pregnant in such terrible circumstances. The family's lower living standards were a secondary concern. Mama's greatest pressure was her feeling of helplessness and the continual sense that she was falling into a dark valley of hopelessness. Mama often said later that she felt sorry for her youngest son because during her pregnancy she was worrying and worrying every day. Her nature was to love laughing, but throughout this nine-month period, she almost never laughed any more.

In February 1954 my poor little brother was born in the small room which was open on all sides at No.7 An Ning Lane. Because Mama didn't even have enough money to pay for giving birth to the baby in the hospital, she had no choice but to find a midwife to help her give birth at home. That year Mama had always been busy rushing about trying to make a living, and she was terribly malnourished so the baby in her womb had also suffered from this. My brother was in poor health and was very thin and weak when he was born. The sound of his crying was very feeble just like a kitten. When Dad and Mama first saw this pallid baby come into the world, even though this was the second precious boy amongst all their children, they could not rejoice; their hearts were filled with distress and grief.

"Oh, our youngest son, our poor son, it is not your time to come to the world!" Dad and Mama looked at him and sighed deeply together, and they couldn't help but cry. Because they were very aware that the abundant life of this family was over, fate decreed that this baby's life would be full of suffering and poverty.

"I will give him the name 'Zu Xin' (Zu was the middle name given to each child, Xin in Chinese means new). For him the life we have now is really a 'new' life we could never have imagined during the past generations," Dad said cynically. Mama didn't say another word, she gave my younger brother another name; it was his pet name 'Mao Mao.' Mama said kittens and puppies are easy to rear because they have a strong ability to survive, so it was fine to just give him a very common name. She hoped god would bless this poor child and help him to grow up to be healthy. Amazingly, this younger brother looked more like Dad than all of the other children. He was handsome. All the sisters took turns carrying him in their arms and loved him. I was only two years older than him; sometimes I also held his hand and played with him.

After giving birth to Di Di (younger brother in Chinese), Mama didn't rest after childbirth for a month as she used to do. She only spent a few days in her bed; then she put a scarf on her head and started to take care of the needs of the whole family again. Each day, after she organized my brother and sisters to go to school, she was busy washing, cooking, cleaning the house, as well as looking after Liu Jie who was two years older than me and the little boy who was just born. If she needed to go out shopping or deal with something, she often carried me on her back and brought me with her, leaving Dad to take care of the other kids. She said that at that time I was just starting to walk, swaying and staggering, and I would easily trip and fall so she did not have peace of mind about me staying home. I would be carried on the thin, weak back of my mama. With Mama's quick footsteps we moved together through so many streets and lanes in Kunming. I opened my eyes wide to stare at this world.

Each time we came home, when Mama unfastened me from her back and put me on the floor, both of us were very tired. Her face and neck were covered in sweat; her hair and the clothing on her back were completely dripping wet. My legs were bound tightly for those many hours. When I was untied, my legs were too numb to get up straight away. Setting me down, she did not even drink any water. She immediately took Di Di who was wrapped up in Dad's arms and opened her clothing to nurse him because Di Di was already hungry and crying.

I often stood beside Mama watching her nurse Di Di, and he became quiet. It took all his strength to suck. But after only a little while, Di Di would cry out again because Mama's milk had dried up. Poor Mama, after Di Di was born she had no opportunity to relax; her body and mind were very strained. She was unable to supply the nourishment he needed.

She had hoped she could nurse Di Di herself, but now her ability fell short of her wishes. When Di Di was only three months old, Mama had no milk left. There was no money to buy milk powder so our youngest brother, from then on, grew up on rice water or rice flour mixed into "rice gruel" which Mama made to feed him. After Di Di ate and slept, she put him to bed, and Mama started to wash and prepare meals. Being without a servant or anyone to help made no difference. She toiled day and night and could still keep life going. The big problem was that after nearly a year the whole family had gone through nearly all the cash in Mama's hand; there was not even enough left to buy one day's supply of food. Every day she worried about the next day, concerned about how she would keep the livelihood of the family going.

Dad, who was bogged down in disappointment and the devastation of feeling as though he was drowning, was going through the biggest test and difficulty of his life's journey. How could he tear off his prestige, face the facts, and accept reality? Could he put on common clothing and muddle along the alley way, and start to live the common life he had to accept now? Would he be able to seek and ask for a job with the shame of doing something he hated to do? Or, could he go back to the factory and have the courage to beg those former workers who were now his bosses to give him a job even lower than working in the boiler room? Weren't there many old friends and colleagues from the business circles who had been respectable in former days, now in order to survive and make a living at this time had already taken this difficult step? It was evident to him that right now, throughout the whole nation of China, people with his social status had been abandoned forever. They would never again be put in any important positions and wouldn't be treated courteously. His fate was already sealed; he would have to spend the rest of his life living like a dog with its tail between its legs.

He often sat staring blankly without speaking. He would think about what had happened during this short time. What should he do? He smoked and smoked, days passed; he still made no decisions, took no action, and had no solution.

Mama would not pressure Dad to do anything he didn't like; she also would not say anything to embarrass him. At that time, there were so many people who needed to be fed at home each day; they could not run out of rice and fuel. And the date for paying the rent was coming soon. Not able to wait any longer, Mama started to sort out the things stacked in the other room, trying to find something valuable. She pulled blankets, silk clothes, a fur coat, and leather shoes from the chest. She ironed and cleaned them and prepared to go and sell them. This was the only way she could think of to keep the whole family from going hungry, and to prevent them from wandering destitute on the street.

It would happen often when there was no more food at home, she would carry me on her back, holding a package with something in it in her left hand, and holding Liu Jie with her right hand. The three of us would appear at the second-hand market in Ru An street in Kunming. After selling something and getting some money, the three of us would rush to go food shopping. Mama would busily buy foodstuff for the family. After she had paid, she would hold one bag and give one bag to Liu Jie to help her and then hurry home. Mama would have to get home to quickly prepare dinner, so the other 5 children could eat on time and go to school again.

One day Mama didn't have any money to buy rice for dinner, there was also only a little food left for Di Di, and she was very anxious. She packed some things in a bag, and asked Dad to go out and try to sell them to get some money to help her cope with the emergency. When Dad held the package in his hand, he hesitated and could not walk out the gate all alone until Er Jie came home from school, and he asked her to accompany him.

Before going out the door, he put on a big felt hat which covered his face. He asked Er Jie to carry the package, and they both went to Wei Yuan Street where there was a place they could set up a stall on the ground to sell used things. They chose a spot and laid out their things. When the things were arranged, Dad immediately squatted with his back to the street. But after a little while, he still felt the ridicule and scorn of the people passing by stabbing him in the back, and he said to Er Jie, "I still feel too embarrassed to squat here; I will stand a little further away. You help Dad to do this. You can sell those old things if the price is not too far off. If the price they offer is very low, you come ask me." He handed over the things to Er Jie with a few words of explanation. Then, he ran to a corner 50 meters away and hid there.

After a while, as expected, there was a person who asked the price. He took his fancy to a small alarm clock made in Germany, which had been beside Dad's bed for many years and cost quite a bit of money. Er Jie was doubtful about the price the man offered, so she told the man to wait a minute, she got up and ran to Dad to ask. When she had the information and came back, to her surprise, the alarm clock and the man had gone.

"Ai Ya, where is our alarm clock?!" Er Jie was scared and cried out. Dad came over and he immediately understood what had happened.

"This is terrible; this world is too fearful," he said as he shook his head. He picked up the other things which were not as valuable and told Er Jie:

"We won't sell, we won't sell, we'll go home!" He carried the package and went back home with Er Jie. Mama knew what had happened to them, but she didn't say anything to complain, and Dad started to talk, "Don't ask me to go to do such things again! Let them snatch away everything we have. With no money to live on, let us all go and die! Living like this, I don't want to live another day!"

Mama knew Dad's personality very well, and after that she did not dare ask Dad to go out to sell anything again.

That year, Liu Jie also reached the age to go to school. Now there were six children studying at the school, and the tuition fee was a big expense. There was no other choice, Mama carried Di Di on her back, sometimes also taking me with her, and we often went to different streets where we could set up a stall to sell the used things she had picked out. At that time, selling something valuable from home to make some money was the only way to support the whole family's livelihood. For Mama, this was the only method she could use now. She continued to search each wardrobe and suitcase at home, looking for something to sell; then she would go to the market to exchange them for some money and return. Firstly, she used the money to pay the tuition fees for my older brother and sisters and to buy some study equipment for them. She thought the most important thing for the whole family was to keep them going to school.

Mama said, "I don't care about my 'face,' my face is worth nothing. If my children cannot go to school, our family will finally come to an end." Mama really resolved to cast aside all considerations of her saving face; she tried by every means possible to earn money to maintain the whole family.

Not able to offer any financial support to Mama, unwilling to go out to find a job to earn money, and even unable to do the housework, Dad felt he was useless and living a degraded life. He had lost the basic confidence to keep his life going. His personality was so fragile. Previously he had very strong self-esteem, and now he was disheartened by everything. He often said to himself, "Ai, I am an unnecessary person; it would be better to let me die." Mama was very sad when she heard Dad say this.

She told him, "No, I don't want you to think this way. I don't want you to say that either. Wait for Mao Mao to grow up a little bigger, and I will go and find a job. Any kind of job no matter how low and degrading it is, I will take it, even sweeping the floor or cleaning the toilet. As long as we can all stay alive. If you don't want to go out and deal with people you don't like, you can stay home with Ling Ling; just help me to look after the house, and it will be fine." She also told Dad, "In two years time, Zu Ying will be finished with her studies, and she will get a job and slowly, bit by bit, things will get better."

"I am still young, I am not afraid of hardship. For our children's sake, both of us need to be alive and well." Mama tried to use every means and all kinds of words to console Dad again and again. Despite the fact that they were in such a low situation, they still loved each other deeply as in the early days. Never at any time had they fought. Often, when Mama came home exhausted from going out, Dad would pass the cigarette he had just lit to Mama since he had a guilty conscience. He would help Mama loosen the tie and take hold of the baby from Mama's back and carry the baby in his arms and stand close to Mama, letting her rest.

"I don't know what to say. I have put you in such a difficult position by allowing you to take on such a heavy family burden." He saw his wife, who was so delicate and emaciated, rushing about taking care of the whole family every day without a word of complaint; now quickly looking older, she hardly ever smiled as before. Dad felt deeply distressed and often said these words to Mama in shame.

At the end of 1954, San Jie (my third sister) suddenly became ill when she was 14 years old. She was diagnosed with bone tuberculosis. After having some simple treatment in the hospital, there was no more money to leave her in the hospital to receive more treatment, and a few months later she died at a young age. With the family reduced to poverty and then to lose a daughter too, my parents were very sad. Dad was in even more pain than Mama. He thought his daughter had developed this disease because they lived in this dilapidated house, and he felt he was responsible for harming her and causing her death. He was choked up with tears for a long time. He took his bed board apart, and made the small coffin for his daughter himself. On the day of the funeral, he was determined to be the pall bearer and together with another laborer, he carried the coffin on his shoulders, sending his daughter to the mountain for burial. For a long time after this, he lived in a state of self-accusation. He could not extricate himself from this predicament, and he looked so wan and sallow, like a totally different person.

Often, he regretted that he hadn't decided to sell off the family property and move the whole family to Hong Kong or Taiwan in the early days. Because of this wrong move, he was now confronted with the family's devastating circumstances. Mama also repented of the past when she had insisted that she wanted the whole family to stay in Kunming. She tried to comfort Dad by saying, "It was my fault; it was my shortsighted thinking which caused this trouble for the whole family. Now we have nothing, and it is too late to turn things around." Dad could not bear hear Mama accusing herself, and because he himself could not do anything to change the family's predicament, he thought that he only had one way to go. He believed his only choice was to die.

From the beginning of 1955, as well as being anxious and depressed, Dad started coughing continuously, and then he developed a fever and began to cough up blood. After a check up, he was diagnosed with pulmonary tuberculosis. At that time penicillin and streptomycin had been introduced into China, and many hospitals had started to use them. If only he'd had the money to go to the hospital and to stay there to receive treatment, this disease could have been healed completely. But at that time, the family had fallen into greatly reduced circumstances, not even knowing where to get enough food for each day. Mama didn't have the money to send Dad to the hospital. She used a folk prescription to boil some Chinese traditional medicine into a soup, giving it to Dad to drink three times a day. During that time, everywhere in the small yard where we lived, there were grains of a Chinese herbal medicine called "Xiao Bai Ji" drying in the sun.

Dad was always reluctant to take the medicine, and Mama knew Dad was sick in his heart. She tried to use the love of the family members to re-awaken Dad's emotional attachment to life. Back then, for most of the day, my older brother and sisters were studying at school. When they came home after class, Mama always asked them to go to Dad, to go and speak to him as he was lying on his bed. When it was time to eat, Mama would move the table beside Dad's bed, enabling him to lean on his pillow and eat with everyone. During the daytime, Mama carried Di Di on her back, ceaselessly bustling about with the house work. In the small yard of that old room in An Ning Lane, I was often called by Mama to stay beside Dad's bed. Mama wanted me, a 4-year-old, to have fun with Dad to give him joy.

I was very obedient to Mama and always stayed beside Dad's bed for a long time each day. I held Dad's hand shakily in mine; I touched his face and spoke to him continuously; sometimes I would sing to him. When Mama soothed me to sleep, she liked to hum some songs. I had a good memory, and now I repeated the songs I had heard from Mama and hummed them for Dad. Mama said my personality was just like the name Dad gave to me - very clever. From my birth any move I made or any action I took would incur the love of people. Also, because big changes had taken place in our family after I was born, and Dad's status had changed, he stayed at home much more than before. Because I had not reached school age, Dad played with me and held me much more than the other children. My older brother and sisters have all told me they remember that when they came home after their classes, what they would see was Dad wearing a long gown and holding me tightly in his arms, or me sitting on Dad's knee. We were very close to each other.

Mama said that when Di Di was very small, he always stayed on her back. In the room there were three beds and some furniture in a very limited space; I would run back and forth and I would be cuddled lovingly by Dad. During the two years after we moved into An Ning Lane, she saw that the very few times Dad had a smile it was me who brought it to his face.

But Dad's illness showed no sign of improving, and most of the time he lay on the bed. He became more and more thin and looked pale. His big eyes which were formerly kind and affable now looked even bigger, sinking deeply into his eye sockets, full of helplessness and despair.

One day, I saw him sitting up and wanting to get out of bed. I ran towards him. I squatted in front of him and used both hands to hold his feet and put the slippers on his feet. After I did this, I raised my head and looked at him smilingly.

"Oh, Dad's angel, I am not willing to part with you!" Dad picked me up and held me tightly to his chest. He kissed my cheeks continuously. Finally, he tried his best to stand up, using all his strength to lift me up into the air. "Ge, ge, ge," I laughed heartily. Dad was very happy too, and he also laughed from his heart. Mama said that was the only laughter she had heard from Dad in those later years. That evening, after Mama had soothed me to sleep, she put me in the middle of the bed between her and Dad's pillows. Dad leaned back in the bed, he fixed his eyes on me for a while, and then suddenly he began to say, "Ai, this daughter is too lovely, but I cannot give anything to my dear little daughter. I...," he shook his head, both hands covered his face and he choked with sobs. To see Dad so sad with bitter grief caused tears to run down Mama's face too.

"If you love this child, you should take your medicine; you should stir yourself up."

"It is too late, it is too late. No medicine can heal me now," he said to Mama weakly.

While Dad studied in the university.

Dad in his study.

I don't know what Dad was really thinking then. Anyhow, he started to refuse to take his medicine. Mama said he just lay on the bed for the whole day, saying nothing. The most sorrowful thing for a person is when he has lost purpose and his heart has died. I think maybe my Dad was in such a state then. When a man's heart has died, there is nothing else that can save his life. Things kept going for a few extremely gloomy months, and then at 11 o'clock on the 14th of October that same year, Dad, who was lying on his bed, suddenly coughed violently. Mama, who was working on the sewing machine, went to Dad to help him sit up. Dad stretched his both arms to Mama and at the same time opened his eyes wide to look at her, and unexpectedly, he spoke to Mama in one painful sentence, "Ruo Bi, I, I feel sorry for you," and his hands feel down limp. At that moment, my Dad breathed his last in that small room he had never liked.

That year, he was only 48 years old. Mama was only 38 years old.

Of the seven of his children, my oldest sister was 16. My youngest brother was not even two years old, and me, I was just 4 years old.

Dad passed away at midnight in that dilapidated old house suffering a great injustice. Dad's death was the greatest misfortune for our family.

That evening, I, just 4 years old, and my younger brother were sleeping soundly. Suddenly, we heard first Mama and then the miserable crying and shouting from our older brother and sisters, the sound breaking into the still of the night. That night, the sad and shrill cries, the sound of everyone wailing and whining, was the initial memory in my immature spirit which would never be obliterated throughout my childhood. It was really extremely fearful. My younger brother and I were too young to know the meaning of death. That day we didn't cry with sorrow, we just felt afraid because we heard the miserable crying of the whole family, and we just cried in fear without stopping.

"Ah! Ah!...," we cried shrilly.

For the whole night, Mama made herself hoarse loudly shouting, "Why are you so heartless, why have you abandoned us, why have you gone? How can I be left alone? You have left us orphans and a widow in the world, how can we keep living!? My god, open your eyes to see, pity me, how can I foster so many kids and bring them up? God! Ling Ling and Mao Mao are just so little, so young; why did you let them lose their father?! Oh, my god! My god!..."

The older brother and sisters couldn't believe their own father had left them forever; they continued to shake Dad's body and cried out loudly,

Dad loved his family.

Dad loved photograph.

"Dad, Dad, you open your eyes, you wake up, you cannot go! You cannot go! Dad, Dad, why don't you care for us?"

"Dad, Dad, wa, waaaa...," my younger brother and I didn't know what had happened right then; we just copied them calling out shrilly.

That night, No. 7 An Ning Lane had lost its peace. The sound of crying and shouting from the orphans and the widow shook heaven and earth; the whole yard was immersed in deep grief.

Dad left the world miserable. It made Mama feel deeply grieved and despairing, and a few times she fainted as she wept.

A weak woman of just 38 years old, she had nothing but the bare walls in her house. She had so many children to provide for; how would she live in the future?

That day and the second day, our home was a miserable picture which was unbearable to look at. We seven kids, the bigger ones holding the smaller ones in their arms, supported Mama with our hands. For a long time we all stood around Dad's remains, just continuing to cry and shout. Nobody knew what our next step should be.

The second morning, Da Jie and Er Jie were sent by Mama to the factory to give a message to the leader about Dad's death. She was too young to deal with such a big event, and she expected that the factory would dispatch some man to come and help her to make arrangements for Dad's funeral. She also hoped that the factory would give her some money to pay for the funeral expenses, because she only had less than two Yuan in her hand at present. Unexpectedly, Da Jie and Er Jie who were crying when they went out were also crying when they came back. Two army representatives and one workers' representative, who all looked like devils, followed them home. In the land of China, in this great struggle of "One social class overthrowing another class," seeing someone dead, for them, was already something that happened often. At that moment hearing that another "class enemy" had left this world was not something serious to them at all. They did come, but they didn't even enter the room. They ice-coldly threw out a word, "He has died, what's the use of crying? Go and find a place to carry him for burial." They didn't leave any money, and after saying that they swaggered off.

"Oh, they are so cruel-hearted. They have taken all the things which belong to our family. Now, even when a life has been taken and we are going through this physical and mental suffering, they don't even have a word of sympathy for us," Mama lifted up her pale face covered in tears.

"Mama is going to buy some poison, we will all take it, and we will all die together," she said to the seven children who were crying with her. And then she walked out of the gate. We seven children were still sobbing and whimpering, waiting for Mama to decide our destiny. A few hours later, Mama came back home quietly, with something in her hand. It was not poison but a bunch of flowers which Dad liked, a piece of black fabric and white gauze, and some sacrificial offerings. She sat at the sewing machine not saying a word and quickly made up 8 black armbands. She put one on each of her children's arms, and also put one on her arm. She seriously told us seven children, "From today, we are all in mourning for your Dad for three months." She stood up and put a table against the wall, spread a white table cloth on it, and set up a mourning site for Dad there. She chose a picture in which Dad was wearing a white suit and looked very handsome to hang over it. Then she cut the white carnations into different lengths and put them in a vase and put it in the front of the picture of Dad. He looked as though he were in the flowers. Afterwards, she burned candles and joss sticks and put them on the table. After finishing those things, she led all of us to kneel at Dad's remains. She spoke to Dad word by word, "Tomorrow, I will bring all the kids to bury you. Your seven children, they don't have a dad, but they still have me, their mama. Ze Gao, I tell you now, you have set your mind to go; you can trust me; I will use my utmost strength to bring up all of your kids. After I have finished my task, I will go to meet you; you wait for me in heaven." While she was speaking, she moved both her hands over Dad's face which looked full of worry, stroking him as if she would like to console him and help him forget his biggest regret before his death. Finally, she covered Dad's face with white gauze. Doing all of those things, Mama was extremely calm, her crying had stopped.

Nobody knows what mental changes Mama had gone through, which brought her from death to life, during the few hours after she left home. Maybe Mama felt she could lean on her instinctive motherly love and her courage, and that she could foster us, her seven kids, and bring us up. As a young woman, how could she imagine that in the following "red years" she would be living in degradation and extreme difficulty! The years Mama helped her children to survive, the hardship and the pain she suffered, now, as I recall it over again, I still cannot bear it; it breaks my heart.

That evening, she hurriedly arranged for her seven children to eat dinner. Then Mama said some words to Da Jie in a low voice and went out again alone. When she came back, it was 10 o'clock. All of the smaller children were asleep; only Da Jie and Er Jie were sitting under the light and waiting for her uneasily. When Mama pushed the door open, her two daughters moved towards her. They saw that Mama looked despairing and sad. They called out, "Mama," and the three of them clung together, crying again. Da Jie knew that in order to pay the funeral expenses in the morning, Mama had gone out to borrow money that evening. Seeing Mama's expression when she came back, Da Jie understood for sure it had not gone smoothly. If Mama didn't have enough money, what would happen tomorrow?

Back then, there were only a few people who chose to cremate because this was an unbearable thing. It meant the family wasn't even able to buy a coffin for their dead. At that time, the equipment used for cremation was also very simple and crude. The body was put into a gasoline barrel, then set up on top of a heap of timber and burned up; it took many hours. Mama certainly didn't want Dad to suffer this kind of torture after his death. But, when she put the money she had borrowed together with her tears and checked the amount, she mainly only had tears. The money was too little to buy a simple coffin. It was impossible to find something costly enough in our home to sell off to buy a coffin. She had no idea who to go to for help. And Dad could not just stay waiting at home. How? How? Mama cried almost the whole night. As a last resort, she was forced to choose to send Dad for cremation on the third day after his death.

That day, our gentle and cultivated father was hoisted into a gasoline barrel, humiliated, and put on a big heap of firewood; he went through 6 hours of burning to slowly be reduced to ashes. This backward technique for cremation meant there were some big bones which did not burn up, they remained at the end. So, the box used for the ashes then was specially made, it was also much bigger than now. But Mama didn't even have enough money to buy such a box. She used a big porcelain vase to reluctantly put Dad's ashes and his remains into. Mama picked up Dad's ashes by herself; while she was doing this she said in a tearful voice to the person she had loved for her whole life, "Heaven bears witness to me, Ze Gao, you forgive me. I have no other choice; I finally had to let you go in this way!" She was holding Dad's ashes in her shaky hands, her tears dripping down into her husband's remains.

What she experienced during those few years was really beyond the limit that a young woman could endure; her nerves nearly fell apart. After bringing the vase with Dad's ashes back home with all the children, for many days, Mama didn't take any food or drink. She sat in a trance and just stared blankly at the portrait of our deceased Dad. The sensible Da Jie and Er Jie took care of the housework; they took on the duty of looking after the younger brothers and sisters. One day, seeing Mama sitting in the same place with a dull look in her eyes again, Da Jie brought all the kids around Mama, crying and saying to her, "Mama, we beg you to eat a little bit of porridge. Mama, if you continue like this, we seven kids will only have a blind alley to go down."

"Mama, Mama…," we clung to Mama together, swaying her and bursting into tears. Mama raised her head, measuring her children up with her eyes one by one. She was astonished to see that each of them had delicate features, but right now, their eyes were full of fear and restlessness. The shadow of death had touched their immature souls.

"Mama, Mama…," we were all aware that in this unfeeling and grim world only Mama could save our lives, could provide for us. We all shouted at her loudly. We had no other words.

"My god, Ah!" Mama held my youngest brother in her arms and also pulled me into her bosom. The cry she had kept down for many days now spurted out like a volcanic eruption, "Oh, my poor kids, my poor kids! You now have no one to depend on, only me. But I am a weak woman. I don't know if I am able to raise you up! Ah, Ah! god! My god." She was shouting and crying; we were all crying loudly together. After a while, Mama took a towel to wipe her tears, and sobbed, saying, "No, Mama will not let you die, never. Mama will take care of you, Mama will bring you up! We will grit our teeth together to keep our lives going on, going on!" Mama's voice was hoarse as she spoke this vow to us. At that moment, we seven kids embraced Mama closely; we clutched her firmly. We all clearly understood that we would continue to live in this world because we still had a Mama who loved us deeply. She would give out all of what she had to protect us. We cried together for a long time, shouting, "Mama, Mama!"

Mama gradually returned to normal; but the issue of the funeral and interment was not finished. Mama had been considering finding a place to bury Dad's remains, to let Dad "be laid to rest." But it was very hard, just like the cremation of Dad's body; I don't know how many times Mama cried. Mama had decided to bury Dad's remains on Mian Hill which is located in a western direction 7 KM from Kunming. For Mama this was also done out of absolute necessity. According to the custom, a person residing elsewhere would finally return to his ancestral home, and Cang Mountain surrounded by pines and cypresses in Dali should have been the last resting place for Dad. But now, Mama did not dare bring Dad's remains to his hometown Dali; no, she dared not. Mama didn't have the money to pay for a place in the memorial park in Kunming. She went out and looked at many places, finally choosing Mian Hill in a bleak and desolate valley. For her, maybe she thought this was only a temporary place for Dad to stay.

One month after Dad died, Mama brought all of us to bury Dad roughly.

Dad's funeral was the most miserable funeral in the world. When he was sent to the crematorium, a group of children and a scraggily woman followed him. The day we went to bury him, it was still those children and this woman, no-one else. That morning as we went to the hill to bury Dad, it was Dad's first son Wu Ge who held the vase with Dad's ashes in both his hands and walked in the front. He was not 10 years old yet, Mama wore white mourning clothes as she walked after him, and following them were four big kids. The two sisters carried the younger brother and me on their backs. This family wore mourning apparel; from when they left home at An Ning lane until they got to the suburbs 7 KM out of Kunming, they endlessly wept and wailed all the way; how miserable they were. Their grieved crying and shouting caused many people to stop in their footsteps and to shed pathetic tears.

"Ai Yo, the little one cannot even walk; the father has died. What a poor family!"

"She is too young to become a widow, how will she keep going on with her life? He has left her with seven children!" they stopped walking and watched. Some shed tears with us.

On Mian hill, when the laborer dug out a big hole and held up the vase of ashes and put it in, Mama found it hard to part and never to meet Dad again, and suddenly she threw herself in the hole.

"Ze Gao, I will go with you," she cried in a shrill voice, and she lost consciousness there.

That day, even those laborers who were used to burying the dead also felt this family's suffering was too cruel. They stopped working and helped Mama up, moving her to sit under a big tree; they gave her water and consoled her, "Eldest sister (this is what people called a woman who was older than them) we pity you; you have a hard lot, but you cannot die. If anything untoward should happen to you, what about your children? You have to provide for seven kids, it is hard for you, it is hard for you, we know." Mama opened her eyes and saw the seven children all around her, their faces already bathed in tears.

"My god, my poor children, my poor children!" Mama struggled to stand up; she held all of us in her arms. We cried together in front of Dad's new tomb for a long time.

"Ze Gao, I cannot even choose to die. For these seven children, I have no other choice but to live! You are in heaven to bless us; you wait for me there, and I will bring your kids to come and visit you each year. When I raise your children up, I will come to meet you," Mama said as she led us to give Dad a kowtow. When we had to leave Dad, Mama embraced us as she said those words to Dad.

Dad and Mama had a very good relationship with people. Why there were no people who came to send Dad off then?

It was because during that time all of the relatives and friends then were classified as part of the same social class as Dad. Most of them were experiencing their own narrow escape; they were unable even to fend for themselves. They wished they could come, but they couldn't. Many people, because of the political pressure, didn't dare to come to visit our family in the day time. They only dared to see Mama in the dark of night without being noticed, and they would speak a few words to Mama and leave quickly.

Mama became a widow when she was 38 years old.

Dad's younger brother, who was appointed as the president of the Xi Zhou branch of the Communication Bank in 1949, took his whole family and moved to Dali then. However, the good times didn't last long. With political movements following one by one, their family was engulfed in it at once. Their situation right now was even worse than our family's because after going through these movements, Si Shu didn't escape adversity. He was innocently condemned and sent to prison. Si Shen had to support five children living by herself; they were in a very difficult circumstance too. Si Shen said they knew about Dad's death 10 days later. She wished she could come to Kunming to see Mama. But, she was too poor to have the money to buy a ticket. Some of the other closer relatives and friends only came for a few minutes. Some were snobs; they were even people whom Dad had assisted and given financial help. But now, when they saw the misfortune this family met, knowing the master of this family had gone, they were so afraid these orphans and widow might trouble them and ask for help. Or they were afraid this family as part of the "bourgeois" would bring them disaster and trouble in the future, so they did not even dare come to our home and avoided seeing us. The person who made Mama feel very heart-struck was Dad's younger sister who had received so much love and care from Dad and Mama; at that moment, she was just hired to be an English teacher in a middle school. She was scared she would lose the trust of the government and fail to get the job. She had to show off how progressive she was and draw a clear distinction from the bourgeois family. She only came to see Mama once after Dad died, and after that she never came again.

The winter of 1955 was the most frigid winter that Mama had suffered in her life. Like losing its backbone, our home looked so lonely and was filled with solemn silence. Without a man to rely on, our miserable life was harder to keep up. The dilapidated and disorderly room instantly had no vigor and vitality with silence everywhere. As a four-year-old, I always used to chirp and run back and forth in the room. At that moment, I became another person. In the last few months, I had heard so much crying, I had become sensitively aware that there were very bad things which had happened at home. I was not happy at all. I only had fear in my heart. Every day, except when I had to sleep, I always held tightly on to Mama's hand. Where she went, there I followed. I continuously raised my head to see Mama's face, and as soon as I saw the tears on her face, I immediately started crying.

"Ling Ling, my little dear, Ling Ling, don't cry." Mama got a towel to wipe my tears for me, but she cried all the time. Each day, in the morning, afternoon and evening, three times Mama put a candle and incense in front of Dad's mourning site. She always carried my younger brother on her back, and I always stood beside her. As the faint candlelight and the smell of three types of incense floated in the air, Mama often could not restrain herself, and she wept in grief and unbearable pain. I pulled Mama's trouser leg and cried with her each time. The older brother and sisters went to school, and Mama hurried to do the housework. The rest of the time she sat cross-legged on the floor up against the spinning wheel, waving her arm by rote to spin. This was the first job she got from the outside. She spun alone silently without speaking, and often, the tears covered her face. She spun and spun, using the spinning wheel to spin some thin thread into thick thread and then wound it into a ball. After she had worked for a whole day at home, she could trade them at the factory for several Jiao in cash. Then she quickly went to buy some rice and came back home to cook for the family. When the meal was ready and all the children were sitting around the table and preparing to eat, Mama customarily put a bowl and chopsticks in the place where Dad usually sat, "Ai, the children's Dad, where are you now?! Why do you not eat with us any more…?" Looking at the bowl and chopsticks, she often shed tears alone. In the still of night, lying down on the bed without Dad's familiar figure on the pillow beside her, she held the pillow and cried again for one or two hours. As a four-year-old, I still could not understand clearly what had happened to Dad. I didn't see Dad for a long time, and sometimes I said to Mama, "I want Dad, I want Dad!"

When Mama heard those words, she burst into tears at once, "Ling Ling, you never had your Dad. Poor daughter, you lost your Dad and you don't even know what death is!"

I really didn't know what death was. It is said when a person is three or four years old, they start to have memories and can remember definite things. But in my immature hear, my first memories of images of Dad and Mama were vague impressions, only the sound was clear. The sound was my Mama's miserable crying. When Dad suddenly disappeared from my life, out of fear, I stayed close to Mama all the time, not moving a step from her. I was so afraid another of my dear ones would disappear again. I remember, I don't know how many times, my younger brother and I would get drowsy and go to sleep with Mama's sobbing. I don't know how many times, we would wake up with Mama's sobbing again. Mama carried us two kids who knew nothing but to cry in her arms, crying out for several hours in succession. During that time, it was simply the thing we must suffer every day. So crying and tears became the two things which regularly accompanied me in my childhood. My big eyes were no longer filled with joy but were full of alertness and worry which was not appropriate to my age; I didn't like to smile any more.

At that time, my oldest sister was studying in the teachers' training school, my second sister was studying in the nursing school, and my fourth sister was just entering the middle school. They were all just in the beautiful years where they were blossoming like flowers. But during this time, they didn't have a day of joy. Every day after school when they came home and saw Mama, they often started to cry because they clearly understood what Dad's death meant for the family. The older brother and the sixth sister were at an age where they were still not sensitive to the affairs of human life, but they had become aware of the misfortune of the family. When they saw their mother cry, they would either cry too or immediately stay silently to one side. My older brother frequently said later that his childhood was finished by the time he was nine years old. It was true. The small room, once filled with noise and excitement in former days, now had no sound of laughing and playing, just crying and more crying. This endless crying during the initial days after we lost our father, the tears of Mama and her children flowed as a river.

In the few months after Dad died, Mama was much thinner and always had rings around her eyes. The black armband she wore for mourning Dad was on her right arm and the arms of her seven children for three months. A little white flower she had also made in mourning for Dad was inserted in her hair beside the ear every day. She had this flower with her for about a year. No matter how other people looked on this man who was the master of this family, in her and her children's hearts, this man would forever be the most precious and loved person.

The inconstancy of human relationships which Mama had realized during the family's urgent and difficult need caused her not to expect anyone to give her any favors. This world had no sympathy and mercy to speak of. She knew from now on everything depended only on herself. She often later said, "When your dad fell down, it made me see clearly into the human heart. After this I vowed no matter how hard life would be in the future, even if I am dying, our family would never go to beg or to rely on any person."

But, in this world, there were still some people who certainly didn't lose their compassion. One morning after Dad died, an old woman from the countryside who carried a basket of pumpkins on her back suddenly came to the small yard at An Ning lane. She walked straight to Mama and called, "Mrs. Yan!"

Mama looked up at her, feeling surprised, "Old sister Ding, how did you get here?" Originally, this was a woman the family named Ding and came from a village called Liang Ting not very far from Kunming. She had often sent some fresh vegetables, especially pumpkin which tasted so good and was only produced in her village, to our kitchen before the liberation. She carried vegetables for sale on her shoulders with a pole; sometimes, she carried her baby on her back too. Mama felt pity for her, always asking her to put down her baby and helping her to carry her for a little while and giving her some water to drink, letting her have a rest before she left. She constantly remembered Mama's kindness, and she sent fresh vegetables to our home every year. When we moved in to An Ning lane, we had naturally broken off relations with her. Now, she called on us by herself. She held Mama's hand and told Mama she had been selling vegetables in the same area where we lived. She also had been asking about the Yan family's whereabouts, but she couldn't find out anything. Today, when she went to the old place where she customarily went to sell pumpkins, she heard some people saying that Mr. Yan had passed away, leaving seven children very pitiful. She stopped selling her pumpkins, and she went and asked several people to get our home address. She carried the pumpkins and came to our home. Mama very much appreciated her but was aware that society had put our families into two different classes now, so Mama said to her, "You must take your pumpkins and leave as soon as possible; our family is now in a bad way, and it is better if you have less contact with us. I don't want to bring any trouble to you."

"Ai Ya, Mrs. Yan, how can you speak like this? I don't care about liberation or no liberation. I only know who is good. You and Mr. Yan both are good people; Mr. Yan died so young, and I feel sorry. I am very sad. Today, I will be here to wait for all the children to come back home. I want to see each of them, and then I will leave. Those children are now painful, how pitiful they are, Ai...," while she was speaking she was crying. When she cried it caused Mama to cry with her. That day, she held my younger brother, whom she had never seen before, and me in her arms. She was continually saying, "It is so evil, poor kids, poor kids!" She words like this. She did wait for all the children to come home and gave her greetings to each child, using her overgrown callused hands to shake hands with each of them and to stroke their heads. Then she was reluctant to leave. When time came to part, she was determined to leave all the pumpkins which she had brought for sale with us; she told Mama over and over that she would come again to look in on us. Sending her off by the gate, Mama led all of us to stand in a line to say goodbye to her. We all looked at her wrinkly face carefully, and in our hearts we were all well disposed towards this old countryside woman. We were all actually looking forward to her coming again soon. During that time, she was really the only one to treat us well and the only person who did not dislike or avoid us.

Bringing up again the past events of Dad's death makes me very sorrowful.

From a child, Dad had received a good education. When he grew up, he had acquired a specialty in study. He could be considered as a hardworking and kindhearted intelligentsia. He was one of the first entrepreneurs to establish the textile industry in Kunming. After his hard and diligent work, he seized a successful career and became an experienced industrialist when he was a little older than 30. He had possessed thousands of millions in assets and house properties under his own name. He didn't spend extravagantly; he didn't go bankrupt and fail. He worked cautiously and conscientiously all his life. Because of his personality and self-improvement, surely, it was impossible for him to make trouble with the new state power while it had just come into power, to do the crime of "tax dodging and evasion" to the tune of high millions against the government. And in this situation where he didn't have any other way to go, he laid down his arms and surrendered and willingly used his own factory and house to refund the "crime" they maintained. But why was he still driven out of his house and deprived of everything? And why was he charged with crimes he did not commit? In 1954, when he was forced to submissively hand over his factory, which he had painstakingly built up for 18 years, to the new state power, he wrote a material account, his last description of his factory, "… there are 54 employees in my factory. The factory produces and sells all kinds of cotton suiting, and processes white fabric, striped cloth, and gauze. The production quantum achieved is 4,500 meter each month. After the land reform, the purchasing power increased, and the products came into a situation where demand exceeded supply in our factory."

It was such a prosperous enterprise, and the owner was also in the prime of his life; but why in such a short time was he deprived completely of all of his belongings and assets? Finally, they bound him, forcing him to his death step by step. The most miserable thing was, when he was dead, his family could not even afford a coffin to put his body in and finally had no choice but to bury him hastily in a small hill in the wilderness.

I cannot keep silent and want to ask - What did he do wrong? Who trampled his dignity underfoot? All of his property, where has it gone? Who was it, and based on what, did they take all of his possessions, and even his life? After so many years, no one dares to make inquiries about those questions, but now, I want to ask. Who can answer me?

Our dear father, how unjust was his death!

Writing this, I think I have answered the question which perplexed the author who wrote that the "Yan family created a business legend" - why until now has not one of the later generations of the Yan family done business? Do they dare!? "Once bitten by a snake, one shies at a coiled rope for the next ten years." For all the people of the Yan family, when they think about the political campaigns of "Three-anti and Five-anti" and "Suppress the Counterrevolutionaries," before their eyes appear the pictures of their relatives dying a tragic death one by one, palpitating with anxiety and fear, absolutely terrified. Not only for ten years, but they will shy away from a coiled rope forever.

Our Father passed away, withdrawing from the world which didn't like him; he also didn't like it himself. But, Mama, how will she bring her children up to live in this world?

Mama was unswervingly faithful to the promise she made to Dad. For the descendants of the Yan family, she exerted her utmost strength to live; her long suffering life's journey will open up from this prologue. During the years after Dad died, she, a 38 year-old widow, worked with perseverance, using painstaking effort in her life to foster and to love us, her seven children. The hardships she went through, I think only a few women in the world could endure. Because the times we were living in were the "red" period when Mao Ze Dong hid the truth from the masses. It lasted not just a few but 30 whole years! During these 30 years, we seven children were classified as "the black puppy of the capitalist," and Mama was someone the red state powers also wanted to destroy. But alive, we all became the lowest citizens and did not receive a welcome anywhere in society. Each day we lived in this ice-cold world, it may be said we trekked on a path overgrown with brambles. Many times we went through dangerous situations, and many times we were in a grave crisis between life and death. But God showed consideration for us; he granted us a great and staunch caretaker and leader to accompany us all the way - she was our mother. Depending on the strong, tough, and flexible strength which emanated from her, we were able to forge ahead step after step to wait until the day when the haze would dispersed like the sun finally shining again after the rain in our country.

For many years, we had lived in poverty and hunger. The tribulation Mama had endured had already made her life extremely difficult, but, even more unfortunate was, in the years after Dad died, Mama and her seven children could not avoid being involved in more and more political movements. Between Mama and her seven children, there were many unexpected turns of events and stories which are inconceivable or should not have occurred. All of these things caused Mama's destiny to become even more miserable and sorrowful. These events I want to particularly record and tell about in the following chapters.

THE CAREER OF SAN SAO,
THE WIDOW IN THE YAN FAMILY
(1955–1979)

J udging by outward appearances, Mama looked like a very thin and weak lady. Her stature was just over 5 feet tall, and she always had a slight figure. When she married Dad, she didn't need to go work in a large organization as she never needed to worry about the support of the family. After Dad's sudden demise, the heavy burden of the whole family, all the basic needs for the survival of so many people, now fell completely on her shoulders. That year she was only a young 38-year-old woman. I suppose Mama must have been able to pull herself together again within a very short time. As well as her natural instinct of maternal love, it was also the good habits she had developed from her childhood of doing things for herself and being enriched by the experience of having a big family after she married that enabled her to do this. All these things had built her up to be a very sensible and staunch woman, more than other women of the same age. It was as if she always had a store of inner strength in the depths of her heart.

By drawing on this reserve of strength, our Mama led us, the group of children, into these times of hardship of "fleeing for our lives" as she often said. She simply coiled up her long permed hair and from then on she never used cosmetics on her face; she looked plain and quiet. Many of her fashionable cheongsams, high heeled shoes, and all the cosmetics she formerly used every day were put into the bottom of the trunk. She wore a set of clothes made of dark blue fabric which the common working women all wore back then. She put on flat heeled black cloth shoes, just like one of the laborers. What didn't change was her temperament which was not vulgar, and she still took care of her appearance from head to toe. Her hair was always combed and was never disheveled; her clothing was always very neat and without wrinkles.

In order to support the whole family's basic needs, for the first few months after Dad's death, apart from spinning on her spinning wheel day and night to make cotton to earn some cash, Mama still relied on the sale of some valuable things from our home to help out with the family's expenses, but it was barely enough to eke out a living. When she needed to pay the rent or the children's tuition fees, she had to find another way. With the first spring coming, she sold all the sets of furniture and sofas which had been moved from the old house. On the one hand she could not find any other way to carry on with life right then; on the other hand, she realized that those things would never be used in our home any more. Later, she began to sell off some of the overcoats, and some clothing which she and Dad hadn't worn. Finally, with tears in her eyes, she took off and sold her wedding ring which she had worn on her finger for years and which had a deep sentimental meaning for her. During that time, all impoverished families were selling off things for survival. There were many people selling, less people buying. Even formerly beautiful and valuable things were no longer selling at a good price.

There were eight people in our family, so it was not easy to maintain them. Even though we continually found things to sell, this only provided enough for half the year's living expenses for the whole family. Then there was nothing of value in our home to sell any more. How to maintain our lives? What was to be done? Mama tried to explore ways to solve the problem. Carrying Di Di on her back and holding me by the hand, she went out into the street. She wanted to see how other people ran small businesses to make money. Immediately, she noticed how some people were setting up stalls and selling small things. After she had tried to calculate the cost, she made her decision. She ran to the shop and bought some cotton print. When she got home, she cut it out and made some underpants and sleeve covers. She sat at the sewing machine to make them, and then ironed each one neatly. The next day, she brought them to the street and to set up a stall to sell them. She also took the opportunity to sell some of her used clothing. That was really a brilliant idea she had. Maybe Mama had business skills, or perhaps her sweet smile and the two kids standing beside her made it easy to attract people's sympathy. From the first day, she would always sell something; she would earn some money to buy rice and to solve the basic food problem for the whole family, now she finally had an assured source of income. At nightfall, Mama would tidy things up and carrying Di Di on her back and holding me by the hand, she carried the cloth-wrappers home in her other hand, always feeling very excited.

"Ai, we were lucky today; I have enough money to buy rice now. Mama is so happy. Quick, let's go home quickly!" She often could not contain her excitement; she talked to me and my younger brother even though we were both still too young to understand. For more than half a year, I hadn't seen Mama with any joy; now to gradually hear Mama speaking so enthusiastically made me very happy. No matter what she said, I always held her big hand and jumped with excitement. Back home, she gave money to Jie Jie, who had just finished school, to go and buy food, and without a pause, she herself started to make something to sell tomorrow.

Gradually, the small business she had set up with her stall moved from the city to the outskirts of Kunming. She had heard that there was a weekly countryside market in Ma Jie and Guan Du that was not very far from Kunming. Those places were bustling with activity and more people went there than the market in Kunming. Shuttling back and forth to the different countryside markets, Mama found out that most of the families in the countryside didn't have a sewing machine, but they often needed some things such as mosquito nets, bed sheets, sleeve covers and children's clothing to be made up. When they asked if Mama could help to make these for them, she immediately took this work. From then on, when she came home from the market in the afternoon, she always carried a big bag full of fabric in her hand. She would come in the door, drink some water, and sit at the sewing machine, with both feet peddling quickly. She wanted to make those things as soon as possible so she could deliver them to the next market day and earn some money.

Mama had good relationships with the people. The things she made were very good and done rapidly, and so more people came to her to ask for help. Sometimes when she went home after the market, the things she brought back were more than she had brought out. She could not carry all of them in her hands, so she would tie some things up in a bundle, and put them on my back to help her to bring everything home. At that time my older brother and sisters were all studying at school. With no-one at home to look after my younger brother and me, she had no choice but to take us both with her each day. By nightfall, when the three of us went back home, we all had red faces, our heads were covered with big drops of perspiration, and the clothing on our backs was wet to the skin. Mama had squatted down on the ground to attend to her stall for the whole day; she also needed to take care of two kids, so she was very tired. But she never relaxed, and as soon as she entered our home, she would very soon be sitting at the sewing machine to start work again. Sometimes there were too many things which needed sewing, and she often worked until one or two o'clock in the morning. Then she would iron each item and fold them in order. When all this was finished, she would go to bed. She was very busy and tired; but this was the only means of supporting the livelihood of the family she could find at that time, and this was the only way she could save the whole family from the menace of hunger, so she seized the opportunity and would not let it go.

This was the most precious trait in Mama's personality. She didn't wait; she didn't rely on anyone else; she never gave up, and she tried to do everything herself, always trying to resolve problems alone. She soon found out that she could catch the first train in the morning to get to the place that had just had a market to deliver the things she had made to the farmers there, and then she could walk to the place that was having the market that day. She could do two things in one day; she could save some fares, and receive the processing charge on time. She decided to try. But she had to leave home for the train station before day break, and that meant she could not bring the two children with her. Early that morning, she could not bear to wake up me and Di Di who were sleeping soundly, so she left a note for Si Jie and Liu Jie and asked them to come home after school and take care of our food. Then she got up and lifted the bags onto her shoulder, and left home. Then she walked out into the dark and quiet An Ning Lane alone. Suddenly Mama thought about me and Di Di still sleeping at home, it was the first time she had left two such small children at home by themselves. "Later, when they opened their eyes with no one there to take care of them, what would happen to them?" While she was thinking about this, tears covered her face, "God, you pity me, pity the two kids now sleeping at home. Bless them and keep them safe as they wait for me to come back. I have no alternative but to go out for our livelihood, to save eight people's lives. I don't have another way out. Please bless them. Ze Gao, also show your presence and bless these two little kids, you look after them. You pity me; I can do nothing about leaving them home; they are so little!" She sobbed all the way to the train station. That day she did go to the two market places, and her income was better. At nightfall, she went home wearily. This was the first day of my life that I had been apart from Mama for such a long time. During the day, no matter how much my sisters tried to coax me, I was not happy; my eyes were filled with tears, and I could only think about Mama. In the afternoon, when they needed to go to school again, they put me and Di Di in the room, closed the door and locked it, and then they left. With the door shut, there was only a dim little light in the room. Di Di and I stayed there, just the two of us. One of us was not five years old, and the other was not two years old. We felt the darkness and were filled with fear. We pushed the two locked doors with all our strength until there was a small crack of light shining between them, and then we burst into tears involuntarily, endlessly weeping and wailing until finally we were hoarse and exhausted, and we could not do anything but go to bed and sleep with exhaustion. At dusk Mama finally came back. When I got the first glimpse of Mama, I took hold of her firmly and cried and cried for about one hour. That day I followed Mama everywhere, I didn't leave her for a single step. Even in the evening, when she worked at the sewing machine, I took a square stool and sat beside her. I was so afraid Mama would run away again. After 10 o'clock, when she saw me doze off, Mama carried me to bed; I pleaded with Mama and said, "Mama, tomorrow I will go with you no matter what, I don't want to stay in this dark room!"

"Ok, Mama agrees with you. Tomorrow I will not leave you two in the dark room." Mama stroked my head and spoke sorrowfully. But the fact was, the second day and after that, Mama didn't take us two little kids to the market with her any more. To support the livelihood of the whole family, she had to go out alone early in the morning and come back home late at night. Di Di and I had to accept this and start living this new kind of lonely life even though both of us, and especially me, were very unwilling.

In this period, a lady Mama knew from the early years often came to visit her. She was the wife of Hu Zhong Ying who was the owner of the famous drugstore "Yong An Tang" in Kunming. Her family had also met with misfortune and was now also impoverished. The worst thing was that her husband had been arrested and sent to prison. This lady was two years older than Mama; she had two children who were studying at school. When we first saw her in our home, we all thought she was very pretty. She was a tall person, and her wavy hair hung on her shoulders. She had also taken off her cheongsam and wore gray clothing like the working women, but she still looked full and round and had an elegant demeanor. She spoke kindly and softly, had a gentle personality, and was easy going. Each time she came to our home and talked with Mama, she always shed tears. Mama understood her difficulties. This lady had never had a hard life, and she didn't have any professional skills. Now her life was so woeful; she was too worried to live. She admired Mama's courage and insight, and when she felt distressed, she often came to Mama to sob it out and to get some advice from her. During those two years, being alongside Mama, she learned about all the methods Mama had used to support the family. Just like Mama, she sold off all the valuable things from her home. Mama now relied on her sewing machine to make some things and would go to the countryside market to make a living. This lady didn't have any skills, so she would go to the mountains to cut wild grass and then weave grass curtains to sell. Doing this rough work did not earn much money at all. It not only caused her hands to become rough and sore, it also destroyed her character and appearance. When she met Mama later, we could see she was sloppily dressed, and there was some thin grass in her hair. When Mama saw her changing, she felt very sad. After only talking for a little while, both of them would cry together.

"You should also try to go to the countryside market like me," Mama consoled her.

"I am afraid I can't. I can do nothing." She had many fears and misgivings. With no special skills and never having left home to grow strong out in the world, she now had no confidence to take charge of a small business. She didn't think she could compare with Mama; she could not do the same things Mama did. Mama encouraged her and started to teach her to do some simple needlework, such as sewing on a button, making a button hole, as well as teaching her to use the sewing machine and so on. They would often both do some handicraft and talk together under the light for the whole night; they became very close to each other.

Only two months later, and only half a year after our father's death, a terrible thing happened in her family. Her husband could not bear the bitter suffering of prison and died of a heart attack there. When the message came to her, she was extremely frightened; the first person she wanted to tell was Mama. That day, isolated and cut off from help, she rushed at Mama when she entered our home and burst into tears. She said to Mama, "Zhong Ying is dead; the thing I feared the most has happened. Ah, I am afraid I only have one way out; I want to die! What can I do, what about my poor children, my two kids? How can I keep our life going? My god, I don't know!"

Mama totally understood the sorrow of a widow. She understood what kind of life she, who had met the same fate as herself, would have to face from now on, and she cried out with a deep sigh, "god!" Mama held her in her arms, and they cried together. They cried for a long time. Finally, Mama grasped her hands to comfort her, "I have more difficulties than you, I have seven children. I don't want to die; you should not think about death, you are forbidden to have such an evil thought!"

"I have had to endure all these hardships in the last half year; I know you can also take it. For the sake of our children, we both have to keep our life going. We brought these children into the world; they haven't done anything wrong. They have lost their fathers; how pitiful they are. We cannot do anything stupid, be sure of that, and leave them without a mother as well!"

"Heaven never seals off all the exits. I believe, if we ourselves do not give up, if we grit our teeth, we will get through any difficulty." Mama's words brought her immense comfort and encouragement. That evening, the two of them had a lengthy talk into the middle of the night. On the second day, Mama accompanied her together with her two sons to the prison to get the dead body and to send it to be cremated. A few days later, Mama together with my older brother and sisters accompanied the three of them to Mian Hill on the western outskirts of Kunming to bury the ashes of her husband just beside the grave of our father. Mama told her the two families could go to visit the graves later. When this disaster fell on her, she had no idea how to deal with this, but together with my strong Mama, she managed to deal with all these things within several days. Later Mama spoke to her, "Our two families have met with the same misfortune, and our two families will get through these hard times together, so don't be so afraid." Mama asked her to go to the countryside market with her. Mama told her, "Well, we'll just work together like friends doing business, who like to spend time together, sharing ideas with each other. We can put our two stalls closer together. After the market each day, if I have food for our family, I will give your family food. Do you think it is a good idea? Come on, you can do this with me."

As she talked, Mama taught her how to prepare some things and package them to sell the next day. Mama's courage and insight, and her generosity filled her with faith; as long as she was with Mama, she could do anything and not feel afraid any more.

"All right, I will follow you; we will go to the market together tomorrow," she looked into Mama's eyes and nodded her head frequently. She started to go out into society to make a living, wandering from place to place with Mama, together "fleeing for our lives," as Mama said. Unexpectedly for both of them, they were tied in a very close friendship. This remarkable and touching friendship between them lasted for the rest of their lives.

In those days, she and Mama were together from morning to night almost every day; they kept no secrets from each other. Their common fate and similar experiences linked them closer and closer, and they became more and more familiar. All of a sudden, they felt that they could not be apart any longer. Having lived amongst a huge mass of people for the past forty years, at that moment, for the first time they had both found a bosom friend in each other. Like Mama, she didn't have any brothers and sisters, so they both determined to become sworn sisters.

One day they both tidied up their appearance and invited some acquaintances and old friends to bear witness as they formally became sworn sisters. From that day the brothers and sisters in our family had a new "Er Yi Ma" (the second aunt in Chinese) who we already knew well but now had changed her status. Her two sons also had a new "San Yi Ma" (the third aunt in Chinese). The children from both families were also getting to know each other. The two sons of Er Yi Ma were the same age as Er Jie and Si Jie from our family. The first one looked smart; the second one was shy with strangers. His name was "Du Du", and when we heard this name we all laughed; we thought it was funny. From then on, Er Yi Ma became the dearest person to us brothers and sisters except for Mama. Er Yi Ma was a very kind person; she was easy to get along with. When she laughed, she had a mouthful of white teeth; she was very sweet just like our Mama. We seven children all liked her very much. We could see her two sons liked Mama very much as well; they were no reserved at all with her.

For more than 20 years after that, both women were very interdependent and faithful as they went through times of hardship together. And the children in both families, despite the fact that we didn't have a father, received double a mother's love from our two mothers. This was indeed a great blessing for both our families; this was a lucky break in the midst of our misfortune!

The time when Mama and Er Yi Ma started to go together to the countryside market became a demarcation line for these two women who had both gone through the deep and secluded valley of death; those days were deeply imprinted on our minds.

In the early morning at about 5 o'clock, Mama would sometimes go to Er Yi Ma's place to meet her, sometimes Er Yi Ma came to our home to meet Mama, and then they would set out together. In our sleep, we all heard Er Yi Ma's voice calling Mama gently outside the window, "San Mei, San Mei, let's go." (San Mei meant the number three younger sister in Chinese. Er Yi Ma was two years older than Mama.)

Mama would also respond quietly, "Coming, coming, I am coming." Then, we would hear a creak of the door shutting.

In the darkness, the two mothers carried the cloth-wrappers which they had prepared the previous evening on their backs as they hurriedly left home. The light was dim and silence reigned supreme as the door was closed quietly; the footsteps of the women could be heard hurrying along the secluded and lonely alleyways. They were always the first to break the deadly stillness under the dim street lamps. As each new day dawned, they had no idea what fate would be awaiting them, but for the sake of their children, these two women continued to do the same things each day. Duty-bound not to turn back, they left home on time, stopped by neither wind nor rain, because there were so many helpless children waiting for and depending on their support, they were the only people in the world their children could rely on.

When the weather became colder, they both put a scarf on their heads before going out, to keep out the wind and the rain. The scarf Mama liked was a light gray underlay covered with a thin brown thread pattern. The scarf Er Yi Ma chose was purplish red with a black brim. During those days, their outward appearance made them look absolutely like working women; however, their features and behavior still exposed their elegant nature which could not be missed. It showed up, for instance, when even if the fabric they needed would only be used for making underpants or sleeve covers, when they went to choose and buy it, they would still pay attention to the design and color. So everything they made always had a distinctive style. It caused their market stall business to do very well. They had an extraordinary ability to get along with others, and more and more handicraft processing came their way. They were both closely dependent on each other, always talking everything over, coming and going in haste every day. The sincere good-will built up between them and gave them a great deal of fresh motivation. The anxious expressions gradually left their faces, and all their children saw the graceful way both mothers carried themselves in their middle age, and this gave them a renewed vigor and hope.

Towards the evening, when they came back from the market exhausted, if that day's business had gone well, they would always bring home in their pockets some sweets, a few cookies, or some small things which they got from the famers in the countryside to give to their children. And then, they would immediately start cutting out the fabric and processing the things which they would sell or deliver the next day. After being taught by Mama, Er Yi Ma could soon do many kinds of work independently. When it became dark, she had to go home to cook for her sons. Before parting, if they hadn't finished their work, she and Mama would divide it up to finish in the evening by themselves. If they had finished all their work, they would make a time to meet the next morning and then take leave of each other. During those days when Mama was back home, I always stayed close to her, and the impression which is still in my memory is that each day when they were parting, no matter how busy she was, Mama always rose and accompanied her older sister as she walked to the gate, their heads nodding as they said good-bye to each other. Watching until Er Yi Ma had walked into the distance,

Mama would then return home. Now, as I recall all those details, I have come to understand this friendship between them, and how profound and sincere it was.

That year, when I was not yet five years old and my younger brother was not yet three years old, we would wake up each morning, open our eyes, and see that there was never anyone with us in the room. Mama left home before daybreak, all the older children had gone to school, locking the door and leaving us there alone. Di Di and I couldn't understand why Mama had to leave us at home while she went to do something by herself. At the beginning, when we woke up and couldn't see Mama, we often sat on the bed and cried for hours and hours. Later, we tried to dress ourselves in a careless way after which we would go to the door and push it open until we could see an aperture between the two locked doors, and we would stand in that gleam of light and wait. After a few days, I became stubbornly unwilling to stay in the locked room. When my sisters came home at noon and opened the door, I ran to the gate of our yard and sat on the wooden doorstep beside the big door, and they could not move me. When Mama found out about it, she agreed not to lock us up in the room and instead let us play in the yard by ourselves or sit beside the gate after we woke up. Because I was a little bigger than my younger brother, Mama told me over and over, "Be sure you do not walk too far away from the house. If you go out of the gate, there are bad men who really like to take little kids away. If they take you away, you will never ever see Mama again."

I kept Mama's words firmly in my mind, and I looked after Di Di carefully. Neither of us went out of the yard, not even one step. At noon, when the older brother and sisters came home from school, we would get some food to eat. After they went to school again, we just stayed in the yard. Each day in the afternoon, when I saw the sunshine moving to the roof of the house, I knew Mama would be coming home soon, and

I would sit on the wooden doorstep facing the alleyway entrance and ask Di Di to sit on the other side. We would always sit very still on those two wooden steps at No. 7 An Ning Lane for a long, long time, waiting anxiously and painfully for Mama to come back.

The waiting time was really too, too long as we gazed with eager expectation.

Sometimes, while we were waiting, we would fall asleep leaning against the gate. The clothing we wore was worn-out and dirty, mucus and tears covered our faces. The neighbors in the lane always said that we, brother and sister, looked just like two little beggars, extremely poor. But no matter if anyone or anything tempted us, we would never take one step from the gate. We had only one thought in our mind, which was to wait for Mama's return, to wait for Mama's return. At about six o'clock, when I saw Mama's figure turn into the lane coming into the line of my vision, I always jumped on Mama at that moment; nobody could know how joyful I was. Sometimes I would get a few sweets, and then I would be even more joyful. When Mama saw me, she would always put the cloth-wrappers aside, hold me in her arms, and kiss me on both cheeks then walk quickly to Di Di, pick him up, and kiss him. Di Di was never a sensitive child. Apart from when he cried, his face never seemed to have any expression. At about three years old, his language skills were still minimal; when Mama came home, he showed no strong response either. Mama would hold him for a little while and then let him go; he would sit silently on his own.

I, however, was totally different from him. To use Mama's words, I was very clever; nothing could be hidden from me. Each day during those times, while Mama was at home even if she had brought some tasty things for me, I would never eat them at once, but I would extend one of my hands to tightly catch hold of one side of Mama's clothing, and where ever she went, I followed. I was so afraid that Mama would leave me and disappear somewhere again.

During my childhood, a feeling of solitude and dread totally occupied my mind when Mama was not there with us. She left us lonely and was always gone; I didn't like this kind of life any more. So, many times, I would try not to sleep all night long, using my small hand to firmly take hold of Mama's pants in the quilts so I would not sleep. It did not help as I was too young; time and time again I would fall fast asleep, and when I woke up Mama had gone. A few times I would wake up once in a while, then I would cry and stir up trouble wanting to go with Mama, but I was always forcefully taken away from Mama by my sisters. I had no choice. For this reason, when I saw Mama, I would never be one step away from her, and I always followed her.

I was too young to understand why Mama had to leave home so early in the morning and what she was going out to do each day. In the night, lying down under the same quilts, I begged Mama over and over, asking her to allow me to go with her to the market place. I promised her that no matter how far the way, I would be able to walk by myself. I even promised Mama that I would help her carry the cloth wrappers and sell things. However, Mama still said no. Mama could not bring two children with her to the countryside market. She could only take me since Di Di was too little, and she didn't have peace of mind about leaving him home alone. Mama talked to me, "You have already helped Mama, little dear; Di Di needs you to stay home with him." How could I understand Mama's heart? So, during the period when Mama went to the countryside market leaving home early and returning home late, I was unhappy every day, and there was no smile on my face. Mama knew the thoughts which were in my mind; she often stroked my head and said to me, "Mama doesn't want to see that you are unhappy, but I have no other choice. The day you are happy, the day you no longer hate Mama, Mama's hard times will be over."

During that initial period when Mama went out into the community going to the countryside market to "flee for her life" each day, I don't know how she got through her days from morning till night. I was too young to have the chance to go with her even once. But, one day Ge Ge took a holiday from school, and he had one opportunity to go to the countryside market with Mama. Many years later he wrote an article to commemorate Mama. The title was "One Day in the Life of My Mother." It narrated the whole of that day.

In his article he wrote that the market place he went to with Mama was Xiao Ban Qiao, which is more than 10 km from Kunming. Mama woke him up in the dark of the night and carrying the cloth wrappers on their backs, Mama held his hand, and the two of them rushed to the train station in the darkness. At 6:30 am a train drove up to the platform. He found out that Mama didn't take him to the passenger carriage where most of the people were getting in but took him to the last boxcar which was for carrying freight. That railway carriage didn't have a footplate for getting up and down, and when the big iron door opened, they threw a wooden board out of the carriage onto the platform and the people. The livestock and the goods were all pushed up to the front together. Mama grasped his hand tightly. It was not easy, and they were both packed into the train, finding a corner to sit down in. Where they were sitting was an ice-cold iron floor covered with traces of animal excrement and urine; it was dirty and smelly. He asked Mama why they didn't sit in the front passenger carriage, and Mama said they could sit here for half the price. They could save half the fare, so she always sat here.

Mama opened up the cloth wrappers and took out some solid food for their breakfast. They ate together there. After one and a half hours, the train arrived at Xiao Ban Qiao station. Mama took him off the train;

they walked about 2 km along a long country track to get to the market place at last. They chose a place to set up a stall on the ground, taking advantage of the fact that there were still not too many people there. Mama asked him to look after the things carefully as she hurried off to her clients, handing out the finished handiwork she had received from each of them on the last market day. When she came back, more and more people had come to the market, so she kept watch over her stall and sold her things. Frequently, people would come to her with some fabric in their hands; they wanted her help to make up some things. She listened to them patiently, taking simple notes in a small notebook. She dealt with her clients skillfully and sensitively, always with a smile on her face. When she had no customers, her hands were not idle but would be stitching the soles for cloth shoes. The countryside market was outdoors; it was not comfortable squatting under the burning sun all the time. After only a few hours, Ge Ge could no longer bear it, and he was eagerly looking forward to going home. He complained the weather was too hot, and Mama said to him, "Hot is good; if it was raining, we would go hungry." Ge Ge saw that Mama sat in the burning sun all day long keeping watch over her stall. At midday, she bought a bowl of pea noodles for him for lunch as she was still busy. It wasn't until around 4 o'clock in the afternoon, when there were less and less people in the market, that he saw Mama take out some solid food - one Mang Tou (steamed bread) she had made at home and some cold water. Ge Ge wrote this in his article:

> "When I urged Mama to go back home, she said, "There is an
> old man who hasn't come to get his mosquito net, we will wait
> for him a while. One hour passed and then the old man came
> and carried two baskets of potatoes on his shoulders. He spoke
> to Mama from far away, "I am sorry I am late. I had expected to

come to get my mosquito net after selling the potatoes, but today they didn't sell out; it delayed me until now."

Mother said to him, "Never mind, you can give me some potatoes instead of your processing charges - it will be fine." The old man got the mosquito net Mama had made for him. He continued to thank Mama and said he had never seen such a kind person.

Finally, he took out a bag of fried beans from his basket to give to Mama and said, "We country men don't have anything special; I planted those beans, they have a good taste." At that moment, I found out that my mother was not only very capable but also got along with people very well. No wonder the people who knew my mother always praised her and admired her with a tone of respect. For her it was a pleasure to help others; this was the thing she loved to do. Even though she was thrown into adverse circumstances, even though she was living in hardship, she still helped others.

"If you give love, love will return; bless others and they will bless you." These were the words my mother left with me like precious medicine; I will treasure them for the rest of my life.

And then everywhere things became quiet. The countryside market was over. Mother packed up her stall at last, and mother and I we set of on foot to go home. We walked along the road we had come on earlier, seeing the same scene as before; then we climbed up into the noisy train. Finding a corner to sit down in, the train started moving crazily in the direction of Kunming. I turned around to see that after only a few minutes, my mother was asleep in this messy and disorderly boxcar. When the sky became dark, we arrived at the southern train station in Kunming.

On the way home, I found out that mother did not walk at a brisk pace as she had in the morning; I knew that this work overloaded her and exhausted her. But when we turned in by the New Kunming Cinema, we could see all of my sisters and my brother standing in rank waiting for mother under the street lamp. Hearing their cheerful voices gave my mother a spring in her step again. For the sake of supporting seven children, my mother's life was full of difficulty. She was doomed to go through countless sufferings, and it demanded that she live this way without complaint and without regret. The only joy she had was to see her children come to her as they did now.

I saw that my second sister hurriedly took the cloth wrappers from my mother's back. My two younger sisters held my mother's hands on both sides. My Si Jie carried her three- year- old younger brother in her arms and gave him to his mother, letting him kiss her. Our whole family of eight people stood together on the central street of Kunming; all the children just wanted their mother to enjoy this few minutes of favor she hardly ever had. In the light of the evening lamps, we were clustered around our mother, like a myriad of stars surrounding the moon; this hero who had returned in triumph. I raised my head to look at my mother. At this moment, my mother looked more like a hen as she was using her wings to protect us jumping and chirping chickens as we walked to the nest. In the ordinary course of events, when she got home, mother should have had a little time for rest since she'd had such a hard working day. But, when mother entered the room, she immediately tied her apron on, and went to the kitchen. Like magic, very quickly, she used some very cheap, very common vegetables and turned them into a table full of delicious food for us. When we seven children sat

together to start eating, mother did not always eat immediately;
for her, sitting close to all of her children was the best way to
relax."

These were some parts of what Ge Ge recalled from that one day in the life of our mother in the initial time after we lost our father. This did not include the work she had to do in the evening.

In less than a year, Mama had completely accepted her fate. Nothing mattered to her but that her children would have enough food and could keep living; she was making great efforts and striving for this.

Five years earlier, the young lady of the Yan family was always clean, elegant and delicate. Right now, muddling along with the lowest crowd in society, she was so tired that she could fall asleep in the dirty and noisy surroundings of a staggering boxcar - the world really has changed!

That impression of Mama's life then was forever fixed in Ge Ge's memory. One day many years later, when he passed by a small shop, he saw a woman whose profile looked very much like Mama, sitting beside a sewing machine and working, and with a slip of the tongue he cried out, "Mama!" Even as a tall man, he could not help but burst into tears in the street.

Ge Ge said then he was too young to really understand Mama's feelings; he recalled at that time Mama was younger than 40 years old, and she was always so delicate and exquisite. She loved beauty, loved to dress up. But, in less than a year, her life of tribulation had changed her to become a completely different person.

Day after day, Mama and her children suffered hardship.

One morning, when all the adults had left home, a thief suddenly pried open the window and entered the room. He got away with the blanket that covered Di Di and me while we were sound asleep. That was the only costly thing in our home then. At nightfall, when Mama came back from the countryside market, she felt so fearful after this event and she repeated ceaselessly, "Ai Ya, that was terrible; it is too dangerous, too dangerous. Thank god, fortunately my two kids were not harmed." She was worried about our safety. A few days later, she made a decision to stop going to the countryside market, but instead to open a shop by the road junction not far from An Ning Lane and sell some Bao Zi (steamed stuffed bun). She wanted to find another way to support the family.

To raise the necessary funds, Mama moved out all the things still in our home which she had not sold yet, and displayed them by the gate of An Ning Lane to sell cheaply. Those things included: furniture, calligraphy and paintings, ornaments, dishware, clothing and many of her cosmetics. Mama urgently needed money, so for all those things, if she only made a small price, it was just fine. After three days, everything was almost all sold. She gathered together the money, added a bit of money she had saved from the countryside market during the past few months, and invested it all into her small food shop. She paid the first three months' rent, and got the key of a room located near the road junction which was only about 5 square meters big. She took the older children and painted the shop front and set up a big board against the wall. In only one day the small room was cleaned up. Later, she went shopping time after time and brought back a big bamboo steamer, a big iron boiler, and a big glazed earthen basin for mixing up the flour and other cooking utensils. In the yard, there was a side room which had been used to store old things, and now it was empty. Mama set up a big board in the center of this room, and prepared a place for putting the raw materials. The little patio behind the room she rebuilt as a kitchen. She found some people to help her set up a big cooking stove and to fix up a long chimney right through the roof of the house. She bustled about inside and out, and just one week later all of the preparations were done.

Er Yi Ma was a woman who loved children very much too. The day she heard that a thief had made away with the blanket that covered Di Di and me when we were sound asleep, she held me and Di Di in her arms, "My god, Ling Ling, Mao Mao, were you terribly frightened by the bad man?" She kept saying, "This is too terrible; these two kids were scared. No, they cannot stay home alone anymore." So, she now supported Mama in opening the Bao Zi shop near our home. During those days, she came to help Mama all the time. When the small shop opened for business, Mama handed over all of the appliances she had used for the countryside market to Er Yi Ma, letting her take it over. At that time, Er Yi Ma went to do this small business all alone.

Mama had always been good at making food. Mama said later, her decision to open a Bao Zi shop was for another reason. She had also been thinking about our health. While we were all still growing, she was afraid we were suffering from malnutrition. If she sold the Bao Zi, she would buy meat which may have some skin and bones left on it to boil soup for us, this way she could give us a little nutrition. Most importantly, Mama said that after that theft happened, she did not feel at ease about me and Di Di staying home alone. If she ran a small food shop not far from home, she could easily look after us. Giving consideration to these two things at the same time, Mama made this decision, and it made me extremely happy. My big eyes glimmered with light again; the broad smile was back on my small face as well. I remember that evening when Mama announced her decision to all of us, I was so excited I jumped and jumped. Mama patted my head and said joyfully, "You are happy now, you will not be angry with Mama, right?"

Nothing could compare to being together with Mama. Di Di and I often suffered cold and hunger, but in my childhood, the thing I most desired was not food and clothing. What I most wanted was to be together with Mama, not to be separated. That day, when Mama saw that my brows had finally unfolded, she happily said to everybody, "Look all of you; this little lark in our family is now joyful again."

I know it was not only me who was happy with the wise decision Mama had made. All of the brothers and sisters were extremely delighted with this decision. All the brother and sisters who were older than me and Di Di were sensible children. They had seen Mama working alone with all her might from dawn to night, and they all wanted to help Mama to do something different for a long time; now the opportunity had finally come. Since running a small shop involved many tasks, each of them could assist Mama by taking on the shopping and processing of the raw materials.

Everything was ready; the shop opened the next day. The evening before that day, our small yard was simply bustling with noise and unprecedented excitement. For the first time, all the lights were turned on everywhere without concern. We seven children were circled around Mama. We watched her boiling the sweet bean paste, chopping up bamboo shoots, mixing the stuffing for the Bao Zi. When the four kinds of sweet and salty stuffing had been put in order on the table, we watched her make four kinds of Bao Zi , placing each of them in a small steam box and then putting four steam boxes one above the other together in a boiling pan to steam them. Our small room was temporarily steaming hot. Even when we had celebrated the Chinese New Year, we hadn't had such an atmosphere of jubilation for several years. Oh, we were almost drooling; we were all so impatient we couldn't wait to eat the Bao Zi. After 8 o'clock, we saw some neighbors coming into our yard one after another.

"Welcome, welcome. Please sit, please sit." Mama smilingly led them into our main room. They were the guests Mama had specially invited. They were asked to come together to taste the Bao Zi she had made and would take to the market tomorrow. Twenty minutes later, four kinds of

Bao Zi, shaped delicately and pleasing to eyes, were lifted on to the table. All the people were filled with a desire for good food and were profuse in their praise. For Di Di and I who had suffered hunger and cold so many times, the Bao Zi we had that evening was the most delicious food we had ever had in our lives.

Mama's craftsmanship was without fault. Every kind of Bao Zi she had made received a good appraisal from everybody.

"Good, good, you like to eat; you come and eat in my shop tomorrow morning," Mama told the people. After she had sent the guests off, she checked everything for tomorrow.

"Fine! We hope for an auspicious beginning of the new enterprise tomorrow." She smiled and spoke loudly, full of confidence in her new business.

In this way, Mama started her own creative independent enterprise.

She would get up right on time at 5 o'clock in the morning, and after a quick wash and getting dressed, she would put on a snow-white apron and sleeve covers, as well as a white hat. She carried a big basin with stuffing for the Bao Zi and hastily went up to her small shop. Generally, she would spend the whole morning and noontime doing business in the small shop. In the afternoon, when my sisters were home from school, if the Bao Zi were not sold out, they would help Mama look after the shop and continue selling. Mama took the opportunity to rush to the market and buy the necessary raw materials for making the Bao Zi each day. Before closing the shop, Mama would use the water in the big boiler to wash all the bamboo steamers and utensils and scrub them clean, and after she had swept the whole storefront, she could go home. This showed her habitual love of tidiness. When she came back home, the work she immediately needed to do was a series of preparative jobs and then make the Bao Zi stuffing - cooking the meat, boiling the sweetened bean paste, chopping up the bamboo shoots into very small cubes and so on. Doing those things was not difficult for her. The biggest and hardest thing for her was to knead the dough. Each evening, she needed to knead a big basin full of the flour mixture and for several hours during the night she would leaven the dough to use the next morning. It was laborious work to put more than 10 kg of flour into a big earthen basin, then add water and yeast powder, and then use both hands to knead continuously. This could not be compared to kneading dough in a small basin for one family to use. The intensity of labor was much greater. Kneading enough dough to make about 200 Bao Zi for the next day took more than one hour.

Often I would place my hands near the big earthen basin and watch Mama knead. Even as a child, I was conscious that kneading the dough was not at all an easy thing to do, especially because kneading such a great quantity of dough was even more difficult.

I saw Mama use her thin hands to continuously turn the paste over and over; her slight figure would sway back and forth without ceasing. After only kneading for a short time, Mama's head would be covered with big drops of perspiration. Both her hands were covered with flour, she couldn't wipe the sweat away, so as I was standing beside Mama, my duty now was to keep a towel in my hand to wipe the sweat away for Mama. Whenever she processed the dough, I always needed to wipe the sweat away several times. After I had done this, she continued kneading again. After a time of kneading the dough, Mama's face became more and more red. Her face and neck were covered with sweat, also making me busily bustle around her. In the end even her hair was wet, and the big and difficult job of kneading the dough was finished. She would then cover it with a piece of white gauze, leave it aside, and wait for it to ferment.

Afterwards, Mama started to mix the four kinds of Bao Zi stuffing in four big porcelain basins. There were two kinds of salty stuffing. One was made by cutting cooked pork and bamboo shoots into small cubes and mixing them together. Another one was made by using minced meat and mushrooms mixed together. The sweet stuffing also had two flavors. One used lard and sweetened bean paste mixed together; another one is used sugar and ham cubes mixed together. After finishing all of this preparation, it was often already one or two o'clock in the morning. Mama was so tired, and when she would lie down on the bed, she fell asleep immediately. And then at 5 o'clock in the early morning when the alarm clock rang, she was always the first one to get up in the pitch black night. Quickly washing and dressing, she picked up the basins with the things she had prepared and hurried to the small shop. The first thing she did there was to split the kindling and add some coals to it, light the big stove, put water in a cauldron to boil, and prepare to steam the Bao Zi. While the water was boiling, Mama started to make Bao Zi. She took some dough and put it on the wooden board and added just the right amount of the baking soda mixed with water to knead through evenly. Then, she rolled the dough into a ball and put it aside for using later. Mama was very nimble; while the stove was burning, she had made some of the Bao Zi including both sweet and salty. In order to distinguish them, Mama would put a little red point on the top of the sweet ones so, when she sold the Bao Zi, she would not pick the wrong ones. When the water in the caldron was boiling, she lifted up four bamboo steamers full of Bao Zi and started to steam them.

Right on time at 7 o'clock, the first steamed Bao Zi was ready to sell. From the first day, the Bao Zi Mama made was very popular. People said the Bao Zi had a fine exterior; just looking at them would be like tasting them. And then after eating one, the taste was simply impressive. They even wanted to eat one every day so that the first round of steamed Bao Zi would usually be bought by clients on their way to work and to school. After the peak selling time, Mama would continue making some more Bao Zi and keep watching the shop until all the Bao Zi had sold out.

Di Di and I, no longer in a state of anxiety, would sleep in, then get up and get dressed, lock the door, and then the two of us would run towards Mama's small shop by ourselves. Giving a loud cry, "Mama!" we threw ourselves onto Mama, and then Mama would pick two white and warm Bao Zi from the bamboo steamer, put them on two plates, and give them to us to eat.

The Bao Zi Mama made was really very tasty, and she knew that I loved to eat the sweet ones and Di Di loved the salty. She always gave me the ones stuffed with the sweetened bean paste or the sugar and ham and Di Di would get one stuffed with meat. After we had eaten the Bao Zi, we both played around Mama. Sometimes Mama would give us some dough just for fun, letting us make something like a star or a fish. What a lovely time we had! The little animal I molded with my small hands always received Mama's praise.

At about 10 o'clock if there were not many clients, Mama would slowly make some Hua Juan (steamed twisted rolls) on the chopping board and steam them. I loved to watch the whole process of how Mama made Hua Juan because I felt it looked like making magic. She put some dough out and kneaded it well, then used a thick rolling pin to roll it continually until it became a very thin big piece, then put on a thin layer of lard and a thin layer of salt and then a thin layer of pepper. Afterwards, she curled this big piece of dough up together, put it on the chopping board, and cut it into equal pieces. This process was not extraordinary; the key was following the right steps. Watching Mama take a piece and use both her hands to stretch it, twist and roll it, dazzled the eyes, and in no time, her Hua Juan was done. This Hua Juan, before it was steamed, looked very common. But when it came out of the steamer, it was just a work of art. The surface was layer upon layer piled up on each other; it was as beautiful as a flower. And then when you had one in your hand and started to eat, you would be in wonder at the taste and the shape. The first feeling was delicious; the second feeling was how is it possible to have so many layers!? When I was a little child and I had one Hua Juan in my hand, I would always break it off piece by piece. I was surprised to count how many layers there were. I felt it was too wonderful. How could Mama use pastry to make such thin layers like paper and to make such a good looking and tasty thing? I adored Mama very much, and sometimes I thought that when I was grown up, I just wanted to be a person like Mama and run a Bao Zi shop.

Nearly every day I stayed around Mama's shop. Once Mama was busy since there were people who came to buy Bao Zi, I helped Mama to sell them. I would stand on my tiptoes, lift the big cover of the bamboo steamer, pick up a Bao Zi with the tongs and put it on one square brown paper which Mama had prepared to hand over to the client, and then I would get the money to give to Mama. At that moment Mama would always laugh heartily and praise me saying, "Good, good, my Ling Ling will become a capable person later on."

I loved the life I spent together with Mama. Even now the picture of Mama wearing a snow-white apron and sleeve covers and white hat and making Bao Zi and Hua Juan with a smile on her face still stays in my mind, lifelike as though it were only yesterday. I also remember that Mama charged three fen for the Bao Zi she made with meat; the ones stuffed with vegetables and the Hua Juan were only two fen each. (One fen is one hundredth of a Yuan) It was really a low price for good food.

At that time all my older siblings were studying at school. Only Did Di and I were at home. But early in the morning and after class, each of them always helped Mama with something, such as helping Mama to carry things, pulling a cart to get the flour and bring it back, going to the market and lining up to buy meat, cleaning and chopping up the bamboo shoots, washing the food steamers, boiling the sweetened bean paste and so on. Each morning, before daybreak, my older siblings would get up after Mama, leaving their warm quilts early or late to follow closely behind Mama to help her do different things. The first thing they had to do every morning was with four people together help Mama carry the big basin with kneaded dough to the shop. Afterwards, one would split the kindling under the street lamp and then help Mama to light the big stove; when the firewood was burning they would hold a big fan in their hands to fan and fan the fire continually until the stove was red hot with flames. Another one went to the well to carry water back on their shoulders and put it into the cauldron to boil. When the water was boiling and Mama's Bao Zi was ready, they would lift the big bamboo steamer up onto the cauldron one layer upon another to steam. When Liu Jie was a little girl about 10 years old, her task each morning was to go to the market and line up to buy meat before she went to school. At 6:30 in the morning, she rolled out of bed; in one hand she held the money Mama had put on the table; in her other hand she carried a big basket and ran toward the Wei Yuan Street food market. She was careful and quick so she completed her task satisfactorily every day. Mama's children did these things to help her each day. When they had to go to school, each of them would have a Bao Zi in their hand. They never complained about this; they felt happy.

In the evening, after they had quickly finished their homework, they needed to help Mama do more things. Under the faint lamplight in the kitchen, they would stand beside the tall cooking range to stir the boiling sweetened bean paste. People may say this was dangerous work because if they were not careful, their hands would be scalded by the sweetened bean paste which was boiling and could spill out. And the work of chopping up the bamboo shoots was also not easy to do; it was often hard to avoid cutting fingers with the kitchen knife. But they all without exception were committed to doing this work. Their hands were often wounded, and they used gauze to twine around them and kept on working. In severe winter, their hands were freezing and would split open, but no one complained of their suffering. Each of them were experiencing a life which was inappropriate for their age, getting up early and going to bed late, living with smoke and the fire burning, but my older brother and sisters worked very energetically. Because this life was the best we'd had in the five years since the liberation, each member of the family really treasured it. Depending on Mama as the mainstay of our family, our lives gradually moved onto the right path. We had extricated ourselves from the bitterness and helplessness of Dad's death.

That was indeed the most unforgettable and precious period we have had! Even now each of us still thinks of this very much. In that short time we were able to be together with Mama every day; no matter what the hardship, we were joyful together, and we didn't have to worry about hunger. After Mama opened the Bao Zi shop, each of the children looked stronger than before. Just as Mama had expected; we could have some meat soup almost every day.

Mama's shop had a good reputation. She had many return clients, and her small business ran very well from when it started. The most important advantage for the shop, I think, was Mama's personality. She was born with a warm heart, always smiling at all times of the day. This was a most valuable characteristic for succeeding in the service industry. Mama was provided with those qualities, and so her shop easily won the favor of the clients. Some of the clients even made friends with her while they sat in the shop to eat Bao Zi, and they often chatted with Mama. Mama noticed this, so she placed two small tables in the shop and added some simple wine which would be served at a vegetarian feast. A cup of wine, a plate of pot-stewed bean curd, a dishful of cooked peanuts, something which was just ordinary, but because of Mama's clever cooking, the taste was distinguished from others, and some clients tasted it once and would come by there every day. Just one month after the opening, Mama's small business was doing very well.

Before long by the roadside next to Mama's busy shop a special booth appeared. A small desk was covered with a plain white cloth. There was an ink stone, two brush pens and some writing paper on the desk. The calico dropped down towards the street side; there were some Chinese characters written on it: "To write documents on somebody's behalf." Who had set up his business near the doorway of Mama's shop? There was a man wearing the standard ink blue Mao clothing with four pockets and the same colored Mao hat on his head, sitting there and reading a book and "waiting for windfalls," waiting for someone to come so he could write something. He was our Da Gu Die (in Chinese, this means the older cousin's brother) who was the husband of my father's cousin Yan Ze Yao. Originally, it was Mama's idea to let Da Gu Die do this to make his living next to the Bao Zi shop.

Before the liberation Da Gu Die had managed a trading company "Shao Xing Xiang" and had always done the local and mountain goods business in Xia Guan. When he was young, he studied very hard at a private school. After school he continued to diligently learn and practice business processes, and he became very skilled in sampling tea. In the business circles of Dali, he had gradually become a recognized appraisal expert. In the spring of each year, when the fresh tea came onto the market, he was the main person to open a quotation and fix a price. The people addressed him respectfully and called him "the master." Da Gu Die was a traditional old type scholar, and he always wore a long gown. He was well-read and a man of great learning. He was voted in as the chairman of the Dali Chamber of Commerce several times.

In 1952 a series of the political movements had unfolded in Dali. He certainly could not escape by sheer luck. One layer after another, like peeling off his skin, he lost all of his property, and his family moved out of their luxury house and had to rent some shabby rooms. But he saw that the situation of other people with the same identity as him was

My parents and Da Gu Die in 1940s.

becoming worse and worse; more and more were taken into captivity, put under surveillance, or killed. He thought, "In this small place, I am unable to justify myself in any way; people will treat me ruthlessly." To try save his life from being destroyed, he decided to come to Kunming to escape for awhile. Da Gu Die had a younger brother in Kunming who was a very successful business man. He considered going to seek refuge with him for a period of time. But when he made the long trip and arrived in Kunming and got to Fu Chun Street the place where his younger brother's family lived, what he saw shocked him. On the door of the nice building his brother owned, there were two paper strips which sealed the door with a cross with a sign saying "building confiscated, no admittance." After making inquiries, he found his younger brother's two children. He was becoming aware that the fate of his younger brother was even worse than his. His brother had met with misfortune for a long time, and he was executed by public shooting by the government a half year earlier, and his wife had died after him. They left two children who were younger than 10 years old; all of a sudden they had become orphans. Da Gu Die held these two young and innocent children in his arms; he could not help bursting into tears and crying out, "Ai, it could be god who sent me from Dali to come and save you!"

He thought of his own children who were older than these two, and they had their mother to look after them, so he decided to stay in Kunming to take on the duty of fostering these orphans of his younger brother. This event had happened in the same year of my father's death. At that time Da Gu Die came to visit Mama, and to assist Mama he did something to help with the funeral. Later, when Mama found out about the miserable situation of Da Gu Die and the two children, she had great pity on them. Immediately she helped them to rent a room in our backyard so they could settle down. She thought if they lived closer they could help each other in the future. The place where Da Gu Die and his nephews lived could not strictly be called a room; it was only a corner of one empty main room in the house. The house owner used some fencing to separate a square area for them (the partitions were not up to the roof), and the three of them moved in. They put a small stove near the door for cooking, which was all they had then. In this way, Da Gu Die brought these two poor children with him, and they also started to "flee for their lives," living in fear not knowing what each day would bring, just like Mama. In this simple and crude place, they also later used some fencing to separate another square and took in Yan Zi Zhen's fourth son and his wife for several years. They were fleeing from the calamity in Yi Bin of Sichuan province and had come back to Kunming.

In order to support the two children, Da Gu Die had to find a job in Kunming. He inquired about this everywhere for a long time but still could not to find one suitable for him. The cash in his hand would soon be used up; how could he keep life going? Da Gu Die walked in and out hanging his head and looking extremely worried. Mama opened the Bao Zi shop to make a living and had a good business, and Da Gu Die admired her very much. In the evening, when he came to our home, Mama talked to him, "You are a calligrapher; you also write articles very well. You should think about this and use your strong points." Da Gu Die nodded and agreed with Mama. But right now, who would use the professional skills of an old scholar, and where could he do this work? A few days had passed, and Da Gu Die still had no ideas. But then Mama finally found the way to do this. It was the sign I have mentioned above that Da Gu Die made saying he would "write documents on somebody's behalf." Such a very simple means to make a living. To do this he only needed to buy some paper, brushes, and envelopes. The total investment was only a few Yuan. While Da Gu Die was still hesitating finding it embarrassing to do this thing, Mama put a small table at the front of her shop and fixed everything up. Da Gu Die did nothing but just go there to "perform." Meeting such a warmhearted relative meant that, from the first day, Da Gu Die had no choice but to sit in Mama's shop and wait there blushing. Facing the street where people came and went, sitting at a small table and writing to make a living, he felt this was a hard job to do. But while he was talking with Mama, someone came to ask about writing a letter. Da Gu Die sat at the table after carefully listening to the visitor tell him what she wanted to express in her letter. He held the brush in his right hand and easily started to write. One standard letter was finished in only 20 minutes and he would charge 8 fen. In the first day he had earned enough money to buy food for the three of them. After that his writing booth was held in high repute in some way. There was an exhibition held in Kunming and the people came to ask him to write the preface for them. When someone wanted to contribute to a newspaper or magazine, they would also come to ask him to edit or amend the article for the writer. So, in this way, relying on this "writing documents on somebody's behalf" job, Da Gu Die brought up his two nephews and sometimes sent a little money to Dali to take care of his children. He had let go of his old-fashioned dignity, the sophistication of the scholar as he hung his noble head and survived in this inclement world.

Er Yi Ma often came to Mama's shop to sit a while after she was back from the countryside. Mama handed her a warm Bao Zi; the two sisters talked and laughed together. However, it was lonely going to the countryside market, and Er Yi Ma didn't want to do this anymore. She was considering doing something not far away from home like Mama. She thought it over and felt that there were many things she was not skilled to do. She saw there were some hawkers selling roasted seeds and nuts on the street, and Mama advised her to choose the simplest thing to try, which was selling roasted sweet potatoes. Doing this small business basically didn't need any skill. The only facility she needed was a bigger stove. Mama and her walked around the streets finally choosing to set up her stall by the gate of the Cultural Temple where the pedestrians continually passed by. This was also closer to her home, only 5 minutes' walk. The first day Er Yi Ma bought 5 kg sweet potatoes from the food market and started to make preparations. She found out that cleaning those potatoes was a big problem. Because the little attic where they lived didn't have a water supply, the water they used for everyday life was obtained by going to the tap water station, paying and then carrying it home on their shoulders. Right then she begrudged spending money on buying water to wash the sweet potatoes. So she had to go to a well in an alleyway in a faraway place to do this. Er Yi Ma carried the sweet potatoes and went there with a water bucket in her other hand. That day, Er Yi Ma drew the water from the well one bucket after another, and after a few rounds, both her hands were blistered by the thick rope. She didn't stop working; she spent about two hours cleaning the clay from all the sweet potatoes with a brush. She forced herself to do this dirty and weary work alone. In the evening, Mama went to her home, and she saw that Er Yi Ma was ready to toast some sweet potatoes on her small stove with the firewood for tomorrow prepared and put aside. Mama was very excited and said, "Ai, you have improved; this existence has forced us to do all this rough and dirty work; we have to do it ourselves!"

"I admire you, I admire you; the little thing I am doing cannot compare with you. I am learning from you about everything." Er Yi Ma said repeatedly. Today, doing all these things by herself, she knew that running a Bao Zi shop was much more work than selling roasted sweet potatoes. She knew the kind of hard work Mama had to do each day. In Er Yi Ma's mind, she had even more respect for Mama.

On the afternoon of the second day, Mama closed her shop early; she held me and Di Di by the hand and went to see how Er Yi Ma was selling her sweet potatoes. When we turned into the Cultural Temple road crossing, in the distance we saw Er Yi Ma dressed in a blue Chinese style jacket with blue sleeve covers on both her arms. She was standing by the big stove and picking up a sweet potato to give to a client. Mama was very delighted and walked to Er Yi Ma quickly. "Good, good, you have started well," Mama said smiling.

"Oh, you have come. Come, Ling Ling, Mao Mao, come and eat the roasted sweet potato which Er Yi Ma has made." Er Yi Ma was smiling too. She picked up two sweet potatoes to give to each of us. While we were eating Mama and Er Yi Ma sat on a small bamboo stool close to the stove and talked. We could see they were both in a good mood.

In this way, Mama and Er Yi Ma, these two widows, at that time bravely strode forward through another milestone of their lives. They tried to use any means to support the whole family. For the sake of their children, they were not afraid of hard work; they made a great effort.

Mama absolutely hadn't thought that by relying on some of her skills and diligence, to her surprise, she would find a way out of a desperate situation. In the evening, when all the people met together, Mama often spoke boldly, "I am not worried. Our whole family, all of us can stay alive. I believe it. This was unexpected. The skills I have are now so useful; how happy I am! Ai, if your Dad had just been able to get through this year, I could have made enough money to heal him!"

Sometimes, looking at my deceased Dad's portrait, she said these words, sighing with emotion. Though she still yearned for her departed husband, everyone could see that as Mama continued working busily from morning till night. Her emotional distress had gradually eased.

In August of 1956, Da Jie had finished her study at the normal school. In order to lighten the burden on Mama as soon as possible, Da Jie gave up her chance to continue her studies at the university and decided to find a job right away. Because in our permanent residency booklet, it showed that we were "capitalists" and of the "black dog" class, she couldn't find a job in Kunming, so she was appointed to a primary school in Wen Shan County which is more than 200 km from Kunming. The day before Da Jie left home, an old cousin happened to come from Dali to Kunming, and he wanted to take a picture of our whole family to show the relatives in Dali. So we all went to the photo studio together with him to have a picture taken. This was indeed a very precious picture because it is the only picture of us seven children together with Mama from our childhood which we still have now. We seven brothers and sisters don't even have one picture of us together with Dad and Mama. When Di Di was the last one to be born, Dad's camera was confiscated by the factory. Even if he had still had the camera, Dad was sick with a heavy heart, and he would have been unwilling to leave any of his images in this world any more.

In this picture of the whole family together which was taken one year after Dad's death, the most striking person was Mama. The expression Mama had in this picture really showed her spiritual outlook while she was running the Bao Zi shop. We can see that Mama had walked out from under the shadow of the departure of her husband. She had straightened her back, her eyes were bright and sparkling, her hair was combed and glossy, her clothing was very neat, and there was a pair of small earrings in her ears. The confident smile on her face displayed her inner strength. The seven children who surrounded her each wore clothing Mama had made herself. The five girls all wore some ornaments on their heads and looked very beautiful. These seven children were all dressed neatly and correctly and seemed unaffected; not one looked miserable or shabby. In this picture, although Da Jie was leaving home, she still had a smile on her face, and everyone could see she had some

Mama was the sun of the seven brothers and sisters' life.

longing and hope. In that moment we all believed that with Mama toiling day and night and with Mama's love, our lives would become better and better day after day.

Da Jie had a job; surely this would lighten the burden on Mama, and it was a good thing for the whole family. But as the day of departure drew closer and closer, Mama's feelings became more and more heavy. She could not bear it that this girl who was not yet 18 years old had to leave her and go somewhere else. Thinking of how this little girl would live alone in a small town far from home, thinking about the earnest hopes she and Dad had wished for this clever and beautiful daughter, thinking of the year after Dad died and how Da Jie had suddenly changed into another person who was now very sensible, Mama's eyes could not help but fill with tears. She felt sorry for this child. In those days, once she had finished the work she had to do for the shop, her mind was on how to carefully prepare the luggage for Da Jie. The best things in the home - bedding, suitcase, and wash basin - anything she might need was cleaned and put aside. And then Mama busily stitched a pair of soles for some cloth shoes, and made a pair of red corduroy upper shoes for Da Jie. The night before Da Jie left, she sat at the sewing machine all the time; she wanted to run up two more jackets and some underwear for Da Jie to bring with her. It was close to 12 o'clock, and she was still busy. Da Jie also felt it was hard to leave Mama. In those days she could see what Mama did for her, and she was touched, and her face was bathed in tears. She stood behind Mama, put her both hands on Mama's shoulders, and full of deep love she told Mama, "Mama, you are too tired. After I have gone, you have to take care of yourself. I promise you when I get my wages, I will send half of them to you immediately, I...," Da Jie was not finished when Mama interrupted her,

"No, Mama doesn't want you to send money to me; you should take care of yourself first. You are too young to support a family. I cannot stand this; I feel sorry." Mama turned her face around and she cried together with Da Jie, "Ah, why do we have to separate? Mama cannot be with you, and from now on you have to take care of everything yourself. Mama will be thinking of you every day. Mama's heart will hang up in the air..." Mama was crying and instructing Da Jie over and over. That evening, the light in our home didn't go out all night. By the time Mama had helped Da Jie to clean up and pack, it was the time she would go to the shop for the day. In the darkness under the faint street lamp of An Ning Lane, Da Jie was together with Mama lighting the fire for the last time.

As she sat on the small wooden stool, automatically waving the big fan at the grate of the stove, she looked at Mama's slight figure working busily in the smoke; she cried all the time. Seeing that the Bao Zi were ready to steam, she and Mama together lifted up the bamboo steamer onto the cauldron. They knew the time for parting had come; no-one said a word, both of them were in tears. After 7 o'clock, there were clients who came to buy Bao Zi. Mama wiped her tears and started to receive them. Da Jie, with eyes brimming with tears, left Mama quietly.

One morning a week later, Mama received a letter from Da Jie which told that she had arrived safely in the small town. One day a month later, Mama received 12 Yuan which was exactly half of Da Jie's monthly wages and which Da Jie had sent home. For many years after that the letter and the money from Da Jie continued to arrive, the only thing which changed was that the money slowly increased. The maximum she sent to Mama was 20 Yuan in one month. While Mama was running the shop, the postman knew that the hostess of No.7 An Ning Lane was there, so he delivered the postal material directly to the shop. I was with Mama every day, and I often saw the scene when Mama received the letter and money. No matter what Da Jie wrote in the letter, just seeing the familiar handwriting on the envelope from her daughter, Mama was always excited. She could not wait to wipe her hands which were covered in flour; she tore the letter open immediately and read it over and over. After dinner when whole family was together, she would open the letter again and read it through for all the children to hear. On the same evening, after she had finished the preparation work for the shop, no matter what time it was, she would spread out some writing paper and conscientiously write back to Da Jie. For many years she did the same.

The income Mama received from working hard in the shop from dawn till dusk plus the bit of money Da Jie sent home was enough to meet the family's basic needs. Only in spring and summer when she needed to pay the tuition fees for four of the children, Mama still could not pay all of this on time. Mama thought that if she worked hard for two years, with Er Jie also finishing school and getting a job, the situation would improve. Essentially, if their lives could keep going like this, everything would be fine. Who could have known that these good times wouldn't last long? In fact, they only lasted for about a year. Mama could never have imagined that the peaceful life we had just started to experience would be completely disrupted by another "wise decision" made by Chairman Mao and the Central Party.

By the end of 1956, "the eighth national congress of the CCP" was held in Beijing, and at this congress, Chairman Mao declared that the three reforms of agriculture, the handicraft industry and capitalist industry and commerce had basically been achieved throughout the whole country. So now China needed to stride from this new democracy into a period of socialism. Yunnan province was always a step behind the rest of the nation and in May of 1957, started winding up the joint state and privately operated movement. According to the experience of other cities, all individual handicraft industry owners must now amalgamate and come under and be supervised by a socialist collective economic category. The Bao Zi shop, the small business Mama was running, Da Gu Die's writing booth, Er Yi Ma's stall where she sold the roasted sweet potatoes - all of these means of making a living were regarded as individually privately operated businesses and were no longer allowed to exist. The people who were doing this kind of business were called together to a meeting to clarify the policy of the party. Mama was faced with a choice. If she wanted to continue using her skills to make money, she would have to take herself and all her equipment and unite with other small food shops to form a collective eating house and become a collectively owned enterprise. The government would appoint a party member to become part of the management. She could then either voluntarily apply to become an employee, or close the shop, be out of work, and stay at home.

Mama didn't want to lose any opportunity to make money to support the family, so after the policy was announced, she stopped doing her business right away. She packed up all the utensils from her shop and hired a tricycle to bring them to the sub-district office to be registered. She was willing to obey the requirements of the government. As long as she had a job and could keep her family, she didn't mind what kind of job; she would take it. A few days later, she was informed that she had been approved as an employee and could work in a new collective eating house which dealt in cooked wheaten food. The shop was on Qin Yun Street and not far from our home. The first day she went to register and report for duty, she discovered that in this collective eating house, the party secretary who was sent by the government to manage the shop was a man, but the rest of the staff were women. Mama now had a formal position; she became an employee in the unit, and she was very glad. She felt that she was a useful person in the new society. During that period she was in high spirits. Every day, before she went off to work, she always combed her hair neatly and put on clean clothing. In her handbag she carried white sleeve covers and an apron ready for use. She was serious about doing a good job from the first day. The new place of work had an 8-hour work system. Everyone was divided up to do different jobs. Mama took charge of the section which made the Bao Zi and Man Tou (steamed bread) while the other women were responsible for the process of steaming and selling. This small eating house was open from morning till night; the wage for each woman was 30 Yuan per month. This money was much less than the income she had previously earned from her Bao Zi shop. According to the prices then, it was just barely enough to buy the basic food for our family of seven people. We didn't have any money to buy clothing and other commodities, or to pay the rent, the water and electricity fees, and there was definitely no money to pay for the four children's tuition fees. Two months later, our life had again landed in a tight spot with our income falling short of our expenditures. The money, a little more than 10 Yuan, which Da Jie sent home each month, at that time was very precious to us. The whole family was longing for the money to come earlier because those who were at school needed pencils and exercise books. Without money to buy these things, they had to wait. The daily needs of toothpaste and soap, even the coal we used to cook with and many other things were waiting for this money to come so we could buy them.

Still, with a job we had some income, and it was much better than nothing. Mama had a job; Da Gu Die also had work in a neighborhood collective laundering and dyeing shop. He was good at writing and helping people to write something, so how could he do this job? Primarily, he was afraid of missing an employment opportunity and running out of rice and fuel. So he told the man from the shop who was in charge of the interview that he was good at printing and dyeing, that he could develop a kind of dye which would not fade. They saw that Da Gu Die's handwriting was very nice, and thought that maybe he could use his ability in their industry in some way, and took him on as an employee. Unusually for him, after Da Gu Die took this job, he studied printing and dyeing with great concentration, and both his hands were always stained with paint and were never clean. As a result of his research, this neighborhood collective laundering and dyeing shop achieved great success in dyeing fabric, and the colors they used were very fine. The newspaper encouraged people to be frugal. Their clothing should be "three years new, three years old, then sew and mend for another three years." All the people brought their faded and old clothes to the shop to be dyed in a darker color so they could wear them again and the new technique Da Gu Die had developed had gained the market for the small shop. Da Gu Die worked in this position until 1970 during the Cultural Revolution.

Mama and Da Gu Die had found a place to earn a living, and Er Yi Ma envied them very much. She didn't have any special skills, and the new policy did not allow her to do an individual small business. To provide even the simple requirements of adequate food and clothing, she now had to look for another means to survive. Her two children needed food every day; she stayed at home and worried about what she could do. She had neither the employment experience nor any equipment to be able to cooperate with others as Mama had. Now she could do nothing but stay idly at home. For two months she was anxious, and sat at home crying. The money she had could only buy some rice, and as she cooked the rice in the boiler, she thought of the children who would come back to a meal with no other dishes for any of them. With her head down, she went stealthily to the food market. She picked up some of the rotten outer leaves of the cabbages the seller had thrown away and brought them home to cook for her children to eat.

"I have to put aside all considerations of my 'face,' my life is drifting along aimlessly. I am alive today and don't know if I will still be alive tomorrow. I have no more scruples," she told herself silently as she walked through the market carrying her basket. But one day, while she was picking up the rotten cabbage leaves, she suddenly saw her second son standing just in front of her.

"Mama doesn't have any money to buy vegetables for you to eat, none but...," Er Yi Ma said as she looked at her son. The sensible Du Du didn't say a word; he bent over and picked up the cabbage leaves together with his Mama.

"Ai, you hurry home to do your homework. Mama doesn't want you to be here; maybe your classmates will ridicule you." Er Yi Ma said to him.

"I don't mind who laughs at me. I will go home together with you." Du Du, who was studying in the middle school, told his Mama. When our Mama heard about this, she always spoke well of this child to us.

Mama said, "It was Er Yi Ma's blessing to have such a kind and honest son."

During that time, Mama often visited Er Yi Ma after her work. With no assured source of income, the two sisters felt vexed again. While they were talking, they shed tears.

"Woe, why is it so hard to live; why can't we see a way out?" both of them sighed together in despair. The women couldn't understand why the situation had changed so quickly. In the last two years, after they had each tried so hard, they had learned to earn their own living and to support the whole family. Their peaceful life only lasted a very short time; why were they not allowed to keep on going? But to earn just a bare living now, they had no alternative but to face the facts. Right now, the important thing was to find a job for Er Yi Ma. They searched for

this everywhere. In the end, they knew there was a neighborhood pickle factory that was recruiting workers. Mama accompanied Er Yi Ma to quickly go and register. It was lucky that they took Er Yi Ma as an employee.

But when Er Yi Ma went to work there, by the second day she felt very disappointed because the job she had to do for 8 hours each day was to use both her hands to make soy sauce and to pickle different kinds of vegetables. Poor Er Yi Ma, from doing this work, not only her hands, but also her hair, her clothing and her trousers were always stained with chili or hot sauce, and you could easily smell the pungent smell which came from her. Spending 8 hours working in a very small workshop, endlessly chopping, mixing, handling chili, soy sauce and pickles really gave her a hard time. The job required that while she was working, she had to wear a pair of high rubber boots and a big plastic apron. Perhaps because the life she now had made her feel nothing was worth paying attention to, sometimes Er Yi Ma would just walk down the street in the rubber boots, which were up to her knees and dirty, and in her sloppy apron. This appearance did not match her image at all. Looking at her made us feel sad. Er Yi Ma had always been an elegant and distinguished and beautiful lady. When she was just 40 years old, she was tall with a full figure and still looked graceful. But because of this job, she looked as she had been pulled through the mud and rolled around; it had ruined her whole body, and she was covered in dirt. Day after day, her spiritual outlook was also lost in the mire as her emotions took a downturn. After just two months, she had changed into another person. She was no longer in the mood to dress up. Every day she would wear very sloppy clothing when she went out. Sometimes she even wore her husband's old clothing which was far too big for her and looked strange. Her hair was disheveled. Her whole appearance was downhearted.

To see Er Yi Ma suffering severely like this, Mama felt very sorry for her. Mama knew Er Yi Ma's life experience. Er Yi Ma was born into a rich family; she was a high school graduate. While she studied at school, she was an eminent girl. At the age of twenty, she married the owner of the "Yong An Tong" drugstore which had the monopoly on the famous "tiger balm" ointment. From then on, she had enjoyed a world of wealth and leisure. When she was young, she went to Taiwan, Changsha, and Guiyang with her husband to open more branches of his drugstore.

She had seen the world. We remember that one day Er Yi Ma showed us some of her pictures of when she was young.

"Wa, how beautiful," we all shouted because we could see that in the pictures Er Yi Ma was dressed in the most fashionable western style clothing of the 1940s. She had a white broad brimmed plumed hat on her head. We all thought that with the style she had then, she really could have been competition for her

When Er Yi Ma was a young girl in 1935.

contemporary Song Qing Ling who was married to Sun Zhong Shan (the chairman of the Kuomintang). She had never known poverty and tribulation. She could not do any housework. She found favor with her husband and only knew the joy of leisure; she was a typical rich lady. After the liberation, when her husband met with misfortune, she was forced to survive by her life's circumstances, so she followed Mama by learning to put her effort into running a small business. She learned to sew and mend and bargain with others in the market. Later, she had to completely put down her "face," when she set up a stall selling roasted sweet potatoes. But even this kind of small business was not permitted by the government. In order to support her family, she had no choice but to take this job. It was really too hard for her to bear this. If she did not continue doing it, she would have no other way out. If she stayed at home, the three of them would go hungry. How difficult was this? Mama knew the hard situation Er Yi Ma now faced. Er Yi Ma also understood that she had no other path to go on; she had to brace herself and walk straight ahead. However, every day she worked in this pickle factory physically injured and mentally affected her, and to her, one day seemed like a year. As soon as she was off duty, she would run home without cleaning up, and then she would often sit with a dull look in her eyes, smoking morosely for long periods of time.

Frequently, Mama went to the small attic which Er Yi Ma rented with her two sons in Min Sheng Street. Mama tried to encourage her, comforting her with a kind and pleasant countenance, sometimes talking with her for two or three hours. I went with Mama to visit Er Yi Ma several times. Mama would coil her hair up on at the back of her head. She dressed neatly and looked capable and full of vitality. Er Yi Ma was different; it seemed that she had collapsed under the pressure of her circumstances. Not just her dress, but the whole of her expression was despondent. Mama sat beside her, patiently talking with her over and

over, "You should not be like
this; you will go down like this.
What about your two kids? Our
tradition tells us, for the sake of
our children, we may become
poor, we may be rebuked, but
we have to recognize that this
is our fate because we are the
mothers of these children. No
matter how hard it is, we have
to bring them up. Our children
now live painful lives. We are
their mothers, and if we break
down, the whole family will
be finished. In this society, the
children could become orphans.

When Er Yi Ma was a rich lady in 1944.

Think about it; how could they survive? There is only a blind alley
waiting for them."

While she was talking, she started to help Er Yi Ma clean up the room;
she even took a comb to fix up her hair. She saw that Er Yi Ma's second
son was painting, and there were many of his pencil sketches stuck
on the wall. Mama praised him for his talent and told him she would
bring some paper and pencils to him later. Each time Er Yi Ma met with
Mama and talked with her and she had sobbed out her troubles, her
mood would always improve. As time got late, Mama would leave to go
home. They were still reluctant to part. Er Yi Ma would keep talking with
Mama as she walked with her towards our home. Mama was worried
about Er Yi Ma going back alone, so she would walk some of the way
with her. The distance between the two homes was about 15 minutes,
and even if they walked up and down several times, they still had many

words to say. They were arm in arm and interdependent. Each time, when they parted, Mama always left these words with Er Yi Ma, "Bye-bye. You go home quickly. Remember, if you have any trouble, you must come and tell me."

Almost every evening, Er Yi Ma met with Mama. The comfort and encouragement from the friendship and love between these sisters helped them to break through their difficulties once again. Bit by bit, Er Yi Ma became calmer; she returned back to her normal state and went to work every day without a worried look. It could be said that she had experienced another transformation.

When I was a little girl, I didn't know that Er Yi Ma was older than Mama because it looked as if Mama was the older sister. She took good care of Er Yi Ma all the time. Er Yi Ma was a simple and kind person; she trusted in Mama and was willing to listen to her advice, and she considered Mama as her dearest friend.

Each year at Spring Festival time on the first day in the morning, Er Yi Ma would especially come to our place. She wanted to give each of us a small red envelop. (This is the traditional way to give gifts to children at the Chinese New Year; the elder members of the family put some money in a small red envelope and give it to each of the children on the first day of the New Year.) We would only receive 20 cents in this lunar New Year gift, but Er Yi Ma loved each of us seven children very much. When she came to our home, she would always pat the shoulders of the older children one by one and talk with them a little while. Then she often picked up Di Di and me and sat both of us on her lap. Whenever Mama went to visit her, she would also bring some foodstuff or appliances to give to Er Yi Ma's two sons and communicate with them, giving her love and warmth to each of them.

These two poor women had each in turn lost their husbands and didn't have a blood relationship, but the friendship they established was profound; it exceeded that of full sisters. They kept the promise they had made to each other. As sisters they helped and supported each other, never abandoning or deserting each other. In their opinion as women, they considered that whatever they needed to do to survive, as long as they gritted their teeth, their children would keep growing up day after day, and finally when the day came when the bitterness was over, the sweetness would come. They didn't imagine at all that on the road ahead of them, they would have to experience one political movement after another. They didn't know that the strategic path they needed to take would not only face them with difficulty and hardship, but with a deadly menace.

At the beginning of 1957, a new political movement called "The Hundred Flowers Campaign" began in China. The Central Party Committee called on non-party people to make criticisms of the government. There were many intellectuals from the university and some of the institutes who participated in this activity. Who could have known that this movement would soon evolve into a powerful and dynamic "Anti-Rightist Movement?" Mama and Er Yi Ma were so afraid of the word "movement," and by studying documents and newspapers in their unit, they knew that there were people who were now experiencing the "cleansing of the soul" (to change their deep rooted capitalist thinking – just as my father had experienced during the 3 & 5 anti time). But the movement at that time was not affecting low level people like them, so they felt especially lucky. At that moment they were worried about the money to buy rice, and the only thought in their minds every day was to have enough food to feed their children. They would patiently attend the political studies in their unit, and when they were finished, they would run home. But it was impossible for them to be protected completely, and they could not escape from the movement which followed.

In 1958, under the direction of the general line of "exert the utmost effort, strive for the best, achieve greater things to build socialism," three movements started on a grand and spectacular scale all at the same time: The Great Leap Forward, The People's Commune and The Steelmaking Movement. This huge movement swept across the whole nation; no family could escape. By the government's regulation, no family was allowed to cook at home. All the people had to join the People's Commune and eat together in the mess hall, both in the country and the city. Each family had to go and register their residence and then get a meal card. According to their residential area, people were appointed to go to the mess hall to eat together at a fixed time, and to experience the "new life of communism," The mess hall that our family was appointed to eat at was set up in a big yard on Qing Yun Street. The scene which is printed in my memory was that each day, when the time came for serving the meal, there was always a huge crowd of people there. Not only was the hall filled to capacity, half of the street was filled with people holding bowls waiting to eat. Because there were about a hundred households who came to eat together, it would take people one or two hours to stand in line and get the rice they needed. Each person had a big bowl in their hands and moved along step by step to get to the big bamboo steamer to receive their ration of rice first, and then they would follow the procession and move along a few steps to the place where they could get another dish. The working personnel would use a ladle to serve the dish and upend it on our rice. Now we had to find a place to eat, there were no tables and chairs in the mess hall. It was not easy for people to finally get their food. Some would eat squatting, and some were standing, holding a big bowl in their both hands either just inside the big yard or on the street outside, hurrying to eat. All three meals were like this. This really was the scene when people ate together in the people's commune.

My older brother and sisters ate together with all the students and teachers in their school. Mama went to work, so she ate together with her fellow workers. Then, although I was not seven years old, it was only on the Sunday of the first week that Mama took my hand and brought me to get the meal. After that I had to go and line up on time to get food for Di Di and me, three times a day. With no one at home to help us, if I didn't go to get the food, we would both go hungry.

These three meals each day did not always provide solid food, sometime it was just gruel. And it was not always rice; sometimes we were given coarse cereals. If we got to the mess hall late, we could only get rice mixed with corn or broad beans. To get rice, people would strive to be the first and would fear lagging behind. When the time came, they all rushed in, exerting the utmost strength, ready to grab. The scene really was soul stirring to describe. I remember every day at around 11 o'clock I told Di Di to wait for me by the gate. I held two big bowls in my hands and went to the mess hall very early to line up for food with many old people and children. But, when it was closer to 12 o'clock, and we saw four strong men coming in carrying the big bamboo steamer with cooked rice on their shoulders and placing it in the center of the yard, people became chaotic. Some young people were afraid to go hungry, and they did not consider the old people and children. Everybody pushed to the front and the mess hall was suddenly in great confusion. I was very thin and small, and I was often jostled aside by the crowd. After a majority of the people got their food I pushed to the front, and could only get some rice mixed with dry corn or broad beans. These two kinds of rice were not tasty. Sometimes to get some rice when the time came, I followed the other people, and without giving it any thought, I pushed to the front. Sometimes I was jostled and fell down; I would stand up and push to the front again. When I finally got some rice in my bowl and held it in my hands, my face and body would be covered in mud. Holding two bowls in my hands on the way home, I had nobody to pour out my grievances to. I gave one bowl of rice to Di Di to eat, I held another bowl of rice, and while I was eating, I was crying. Going to the mess hall to get food day after day was just like going to fight. Because I was still too small and weak to jostle those strong adults, the food I got was often just some coarse cereal. And when I hastily ate that coarse cereal while I was weeping, slowly I would start to feel bad, and I would immediately throw up the things I ate. Dry corn and broad beans are foods which are not easy to digest, so when I ate those two things I would immediately get a stomach ache with the pain getting worse and worse. People said I had serious stomach trouble. I became thinner and thinner, and often vomited. Mama was very distressed; she wished she could be home to take care of me. But to provide for all the family's needs, she worked every day except Sunday, and she did not dare to ask for leave. If she did it could be deducted from her pay or she could even lose her job, and it would bring great trouble to the family.

I often had a stomach ache, and when it happened, I didn't eat anything. I would just cover my stomach with my hands, or squat or lie on my stomach on the bed, and cry loudly for a long time.

"Ow, it is too painful, too painful, Mama, Mama! I have an excruciating pain in my belly, come, come and help me!" I was crying loudly, and my head was covered with big drops of perspiration. The one and only thought in my mind was looking forward to seeing Mama come home quickly. Mama come back home quickly!

Mama finally came back home, she didn't have any medicine to give me; but she would immediately give me some warm water. Because food supplies had stopped there was no rice in our home, Mama couldn't cook anything special for me, and often I didn't eat any food all day. I remember that Mama held me in her arms, she would put the dry corn or broad beans which I got from the mess hall and hadn't eaten in her mouth, she chewed them up and then fed them to me from her mouth to my mouth, and it helped me to digest the food. It was amazing that in the many years while I had a stomach ache, Mama didn't have the money to send me to see the doctor or to buy any medicine for me. She also didn't give any special food to me. The most treatment I received was to put a bottle of hot water on my stomach to keep it warm. But with each bout of pain, if I only heard Mama's footsteps, if I only threw myself into Mama's arms, my stomach ache would soon be on the mend. As Mama held me in her arms, looking at my sallow face and listening to my feeble breathing, tears would cover her face and big teardrops often dripped on my small cheeks as I looked up at her. I lay down in Mama's arms, both hands firmly grasping Mama's clothing like grasping for life, and in this way I endured this pain over and over again.

After I had grown up, Mama would often tell me, "It was god's blessing He didn't let you die. He didn't let you leave Mama when nobody believed that you would survive." Yes, it was the God in the unseen world who blessed me; it was the deep-felt love of my Mama which made me feel sad to leave her and unwilling to leave this world.

Misfortune continued to come with the deafening sound of the gongs and drums of "long live the three red flags" (the Great Leap Forward, People's Commune and Steelmaking Movement were called the "three red flags"). Chinese people now encountered the dreadful period called "three years of natural disaster" which was brought about by the government. This great famine set a world record, and in the data which has now been published, the government admitted that there were thirty million people who starved to death throughout the country. There were floods and insect pests to varying degrees in some provinces, which resulted in a reduction of grain output. But actually the death of so many people was due to the economic policies and inexpediency of the state. Several years after the liberation, the authorities had exported most of the agricultural products to trade for steel, so it meant there were no grain reserves in the national treasury. Thus, it caused a great famine. All the people who experienced this could remember what a very fearful period these three years were for the whole nation, everyone in China was hungry. Finally, even the unpalatable dry corn or broad bean had run out and people started to eat anything they could find even grass roots and bark were dug up to allay their hunger. The mess hall didn't provide solid food for a long time. All three meals consisted of a kind of soup made by boiling up a little bit of staple food mixed with a lot of melons and vegetables. It was cooked in water and looked like something for pigs. Each day when meal time came, all the people went crazy trying to snatch this light tasteless soup. The old and infirm people or the little children like Di Di and I didn't have the strength to get in and grab our food together with those people. What ended up in our bowls was only some boiled water with no vegetable leaves. Many people in the city struggled, their stomachs rumbling with hunger every day. The circumstances in the countryside were even worse than in the city. There were some villages in the north where the whole population had already starved to death, or where all the people from one village would go out together to beg for food. In a few villages, it even happened that people started to eat people because of this miserable situation. People were starving to death everywhere in every place, both in the city and the countryside. Amongst the people who were still alive, grievous undernourishment caused thousands upon thousands to develop dropsy. They looked plump but they were too weak to walk, looking as if the wind could blow them over. On the street, we often saw these strange looking people. Unfortunately Er Yi Ma had dropsy; when she walked 10 minutes to come to our place, she would be out of breath.

At that time in Kunming, we heard of or saw people starving to death every day. In secluded places like alleyways, we often saw hungry people who had fainted or people who had dropsy; their appearance was very frightening. They roamed about in all directions like ghosts with greedy eyes searching for any bit of food. My older brother and sisters shared a little bit of the liquid food from the mess hall at the school each day, it was not enough to fill up their stomachs. Each of them lost weight and looked thinner and thinner. The taste of suffering from hunger is hard to describe. No words can express the feeling; it was so bad. I remember during the most difficult times in order to bear the hunger, Di Di and I did nothing but drink cold water continually, sometimes even gnawing the edge of the table. Because of the lack of food, we often ate many dirty things and roundworms grew in our stomachs. When we went to the lavatory to defecate, the worms would come out. My stomach trouble was getting worse and worse, and I became even more emaciated. My big eyes looked like they were protruding from my face. But sometimes I could not open my eyes; I would be in a stupor and sleep on my bed all day. With my illness and the added hunger, I was approaching a condition of total collapse, almost at my last breath. Mama would come home after work, holding me in her arms unable to take any of the measures needed to get me out of danger, other than to cry, "Oh, this kid is in danger; what a terrible thing this is!" She felt very anxious. I opened my eyes feebly and stared at Mama blankly, wishing she could save me again even though I could not even say anything. Only two lines of tears flowed out from the corners of my eyes. How could she get a little bit food to save this child? Mama talked with the leader of her work place. She asked for permission to keep the food she received from the unit and bring it back home to give to Di Di and me to share. According to the regulations, the staff who worked in a food shop was not allowed to take any food in and out. I had been in her shop; they all knew that I was not doing well and often had a stomach ache. So the leader agreed to Mama's request. From then on after work Mama carried some food in her metal jug with a lid and ran home in haste. Relying on this little food Mama endured the torments of hunger to save us. She fed me day by day, and I unexpectedly recovered.

Goods were in short supply in the small food shop where Mama worked. Because of the shortage of ingredients, the shop was only open two or three days a week; but before day break each morning, there were hundreds of people lined up there waiting. The most urgent thing for all the people back then was solving their hunger problem.

It was under these circumstances that on September first of 1958, Mama took me by the hand and brought me to the Jing Xin primary school to register and start my studies. To look at me, my head was big, but my body was small, and physically I was not very well developed.

Mama was concerned about Si Shen's (my father's younger brother's wife) family who lived far away in Dali. She often said, "I wish the little town of Dali was better than Kunming; I hope your Si Shen's family is all safe." It was sad; Mama waited and then heard the miserable news that our younger uncle had starved to death in the prison. While all the people were hungry, the food situation for the prisoners was even worse. In Kunming, people heard that there were many people who had starved to death in prison; they had to use trucks to take them out to be cremated every day. But nobody could have imagined that Si Shu, who had been in good health before, after a few years in prison, deteriorated into an ever worsening physical condition. Finally, he could no longer survive starvation, and he died in the cruel prison.

When Si Shen went to the prison to collect his body together with her two kids, she couldn't identify her husband. Having suffered famine for such a long time, Si Shu had developed dropsy; his whole body was swollen and pale, with no color in his skin at all. Since the medical treatment and the sanitary conditions were very poor, both his legs and arms were swollen, had ruptured, and were oozing pus. The dropsy resulted in blood poisoning; he died a tragic death in a somber cell. Si Shu lingered close to death for many days, but he had none of his relatives beside him. How miserably he died. Our father's younger brother - this talented and romantic scholar when he was young, who always had a broad smile on his face in all the photos with an optimistic and humorous character; he was called the "banker" by the people when he was only 30 years old. He was the second child of the Yan family and was sent into the prison on a fabricated charge. After just a few years, he went so far downhill that he died in this terrible way. Both the Yan brothers had now become like ghosts; it was just too cruel. One more family was now without a father and a husband. How can they keep their life going? Mama choked with sobs when she heard that Si Shu had passed away, "Ah! god, why could the Yan family never escape this misfortune? My god, how can Si Shen earn even a bare living for herself and her five children?"

Two great women from the Yan family - Su Ruo Bi and Yin Gui Zhen.

As the elder brother's wife, she wished she could go to visit Si Shen, to comfort her and help her to take care of the funeral arrangements. But just like Si Shen before, she didn't have enough money to buy a ticket, so apart from crying ceaselessly, there was nothing she could do. Mama deeply regretted that she couldn't go to the funeral of her brother-in-law. She felt so sorry for the widow of Si Shu, her sister in law, because they had always been on very intimate terms with each other. Mama knew that Si Shen was also a gentle and feeble woman; the difficulties she needed to face right now were far too great for her. Si Shen would now have to wear the label of "the prisoner's family," and to survive in this community life in the years ahead would be very hard.

Mama wrote a long letter to Si Shen. Using herself as an example, she told Si Shen how she had experienced the hardship of losing a husband and had to overcome her difficulties and keep going. She encouraged Si Shen, and wrote in the letter, "For the sake of the children of the Yan family, we can't retreat; we have to grit our teeth to keep our lives going." Mama waited for a reply from Si Shen every day. One day, a letter came from Dali into Mama's hands. While Mama read it she was crying. "Good, it is good. Your Si Shen is standing firm," She said to us loudly.

Si Shen and Si Shu had been an affectionate couple too, and she told Mama in her letter, "For the sake of Ze Wen's children, even if I have to beg on the street, I will take great pains to bring them up. San Sao, you are my good example." With the comfort of her relative and the tears of her five children, Si Shen awoke from her grief, and she stood up. That year, she was just 40 years old, and her youngest daughter was not yet 5 years old. During the

My parents and Si Shu's family in 1940s.

long period of time that followed, the suffering that Si Shen and her five children experienced in Dali was also a sad history to remember. For many years the whole family lived on 26.5 yuan a month. This was the monthly salary Si Shen got from the primary

Si Shen became a widow when she was 40 years old. She brought up five children on her own.

school where she worked. In her later years, after she retired, Si Shen tried to write down what had happened in the past. But, in 2006 during the writing of this book when I went to her place to interview her, she told me, "I was unable to continue writing; when I started to recall the memories of my past life, I could only cry. Just tears and more tears," So in the end, she couldn't put her life story into words.

During the many years until Si Shu passed away in 1970, Mama and Si Shen had met together only once. But during the years they were apart, they wrote to each other and kept in contact continually. They communicated information about their children, encouraged one another, and faced up to adversity. They were so courageous as they brought up their children and never gave up. In 1956 after Dad had died, Si Shen had sent Mama one photo which she and Mama had taken together in 1940 and wrote these words on it, "San Sao, this is an old picture, but I hope we are still as close as we were in the past. Your sister Gui Zhen." At that time, the photo and those words brought great warmth and comfort to Mama. In 1966, Si Shen sent another photo of the whole of their family in a letter to Mama. In this picture Mama could see her five nephews and nieces again after being apart for more than ten years. She took the photo in her hand and was so excited as she looked at it over and over. Afterwards, she called all of us together and introduced each of us to our cousins. The children of the two families had come from the same root but had gone on to live in different places, and we almost didn't know each other.

Si Shen and Mama were not named Yan but may be considered to be the great women of the Yan family. They worked with their frail bodies, encouraged and influenced each other, forcing themselves to bring up all of the next generation, a total of 12 children; each of whom grew up and matured day by day. This was the situation before the Cultural Revolution came to China.

Later, as the whole of China would head towards an even more unimaginable state, neither of these women could understand why so many terrible things continued to happen in their land. In their letters they could but sigh in despair, "As we watch our children grow up day after day, why does this world become more and more fearful? When will the suffering this world wants us to endure be finished?"

Throughout the years when the whole nation was in famine, Dali did not escape, but even though Si Shu died in an accident in prison, the five children and Si Shen were fortunate to survive. In our family no one had an abnormal experience either. The little food Mama was able to get from her work place, no matter what kind food it was, she would put in her small jug and bring home. I, the sick child, was always the first one to get some. Then she used some water to dilute the rest of the food, and would give a little bit to each of the other children, finally she would eat what was left. So, I believe this "small jug" which Mama always held in her hand helped us to overcome our hunger and saved all our lives. We were all surprised that Mama who only took so little food each day, still had the energy to go to work as well as do all the housework. Mama said, "Heaven was fostering me."

When "The Great Leap Forward Movement" was unfolding like
a raging fire everywhere in China, one motivational slogan we saw
everywhere was: "To surpass Britain within three years, to catch up to
the United State of America within five years." The newspaper publicized
that the aim of the Great Leap Forward was to make China "catch up
to all of the capitalist nations within a very short time and to become
one of the most advanced and prosperous and strong countries." In
order to surpass Britain and catch up to the United State of America,
the first thing needed was industry, and the state was starved for steel.
Throughout the nation all the people responded to the call of the central
party and threw themselves into the Steelmaking Movement on a grand
and spectacular scale. As a practical way to vigorously support the state's
construction requirements, each family had to hand in everything which
had any metal in it to be sent to the steel smelter. I remember in An Ning
Lane where we lived, each family had to send in iron bolts, iron locks,
the frying pans and ladles used for home cooking, the frames of bicycles,
even the hair clips women used. These strange things which, even if
they only contained a little bit of metal, were piled up like a small hill
in front of the sub-district office, waiting to be thrown into the stove to
make steel. This attracted all of the children, including me; we were all
gathered around there to look at these things.

It seemed like something from Arabic mythology (a story which
could not be believed), but back then, no one dared to question what was
happening. The "Anti-Rightist Movement" had just finished and people
had seen that there were many men of insight who had answered the call
of the government and made some criticism or spoken the truth about
the current policy, when in just one day things had changed. Suddenly,
they were classified as "the rightists," and their status had suffered a
disastrous decline as they became the enemies of socialism. The deterrent

force of this proletarian dictatorship was so strong that all the people had learned how to endure and just obey what the government said.

The inconceivable thing now was that each family had to send someone to take part in the steel-making. Everywhere we looked we could see small blast furnaces as their flames lit up the sky. Right near the corner of the lane where we lived, there was also a small blast furnace. The old ladies of the residential committee, some with bound feet who walked with a limp, were also there enthusiastically taking part in the steel-making process. They threw each family's ironwork into the small blast furnace. They added coal and firewood and then worked the bellows with their two hands to start the iron smelting. For many days and nights they continued to add coal and keep the fires blazing, they took turns on duty to keep watch by the blast furnace. They all hoped they could smelt some piece of steel to support the state's construction industry, even though they knew that the steel smelted in one of these "earth blast furnaces" at best would become pig iron and nothing more; perhaps most of the things they made after all their hard work would not even qualify as pig iron.

Then all the students from the middle school and university were organized to take part in a different steel-making movement after school. People like Mama and Er Yi Ma worked with their unit; they were organized to go to the formal site and join the steel-making.

Mama was sent to steel-making for two months. The place she had to go to was called Xiao Hong Shan in suburban Kunming. That year the hill of Xiao Hong Shan was covered with small blast furnaces from its foot to its peak; the flames lit up the sky. The sky had a red glow in the evening and even from a distance a mixture of flames and steam could be seen. The day that Mama was told to go and register at Xiao Hong Shan, she went home quickly in the afternoon to get some clothing. According to the stipulations, she had to stay there and take part in the steelmaking for a week and then she could go home once. Mama was going away again, Di Di and I, who were still so young, didn't want to be separated from Mama, and our eyes brimmed with tears. We grasped the side of her coat and followed her as she walked to the crossing of Zheng Yi Road. We had to say goodbye to her, and then we walked home with a long face. We could not force Mama to stay home with us. No one dared to defy the activities the government organized. Mama missed us very much when she worked at the site. Sometimes she would quietly come home to see us late at night, and then go back hastily to the site the next morning before daybreak.

One night it was freezing and outside the window there was a flurry of snow. At about 9 o'clock, all of us brothers and sisters were suffering from hunger and cold, crouching under the quilt early and ready to go to sleep. Suddenly we heard a "creak," and Mama burst through the door and came into the room.

"Mama!" We were all overjoyed and jumped off the bed immediately, all of us jumping on Mama. We surrounded her completely in the center of the room. There were many small pieces of ice on her cotton-padded clothes, and the scarf she wore on her head was dripping wet. Both her hands were freezing and red; they were ice-cold when we touched them. We helped Mama to undo the scarf and held her hands tightly, getting a chair for her. Mama didn't sit down, she asked Si Jie to go and get six small bowls. She quickly drew the small jug out of her handbag and talked to us excitedly: "This evening we had a dinner party, and I received this little Hong Shao Rou (pork braised in brown sauce). Mama didn't eat any of it; after the political study was finished, I ran back home to give it to you to eat." As she spoke she separated the pork into six pieces and gave one bowl to each of us. (Da Jie had already left home to work in another place and was not in Kunming). We hadn't eaten any meat for a long time. We took the bowl and wolfed down the two or three small pieces of meat in less than a minute and licked all the juice in the bowl until there was nothing left. Mama looked at us smilingly as we ate. She didn't eat anything at all; she only poured some hot water into the small jug, rinsed it and drank the water. Afterwards she told us that she had to leave for the site at once because she was on duty and had to work on the night shift at 12 o'clock, and she could not be late. The time Mama stayed with us was less than 10 minutes; on such a cold and dark night, she would leave again, and we could not bear to part. We were very upset especially my younger brother and I, and we took hold of Mama's hands and burst into tears, "Mama, don't go, don't go!" We hoped that Mama could at least stay a little bit longer with us. But in that year, Mama could never stay home; she had to go. Mama patted our two heads, put on the scarf which was still not dry, and quickly walked out of the gate.

"Mama, Mama,…" we were crying and shouting as we followed her to the front door, reluctant to part. We watched as her emaciated figure disappeared in the dead of night as the cold wind chilled us to the bone.

Today, as I am writing these words, the scene of that evening still leaps up vividly before my eyes. I cannot control my emotions… I am filled with deep sorrow.

In order to bring that small jug of the meat to all of us hungry children that day, Mama had to walk alone from a desolate place about 10 km outside the town, braving the cold wind and snow.

Whenever I think about that evening of wailing wind and weeping rain, remembering the small jug of Hong Shao Rou Mama held in her hands, I always immediately feel the deep love she gave to us. I will remember this for the rest of my life; it is indeed like a warm current which will stay in my heart forever.

When Mama came back from the battlefield of steel-making, she only looked a little black and thinner than usual. But after Er Yi Ma had finished working at the steel-making site, she had totally changed into another person. Because she had dropsy, she felt weak in her four limbs. She worked at the site for two months and had to carry coal and steel ingots. This strenuous manual labor made her so tired, she felt as though her body was falling apart. Her sickness was getting worse, but she didn't dare to ask for a day of leave. She held on firmly despite extreme pain. The day she had finished her steel-making task and came back to Kunming, she walked directly to our home because she had been sent to another site and hadn't seen Mama for a few months. That day she wore an old dark gray coat which was called "Lenin clothing" back then. Maybe she just felt so cold; she used a rope to fasten the coat at her waist; it seemed as though she had tied together clothes which did not fit her. One of her trouser legs was too long, another was too short. She wore a pair of army shoes which were covered in slurry. When she came in the door of our home, we children were all surprised when we looked at her. We hadn't seen her for just a short few months, and we found that Er Yi Ma looked like a sick person. Her spongy face looked unresponsive and exhausted; her elegance and beauty was gone. When Er Yi Ma met with Mama, she started to cry, "I cannot endure any more, San Mei; I am dying." She stood before Mama with disheveled hair.

"Ai, how can you be like this?" Mama asked her with some reproach.

"I don't care about anything else. I am going under. I cannot keep living like this. I am really to go to die. I want to die." Er Yi Ma could not contain her emotions and burst into tears. Mama gave her a cup of water and pulled her to sit down. Seeing how this weak and kind woman had been ruined by society step by step, finally ending up looking like this, Mama felt pity for her. She wept together with Er Yi Ma. She helped her older sister unbind the rope from her waist, and handed Er Yi Ma a hot towel to clean her face. At the same time, she took a comb to fix her hair, and said some words to console Er Yi Ma. She told Er Yi Ma that tomorrow she would take her to see the Chinese doctor. After quite a long time, Er Yi Ma gradually settled down. We all heard Mama reiterate to Er Yi Ma loudly with one sentence, "We cannot die; for the sake of our children we must hold on right to the end! We cannot choose to give up!"

In the summer season of 1960, during the most difficult period, the old lady, Mama's sister Ding from Liang Ting village came to visit our family again. She wore light blue Chinese style clothing with a scarf of the same color on her head; this is the style of dress which was very popular in the countryside near Kunming then. She carried a basket with some fresh corn on her back as she came to our home, and she spoke loudly to Mama when she came in the door, "I am concerned about you all; the kids are starving, and I pity them. I have come because I just want to see each of you. We obtained some fresh corn today; I am now sending you some for the children to eat."

Getting this unexpected food made Mama especially happy. She cooked the corn at once and let us eat; we devoured it ravenously. Sister Ding told Mama that the piece of land which each peasant had been given by the government after the liberation had already been "cooperated" for two years. In the countryside each family's plot had been canceled and all the peasants had already joined the cooperative. Now all the peasants were working together to join the collective labor force to gain a point each day, which enabled them to get their provisions to live on. In the countryside, depending on their age, whether they were young or old, a man who worked in the field could gain 6-10 points a day; a woman could gain 4-8 points. At the end of the year, they received a grain ration according to the points they had accumulated. No family had a piece of their own land; for a long time they could not grow melons and go to the city to sell them. Seeing sister Ding always smiling and talking frankly, Mama knew this countryside woman was really a person full of deep affection. Even now in such a difficult period, she still came to bring food for us. It meant taking away some food from her family's mouths. After deeply thanking sister Ding, Mama told her that we would never forget her. If she would like, our family could be her home in the town. She welcomed her to come at any time. As expected Sister Ding wanted to make friends with our family. She, the poor and lower-middle class peasant, didn't care about politics; she took pleasure in being with people like us and wanted to spend more time with us. Afterwards, she came to visit us once or twice a year, and always brought us some special local products from her village. Sometimes, she would stay with us for one or two days and then go back home. When she came, Mama would arrange for us to take her to the Yuan Tong Zoo or Green Lake Park to play for a while, or she herself would accompany sister Ding to the department store to buy something to bring home. From then on our family had a relative from the countryside because Mama told us to call her "grandmother Ding." We all went to her home in the countryside during school vacation, and sometimes we stayed there for a few days. Our two families built a very good relationship with each other. I remember one year Mama knitted a red sweater for her, and she came to our home to receive it in person. That day Mama's sister Ding looked like the grandmother Liu in *The Dream of the Red Chamber*. (This is the title of a famous classical book in Chinese literature; grandmother Liu is an interesting role in this book.) Her every move and action made us laugh heartily.

During the following difficult period, Mama tried her best to find a solution to give all of us some nutrition. One day, she got a couple of chickens from sister Ding, so she built a henhouse in our back yard for them. She left instructions with us to close the door tightly, and not to let the chickens get out. Because the family was not allowed to have any kind of sideline including raising livestock, we were not even allowed to breed a chicken. Both chickens grew up day by day. The hen began to lay eggs. Mama was very happy; she watched the hen laying an egg every day, picked it up day after day and put it into a special crock. After gathering together 6 eggs, she would choose an evening to use the rationed brown sugar and cook them, giving each of us a small bowl with some sugar soup and one egg. During this time of famine, having a bowl of sugar with an egg for us was like having a great holiday at home. After we had eaten it, we would start counting when the second time to have it would come. Ah, this was indeed the most delicious, tastiest food for us. Each time when Mama put the small pan on the fire and was boiling the sugar soup, we all stood around the stove to watch. When the cooked egg was put in the bowl and we held it with both hands, we could never wait, even if it was very hot. We were too impatient to wait and hurriedly put it into our mouths. Mama saw how greedy we were, and she couldn't help but smile. Each time we were eating, we hoped Mama would also have a share, but there was no egg in her bowl, just a bit of sugar soup. She told us with smile, "Mama ate too much before; now my stomach is still full. You eat, you eat."

Seeing that all of us had something to eat and having us around her gave Mama the most pleasure. Only in those moments would we see a rare smile on her face.

"Oh, if Mama could have any other way to find some more food for you, I would be happy," she often said to herself.

For so many years, to give all of us children one more bite of rice, one more spoon of soup, Mama always restricted herself to an extremely rigorous degree. Later, her weight dropped to 40 kg, her previously emaciated figure now looked even more thin and weak. She could not fill her clothing and pants when she put them on. Seeing Mama's health gradually fall into decline, in 1965 my older sisters who already had jobs made a decision to pool their money together and to use three Yuan each month to order half a pound of milk to give her as a tonic to build up Mama's health.

Each afternoon after 5 o'clock, I often carried a small jug in my hand and went to the sub district office on Wen Miao Street to get it. The half pound of milk only filled a small part of the jug. Every night when Mama boiled the milk, she would always give each of the children a bit to drink first, and then she would take the rest. Even if we were already in bed, she would hand over the milk to us, asking each of us kids to take a little bit. At that time Wu Ge, Liu Jie, Di Di and I slept in the small room together with Mama every day, and we all took the milk Mama passed us in our bed. After we each took a bit in turn, the milk left over was only a very little.

It was in this way that Mama worked her heart out just so we brothers and sisters would not fall down because of the famine!

We were growing up under the protection of Mama's sweetness and kindness. The words Mama often spoke to us were:

"Mama loves each of you. For you, Mama could endure any suffering."

"Mama will never fall down; Mama could not allow you to become orphans. I will try my best to bring you all up until you are grown."

"You must remember you still have Mama. Even if Mama is only alive for one day, none of you would ever starve to death."

"No matter what happens outside, you still have a home. The word I have promised your Dad I must keep until it is completed."

In 1961, the cooperative shop Mama worked in was amalgamated into "The Kunming Min Sheng Clothing Factory." Because she was able to make food, she was assigned to work in the mess hall of this factory. Her salary was still 30 Yuan per month. This income, after paying the rent, water and electricity fee, could only buy a little food supplies. At that time, my youngest brother had reached the age to go to school, so she sent him to school on time too. Then, even though Er Jie had found a job, there were still five children studying in school, and for Mama, the burden of the cost of living was still very heavy. In our home for many years, we didn't buy any new bedding and appliances, and the clothing and pants each of us children wore were mended and patched.

The status on her identity said that Mama was "the rotten wife of a capitalist." In this factory, which was bigger than the unit she worked in before, she was bullied. There were about 100 people who ate in the mess hall. Every day Mama had to do all kinds of hard tasks which she had no choice but to do. In order to get her meager income, she forced herself to go in to work every day. To support the whole family's basic living costs and to pay for five children's tuition fees, the heavy burden of life pressed down on her nearly leaving her breathless. We seldom saw a smile on her face; where before she was always full of enthusiasm and optimism, now her nature had changed. She became silent; for many days we often did not hear her speak a word.

"Worried, I am worried; I have so many things I need to worry about!" Sitting on the bed, this was what Mama often said to herself.

One evening late at night, we were awoken from our dreams by a sudden clap of thunder. Along with flashes of lightning, torrential rain poured down, and there was a clicking sound in the small room we lived in as the roof started leaking. Our quilt was immediately splashed with water. Mama called all of us to get up in a hurry. She turned over quickly from the bed to put a washbasin and a water bucket to catch the rain water in the place where the roof was now seriously leaking. And then she handed a dish or a bowl to each of us, making us sit on the bed to catch the rain water. Our family was too poor to pay to fix our house; we couldn't even buy a piece of plastic to keep the roof from leaking. All of us were mobilized, but when this heavy rain was over, the small room was filled with a vast expanse of water. Everything in our home had gone through the storm and was now damp.

When bit by bit the rain drops became smaller, we lay down again under the half dry and half wet quilt. Mama also lifted her quilt and as she went to lie down she saw the water marks all over the bedding and sighed with great emotion, "Oh, my children are too poor. How can they get through this night; they don't even have a dry place to sleep!" Straight after that, she couldn't help bursting into tears. While she was crying she called out loudly, "Lord, give us a way out; help us to keep on living!"

"I don't have any means, our house has a leaking roof, and I don't have money to fix it up. I don't have money to buy any more bedding, and now we are all sleeping under wet quilts. My god, who can take pity on us, take pity on this poor mother and children!" That night, Mama's bleak cry flew through the sky of our small yard for a long time. Along with her cry, there was the ticktack sound of the roof leaking. It continued to fall down into the different household objects we were using to catch the rain water in the room; it lasted till day break. That night each of us children were also weeping under the wet quilt; no one could sleep; only none of us cried out loud. We all knew that our home was indeed the most pathetic home in the world.

In that beat-up small room during the first few years after Dad had died, that distressed cry for help and our helpless tears often cast a shadow over everyone's heart; we were living in circumstances of extremely constraint and incomparable difficulty.

When she felt helpless, Mama would often cry. Now, from a medical point of view, Mama's sobbing could help her to break down the melancholy and pressure, so it was very good. But in my childhood, the most fearful thing for me was to hear or see Mama weep in grief; every time I saw it, I would follow her and cry with her.

On Tomb-Sweeping Day each year (April 5th), Mama would choose one day to bring all of us to go and visit Dad's grave. This lasted for years and would never be interrupted. Er Yi Ma's husband was buried close to Dad's grave, so many times Mama also invited their family to go to visit the grave with us.

The day before we went to the grave, Mama would always prepare something to eat and put it in a basket. Sometimes she would have a bunch of fresh flowers on the table. The next morning, she would put on some neat clothing; she also asked each of the children to change into some clean clothes, and the whole family would pick up the things and get going. Usually, we walked from the city to the western suburbs and went along the railway line straight to Hei Lin Pu. Then we would start to climb Mian Hill. Each time, when we had just set foot on the bottom of this small hummock, Mama could not help bursting into tears. While she was crying, she quickened her step and led us quickly along several narrow meandering footpaths to get to Dad's grave. Dad's death was so miserable, his grave was just a big mound with no gravestone or any stones mounted around the grave, and it was overgrown all around with weeds. But, each year, Mama would take us straight to Dad's grave. The way to get there was etched in her memory. As we got closer to Dad's grave, the scene we would see was Mama leaping towards the grave. She would lie on the grave as if she had thrown herself on the bosom of her husband. She would cry out involuntarily she was so sorrowful; many times she would even lose consciousness. She brought her grievances, her grief and indignation, and her desolation and poured them out completely on her husband, "Oh! Once a year I can come to you to vent my grievances, Ze Gao; you listen to me! You left me alone, and you sleep here. Do you know what kind of life I have? When will my hard life end? You tell me, you tell me! eh, eh!" She would hold both her hands high and flap them at the grave and cry out in distress, overwhelmed with sorrow. Each time, it always took about half an hour, and then Mama's emotions would gradually quiet down. She would lead us in cleaning up the grave, pulling up the weeds, and neatly sweeping the surroundings. Then, Mama would lay the offerings she had prepared in front of Dad's grave herself; there was always a small piece of food which was Dad's favorite,

242

and one cup of tea, and one cigarette. After she had spread a clean cushion in front of the grave, Mama would first give Dad a kowtow, "Ze Gao, I have brought all your children to come and see you; you see, we are all right; we all miss you; we are thinking of you every day," Mama respectfully faced the grave to kowtow three times, tears covering her face. After Mama rose to her feet, each of us children took turns to give Dad a kowtow. When each child knelt down before Dad's grave, Mama would say the child's name to Dad very seriously, "Now this is your child who will give you a kowtow; you bless them in heaven." Usually on that day each year, the whole family would stay for the whole day by Dad's grave and be back home by dusk.

That day each year was the most heart-rending day. Mama was deep in sadness from when we set off through the gate. When we arrived at Dad's grave, she started loudly talking to Dad, telling him about our life and the recent situation of each child. In the afternoon, when the time came to part, Mama always found it hard to leave that place. Her talking changed into sobbing; many times, the sobbing she did before Dad's grave could last one or two hours; nobody was able to hinder her. At nightfall when we had to leave for home, as we went down the hill, Mama's dreary and plaintive cry could be heard in the mountain forest, she continued to talk to her husband until the last moment, "I have brought your children, and we are leaving; we will come to see you next year. You bless each of us. I can only talk with you once a year; I don't have anyone to pour out my woes to. For the sake of your children, I grit my teeth and stay alive; I am living in this world just like the cattle, like a horse. You tell me what day this kind of life will be finished! Oh, oh..."

All the way home on the 7 km long road, Mama whimpered until we were back in our house. A few days later her emotions would still be consumed in sorrow. Except to go mechanically about her work, she

The Mian Hill, where Dad is buried, knows how much suffering Mama had.

often sat without saying a word for many days. We all knew that she was thinking of Dad.

Our poor Mama, she was like a machine in operation every day. And she was just around 40 years old. Actually she was a weak lady who had no one to turn to for help, and she lived in solitude. Her body and mind also needed the caressing and consoling of others, and those were things her children could not to give to her. Therefore, she only had an opportunity once a year to go to Dad's grave; this gave her a chance to get the suffering off her chest. Back then we couldn't understand this.

I never liked to go to visit Dad's grave because I was so afraid of Mama's wailing and pain. In my mind Mama's cries of distress and helplessness were the most miserable sounds in the world. But, this was the kind of cry which accompanied us from year to year.

One day in the summer of 1973, my three older sisters brought their children to Kunming. Dad's younger sister-in-law, our Si Shen, also had a chance to come to Kunming from Da Li. She and Mama made a decision to go and visit Dad's grave together. That day, Mama had prepared many things as she was accustomed to doing, and she brought the whole family, including five grandchildren, to walk to Dad's grave as usual. Ge Ge borrowed a camera that day and took one picture which recorded the scene where we were all together around Dad's grave. In the picture, we all look heavy hearted. Maybe Mama's crying scared the little kids, these children of different ages, Dad's grandchildren; each also looked very serious, with no smiles on their faces.

This is the one picture which always made me feel sad. On the desolate mountain ridge, all of us are sitting in front of Dad's grave staring blankly. From the picture you can see that our Si Shen had experienced the hardships of life; the tribulations of her life had taken away her dignity and good looks. Before her San Ge's grave, her eyes revealed only bleakness and distress. And our bitter Mama, she had cried the whole day again, and her wrinkly face was stained with tears, and this was even 20 years after Dad had died.

Because I always slept with Mama in the big bed, I think I knew Mama's moods more than my brothers and sisters. In the still of the night, Mama often leant against the head of the bed to cry. When I grew up I still slept with Mama in the same bed; I would try to comfort her whenever I saw her crying, and she would say to me, "You can't understand, just let Mama cry; after crying, Mama feels better."

Yes, we, the young children of our Mama, were unable to understand the inner sufferings and struggles of a woman who had lost her husband. Mama also needed love, needed to pour out her heart, needed a massive shoulder to lean on, and to be able to relax. It was just as Mama told us, "Even if your Dad did nothing, he could stay home. I would go out to work no matter how hard it was or how tired I became, and I could take it. If only he were here to talk with me when I come back home. However, he has completely left me, left me alone to face everything by myself. I don't have anyone to talk things over with, to complain to. What a poor person I am. Why has this become my fate?"

Our poor Mama, no matter how hard and painful her inner suffering, on the second day she would wipe her tears. She still had to face her grim life by herself.

The money Da Jie sent home each month really helped Mama a lot. Mama's salary which needed to be shared amongst each of us was less than 5 Yuan, this little money was not even enough to buy basic food supplies. So the money Da Jie sent home often meant we did not run out of rice and fuel. We would often come home to find Da Jie's money had arrived, and we could go to buy the food supply for the day. When the new term began, all the children also depended on the money to pay the tuition fees and buy textbooks. Since I was now at an age where I could understand, I knew clearly that Da Jie was the benefactor of her younger brother and sister. If Da Jie had not insisted on sending money home, Di Di and I might not be able to go to the primary school. When I was 10, and we received Da Jie's money order, Mama sometimes asked me to go to the post office to get the money. I held the money order in one of my hands and carried Mama's seal and residency booklet in my other hand. I would always run to the post office as fast as I could, get the money, and hold it firmly in my hand, running back home at my quickly again to put the money in Mama's hand. I knew Mama was in dire need of this money.

Da Jie had left home to work in a small town far away from Kunming, and Mama was missing her so much. She kept in contact with Da Jie by letters for years. Da Jie has still kept a few of Mama's letters. Mama wrote with beautiful handwriting in her letters, and they would touch one deeply in the heart. At the beginning of each letter she always wrote, "Dear Yin, my dear daughter." Her inscription at the end was always, "I long to see you again, signed, Ruo Bi."

The first Chinese New Year after Da Jie had her job was also the first winter vacation for her. We were all looking forward to seeing Da Jie come home to spend the holiday with us. Da Jie also missed home very much. But, after she had calculated the return travel expenses, she decided not to come home but instead sent some more money to us. When Mama received the money order and read the few words on it, she felt very sorry; her eyes streamed with tears. She chattered incessantly. Your older sister is too sensible, too sensible. Then she walked out the door alone.

She went to the post office to get 20 Yuan and went straight to a shop; she picked out some nice fabric to take home and sat busily at the sewing machine to make something. Half a month later, Da Jie received an unexpected package; in it were a shirt in blue with cotton prints and some pants in a gray color which Mama had made up herself together with a letter from Mama.

Mama wrote to Da Jie, "Dear Yin, my dear daughter, my desire to see you far exceeds my desire to see the money. In the next Chinese New Year, you must promise Mama that you will not send money home but you will come to Mama's side. Mama misses you every day. With love, Ruo Bi."

This heartfelt letter Mama had written and the new clothes which were soaked in a mother's painstaking care brought incomparable warmth to Da Jie who was just 18 and lived alone in a strange place. And it was something Da Jie remembered for the rest of her life.

Due to the poor economic situation in our home, for many years, all the clothes and shoes we wore were made by Mama from a cheap fabric. Usually, we only had one set of clothing each year. No matter whether it was spring, summer, autumn or winter, we wore them every day. If we needed to wash them, we always chose a day with sunshine; we would wear some undershirts or old clothes, waiting for this set of clothing to dry in the sun. Then we would put them on again.

It was always at the Chinese New Year each year that we brothers and sisters would get a set of new clothing and a pair of new shoes like all the other children on the first day of the New Year. To prepare those things for us, Mama's hands were never idle at any time when she came home after work.

One New Year's Eve when I was 8 years old, I saw that each of my brothers and sisters had a set of new clothes beside their pillows, but I didn't have any, so I waited up and could not go to sleep. That night, the lamp at home was lit up and Mama worked through the night until about 3 o'clock in the morning. I was so sleepy I fell asleep. Later on in a haze I heard some noises outside the door so I knew the day was breaking. I rose up and sat on the bed and saw Mama leaning against her pillow; her hands were still sewing a button on the clothes. She saw me wake up and spoke to me, "I knew you were anxious about your new clothes and that you could not sleep well. I have made them, I have made them. Come and try them on." As she was speaking, she finished the last bit of sewing. She handed over a nice cotton coat in purplish red to me. I didn't get off the bed; I stood up on the bed and put on these new clothes in a hurry. When Mama saw that I was so happy, she asked me, "You see those buttons - don't you think they are beautiful?" While she was saying this, she helped me do up the six buttons; it was a Chinese style jacket with buttons down the front of the garment. She had used many leftover bolts of cloth to make and then to sew them onto the clothes, they took a long time to make. Wearing the new clothes, and having these special buttons, I was very happy and nodded to Mama. Mama looked at me and said, "Happy New Year! How pretty our Ling Ling is today."

I knew that Mama didn't sleep at all that night just so I could also have some new clothes, clothes which were even more beautiful with those buttons, which she had stayed up all night to make. But then, after putting on the new dress, I didn't even say "thanks" to Mama as I flew outside to play. All the brothers and sisters were the same as me. For all of us, seeing Mama working in the night or staying up all night, we just thought it was her habit. Mama working hard day and night was a common sight we had seen for years and years.

Despite the fact that Mama toiled day and night, we still relied on her very small earnings, and for many years poverty was our companion. We were often unable to get enough food, and sometimes as it grew closer to dinner time, we didn't have any food in our home. We boiled some water in a boiler waiting for Mama to come back home after work so we could have some money to go and buy half a kg of rice or 50 grams of oil to cook a meal for the day. This kind of thing happened often. We were also unable to buy the coal for cooking anymore, only when Mama had money could we buy a small basket of it. Our clothing and pants were always mended over and over. No matter how cold it was, we still only wore one set of clothes to school; we never had any extra clothes to add. It was normal for us to go to school with bare feet, because each year we only had one pair of cotton shoes which Mama had made for each of us. If they broke we had no more shoes; even in the winter we had bare feet. In the rainy season, Mama had no money to buy umbrellas for us, so we were always exposed to the rain on the way to school. We could not pay the tuition fee on time, so we were always treated badly at school. For many years, we used salt to brush our teeth; I did not know the taste of toothpaste until I was 15 years old. The enamel basin we used to clean our faces and feet every day was used for so many years that it had broken. There were some small holes in the bottom and water would leak out; we used some cotton to fill in the holes and kept on using it. The holes became bigger and bigger and we actually could not continue to use it, so because Mama didn't have enough money to buy a new one, she used 2 Jiao and bought an earthen basin which she brought home. From then on we used the earthen basin to clean our face and feet. The bedding on our beds had been used for such a long time, it was too tattered to use. Mama couldn't buy any more for us and one day she pulled a cart with some straw mats to our home and spread them on the bed. Sleeping on the straw mats was not comfortable, but we had to accept it. The worst thing was when fleas began to wreak havoc, and we were bitten by them and often had red spots all over our bodies. Mama didn't have the money to repair the small room we were living in for years, so when it rained, the roof leaked and dripped continuously. During the tenth year after the new country came into existence in around 1960, our lives had really reached extreme poverty. Every day we experienced the blow of being impoverished; it was hard for us to grow up with this tribulation.

However, even now, when we remember the events of our childhood, we still immediately feel joyful in the bottom of our hearts. We sigh with emotion, so lucky to have had a Mama so we didn't become orphans wandering about destitute on the street; we had a home which belonged to us. Although, it was a very simple and shabby home, it still left us many indelible memories.

I have mentioned before that Mama was an enthusiastic and optimistic person. Whenever she laughed to her heart's content, the sound was very bright and infectious. When she was young she revealed in Beijing opera. She was part of a group of people who loved to sing amateur Beijing opera, and we could see her elegant demeanor from the old pictures which still remained in our home. She loved literature too. *Dream of*

the Red Chamber was the book she always put beside her pillow. We all
remembered that she could recite the entire "bury flower ci" (a Chinese
poetic genre) written by Dai Yu in the *Dream of the Red Chamber*. While
she was reciting, her emotions were completely absorbed in the dainty
rhythm of the poem. She understood every word and sentence so well.
And her dress, her style of conversation, and her habits all demonstrated
her noble taste and culture. But in those years, because of the daily need
to support the whole family's basic food and simple clothing, the grim
reality of life hung around her neck. It was impossible for her to have
any recreation or hobbies. She worked hard from morning till night; we
rarely saw a smile on her face. The little time of relaxation she had would
be to sometimes sit together with her older sister, our Er Yi Ma, to have a
talk.

I was growing up day by day, and I habitually watched Mama's
expression which never changed. I looked at Mama's face every day and
hoped that Mama would have a smile on her face; I hoped that she could
have even one happy time, even if it was very short! One day Mama
indeed had a very pleasurable evening; it was the only time I ever saw
Mama feeling happy and excited, so I never forgot it.

This was an evening in the summer of 1960 when I was in the second
grade. That day, our whole family ate dinner ahead of schedule; Mama
changed her dress, cleaned up, and quickly put on some light make up.
Then she also cleaned me up and helped me comb my hair. She told me
that she would take me with her to go to The Victory Hall to see a Beijing
Opera performance. I had never been to a theater to see any kind of
performance; I was very excited and held Mama's hand as we cheerfully
went out the gate of our home together. On the way, Mama told me very
particularly that when we entered the theater I should bend my body over
as low as possible. If I was checked and exceeded one meter in height by
the ticket inspector I could not enter the theater and would have to go

home alone. (Back then the theater allowed each ticket holder to bring a child less than one meter high to come in and see the performance.) Mama held my hand, as we went through the entrance, I lowered my body (actually I had a slight figure.) It all went smoothly, and we both walked into the theater successfully.

I remember our ticket was in the middle of the last row on the second floor. We found our seat and sat down, Mama put me on her lap, and we waited for the play to come on. All at once, a deafening sound of gongs and drums resounded through the hall. The lights suddenly went out, and the whole audience was quiet. Only one big spotlight shone on the red curtain on the stage. For a while a huge caption was shown on the straight screens on both sides of the stage: Famous Beijing Opera Artist Mr. Shang Xiao Yun to act in the leading role "Zhao Jun goes to the frontier fortress." I was a second grade student; I knew all the words, so I read them loudly. Mama hinted that I should not read aloud. This detail remains fresh in my memory until now.

The big curtain opened up slowly. Mama and I fixed our eyes on the stage and began to enjoy this Beijing opera. On the stage, we saw a female wearing a gorgeous, richly ornamented dress with two pheasant tail feathers inserted in her hair. She had a bright red mantle draped over her shoulders. She was dancing while she was singing, and she held the two feathers from her head in her hands, moving back and forth, and moving into different postures. Along with the strains of the music and accompanied by drum beats, she struck a pose in the center of the stage; she looked very beautiful. When I turned around to look at Mama, I saw that while she was listening to the drama, she was moving her head from left to right along with the drumbeats and one of her hands was beating time on my knee. She was really enjoying the drama so much. But after about 10 minutes, I was not interested in this drama at all because I couldn't understand the meaning of the performance and the lyrics of this opera. For a while I slept on Mama's bosom. When Mama woke me up, it was already time for the curtain call. Mama stood up clapping her hands together with the rest of the audience for a long time. The leading lady Zhao Jun shifted her posture and position in answer to the curtain calls a few times but still didn't go off the stage. The gong and drums were beating more and more lively and loudly. The emotions of the players on the stage and the whole audience were coming to a climax. I raised my head to look at Mama again. I saw both her eyes were gazing at the leading lady, and she was engrossed and laughed in adoration, shouting with joy with sounds of "Oh, Oh" together with the rest of the audience at intervals just like a child.

That day I saw Mama the happiest I had seen her in many years, and I felt very happy too. The big curtain had closed, the people started to exit, and while we were walking, Mama was saying, "It was so beautiful, so beautiful."

She held my hand and walked out of the theater. But when we walked into the big courtyard, Mama didn't continue walking toward the street, she said to me, "Let's wait here for a moment; I want to see Shang Xiao Yun after he has removed his stage makeup and costume."

Outside the theater there were many people, both old and young, who were fans of the leading lady as Mama was. They were all waiting for the player to appear. About 20 minutes later, we saw an old, short man in a gray tunic and trousers come out through the exit of the dressing room with many attendants crowding around him. Someone suddenly shouted loudly, "Coming, coming, he is coming!" Mama held my hand and rushed towards the man together with all of the theatre fans. But we didn't see the person's face clearly; he had disappeared into a saloon car which stopped by the exit of the dressing room. When we ran up close to the car, it took off in a hurry. All of the people who had been waiting now followed the car, running after it through the gate into the street until we saw the car had turned a corner; they stopped and were talking about it excitedly.

I was confused by this event, just now on the stage there had been a lady in a beautiful theatrical costume, looking pretty. Why now was it an old man? And, he was such a short and old man. Why had so many people gone into raptures, including Mama? But Mama had a really good time which she seldom had; I didn't need to be concerned about anything. I held Mama's hand joyfully as we went home.

Later I found out that this was the first time one of the famous Beijing Opera's Chinese performers, Mr. Shang Xiao Yun, had come to Kunming to perform. Mama loved to sing Beijing opera when she was young; she was good at playing the female character "Qing Yi." Mr. Shang Xiao Yun was indeed one of the four famous female character types of Chinese Beijing opera, and he was well-known throughout the country for his melodious "Qing Yi" singing. Mama really was one of his biggest fans.

Mama said later that on that day she had hesitated for a long time, finally making the decision to spend 5 Jiao and buy one of the cheapest tickets. When she took me with her, she fulfilled a dream she had since she was young of wanting to see such a master's performance. This was the only time she used 5 Jiao for herself for something luxurious and selfish during those hard years she took care of us. That evening she even told Dad the story of her visit to the performance of Shang Xiao Yun. Mama said when she was young Dad had promised her many times that he would take her to Shanghai or Beijing to see a performance of the four famous female character types of the Chinese Beijing opera. Because Kunming was such a small place, those famous performers would not come there. With the changes in the political situation and her husband's death, Mama thought that her desire would always only be a dream. She absolutely didn't expect that one summer night in Kunming, her dream would come true.

I hoped that Mama could have more and more of these good times. One evening, I snuggled up with Mama on the bed and looked up at her and asked, "Mama, apart from seeing the Beijing opera, is there anything else you would also really like to do?"

"I would like to go to Beijing to see the Forbidden City where the emperor used to live; I want to know what it looks like." Mama answered me full of longing. But, she immediately shook her head and said, "It is impossible; it will always be impossible; this is Mama's wishful thinking." I knew Beijing was the capital of China and that it was far away from Kunming, but I still didn't know where the Forbidden City was or what it looked like.

And I didn't understand what "wishful thinking" meant so I told Mama, "It is possible; when I am grown up I will go with you to see this place."

Mama cuddled me into her bosom and muttered to herself, "Fine, let's have a dream tonight and go to there once."

Ah, the memory of that conversation with my Mama during my childhood that evening makes me feel so sad.

Mama experienced so much bitterness and so little joy. But always composed and indomitable, the self-respect and confidence she showed every day had an edifying influence on us; we were deeply affected by her nature as we were growing up. We were poor, but we were never felt inferior, and we never looked down on or despised ourselves. Mama urged and exhorted us again and again, "We are orphans and a widow, but we are not inferior to others. You should all remember this; you should try to look good!"

"You may be wearing worn-out clothes, but your heart is not tattered; you are not a worthless person. You are from a decent family; your behavior must be open and above board!"

Those words resounded in our ears almost every day.

Although our housing and living conditions were exactly like that of the urban poor, our intellect and appearance was still different from other children. In school, we were all hardworking students, and all of us had some special qualities. The most excellent students in the school back then were called "the three best students." This meant the student was the best in three areas: they had developed well morally, intellectually, and physically. Each of us brothers and sisters received one of these awards and brought a certificate of merit home. I myself, from the first grade to the sixth grade, was one of the "three best students" in our school. And I was always one of the "class leaders," which meant I had two red lines on my arm. All of us brothers and sisters loved singing. Er Jie and Ge Ge were talented with musical instruments; Er Jie could play the guitar. Ge Ge could play the flute, the erhu (a traditional Chinese instrument), and the harmonica. So while we lived at home together, the sound of singing, fluting ,and laughing could always be heard coming from our small room.

In An Ning lane where we lived, most of the people were from the working class. They would do handicraft to make money to support their families. When we moved into No. 7 An Ning lane, there were only two families. Our landlord and our family lived in the front and backyard. Because of the new policy, privately owned houses were taken over by the government, so this little yard was taken over by the state. By the middle of 1960, there were 7 families who had been settled in this yard by the government. It had been turned into two yards which were now occupied by many households. Old and young, more than thirty people lived there together. The families who moved there were mostly working class people. There was the Wang family. Mr. Wang made a living by helping people carry heavy loads with a "carrying pole." The Zhu family was bricklayers. And the Cheng family used a tricycle to transport freight. And one old lady from the Lao Gu Ma family washed people's clothes to make a living. One family named Gong, who was carpenters, moved into the front yard when only our family lived there. The Gong family moved into the room on the east side, so we had to squash into the room on the west side which was less than 30 square meters. Mama used some wooden blocks to divide one room into three, the right and left sides were our bed rooms, the middle of the room was set aside as a small space for eating. Fortunately, behind our living room there was about 10 square meters of long empty space, this became our kitchen. Gong was a typical boor; our yard lost the peace we had previously when his family moved in around 1962. He set up his big wooden table which took 2/3 of the space in the yard so he could do woodwork. Every day he made wooden shoes in the yard. Our yard before was neat and clean, from then on it was strewn with wood shavings and the wooden shoes he made. He made the wooden shoes to support his family, so everyone understood. We lost our play space; Mama told us we should exercise forbearance and go and play in the lane. But we couldn't understand why once a day he would beat his children to his heart's content. It was hard for us to bear it. He drank alcohol every day, and when he was drunk, he would hold a wine bottle in one hand and a strap in the other hand. If anything was not as he wished, he would use the strap to thrash his children. Therefore the small yard was always filled with the crying and shouting of his children. His family had six children aged from 3 to 15 years old. Even the oldest one, the 15 year old daughter, was beaten with his strap. The two youngest were always acting up. Gong even used a broom and a rattan rope to beat them. When they were walloped, they sometimes came to hide in our room. Mama always tried to offer advice with the best of intentions, continuously helping them to calm down the conflict.

The neighbors wondered why they never heard the sound of beating and scolding from our Mama, and why each of us looked nice, studied hard, and why our behavior was more cultured.

"Mrs. Yan, how have you taught your children to be so nice?"
Old Gong often asked Mama for advice. Old Wang who lived in the
backyard also gave his children a scolding because they did not study
hard. "Why are you not like the children of the Yan family? They are
all good students at school; they are a good role model for you." Yes we
brothers and sisters, by looking at the clothing we wore, were almost the
same as the children of the other families in the lane, but our style of
conversation and habits made us very different from the other children.
Some people even said that just from our appearance they could tell that
we were the children of a rich family.

Now, of course I knew why we were different from other children.
The main thing was that we were held together by Mama's strong love;
therefore we were shaped differently from other children. For many years
in our room, there were some things which we had preserved which did
not match our surroundings; these things also made our family seem a
little different from other families. For instance, there was a delicately
made western-style square table, as well as several beautiful old china
plates which we used every day. Those things were easily recognizable as
being from a rich family. Those few things had often been put up for sale
but weren't sold so they were preserved and stayed with us. In addition,
there were many brightly colored and high quality neckties of Dad's,
and many pretty stockings of Mama's as well as a number of Mama's
face powders in a nice box under the bed and in the bottom of the chest.
Those things were not used by anyone in that society, and even if they
were sold cheaply no one would buy them, so they stayed in our home.
When we were growing up, we had no money to buy belts, but it was
all right because we used Dad's beautiful neckties. We each wore one
around our waist. Mama's stockings became the bags for us girls to put a
kind of fruit pip in; this was a game we played with our fingers. Each girl
had one or two of these bags next to their pillow. As all the girls grew up,

they loved beauty. Liu Jie, who had studied chemistry, mixed Mama's face powder with some glycerin and turned it into a nice cold cream to put on our faces.

The time when people ate together in the mess hall had finished, but all the commodities were now rationed. We brought back the foodstuff, and the whole family could eat dinner together again. Mama arranged for Si Jie and Liu Jie to take charge of the shopping. Our lunch was simple, but each dinner time we always waited for Mama to get back home to make a fried dish; then the whole family would eat together. Since Mama worked in the mess hall, it was usually after 7 o'clock by the time she had finished serving and cleaning up the kitchen, so our dinner was always later than others. But then no matter how late, we liked to wait.

At 6:30pm each afternoon, we knew Mama would be back home soon. My sisters would start getting things ready for Mama to cook. The thing I loved to do the most was to go to An Ning Lane crossing of Qin Yun Street to meet Mama. My eyes would stare at the street corner waiting for Mama's silhouette to appear. Every day Mama was the same; she always held a small canvas bag in her hand which held a jug with the food she had in her unit. As soon as I saw Mama's figure come into sight I would run towards her. I would take the bag from Mama's hand and hold it in one of my hands, and use my other hand to hold Mama's hand firmly; then we would go home together. I always felt incomparably happy. In the cold winter season even if it rained or snowed, I still went to the street crossing to meet Mama. In those conditions I would put my hand in the place close to my heart to warm up, when I saw Mama I extended my hand to hold her ice-cold hand in mine so she could quickly warm up. We walked hand in hand for about 200 meters, and when we could see the gate of our yard I gave a shout, "Mama is coming."

We knew then that the happy time for our family was coming. Mama came into the kitchen and started to cook; the good smell would immediately spill over and fill the whole yard. Even if it was a vegetable dish, she would make it tasty. While Mama started to cook the dish, we were busy putting out the bowls and chopsticks and the meal Mama got from the mess hall on the table. Then as we all sat around the table, the sound of happy laughter was everywhere. When the dishes were put on the table, the whole family would eat together.

In those days no matter what food we ate, the people around the table were always talking and laughing, enjoying our meal together very much. Mama would always pass something good to each of the younger children, and pour some juice from the dishes onto our rice. If we had meat with the dinner, she would divide some into each of our bowls. The juice Mama made with the meat simply was the most, most tasty thing we had back then; we would eat each meal with great relish.

Each month on the day when Mama got her salary, she always used the fixed quantity "sugar ticket" to buy 200 grams of fruit drops to bring home. She would put them on the table and count how many there were, and then she would divide them up and give each child a share. When I got my share, I always quickly peeled off the paper and put one in Mama's mouth. But she never ate it, she would only bite off a little piece and put the candy into my mouth.

After dinner under the faint lamp, Mama would start to do her handiwork, making clothing or shoes for us. All of us brothers and sisters would sit around the table in a circle to do our homework. We were all huddled together around the only eating table in our home. If it was a cold day and there was a small stove burning in the room, Mama's seat would be moved beside the stove. She would sometimes speak to us while she was doing her needlework. Behind the closed door, the atmosphere inside our small room was very peaceful and warm.

Whenever any of the children had finished their homework and packed up their school bag, they would move to sit beside Mama. We hoped we could try to help her wind the threads or thread a needle. Sometimes we would also put a thimble on our finger and try to make a stitch in the sole of the cloth shoes. I remember in our home we had a sock board which was made out of wood and shaped like a real sock. Mama would often slip our torn socks onto it and repair the holes for us.

At least once a year Mama would make one pair of shoes for each child. It was not an easy job to make those seven pairs of shoes. First, she needed to find some old clothes or used bedding and cut them into small pieces, then she would use rice water to stick them down one layer on another, to make them become "Ge Bu"(a hard and durable cotton material). After this material had dried, she would put more layers of new fabric on both sides, then Mama cut the shape according to each person's size and would stitch the soles of the cloth shoes. She used a needle to drill through the thick cloth cover to stitch the soles of the cloth shoes, one stitch at a time. The stitches needed to be thickly dotted and even; this not only required skill but need strong hands; it was very difficult to handle. I tried and tried, and often broke the needle and punctured my finger but still could not drill even one needle through the thick, hard sole. I could imagine how much hardship it was for Mama to do this job all year round. From when I was a little girl, I understood that Mama was a very, very hardworking person. However, I was too young to help her. I always felt sad because I could not share these burdens with Mama.

All of us children knew that our lives would be very limited, we did not care about what kind of food we would eat or what kind of clothes we would wear. None of these things were important to us, as long as we could be with Mama; that is what satisfied us.

Mama was the sun who always gave out light in our lives, day after day. When spring had gone and winter was coming, because we had this abundance of warm light, even though the world outside was as hard as nails and ice-cold, we did not completely live in the dark. We were like the small blade of grass in the crevice of the rock; we were growing up tenaciously day by day under the sunshine of my mother's love.

When I was ten, my music teacher found out that I had a singing gift, so he gave me individual training after class. On "Children's Day" in 1961, he decided to choose me to represent the Jin Xing Primary School and take part in the gala celebration performance for the children of Kunming. As a dress rehearsal one morning, he took me to the teachers' office and asked me to sing for all the teachers the song "The Beautiful Havana," which was the solo that I would perform at the gala celebrations. To the rhythm of the accordion, I stood in the center of the office and started to sing with expression. When I had finished ,all the teachers applauded.

Then my mathematics teacher drew me to her desk and said to me, "Wait a moment; don't go home right away; come to my home with me first." I didn't understand what she meant, but I waited beside her. I saw that she tidied up her desk in a hurry, then she held my hand and walked to her home in the school. She fetched some adult clothes for me, and asked me to give her the clothes I was wearing. I did what she said. She put my clothes on the table, straightened the two sleeves evenly, and used the scissors to cut out part of the sleeves. Then she took some of her old clothes and also cut out two sleeves. She sat at the sewing machine and started to work. At that moment I understood what she was doing for me.

Because I had been wearing these clothes all year round, the elbows in my clothes had been torn for a long time, now these two holes were getting bigger and bigger. Perhaps while I was singing, she saw the big holes, so she had pity on me and did this for me. I thanked the teacher and felt very satisfied as I went home wearing my clothes with two colors on my sleeves. Mama saw it in the evening; she asked what happened and was touched. The next day she went to the school with me and expressed her thanks to the teacher. The teacher was named Yuan. She was the teacher in charge of our class, and since I could never pay the tuition fee on time for each new term, she knew our family's living situation. She spoke to Mama, "No, you don't need to thank me. We all know you have so many children, and it is not easy for you."

And yet, living in these impoverished circumstances did not mean everyone was kind to us. The teacher in charge of my fifth grade class was very harsh towards me. Because the burden of making a living was too heavy for Mama, she could not pay the tuition fee for all the children at the same time. Often, some of us had to wait one or two months before we could pay. The kind teacher had pity on us; she did not press us for the tuition payment, and she would give us new books each term. But the teacher of my fifth grade class was not like this. I don't know why, but she had a kind of inherent animosity toward the poor students who wore tattered clothing. If you could not pay the tuition on time, she would not give you the new books. If you didn't have books for one or two months, it was difficult to do the work in class and to do homework. I was a child who loved to study. For a long time I didn't have books, and I was not happy at all.

I wanted to get the books as soon as possible, so to pay the 2 Yuan tuition fee, I saved the 2 fen breakfast money that I had every day for a long time, but it was still not enough. So almost every day I asked Mama when I would get my tuition fee. I would try everything. For example, I would leave home with Mama when she went to work each morning, and on the way to her factory, I would catch hold of her clothing and not let her go, trying to pester her all way just wanting her to give me the money to pay the tuition. But as I followed her and we arrived at the gate of her factory, she still could not give me 2 Yuan. She was in a hurry to get to work, so she had no choice but to try to fool me and say, "Tomorrow, Mama will give you money tomorrow."

I had no choice but to let go of Mama's hand. I always went to school with tears in my eyes and with loathing. However, the next day Mama would say the same words again. In my childhood, this was the one thing I didn't like about Mama. I felt she deceived me by lying. Of course, I was wrong to blame Mama. Because her salary was only 30 Yuan per month, just supporting our daily lives was already very difficult. Six children needed to pay the tuition fee; where could she find the money for us? But back then this tuition thing really depressed me.

The beginning of second term of the fifth grade was coming, and Mama gave me the tuition money on the day when the new school term began. That day, with the money in my hand, I was so happy; I almost sprinted to the school. For the first time I queued up with my other classmates to pay the tuition and to get the new books on the same day. But when I opened my small hand and gave the teacher the 2 Yuan I had been clasping for a long time, she refused to accept it and said, "How come you have the money, did you steal it?"

I couldn't believe the teacher would say this with such certainty. I felt wronged, and I answered her loudly, "No!" and immediately burst into tears. That day, with the new book in my hands I left the school to the whisper of my classmates. I was not happy at all. In the evening, Mama saw that I was not my usual self. She thought this was very strange and asked me, "Ling Ling, this year you are the first one I gave the tuition fee to, why are you still unhappy?"

I sprang onto Mama and burst out crying. I told Mama what the teacher had said. Mama was very indignant and said, "This teacher is not a human being! Tomorrow I am going to confront her!" Listening to

Mama say this immediately released the grief in my mind, and I went to play outside again.

This was the sharpest and most abusive language I ever heard Mama use during the years I was growing up. If anyone dared to humiliate or hurt her child, she would not be forgiving. She would rise up and roar like a lioness. No, this teacher was not a human being. The degrading and damaging way in which she treated me was really humiliating and hurtful to Mama. I knew Mama had gone to the school and met with this teacher to talk this thing out with her. This irritated this teacher even more because later she frequently treated me with freezing sarcasm and burning derision so that some of my classmates began to wonder if I really was a thief. Naturally, this middle-aged teacher named Yang, who had a face full of freckles, became the only person I totally disliked throughout my life.

Just like most of the people who experienced poverty, we suffered from fabricated accusations and were looked down on. Luckily in our childhood, we had a Mama who was clear about what to love and what to hate. She always kept the evil arrows away from us, and protected us intensely. It helped us and meant our sense of self-respect was not destroyed and did not die. The shadow of an inferiority complex which was easily caused by poverty didn't take root in our hearts. The inflexible attitude with which Mama faced poverty has very much influenced the personalities of each of us.

When Er Jie was 18 years old, she finished her studies at the nurses' school. To lighten the burden on Mama, she decided, just like Da Jie, to find a job instead of continuing her college studies. Because her family origin was not good, she did not qualify for a job in Kunming. Mama thought it would be better if Er Jie could work in Wen Shan and be together with Da Jie in the same town, and then they could take care of each other. She went to the school to plead for favor, whereupon Er Jie was appointed as a nurse in the Wen Shan county hospital. She did the same thing as Da Jie and sent half of her salary to Mama to help with the family expenses from the first month she started to work.

Out of concern for Da Jie and Er Jie who were absent for many years, Mama kept up regular correspondence with them. In Mama's letters she would tell of everything that happened at home and the latest news about each of their brothers and sisters. Mama also asked them to write to tell us about their work and life. When Mama received a letter from the older sisters she always read it aloud to us.

Once, in Er Jie's letter, she wrote that one evening, when she and a few nurses were on night shift, they were so hungry that they stole some cabbages from a farmer's field. They cooked it on an electric stove in the nurses' office and ate. She described the details very vividly. While Mama was reading it to us, we all laughed until we cried.

In those years we were living far apart from our two older sisters but the bond of relationship was held together tightly by Mama, the warmth and care between us was never discontinued.

In the holidays, to send the family's blessings across the distance to both the older sisters, no matter how difficult the economic situation was in the family, Mama would always prepare something to send to them. She would go to the post office herself to send off the packages. The years when Da Jie and Er Jie were not beside Mama, the things she sent them were varied and even included hairpins which girls love. Particularly during the moon festival each year, they would both receive a package with some moon cake and a few other sweets. For many years Mama never changed this habit of sending some moon cakes to her two daughters.

In those lonely and doleful years, young Da Jie and Er Jie were living in a small town far from their home and apart from Mama. For many years they were inspired by the kindness of those letters and packages which were full of Mama's deep love. The moment they received a letter or a package was the happiest time for them.

"The most beautiful sound in the world is the voice of a mother." It was true that they received continual love and care from Mama as they grew up day after day in that far off small town. Soon both of them stood out conspicuously, showing not only exceptional ability and a striking appearance, but their behavior also won the admiration of their colleagues in their units.

Da Jie said that because her family origin was not good, from the first day she started to work, she exhorted herself to be cautious and meticulous. Her conduct was like a dog with its tail between its legs, and by no means could she make any mistakes in her work. Most importantly, she knew she must try to make a good impression for Mama with every word and action. She absolutely should not give Mama anything to worry about. Why should a girl in her prime exhort herself to "live like a dog with its tail between its legs" when she had just stepped out into the community? This was because when Dad died she had to wear black gauze on her arm to mourn over his death. Immediately she was criticized as "the unworthy offspring of the bourgeoisie" by the branch of the Communist Youth League in the school. The monitor of her class who wrote a short letter to comfort her was informed against, and then the broadcast station at the school warned all the students three times a day that they must "draw a demarcation line with the bourgeoisie." She was conscious that the good life she had before the liberation meant she had enjoyed "the decadent and dissolute life of the exploiting class." Deep in her heart while she was just in her youth, the mark it left on her was this: the family she had grown up in had committed a crime against society; she belonged to the bourgeoisie blood line, so she was also a sinner in this society. From then on she never dared to laugh at school, and always hung her head as she walked. With everybody's help she clearly knew that she only had one choice, which was: she had to thoroughly remold herself, then she could be accepted by the new society.

She wrote a self-criticism over and over and made an application hoping to join the Communist Youth League. She wished by her practical actions to indicate that she was willing to draw a clear distinction with her bourgeoisie family, and sought to ask for a new life. However, no matter how well she behaved herself and displayed good character and scholarship, at no time was she accepted as a member of the Communist Youth League. She tried to seek refuge with this progressive force, but the door was shut. So to gain a foothold and keep living in society, she considered she could only live like a dog with its tail between its legs. In the many years that followed, she always lived this way. But, how did she put this into practice? Da Jie said the way for her was to speak less and do more. She could never think about getting any benefits in the work organization, such as receiving official promotions, getting a raise, or getting an apartment from the unit, but if she worked hard with all her heart, then nobody could pick fault with her. She had to be strict with herself and lenient towards others. (In Mao's time, generally, each unit would provide living quarters for staff and workers. But it always happened that if the person's family origin was good, for example if they were farmers, workers or in the army, they would get nice and big living quarters. If the person's family origin was not good, such as ours, they would share one room with another person.) Da Jie conducted herself in this way throughout her whole life. Da Jie said that it was lucky that if she just lived like a dog with its tail between its legs, she could dodge the calamity of "the Anti-Rightist Movement" and "The Cultural Revolution" later on. At her young age she knew how to live so rationally in this world, and it set Mama's heart at rest. And Da Jie's behavior helped her professionally as she strived for perfection. She was outstanding in Wen

Shan County. She started by being employed as a teacher in the primary school; later she became a teacher at the university and was greatly loved and esteemed by the students. One unexpected thing which happened in 1983 was that after 27 years of living like a dog with its tail between its legs, the price she paid gained her the greatest return. That year Yan Zu Yin, the first born of the Yan family, was chosen as a model woman of the People's Republic of China, and she went to Beijing to receive the commendation in the Great Hall. In China this is the top commendation for a woman who has both ability and political integrity.

Mama was a woman who was innately very traditional in the way she handled housework. She took great account of the Moon Festival and Chinese New Year each year no matter how strained our circumstances. When these two festivals were coming each year, she had to give our home a little festive atmosphere. For Chinese New Year, she always bought a bunch of camellias that were blooming and put them on the table at home. On New Year's Eve for dinner, the whole family would always have two traditional dishes, chicken and fried rice cake, which she cooked herself. For the Moon Festival, each of us would have a little piece of moon cake with some cooked chestnut and green soy bean which was nice and warm. We all sat around together and ate cheerfully. This was food that Kunming people used to have during the festival. She always tried by any means to let us to have a little bit without exception for many years. An interesting thing that happened at home was that no matter where Mama stored the food she prepared for the festival, it was always found by us hungry children, and we would take some of the food on the sly without being noticed before the festival began. I remember one year Mama had bought one kilogram of chestnuts. When she took them out to cook on the evening of the Moon Festival, she was surprised because there was less than half a kilogram of chestnuts in the bag. "Ai Yo, there are so many mice in our home; they ate almost all of my chestnuts!" Mama said, not knowing whether to laugh or cry. The person who had taken Mama's food on the sly was among us. We looked at each other with wide eyes and our tongues poked out. Each year on the second day of the Moon Festival when we got up, we would see some small pieces of moon cake in pretty wrapping on the table. Mama had placed them there and gave them to us for breakfast. The moon cake which was stuffed with ham and sugar was the tastiest, but it was too expensive to have in our festival. Usually, the moon cake we had was stuffed with sesame and sweetened bean paste of two kinds. On the second day of the Moon Festival, we had a little piece of moon cake in our hands as we went to school, and we always felt very happy. We ate the moon cake bit by bit and enjoyed it slowly because during the years we were growing up, we only had the chance to have breakfast a few times.

At these two traditional festivals, Mama would also take out a small memorial house which was made from wood with the memorial tablet of the Yan family's ancestors inside. It was hidden somewhere in the roof. She made offerings of water, wine and food, and burned incense, and then she prayed. She always prayed, "Souls in heaven, I am here now on behalf of Yan Ze Gao's family to offer sacrifices to you; bless all of us people on the earth with peace and safety. I pray that you will especially bless my two daughters, who are apart from me; bless them to have peace and safety. I thank you!" Mama believed that the human being has a spirit. Apart from believing in the Buddha in the temple, she also believed in the souls of the dead ancestors. She missed her two daughters who were not beside her each day; she had no other means to make these requests, other than to pray to those souls for help.

From my memory, after Da Jie and Er Jie left home to go to work in Wen Shan, we didn't have a family reunion on any of the Moon Festivals.

On the evening of the Moon Festival each year, with a bright moon in the sky, Mama would put some moon cakes, chestnuts, and green soy beans on the table, and she could never refrain from missing her two daughters who were not beside her. She often said, "Ai, I hope your older sisters are also eating the moon cakes Mama sent to them under the moonlight now; I hope both of them are together having a Moon Festival! Mama misses them very much; I hope there will be a year when the whole family can have a real family reunion during the Moon Festival!"

Sometimes, while she was speaking, her tears would flow......

Our mother existed for us. She had come into the world and lived in the world for her children. Her children were her center; her children were everything to her.

Naturally, the thing which made Mama the happiest was having all of her children beside her, and that only could happen at Chinese New Year. Because of this my two older sisters always planned their annual leave to be close to the Chinese New Year. They could stay home for 12 days. Only during these 12 days could all of us seven children be together with Mama and have a reunion dinner.

When the two older sisters were back home from Wen Shan, for the whole evening all five of us sisters always got together on very intimate terms with each other and chirped and talked without end. As Mama looked at her daughters one by one, her five daughters, each one looking like a flower blossoming to attract attention, she was really not willing that any of them should be apart from her. Her greatest hope was that they would all be around her every day. So, when two old sisters had to go back home, we rarely saw a smile on Mama's face; she also sighed with feeling again. "If our whole family could meet together every day like this, how wonderful it would be!" She often said.

During the years my two older sisters were not in Kunming, as soon as we received a telegraph to say they were coming, Mama would immediately organize us to sweep the rooms, clean the bedding, and prepare everything to welcome them back home. Usually all of us would start working together, using some old newspapers to repaper the ceiling and walls of our small room. And then someone would sweep the floor, and another would clean the windows; right away our small room looked brand new. As the time of their arrival drew closer, all of us brothers and sisters would go together to the train station to meet them. Mama would stay home and start to prepare the reunion dinner for the evening.

We met the older sisters and clustered around them, carrying their luggage home. When they shouted out, "Ma!" and held Mama's hand and warmly embraced her, it always made Mama extremely excited. Hand in hand, she looked at them carefully; she only saw them once a year. It often happened that when she was looking at them, her tears would flow because in a whole year, they could only spend these few days together. During their first days at home, she always talked with Da Jie and Er Jie until 2 or 3 o'clock in the morning. Da Jie and Er Jie were big girls now, about 20 years old, but when they were home, they still liked to sleep in the bed with Mama. Both older sisters thought the happiest time each year was when they could be close to Mama, snuggled up to her, sharing many of their secret thoughts with their dear mother. The unfair treatment they had received on the outside, the grievances and the difficult events which they could not resolve by themselves, they could now settle and thoroughly release. Mama was always a magnanimous and wise person; she always understood others and could solve problems with a sensible attitude and resolute action. Talking anything over with her would always result in objective guidance and a wise solution.

Therefore, despite the fact that my older sisters had left their home and relatives at a young age and had no care and advice from their father like other children, their personalities had developed in a healthy way, and their attitude towards work and life was always positive and optimistic. Their manner was well received by their colleagues.

"Mama has influenced us so much," they said, even still into their later years. However, back then, when they came home each year, they were always worried about Mama's health. They noticed that Mama's body was getting thinner and thinner, her hands which never rested had become so rough and inflexible, and her joints had become deformed. The older sisters saved some money and bought some "three seven" or "the root of three seven" which grew in Wen Shan and enriched the blood and sent it to Mama. (This is a Chinese herbal medicine, which only grows in Wen Shan county and has a growing period of three years and seven months, so it is called "three seven.")

"Mama works too hard. Mama is too thin. Mama has to have more rest; she needs to eat more and gain more weight," they often told Mama.

"It is because you are growing so fast; you are both tall and big. Compared to you, I look small. Mama is fine. You see, I am full of energy," Mama would answer.

During those years, some foodstuff including sugar and bean curd was rationed. Each person was only supplied with 200 grams per month. The staple food supply was also rationed, such as maize, potatoes, broad beans and pumpkin and so on. Eating rice was considered to be a luxurious big meal. However when the older sisters were home, Mama would try to make a table full of dishes every day and let all of her children have a good meal together.

And the dinner on Chinese New Year's Eve each year was the most memorable of "Mama's big meals," which can still make your mouth water to think of it even today. That day, the chicken Mama had raised for about one year would be killed. This was the main course for the family reunion, and this was the dish we all looked forward to each year. As the time drew closer to the New Year, we would think about this dinner every day. The smaller children were greedy, and as we stood near her, we watched Mama put the chicken into the earthenware dish to cook. Then, we all sat around the table silently and waited for the cooked chicken to appear.

Ai Ya, what a delicious dish that chicken was. We only ate it once a year with the whole family together; it was really unforgettable. Also for this dinner Mama would cook a cauldron of hotchpotch soup which Kunming people called "Chang Cai." It was a soup of different vegetables cooked together with chicken stock. It was quite strange; those vegetables were very common and eaten almost every day, but in the Chinese New Year when they were boiled in the chicken soup and eaten with all the people together, they were much tastier. Especially when it was cooked by Mama, we all enjoyed the meal so much; we could not find the right word to describe the feeling.

All of my brothers and sisters remember how in our childhood, the most anticipated date of the whole year was the Chinese New Year. Only then could the whole family meet together. We would have new clothes, and we always had some good food to eat.

However, after the Chinese New Year, the time for parting would come since the older sisters only had 12 days of time off. Mama really hated the time when her daughters would leave again. Each time they left, she always shed tears and would grieve for many days. As she started to put together the things for the older sisters to take with them, Mama's eyes were always red.

"Ai, I will not be able to see my two daughters each day. I will be deeply concerned for them and miss them day and night," she often said. When I was 10 years old, and saw Mama grieving, I always tried to console Mama and tell her not to worry about them, they had grown up. But Mama told me the following words, "I feel sorry for your older sisters, allowing them to leave home when they were so young to make money and to subsidize the family." She also said, "When you are grown up, you must remember to repay your older sisters. Without them sending money home, you younger brothers and sisters could never go to school."

Mama was troubled by the thought that her two daughters had been treated unfairly. She always wanted to do something more for them. Later, when both of them were married and gave birth to a child, Mama asked for leave to go to take care of them while they were in confinement. She was so careful and considerate with them.

In 1960, in the remote and small town of Wen Shan, Da Jie got married. Soon, her daughter Lan Lan and her son Le Le were born one after another. When the time was close for her to be confined, Mama asked for time off from her unit and carried many useful items and food which she had prepared. She went to Wan Shan alone. In the small room where Da Jie's family lived, they added a stretcher in the evenings, and Mama's figure started to busily shuffle back and forth.

They didn't have a kitchen, so Mama cooked for them on a small stove just by the door of the room. When Mama was making food there, the good smell attracted the admiring looks of the neighbors. Mama bathed the baby, took the utmost care of her, and taught my older sister with her example how to be a good mother. Da Jie said that while Mama was together with them, the pleasure she brought to them was more than that. While she was there on the weekend, she often asked Da Jie and her husband to invite all of the unmarried teachers to come to that small room and to eat a meal she had prepared. She knew that most of the teachers had come from different places. She said, "It is not easy for those young people to work in a place far away from their home and relatives;

while I am here, we should let all the people have a good time together." Even though they had limited resources, Mama still had the ability to make some special dishes for them to eat. While Mama was there, the small room was often crowded with guests. Mama's arrival helped to draw the relationship closer between Da Jie's family and her colleagues.

"Wherever Mama had been, she would leave her special perfume," Da Jie said. Of course the perfume she spoke of was not a fragrance Mama had on her body which people could smell. It meant Mama's personality and charm. It was true; wherever Mama left her footprint, "the fragrance" would be left there too. Although Mama had been to Wen Shan only two times, this harmonious relationship was built up there. Since then, Da Jie's family and colleagues from the school had a very good relationship. Afterwards, some of the colleagues had a chance to come to Kunming. They all came to No.7 An Ning Lane to visit Mama; they would never forget her.

Mama was a born mother; as soon as she saw a child, she would immediately have a beaming smile. As each new life in the Yan family came into the world, Mama devoted all her love to them. She reared 8 children, but she never complained about the hardship and travail of bringing us up. What she enjoyed and appreciated was the joy and pleasure of the process.

During the Cultural Revolution, I once went with Mama to the place where Da Jie and Er Jie were. Although the distance from Kunming to Wen Shan was only about 200 km, to get there was not easy back then. We first had to take the night train and stay in the crowded and noisy "hard seat" carriage for 10 hours. Then we had to change to a long distance bus and drive about 9 hours to get to Wen Shan. I don't know if there were any "hard sleepers" on the train, but even if there were, we didn't have the money to pay for them. I remember that evening as Mama and I got into the small train and put our things down. I could not suppress my tiredness, and at about 11 o'clock, I rested my head on Mama for a while. Then for a while I leaned on the chair and started to doze. During the night, the small train had to stop at five different train stations. People entered and exited, and actually no one could sleep.

As it was beginning to get light the next morning, the sound of the prelude "The East is Red" came from the loudspeaker, and a train attendant held a Chairman Mao's red book in his hand and stood right at the front of the train. He called out loudly for everybody to stand up. I was too sleepy to stand, so I still sat on the seat. Mama exerted all her strength to shake my shoulder and asked me to quickly get up. I stood up and saw that in the whole carriage all the passengers were already holding a small "red book" in their hands and standing in line to face the loudspeaker. All the people followed the tweeter together to sing the song "The East is Red," which all the Chinese knew. When the three verses were finished, the train attendant very seriously held the treasured red book up high, speaking loudly in a modulated tone, "Let us respectfully wish our very, very esteemed and beloved Chairman Mao a long life!" He didn't need to tell the people anything. All the men and women, old and young, in the carriage held the treasured red book up high like he did, and while waving it from left to the right, with one voice repeated his words, "A long life, a long life!" Then he spoke the second sentence slowly and at length, "Let us respectfully wish our very, very esteemed and beloved vice-commander Lin good health." All the people repeated the same action and followed his words with one voice, "Good health forever; Good health forever!" At that moment the train was going forward swaying and staggering. All of us with one hand holding high the treasured red book and with the other hand grasping each other, stood unsteadily with not even a tiny bit of a smile and automatically performed the ceremony of "asking for instructions in the morning," which would happen in every place, every morning in the whole of China. This is something everyone had to do during those years.

At 8 o'clock, we got off the train at a town called Kai Yuan. Mama and I carried our bags and ran to the bus station in a hurry; we had to catch up the bus that departed at 9 o'clock to go to Wen Shan. This time, Mama planned to go and visit both Da Jie and Er Jie, so she had prepared many things to bring with her, including pickles prepared in two pots, one for each of them. When we arrived at the bus station in the center of the town both of us were tired out. But we finally caught the bus. While we sat securely on the bus, Mama took out some solid food she had prepared at home, and we ate a small piece each. We arrived at Wen Shan at nightfall that day.

This was how we travelled to Wen Shan town. And back in 1965, because our family origin was not good, when another small town Guang Nan hospital needed medical personnel, Er Jie transferred to that place at once. This was a very small town which has not been developed; the living and working conditions were much more basic, and there wasn't even electric power there. To get there from Wen Shan involved a one day journey through the mountains; it was a very difficult trip. But Mama didn't care about this. In order to see her daughter, even if they could only spend a few days together, she faced any difficulties calmly.

In August of 1968, when her first daughter was only one and half years old, Er Jie had her second child in Guang Nan. At that time her husband worked in Kunming, so the family was separated in two places. She needed to go to work and to look after two babies, so the situation for her was very difficult. But Er Jie said that this time she did not expect Mama would come to her to take care of her in her confinement. With the Cultural Revolution going on then and the rebels having divided into different groups in order to safeguard their point of view, there were many military confrontations. Both far and near they were using force;

people were being killed everywhere, so to try to travel anywhere meant putting one's life in danger. And the public bus then had been stopped, so even if Mama wished to go, she could not do it.

But one evening Mama was presented to her like a raindrop from heaven.

"Ma..!" she could not believe her eyes, and after crying out, her tears started to flow.

Er Jie said Mama's arrival was really as though a savior had appeared to her because after she gave birth to her second son, she came down with an illness. And her first daughter had a fever so the three of them stayed together in a sickroom at the hospital. She was a patient and had two babies with her - one was sick, one was just born. In those days, she was struggling with this hardship with tears in her eyes. Just at that moment, Mama came.

"I knew it was impossible for any other person in the world to come to me at that time, regardless of danger and hardship." Er Jie said about this afterwards.

The relationship between Mama and her children was really like ten fingers joined together; so firmly did they depend on each other. She knew when her children had been wounded or had pain; she always had a premonition when her children were stuck in a difficult position, starving for help. She would then travel at double speed to be there without giving it a second thought.

That year, on the trip Mama took from Kai Yuan to Wen Shan, then from Wen Shan to Guang Nan, she experienced all of the hardships. She said she stood by the roadside, begging truck drivers again and again to allow her to hitch a ride on the canopy of the truck a bit of the way, and then hitching on another truck a bit of way, slowly moving to Guang Nan one step after another. For the last three hours of the trip, she sat on top of goods that were two meters high. She took hold of the ropes which bundled the goods together firmly and bumped along the mountain road; it was really not easy to finally get to Er Jie's place. She said there were fights in many places on the way with the sound of gunshots everywhere. "I was going to visit my daughter; my daughter is in trouble and needs help. God will bless me to get there safely," she told Er Jie.

Er Jie was very touched. Mama told her, "Mama is coming; while Mama is here, you do not need to be afraid of anything."

Yes, together with Mama, there was nothing to be afraid of. Er Jie's tears welled up like a fountain as if she was relieved of a heavy load. That year, their family of three fortunately received a timely salvation from Mama, and they all recovered day after day.

After taking care of Er Jie's confinement, Mama thought she should help Er Jie get through her difficult period, and she decided to bring the first baby to Kunming so she could look after her. Mama considered that because Er Jie was part of the medical affairs personnel, and she needed to take the night shift, having two babies with her would be difficult. She wanted to share the burden with Er Jie. Therefore, Jin Jia, Er Jie's first daughter, was taken to Kunming and grew up beside her grandmother from when she was one and half years old.

Three years later, so their whole family could be reunited, Er Jie and her husband were forced to each leave their working unit and to transfer to a small factory which produced sodium thiosulphates in Lu Quan County which is quite close to Kunming. It was a new small factory just starting production; the road had not been built, so to get to the factory meant hitching a ride on the public bus to get to the main road, then walking on a bumpy and narrow meandering footpath for more than one hour. And the housing the unit offered them was not really a proper house; it was just the temporary shed which used some asphalt felt and straw mats to make a partition, with asbestos as the roof. In this situation, Mama also often tramped over hill and dale to visit Er Jie's family and lived together with them in this very simple temporary shed. And in this type of room, Mama helped Er Jie deliver their third child into the world.

After Da Jie and Er Jie got married and had children, Mama insisted she didn't want them to send money home any more. Later, Si Jie and Wu Ge also found a job, so they were able to support themselves. Then we youngest three children still depended on Mama's income for our living expenses and tuition fees. So each time Mama asked for leave to go to visit the older sisters, she could only take about one week. Because she asked for "private affairs" leave, this would be deducted from her wages. When her income was reduced, life was hard to sustain. Despite only having a short leave from the work environment, which Mama didn't like but had no choice about, it always made her very joyful. We could see that after Mama came back home after meeting with the older sisters, she looked as if she had gained some weight and her mood was also better.

Er Jie was unlucky, and after a short time, something bad happened to her again. One evening the whole row of temporary sheds where they lived caught fire, and the people escaped from the fire safely, but all of her family belongings had suddenly melted into ashes. Er Jie was thrown into panic and confusion and ran back home to pour it out with Mama. Mama was as grieved as Er Jie. They wept together in each other's arms. At that time, to even purchase the basic articles for daily use was no doubt a huge expense for Er Jie who now had three children. Er Jie's life was suddenly in a woeful predicament. But how could they lift the gloom and resolve the problem? Mama was very calm while she was comforting Er Jie. She went off and bought some nice bowls and plates. She packed up some old things from home, and decided to bring those things back to that small hilltop with Er Jie to rebuild their home. She told Er Jie who had a worried look, "Crying helps nothing, life must keep going, your three kids need you, don't worry. Mama will help you to go through this difficult period. Let us restart!"

From not owning anything in the world, Mama helped Er Jie and her husband together to rebuild their shabby home.

To this day Er Jie has continued to use the bowls and the plates Mama gave to her. When she looks at them, it always brings to mind the calmness and staunchness Mama had then. Mama may not have realized that it was her love, as strong as a mountain, which she firmly and deeply gave to her children so many times built them up and helped them to rise up again from adversity.

THE STORY ON AN NING LANE
(1955–1970)

After we moved into No.7 An Ning Lane in 1953, it seemed that we were destined to take root there. All of us seven brothers and sisters spent most of our childhood and youth in that place. The courtyard, which looked more and more dilapidated, recorded our many stories.

In 1961 my older brother finished his studies in the middle school and was admitted to the high school which was affiliated with the Nationality University. The whole family was very happy when he received his admission notice, but our happiness was short-lived. The pressure of the tuition fee made our smiles vanish. Because this was a boarding school, it required the students to pay 18 Yuan for tuition and housing once a term. This was more than half of Mama's monthly salary. Ge Ge saw the anxiety behind Mama's smile, he also knew that he would need to pay this high tuition fee for the next three years, and he knew for sure that it would be very hard for Mama to bear. Even though it really grieved him, he still decided to abandon going to school. He thought he should find a job because this was the best way to help Mama.

Therefore, at only 15 years of age, Ge Ge started to work. The first job he found was as a storekeeper in a storehouse. Because of his intelligence and wisdom, very soon he was promoted to the position of price administrator in the Jin Zhi grocery store in Xiao Ba in Kunming. Naturally, as the eldest son of Yan Ze Gao's family, all the best hopes and desires his parents had for him, had now completely gone up in smoke.

As I have mentioned before, my older brother was the first son of my parents, and he was born in the year when our family was the most prosperous. From when he was born, he was looked upon as a pearl in their hands. As the eldest son of the parents, in a feudal and conventional family, he had received very special nurture and care from his childhood. He was the one on whom my parents had put their maximum expectations for a bright future, and he would inherit the family property. He was also naturally gifted and extremely intelligent.

After Dad died Mama continued to show him favor. As Ge Ge grew up day by day, Mama started to raise Ge Ge up to play the role of the father which this family had lost. "The eldest son serves as the father in our family," she would tell him. Ge Ge had taken the status of the father, and it was Mama who gave him this absolute authority. She taught all the girls, especially the brother and other sisters who were younger than Ge Ge, that they must be obedient to what he said even though Ge Ge was only 10 years old. No matter what happened at home, Mama always took great account of his opinion. Mama also did her best to give Ge Ge better food and clothing than the other children. All of this caused Ge Ge to become self-confident and arrogant, and even my oldest and second sisters who were many years older than him, often held him in awe and veneration.

The whole family had a bleak future, but in Mama's mind, the destiny of this son should be different from that of the other children. Now that Ge Ge had made his decision to abandon a more advanced course of study and to stride forward in a society that could barely provide enough to fill up his stomach and live, this doubled Mama's grief and disappointment. For Ge Ge to abandon his studies and to start work so young just like his two older sisters was the one thing Mama absolutely didn't want to see. When she saw that Ge Ge had resolutely and determinedly taken up his employment position, her emotions were filled with pain and remorse, and she had no peace, "Ai, destiny has forced me to be unable to let your brother go and study in the university! That

Mama could not bring up your brother to become a useful person is indeed something I will regret for the rest of my life. This son of mine, he was born for greatness. Ai, he is unlucky to be born at such a time! Don't say anything, only this one thing, I feel so sorry towards your father!"

For many years Mama continually said these words. This kind of abnormal favoritism she showed to Ge Ge, which was like a blind obedience to him, growing stronger and stronger and coming from the depths of her heart, showed in all Mama's words and deeds.

Once Ge Ge had a job, Mama made a decision that his younger sister and brother, who had shared a room with him up until then, should move into the small room she used; she wanted her "man" to have his own room. That year, she put in an application which was approved by the housing administration office. Mama hired some plasterers who removed one side wall and the roof of the room where she lived, and extended it about 2 meters in the direction of the small kitchen which was behind it. This space then became the place where she put her big bed. She now put a small bed for Di Di next to the window in her room, and the long table against the wall now became a bed for Liu Jie to sleep on. This room was now very crowded with the big bed and the small bed; there was no more space for anything else. Everyone was huddled together in one room just so Ge Ge could have a space all to himself.

The small room was emptied out and the brothers and sisters painted the wall, papered the ceiling, opened the window, and immediately that room became bright and neat. At the left of the entrance to the room, there was a mirror on the wall, and it was turned into a little dresser. A small bedside cupboard and a five drawer wardrobe were also moved in; the small room was decorated very nicely.

Ge Ge accepted the privileges Mama bestowed on him and felt very comfortable and deserving although he was only a little more than 15 years old. Perhaps the special treatment he had received since he was born had formed or influenced his personality. This eldest son of our family both in his appearance and in his heart was always filled with a kind of superiority and self-will without any kind of cowardice or sense of inferiority. Even in the situation where the family's economic status was quite bad, his speech and actions were still to stick out his chest and hold his head high. He never played with the dirty children in the lane. Whether he dealt with people of the same age or others from the neighborhood, he always presented himself in a commanding way to the public.

When he had a job, Ge Ge flaunted himself with a valiant appearance, striding as if he had indeed grown up and was on his way to do something special. Each morning, he wore a gray tunic and trousers that Mama had made for him and carried a grass green bag as he went to work in all seriousness. Before he went out, he would always stand in front of the mirror to freshen up, styling his hair like an adult and straightening his clothes. He had a manner that seemed as though nothing was worth a single glance from him as he walked down the lane; it made many people look at him with new eyes.

Each month when he was paid, Ge Ge bought more and more new clothes. At the head of his bed he fixed a pothook so he could hang up his clothes, and he used a beautiful gauze kerchief like a curtain to keep them in. He added some more things to his small room as well. A new single sheet was spread on his bed; there was a yellow towel which covered his pillow. On the dresser we started to see toothpaste, a new toothbrush, fancy soap and cold cream. He had his own facecloth and washbasin. Soon, his room also had a phonograph, radio, and plastic flowers in a vase. The cement ground now had a wooden floor. This small room was changed into a higher and higher level. There was a great disparity between his room and the room where we lived. If we, his younger brother and sister, wanted to "enjoy" the life of that room, we could only do it when he was not home. Then we could enter the room and sit in the chair for a little while or lie down for a few minutes on the bed which belonged only to him and was very comfortable. Mama told us clearly that Liu Jie had to take charge of washing all Ge Ge's clothes and bedding, and cleaning his room was my duty. Ge Ge's small room was very neat; there was not a speck of dust anywhere.

Ge Ge had high aspirations in his mind. He believed that by depending on his capacity our family's situation would change bit by bit. It was true very soon as his position and rank were adjusted, and he received 30 Yuan in wages per month, just as much as Mama's. Apart from improving his living conditions, he also used his income to buy some new appliances for our home. The second porcelain enamel washbasin we had was bought by Ge Ge. We didn't have toothpaste for years; now sometimes Ge Ge also would buy some for us. He not only helped Mama materially, but the more important thing was that he presented himself with the image of a dignified man in the eyes of the people.

Another man from the Yan family had finally grown up. Looking at Ge Ge's figure brimming with confidence and youthful vigor, Mama's face started to smile. At dinner time she would cook some dishes which were Ge Ge's favorite. Then, waiting for Ge Ge to come back home, the whole family would have a meal together. At the table, the logical seat for Ge Ge was of course opposite Mama. That was always how it was; nobody would take those seats. After Ge Ge had come home from work while the whole family was eating together, the most pleasurable thing for Mama was the time when all of us would listen to Ge Ge tell of what he had seen and heard on the outside and the things that had happened in his unit. Mama would look at her eldest son full of expectation and satisfaction. After dinner the rest of us would stand up and tidy up the dining table or go to wash the dishes, and because Ge Ge didn't need to do any of those things, he would always naturally sit with Mama at the table. After a little while Liu Jie or I would offer them tea, one cup of hot tea for each of them, putting it in front of them on the table. For many years this became the natural custom in our home. The status Ge Ge enjoyed and the way he carried himself showed that he was indeed the elder member of our family.

When Ge Ge started to work, Liu Jie was 14 years old. She studied in the 24th suburban middle school. She lived at the school and only came back home for weekends on Saturday evening. I was 10 years old, and Di Di was 8, and we were both studying at the Jing Xin primary school. Each month after Ge Ge got his wage, he bought some candy or something to throw to me and Di Di. We really enjoyed that day as if it were a festival. Sometimes, he gave one jiao (1/10 of yuan) to each of us. We would quickly go and buy a new pencil or exercise book; in our hearts we were full of appreciation. My impression was that Ge Ge was always serious in his speech and manner; his apparel and his style of conversation were sanctimonious. He really did not look like someone from the same generation as us, but he looked more like "the strict father" in our family. Sometimes Di Di did not study hard and his speech and actions were lazy, so his school results were not good, and his character was weak. I don't know how many times he was rebuked by Ge Ge. To be honest, we were all a bit afraid of Ge Ge.

During the summer season one year, we three younger siblings all stayed home for our summer vacation. One day at nightfall all of a sudden, Ge Ge brought home a big schoolbag full of Iraqi dried candied jujubes. He poured many of them out on the table and said to us with a smile, "Come, come, just eat as much as you like."

For many years because the economic situation had not been good in our family, we almost never had any money to buy any kinds of snacks. In my childhood, the only food I had to nibble between meals was white sugar. I would beg Mama to give us some sugar and put it into a used match box and bring it to school. When I would put a little bit into my mouth and suck on it slowly, the day would seem very joyful. Now Ge Ge said we could eat this Iraqi dried candied jujube, which we had never eaten before, as much as we liked. How happy we were! All three of us immediately sat around the table and started to eat. We ate it for about an hour and really ate too much. There was not much left, but we brought it to the school the next day and continued to eat. Three days later, Ge Ge brought another schoolbag of Iraqi dried candied jujube for us to eat again. We ate Iraqi dried candied jujube every day for about a week. I don't think many people have eaten that much candied jujube in their whole lives. It was a record for us three children to have eaten so many sweet things in such a short time since we were born.

We asked Ge Ge afterwards why he brought so many candied jujubes home for us to eat, and he told us the truth. It was because they had been piled up in the storeroom of their shop too long and they were out of date, so, as the price administrator, Ge Ge ordered the shop leader to quickly sell them at reduced prices. But after many days they were still not sold out, so, they dealt them out to the employees at a very low price. Ge Ge also got two bags, so this allowed us to have the experience

Er Jie and Si Jie in 1969.

of eating Iraqi dried candied jujubes extravagantly that summer. After many years had passed whenever I saw Iraqi dried candied jujubes, immediately, I would remember this experience, and since then I never liked this food anymore because we ate too, too much that summer.

In 1964, Si Jie finished her middle school studies. She attended an accounting training course and then found a job in a farm machinery factory at Cheng Gong County 20 km from Kunming. It was the same as our older siblings; she also went to work when she was less than 18 years old. The gift Mama gave her to take to the place where she would settle down was some cotton wadding, the color of which had turned into gray and black. It was old cotton wadding which we had used for more than 10 years at home, and it was also the only thing Mama could find at home to give to Si Jie.

Mama watched Si Jie walk out of the gate with tears in her eyes, seeing another of her daughters, as beautiful as a flower, now also entering society and leaving her to go to another place, made her feel sad and unstable. "Mama feels so sorry for you; I could not give you anything nice," she told Si Jie. "Next year when I have saved enough money, I will make some new cotton batting for you. Right now two of your younger sisters and your younger brother are still studying at school. You need to forgive Mama."

No, Mama didn't have money to buy anything for Si Jie because back then Liu Jie had gone to study at the Chemical Technical Secondary School, I had gone up to the Kunming Girls Middle School, and Di Di was still in primary school. The expense of the tuition fees for the three of us was still a big economic burden for Mama. Ge Ge and Si Jie could get their wages each month, and they could support themselves, so it had lifted some of the burden from Mama, but she was still unable to relax. To get her salary, even though it was only a little, she had to go to work every day.

My older sister Si Jie was a very kind person with a sense of filial duty. The year of Dad's death, she was only 8 years old. She wanted to help Mama financially, and every evening after school, she would go out and push a cart for the people who were hauling coal. She would run after the cart, and when it went uphill she used all her energy to push it. Each night the length of the road she had to run on was about 10 km, so she always

When Si Jie started to work.

came home around 1 or 2 o'clock in the morning. With black face and clothes she would hold the 2 Jiao she had earned in her hands and give it to Mama. Because she didn't get enough sleep, she always fell asleep while she studied in her class the next day. Mama would not allow her to continue doing it, so she had to stop. So right now, she carried her very simple luggage and registered in her unit in Cheng Gong. She understood Mama's difficulty. She never complained to her; instead, she just wanted to show her consideration for Mama and to care for her.

The accounting position Si Jie had in that factory introduced her to some of the cadres from the organized body and the farmers from the countryside who wanted to buy agricultural machinery. During that time those products were not easy to buy; the quantity which was produced and sold was limited. People who wanted to buy those products tried to get "back door" deals and would send some special local products to her. This was really a great thing which we could never have imagined.

When Si Jie got those gifts, the first person she thought of was Mama. After work she carried the things and ran to the bus station to come to Kunming. At nightfall Si Jie often appeared at home unexpectedly carrying a basket in her hand full of fresh melons and fruit or fish and goat's cheese. Mama was very delighted when she saw those things. Sometimes she would immediately go to the kitchen and cook it, and the whole family would eat together joyfully. Sometimes when Si Jie got back home, it was too late, and she didn't catch dinner time. At about 9 o'clock, Mama would go to the kitchen to busily cook something. When we finished our homework, before we went to bed, the "night snack" Mama had prepared would be put on the table. Each child always got a share. How excited we were, and we would use both hands to hold the bowl and enjoy the food so much.

In those years all foods were rationed, and we often had rumbling empty stomachs and were too hungry to sleep. In our family, not only did we have an older sister of Mama's who sometimes sent something to us from the countryside, now, unexpectedly, we had those treasured things from Si Jie. Some of these were things we hadn't dared to think about in the past 10 years and were very costly, like fish and goat's cheese. But right then they had inconceivably appeared on our dining table, and each of our family members ate those foods, full of gratitude. Mama often said with a smile, "Ai, we are benefiting from you, Si Jie; this is an additional blessing god has given to our family. We really have good luck!" Mama was very happy; she felt so happy that Si Jie had found a nice job.

We knew that the place where Si Jie worked always had good food to eat. On the weekends, Mama would take us younger three and go to Cheng Gong to spend a day there. Er Yi Ma also went there with us sometimes. We would have a local meal in the home of a peasant Si Jie knew. We would go to the countryside market or go to the village close to the Dian Chi lake to sit for a few hours and then go back to Kunming in the evening.

During those years, it seemed that the State had started to resume the economy. The peasants opened up some small pieces of the wasteland for themselves to plant some vegetables, which they later sold in the city. A few free markets began to quietly appear in Kunming. I felt that Mama and all of her children had a bit of physical and mental relief for a while. The dimension and scope of the political movement was much smaller than before. For example, the "Four Purges Movement" of 1963 – 1966, which was a socialist education campaign to overhaul the fields of politics, ideology, organization and economy, was mainly carried on in the countryside, so there was nothing that affected us. The economic situation of our family was much better than before, and our family circumstances were going in a better direction. But whenever we had a big expenditure, Mama still did not have enough money to pay for it since her monthly salary was only 42 Yuan.

The National Day Parade was the most important event for the people of China. As students, on the first of October each year, we had to attend the parade. According to regulations, we had to attend the parade wearing specified unified clothing; with this we could not be careless. For many days the school required everyone to wear this clothing and attend dress rehearsals. Where could Mama find so much money to buy these special "actor's costumes" for us each year? We were always in an embarrassing position when we attended the parade. When I think about it, I still feel like laughing. We all had a white shirt as this was the most basic dress requirement. Of course we begrudged wearing it, always having to fold up it nicely and put it aside and preserve it year after year, only using it when there was some important celebration activity. We were getting taller and taller, but the white shirt was still the same one. Finally, the shirt was too short and too small to wear. When we wore it, no matter how we pulled it on, the buttons could not reach the button holes on the other side. We used some small pieces of tie to link the button and button hole together, and then would wear a red scarf (the sign of the Young Pioneers in China that all school children wore every day) to "cover" this secret at the front of the shirt. But the sleeves could not be covered up; often they only covered half of our arms. It didn't matter. We still wore it. So wearing this white shirt looked stupid and very funny. As if this was not bad enough, at the same time, according to the regulations, in order to attend the National Day parade, we also needed to wear black trousers and shoes. Normally, we always wore black trousers so it was easy to make do even if we needed to put some patches on them. The shoes were the big problem for us. The shoes we wore were made by Mama, and we had only one pair of shoes per year, and the color was not always black. The pair of shoes we used from the beginning of the year to October was already broken, and our toes were showing. Therefore, when the time drew closer to the National Day, we tried with all our might to save money and pestered Mama to get a little bit from her, hoping to buy one pair of the "necessary cloth shoes" which were specially made for the parade and very popular then. "Luckily" we were all able to wear these kinds of shoes. They cost 5 Jiao for one pair and looked fine, but the quality was so poor since the soles of the shoes were made of one layer of strawboard. We put our feet into these shoes, walked from Dong Feng Road to the reviewing stand, looked at the leaders who were sitting on the rostrum jump and leap for joy, then walked to the building where the department store was, and then the shoes' usefulness was finished. We would feel the soles of the shoes and the upper part start to slowly come apart as we kept on walking to Xiao Si Men where the parade stopped. By then the whole sole of the shoes had completely disintegrated, and we didn't know where they were; only the upper part of the shoes still covered our feet. Ai, now what could we do? There was no choice at that moment. Still wearing these special shoes that nobody knew had no soles, we limped along the street with only one thought in mind which was to hurry home. The whole distance of the National Day Parade was about 5 km; it finished at noon, and to walk barefoot on the dirty and boiling hot road was not like walking in the water barefoot on a rainy day. The feeling we had, this kind of suffering, only we ourselves really knew.

Anyway, we still grew up day after day, although each of us looked as emaciated as a fowl. Mama gratefully had no diseases. Only sometimes she caught a cold, so she boiled some Chinese traditional medicine to drink, and she recovered. Mama often met Er Yi Ma, and the topic those two talked and talked about most was their children. Now Er Yi Ma's two children would have to start finding a job sooner or later. Her eldest son who was very intelligent was praised by my older brother. After he finished his high school studies, he found a job in a chemical plant. He was a clever and handsome young man, but the job he was appointed to do was to burn the boiler. The second son "Du Du" had a talent in art, and he painted very well. He took the examination for the Yunnan Art University two times, but as a result of the class status of his family, he was not accepted. This sensible boy gave up his interests and found a job in a primary school and went to work quietly. Er Yi Ma knew the reason her two sons had to step into society so early, and she always sighed with regret for the fate of her two sons.

"Oh, we have suffered so much, is it not enough? The kids have no chance to develop themselves, at such a young age; they are living in depression. Thinking about this makes me feel sad."

"That all our family members are safe is our blessing; we have to learn to force ourselves to straighten out our thinking." Mama often comforted Er Yi Ma in this way. Listening to the two mothers' conversation, we hoped we could grow up quickly. We wished we could have a job at an early age just like our older brother and our sisters. We wished we could support ourselves and let Mama relax a little bit. At that moment, this was the biggest desire in our minds for we three were still minors.

But in Mama's mind, she never wanted us to go to work in a hurry. There was a secret concealed in her mind. That was, she still hoped that in our family we would have at least one university student. Mama often said, "Your Dad was a 'name brand' university student, and he also studied abroad. Among all of your brothers and sisters, we should have at least one person go to study at the university; it would be worthy of your Dad. No matter how difficult, I am willing to support a university student for the Yan family." Then, she placed this hope on me because since I had begun my studies in the primary school, my achievements had been excellent. Study for me was always a very easy thing to do. If the political situation in China did not expand and turn terribly to the left, perhaps, Mama's desire could have become true.

But, when I had just started studying in the second grade of the middle school in the summer of 1966, nobody knew what was happening in the superstructure of the political circles of China. Mao Ze Dong flared up and initiated an "unprecedented proletariat cultural revolution and demanded to seize power from those in power who were taking the capitalist road within the party." However, this "revolution," this internal turmoil in the land of China, lasted 10 years from start to finish. The people who were involved in it and fell under attack and persecution were not only the capitalist roaders within the party. The later leader of the Communist party of the China Political Bureau, Ye Jian Ying, made an admission of fact in the central working conference and summed up the Cultural Revolution on the 13th of December in 1978. He said, "During the Cultural Revolution, including the people to be implicated internally, there were more than a hundred million people who fell victim; it accounted for 1/9 of the population of the whole country." (Note: this number was according to the nationwide population then).

This political movement engulfed the whole of the nation. All the people no matter if they were men or women, old or young, all participated in it. The life of Chinese people had only just become a little calmer in a way; this caused the big wave to surge again.

Under the social ideological guidance of "the class struggle was the guiding principle." People like us who were born in the "black" family were always the first target of attack when each political movement came. In school, the movement started with the first step of checking the class status of the family you came from according to your permanent residence booklet. According to the principles of the famous slogan: "If the father is a hero, the son is a hero. If the father is a reactionary, the son is a reactionary." They would ferret out enemies and friends based on their blood line. The class status of my family was recorded by my father's position of "industry and commerce" on the residence booklet. Just the day after I registered, I was labeled as "the black puppy of the capitalist," and I was moved to another seat on the right side of the classroom. That year, all of my classmates were about 15 years old. I don't know whose idea it was, but they thought the students who came from a red family should sit on the left side of the classroom (this stood for leftists), and the students who came from a general family could sit in the middle of the classroom, and students like me who came from a black family should sit on the right side in the classroom (this stood for rightists). Separating where we sat made it easy to differentiate between enemy and friend just by looking. Each class rearranged their seats, and it was the same in the whole school. (Note: In China, during Mao's time from 1949 - 1979, the person who was born in the family where the father was a worker, a peasant or an army member was regarded as coming from a good family. The person who was born in the family where the father was a capitalist, a landlord, a counterrevolutionary, an evildoer or a rightist was regarded as coming from a bad family. The person who was born in the family where the fathers did not belong to either of the above two families was regarded as coming from a general family.)

It was only a few days later that Bai Zu Shi, the principal of the No. One Girls School was exposed as a reactionary gang member, and he was forced to wear a tall paper hat (worn as a sign of humiliation), and sent away under escort onto the stage to accept repudiation by a girl who was a Red Guard from the High School. Because of the articles in the "People's Daily," the students learned that the school was controlled by "the capitalist intelligentsia," and now it was the time to throw them down to "beat them down on the ground, and to set foot on them!" Those young people with restlessness and violence in their blood were very easy to incite. Right now, they were bearing the brunt of it, and they started to charge and shatter the enemy positions to safeguard Chairman Mao.

In my class, only 6 students were classed as being from a "black" family. Each day when we entered the classroom, we sat on the right side leaning against the wall, sad and solitary, and we felt very much embarrassed. All the classmates in our class had previously played together cheerfully. Now all of a sudden, we were divided into opposing groups and were enemies with each other. We did not dare to talk and play together carefreely anymore. In the beginning, not only me, but even those who were born into a red family and had put on the red sleeve covers to become "red guards," were not able to adapt to this straight away. After the class, some would still talk with us "black puppies" for a while. We were too young to understand why we had to separate into two kinds of people like this. But the seed, "our treatment of the enemy must be like the severe winter, unfeeling and cold-blooded," which Mao Ze Dong had sown for many years, at that moment adapted itself to the circumstances immediately. The situation was pressing, and very soon, indeed it was very soon, all the people, either positively and on their own initiative, or negatively and passively, had come to accept the role they were supposed to play. Before, the classroom would be cleaned by all the classmates in turns. Now the red guards declared publicly that from now on this physical labor should be done by the 6 black puppies every day. This was because they needed "to betray their reactionary families and to rebuild and become a new person." And the physical labor was only a part of our re-education. After the class every day, we had to report to the Red Guard in our class on what we had been thinking about that day; this was the most important part of the ideological reconstruction. Since this Cultural Revolution was the "great revolution to touch people's souls," we black puppies must expose the dirty thinking in our innermost soul, and let everybody help and retrain us. At the beginning, when we reported what we had been thinking about during the day, we were negligent, had a little smile and grimaced. We were just teenage girls; what could we be thinking about in our minds each day? So, when we talked with them we were careless. But as the punishment showed our attitude was not proper, we would be helped by a group criticism meeting. When the black puppy was receiving criticism by others, you had to sit in the middle among the group members just like a defendant surrounded by the people. And when the meeting started, you had to say the following words first, "I am the black puppy of the capitalist; I am the son of a bitch. I am willing to receive all your criticism." Certainly, nobody could have an easy mood any more. And then, the classmates started to criticize you one after another. They departed from a little girl's normal gentleness and softness in former days; they would deride and hurl invectives at you with animated gestures. The movement had just begun a few days earlier, yet they had all changed into different people and seemed as though they had received some training; each of them was very serious. From this I have realized one principle which is: human beings are easy to change. In our class, those who were born in a good and glorious family had a Red Guard sleeve-cover on their arm; one day they appeared like this. They were asked to the Red Guard headquarters of the school to have a meeting, making it clear what they should do, and when they came back to the classroom, they talked to us with arms akimbo in an awe-inspiring manner. We, the people born into a bad family, were now certainly clear and definite that at that moment we had become the "object of ridicule" in our class. We did not dare to laugh, we did not even dare to speak, and when we entered or left the classroom, we hung our heads. When we were sitting in our own seats and thinking about how we would spend this day, we trembled with fear. Oh, even though so many years have passed, when I recollect those days, I still have the feelings of those very terrible times. And one thing I feel is even more pitiful is that at this very young age we were filled with hatred for each other because of this man-made movement. Because from then until now, these two kinds of classmates who were divided as "red" and "black," never had contact with each other any more.

The middle school where I studied was a girl's school; however, the manner of dictatorship that these Red Guard girls exerted was very cruel, and they were by no means inferior to any other middle school. For instance, when they had finished the meeting where they accused and denounced the reactionary gang of the principal, they went after the former dean of studies of the school and the teachers who were born in "bad" families. They would compel them to hang a heavy blackboard in front of their chests and to stand in line under the burning sun for many hours in succession. They themselves were hidden under the shade of a big tree, laughing and joking. They held a leather belt in their hands and in order to show their power, at intervals whipped it on the ground straight from the shoulder; the noise was everywhere. We could see from a distance that those teachers were baking and sweating profusely, big beads of sweat dripped and fell at their feet. One day, one of the oldest women teachers was so hot that she fell in a faint on the ground.

Formerly I loved singing and often sang in the theatrical festivals of the school. One day, the Red Guard leader in my class officially declared in the class meeting that I was not allowed to sing anymore. She pointed at me using her finger and said, "Your body is flowing with the blood of the bourgeoisie; therefore, your singing is also the bourgeoisie's; it is dirty. Previously, when we sent you to perform on behalf of our class, it was simply the shame of our class. Actually, you did not deserve to have this right; you were not qualified to sing at all…" and so on. After the speech, she asked me severely, "Yan Ling Ling, will you obey this?"

I stood up and answered her, "I will obey; from today I am not going to sing any more."

Every morning I had to go to the school early to clean the classroom, and to sit on the right side alone to have class. After class I was not allowed to play and talk with the other classmates; before I went home I had to report what I had been thinking that day, and now with this announcement, I was not allowed to sing. In those days, I didn't like to go to school any more, or I could say that I was so afraid to go to school. On the way to the school, I often did nothing but cry. When I walked alone to school I always moved slowly. One evening I told Mama what had happened in school, Mama was very sad, she said, "Utterly devoid of conscience! You are just a child; why can't they let you off? You are 15 years old, and you never even had one pair of presentable shoes. You grew up steeped in Mama's tears; you were always unable to get something to eat; and you were always unable to have warm clothes. What bourgeoisie? You have nothing to do with the matter!"

Yes, before the Cultural Revolution came, I never had a pair of presentable shoes. I remember when I was 12 years old, the teacher from the children's "after school sports school" came to Jing Xin primary school to select a person with sports ability. They chose me and asked me to go to train in gymnastics in the sports school. I went there only two times and gave up because I did not have a pair of gym shoes. That day I wore a pair of "sandals," which had several pieces of worn corduroy sewed onto a broken rubber sole by Si Jie, to report for duty at the sports school. When I was practicing running to warm up with my other teammates, in less than 10 minutes, my shoes had broken into fragments. I threw them off and persisted in running in bare feet, but the teacher did not allow me to do that and, I had no choice but to go back home, my eyes brimming with tears.

When I was studying in the middle school, there was a swimming pool in the No.1 girl's school, and the physical education class sometimes had swimming. But I could only sit hopelessly by the pool and look at the other classmates enjoying the water, since I did not have money to buy a swimsuit. During the years that I was growing up, even in the severe cold, I always wore a single garment throughout the winter. I have worn a thick garment only once; it was when I was 14 years old that I had the chance to wear some old silk and cotton padded clothes which belonged to Mama that she had worn for over twenty years. That year, Ge Ge used his savings of many months and bought one knitted sweater for Mama, and Mama gave these thick clothes for me to wear because the winter that year was very, very cold. Because it was in the old people's style and color, when I wore it I was ridiculed by my classmates. I could relate many more pitiable things from the years when I was growing up, such as the only fruit I ever ate was tomato. I never had any toys. When I studied in primary and middle school, I never had a formal schoolbag; the bag I used to put the things in for the class was a string bag which my older sisters weaved with some plastic belts. I often could not afford 2 fen to buy a pencil; the length of the pencil was only a few centimeters and too short to hold, but I still used it. Many times, while I was singing and

standing on the stage, my voice was sweet and my actions were graceful, but I never had a set of presentable clothes. I was always the shabbiest person among all of the little players. It was not only my tattered clothes; often I didn't have shoes on my feet. I stood on the stage in bare feet...
I really had nothing in my life. The life which I experienced could have been considered the life of the poorest child in the slum. What connection did I have with the "bourgeoisie" which we had heard of and which is described in the book?

The situation was the same throughout the whole nation; by reason of the class status of their family, thousands upon thousands of children came under unfair treatment. The revolution was just starting. Even if we were completely unwilling, no-one dared not to go to school. If you were absent from class and stayed home, it was tantamount to resisting the proletariat cultural revolution; nobody could bear this kind of accusation. Thus, every day I still went to school sulkily. One day, on my 15th birthday, something happened which I will never forget. On that day, I was called out to rise up and stand in the center to accept criticism once more; they put their chairs in a circle and completely surrounded me. The central issue of the meeting was to make me spell out what I really thought about being a "black puppy" lately, as they had found out that I had recently had a worried look on my face, and they were sure that I was "pleading not guilty in the mind."

While I was hanging my head to accept the severe criticism and rebuke by my classmates one after another, I had to say to them over and over these words which I uttered against my conscience, "I was not pleading 'not guilty,' I was a little afraid. Henceforward, I am willing to struggle against selfish ideas and personal considerations to repudiate the revisionist trend. I am willing to utterly draw a demarcation line with my bourgeoisie family, receive the supervision of all of the classmates, and take a stand on the Chairman Mao's revolutionary line." After class,

I did indeed plead not guilty. I sighed with regret for my fate in my mind again and again, and I wrote down one sentence in my Chinese book: "Lackaday! My 15th birthday!" But when I came home with a long face, I received a bowl of delicious noodles to celebrate my birthday from Mama. Mama always remembered each child's birthday. No matter what kind of circumstance we were in, on that day each year, every child would get a birthday blessing from her. That day, when I saw Mama's smiling face, when I held the birthday gift from Mama with both hands, I exhorted myself not to tell Mama about anything that had happened at the school.

On that same day, as the people in the world treated me with two kinds of attitudes which were so completely different, it made me grow up instantly, and I became sensible. I told myself that for the sake of my love for Mama, from now on I must learn to face tribulation and frustration by myself, alone. I must be as brave as my other brothers and sisters and let Mama have her heart at rest with everything and not worry about me.

Just like me, Liu Jie and Di Di also came under the same unfair treatment; they also had to wear the "black puppy" label and also went to school with deep feelings of grief each day. They also had to accept the treatment and re-education which was different from their classmates of the same age.

One day at the end of 1966, all of us of the "black puppy" class at the No. 1 Girls' School had to form a line and were taken to another middle school. Together with the principal and the teachers who had been exposed and criticized at our school, we had to walk to the other middle school to attend an outdoor meeting to "contrast our past misery with the present happiness." When the meeting started, some Red Guards went up on to the stage one after another, narrating the life of the working class people in the old society in tearful voices, as well as the extreme hardships and difficulties the Red Army had gone through on the "long march." In a corner of the playground, a group of Red Guards set up a cooking range, and started to cook something in a cauldron. They said these were the things that the Red Army had eaten when Chairman Mao led them across the grasslands. They put some grass roots and bark into the cauldron. Suddenly one Red Guard said that during the most difficult time the Red Army even ate their leather belts and leather shoes. Immediately some people took off their belts and shoes and threw them into the cauldron. They added more firewood and brought this "soup" to the boil. At first I thought that this process was just to illustrate what had happened back then and to educate all of us. Unexpectedly, when the meeting was over, one Red Guard loudly proclaimed, "All the "black puppies" and the people who have come to be criticized in this meeting today must drink a bowl of this soup which was just boiled in the cauldron." She said, "Doing this will teach you bourgeoisie nobles and reactionaries a lesson and will let you know that the victory of the revolution was hard-won. We don't need to drink this soup; we, the descendants of the proletariat revolutionary, shall "never forget the proletariat suffering and will keep tears of blood and hatred firmly in our minds."

When she had finished speaking, the Red Guards cried out loudly, "Rise up, stand up, go, go and get yourself this soup!" Without any complaints or resistance, those teachers who were wearing the tall paper hats on their heads and white sleeve covers on their right arms were the first to go obediently to the cauldron and take a bowl of the soup and drink it. When the teachers had finished drinking and sat down, it was the turn of the "black puppies" from each school. We lined up one after another and got a bowl of black soup with grass roots and leaves floating in it. Without excuse, I drank that muddy soup which was very difficult to swallow.

That evening, although I hung my head and went home with a heavy heart, I didn't relate the things that had happened that afternoon to anyone. My habit now was that, no matter what happened to me, things which formerly I would always tell Mama, I now had learned to handle patiently by myself.

Fortunately, this kind of life only lasted for half a year. At the beginning of 1967, all the schools in the nation actively responded to the call of the party and "suspended classes in order to carry out the revolution." The Red Guards in each school now no longer paid attention to us "black puppies" and the "reactionary" gang at the school. They wanted to create a bigger revolution in the community. When we heard the news of the suspended classes, we were incomparably happy because we no longer needed to go to school feeling dejected and to be the "black puppy" or have to report our thinking each day. Despite this, in all the public places and shops, including the barbershops on the street, big slogans were now seen with words like: "Proletariat, please come in! Bourgeoisie, get away!" But we were not afraid any more. Our faces didn't show what family we came from. If it only depended on the clothes we had on we could pass ourselves off as the proletariat really easily, no problem at all. We often went out into the street to watch all the excitement along with the other people. We saw there were some people who had long hair, wore narrow pants and cusped leather shoes being taken down by the Red Guards from the street. They were forced by the Red Guards to cut their hair short, to cut off their narrow trouser legs and to take off their leather shoes and hold them in their hands. Day after day, there were more and more people on the street wearing the grass green army uniform that Chairman Mao wore and which had been promoted in the newspaper lately. Even if they only had one set of this clothing to pull on, it meant that they were one of "the Leftists," how awe-inspiring they were!

Following closely behind the factories, enterprises throughout the whole country also began to participate in this revolutionary movement. Many different factional organizations with various names suddenly appeared in the streets and lanes of Kunming with big signs which read "xxx Revolutionary Rebel Headquarters" or "xxx Red Guard Headquarters." Under the verbal command from the top captain Chairman Mao that "Revolution is impeccable, insurgency is right," the Red Guards started to do whatever they wanted to. The exercise called "breaking with four old, setting up four new" took the lead in revolutionizing the whole nation. In the newspaper the "breaking with four old" was interpreted by the government as breaking with the old culture, old customs, old habits, and old thinking. But in Kunming the breaking of the first of the "four old" was catastrophic when the Red Guards destroyed the two most beautiful and famous pieces of architecture - the Memorial Gateway of the Golden Horse and the Blue-Green Chook. These two big wooden gateways, with their 400 year history and their carved beams and painted rafters, stood high on Jin Bi Road, but in one evening some Red Guard girls poured gasoline on them and lit them up as they laughed merrily. That evening, there were hundreds of stupefied Kunming citizens standing beside them just looking at them melting slowly into ashes and finally falling down with a loud crash…nobody dared to say a word. Because our home was only several hundred meters from Jin Bi Road, I ran to the scene and witnessed with my own eyes as these two nice gates were burned and were irretrievably destroyed by fire.

If such a valuable building could be burned so suddenly, what else could not be burned? In all the streets and lanes people would see scenes of fires during the days and in the evenings, old style furniture, old books, foreign literature books, anything which was stained with "feudalism, capitalism, revisionism" or that belonged to the "four old,"

The Memorial Gateway of the Golden Horse and the Blue-Green Chook in Kunming.

were all thrown into the fire and consumed by the flames. The Beijing opera had been regarded as the quintessence of China, but now it was criticized and was called the tool which sang the praise of the emperor and generals. The theatrical costumes and stage properties, all those brightly colored things, were burned in a big fire. Not only were there fires on the street, people were burning things in their gates both in the day time and at night. Because the newspaper and the Red Guards were calling on people to sweep the "four old" away from their consciousness, each family had to take their old things and burn them themselves. If they did not do so, it meant you had a grudge against the movement and it would give you big trouble. We saw how families had their houses searched and their property confiscated by the Red Guards in the streets and lanes of Kunming. Some of their property was taken away by tricycle by the Red Guards. Some of their things were just piled up by the gates of their houses where they were set on fire and burned in front of the owners. This movement was bearing down menacingly. Our narrow An Ning Lane was also filled with firelight. Each family quickly cleaned out the articles from their home, everything which was considered to even slightly touch on the "four old," such as old books, calendars which had beautiful girls on them, Chinese calligraphy and paintings which before had hung on their walls, gramophones, nice clothing with decorative patterns, tables and chairs with carved dragons or phoenixes, and so on, and so on. Many, many different things now were all put into the fire at the gates of their houses. In this way they notified that they had actively responded to the call of the communist party and Red Guards. One evening Mama not only burned the little wooden house which had the ancestral memorial table in it, but afterwards, with tears in her eyes, she put her stage costumes into the fire, those nice clothes she had treasured up for nearly 30 years.

"No, it is impossible to wear them again, it is impossible! Burn them away, burn them away." Mama was frightened and said this over and over, sighing with emotion. Just that same day in the afternoon, she had seen for herself that Guan Su Shuang and Xu Min Chu, the two most famous players of the Beijing opera in Yunnan, had both had half their heads shaved, and wore a few chi (3 chi =1 meter) tall paper hat as they were paraded and denounced at a meeting on the street. Right on the street, a pile of their beautiful and inimitable theatrical costumes were thrown into the fire and burned. Mama clearly understood that in the last half of her life she would have to part from the Beijing opera forever; it was time to burn her stage costumes. After she had burned those two things, our home, which was already impoverished and poor, had nothing else left which could bring trouble for the family. But some of the old photo albums Mama had treasured for years, should she burn them or not? This question disturbed her in those days and gave her no peace of mind. According to the newspaper, those old photos which were taken in the past certainly belonged to the articles of the "old four," and should be cleaned up. She knew, if the Red Guards saw those things, she would be accused with the "vain hope the world could change in one day," and it may cause a horrible result. Many times, Mama held the albums in her hands, wanting to commit them to the flames. In the end she could not find it in her heart to burn them. Finally, she hid them in a very secret place. Mama told Ge Ge something about those albums; they did not only have some old photos in them which had been put in order and stuck in by Dad, but most importantly, there were some inscriptions that Dad had personally written under each photo. This was the last thing Dad had left behind in the world. It also recorded the family's life, and she didn't want these to be completely erased from her life or our lives. So she racked her brains to think of a way to store those old photos. As the time went by she treasured those photo albums even more. Certainly, during the years of the red terror, she never showed those photos to anyone; she just kept them silently in a place only she knew about in our humble room. When she passed away, Ge Ge cleaned up the things she had left behind in every nook and corner of our small room, and he found those precious things. Earlier, Mama had used some fabric to wrap those albums and used some ropes to tie them under the rattan mattress of her bed; those photos were just under her pillow and were close to her every day where she could keep watch over them. That is how she preserved those old photos in our home. The bed Mama slept on was so tattered and so old that no one could believe there was something precious hidden there.

From 1949 until now, more than 10 years later, there was a never-ending succession of political movements in the land of China. Right now the Cultural Revolution had created such a hellish situation, how would it ever end? Nobody knew. On the street we saw nothing but a red ocean. The young people who wore green army uniforms each had a treasured red book in their hands. (The Quotations of Mao's works had been published in a small size with a red cover. In the beginning only Red Guards held one in their hands. Later, everyone, including the children and old people had to carry one at all times every day. It was called "treasured red book" during the Cultural Revolution.) They waved these small treasured red books and red flags and sang the songs of praise to Chairman Mao, shouting slogans, marching in orderly rank toward the City Government Offices and the yard of the Provincial Party Committee.

The front page of the "China Daily" issued the "most important instructions" from Chairman Mao. Also the leading editorial each day was about what Chairman Mao wanted to do so that the people of the whole country could closely keep up with him. Da Zi Bao (large banners) were put up in an overwhelming manner by the Red Guards in all the streets, at all the schools, and in every unit: "Down with those in power taking the capitalist road," "Taking up the pen is like a weapon," "Condemn both speech and writing." Nan Ping street and the place around the department store that was the main street of the city and not far from our home had previously been full of shops. Suddenly, all of shop fronts seemed to disappear. All the showroom windows and shop fronts that faced the street were enveloped and covered perfectly by every kind of Da Zi Bao. It was all right because the employees in those shops didn't need to go to work anymore; they had spontaneously devoted themselves to this great revolutionary movement. In the whole of Nan Ping street and in the doorways of the department stores, only two things could be seen. One was the Da Zi Bao that looked as though they had blotted out the sky and covered up the earth. Another was the crowd that was looking at them. Of course, there were also the parades of representative characters of "feudalism, capitalism, revisionism" that had been exposed in each of the units. They now wore tall paper hats and were being marched under escort on the street. The troops who escorted these parades didn't care about traffic rules or traffic jams. They just walked on the main street one after another where the cars normally drove. The cars had no choice but to stop at the side and let them walk by. A one km area around Nan Ping Street and the doorways of the department stores were simply a big stage; you could see all kinds of farce there. There was an assortment of content on the Da Zi Bao. In time varied and authoritative information and hearsay about the movement, especially "important instructions" from Chairman Mao, appeared even more flamboyantly on the Da Zi Bao.

Very soon Liu Shao Qi, the vice-chairman of the CPC and one of the top leaders of the nation who had gone through fire and water with Mao Ze Dong for years and together with him had seized political power by force in China, became "the most powerful person in China who is taking the country in the direction of capitalism." In front of his name were put the adjectives "traitor, agent provocateur, scab." Later, different levels of leaders from different provinces, cities, universities, organizations, and units, also suddenly had a red X put by their names. The facts about their crimes were published for all to see on the street; they also became the "capitalist movers." Those former powerbrokers had now all reached rock bottom. They were forced to attend various meetings to be accused and denounced, and then they had to wear a tall paper hat and hang a big signboard on their chests and be paraded through the streets. Some of them were forced to dress up as a clown; some of them were escorted on a donkey with their heads facing the donkey's tail. When they were paraded through the streets to the beating of drums and the striking of gongs, they shouted slogans like, "I want the restoration of the old order; I am a capitalist mover." The distance from Nan Ping Street to our home was only 5 minutes' walk, and when we heard the noise, we often ran out to look. I saw that the words used to describe those capitalist movers on the Da Zi Bao on Nan Ping Street or on the slogans hung in front of their chests were very expressive. Some read: "strike xxx down, and to set foot on him!" Some said: "break xxx's dog head!" and "deep fry xxx!" and "set fire to xxx!" One day I saw a sign on one of the capitalist movers which actually read: "steam xxx!" I thought it was very funny. How could a living person be fried, set on fire or even steamed? The Cultural Revolution used "culture" in such a low and vulgar way that anyone who had received a basic education could immediately see how absurd and unintelligent it was; it was easy to see how backward the situation was. But at that time, people felt differently; they thought using language like this was right. This was "revolution"! In the evening I told Mama what I had seen and heard. Mama also thought they were laughable, but she was a person who had experienced political movements; she knew what was hidden behind the craziness.

She told me, "Don't get involved; when you come across these things you should not laugh! Remember that!" Every day, I saw the people taking part in these "proletariat cultural revolution without precedent in history" activities. I was just 15 years old and with my big eyes I saw so many unimaginable things happen at the turn of a hand, and naturally I could not understand why. This was the first time I had gone through a "revolution" myself. I have to say the things I saw and experienced during this revolution were shocking to me!

At the beginning of 1967, a young man named Yu Luo Ke published a lengthy treatise, The Theory of Class Origin, to vigorously criticize "the theory of blood lineage" that was put into practice in our nation. This article was hand copied by many people and posted everywhere as his point of view had obtained very strong support by thousands of people. But in April of that year, this article was called a poisonous weed by the Center of Cultural Revolution Leadership in Beijing. Yu Luo Ke was arrested and sent into prison as an "ultra-reactionary" guilty of publishing counterrevolutionary thoughts. He was given the death penalty which was enforced at once in Beijing Worker Stadium. He was 27 years old. The picture of the execution by shooting and the news of his death were publicized on a great scale. For those of us who came from the 'bad' families, it was a warning sign that said, "In this society you will never have any good prospects and not any chance to defend yourself; you have nothing but to accept your destiny and allow yourself to be trampled upon."

From age 15 to 25 should be the most precious time in anyone's youth. But those precious 10 years in my youth were the same 10 years of the Cultural Revolution's "great calamity." Where could I find any happy memories in my mind during those years?

Back then, even though Mama and Er Yi Ma had lived in the world for more than 50 years and had experienced many movements, they looked at the things which were now happening before their eyes and were still unable to make sense of it; they felt as if all the people had "gone mad." They really hadn't known what kind of terrible things would happen next in this world.

In November of 1966, Chairman Mao started to receive the Red Guards in Tian An Men Square in Beijing; he called on all the young people throughout the nation to collude with each other. People could go out the gate of the school and go out from their homes, catch a train, and just go anywhere they liked for free. Large numbers of students from university and middle school rushed to Beijing to go to see "the most red, most red sun in our minds - Chairman Mao." In the meantime, rebels from all over the nation rushed to different cities and counties too; rebels also came to Kunming "to sow seeds of revolution" in this small city located in the border area. Our former way of life order was now totally upset. Kunming was a small city and not very busy; now there were people filling the streets with mixed accents. People waved the "red treasured book" of Chairman Mao, and wore a variety of Chairmen Mao badges on their chests, and participated in this revolution. A great revolutionary movement had unfolded in the whole country.

When Liu Jie had not yet finished her studies in high school, and I had not yet finished my studies in middle school, my younger brother had just started studying in the 6th grade of primary school. We were forced to stop our studies at school and had to stay home. Our Mama had lived as a widow since she was 38 years old; she had built up our family from nothing, and through years of difficulties and hardships, she had brought up her seven children. She thought maybe now she could have had an easier time. She could not have known how the situation would become more fearful and disorderly. She could not imagine the future and could only face each day with trembling and fear.

"Ai Yo, it is too terrible, too terrible." Seeing so many unexpected things happening she told us clearly again and again, "Just stay home, do not go out, and keep quiet when you go outside." Especially, we could not admit that we were the later generations of the Yan family in Dali because she had heard that many of the surviving members of the Yan family were experiencing a new "political ablution" once again and were facing misfortune again.

The whole nation had relapsed into a confusing situation. Nobody knew what the final purpose of this revolution would be; nobody could predict that this revolution would start with the ablution of the classes, then the breaking with the "four old," the searching of people's houses and confiscation of their property, the overthrow of those in power who had been taking the capitalist road, then going into a civil war, the jostling between the rebels, the refuting of Lin Biao and Confucius (Lin Bo was the Chairman of the Central Military Commission before 1973, Confucius was one of the great thinkers in Chinese history), and finally the collapse of the Gang of Four. In total this movement lasted a whole 10 years. Innumerable mothers in the land of China, including our Mama, had all their nice expectations and hopes for their children completely vanish like soap bubbles. Many families were ruined; people divorced and lost their children in this unprecedented movement.

In the first phase of the Cultural Revolution, all the members of our family could live in peace. We didn't become targets; it has to be said we were lucky because the people who identified with "the capitalist movers" would always unavoidably become the "class enemies" of society. Mama saw some acquaintances or friends whom Dad had known before now being pulled out into the street to accept accusation and being denounced at meetings time after time during this moment. After the meeting, they had to wear white sleeve covers on their arms and to hang a black wooden board in front of their chest to receive labor re-education, and they had to drag their aged bodies along to sweep the road or to clean the public toilet. She sighed with emotion, and she often said,

"If your Dad hadn't died early, he would not be alive now. Ai Ya, it is terrible; it was better he died early, disentangled from this early!"

Our Da Gu Die who lived in our back yard could not escape his doom now. During the first movement of "combing out the class ranks," Da Gu Die was given the label of "escaping unpunished landlord." He was tied up and had a big black board hung on him, and he was made to wear a tall paper hat and was paraded through the streets time after time. When he came back home, he had the white sleeve cover on his arm, and in both hands he carried the tall paper hat and the big black board. As he was walking across the yard, his head was bowed, and he looked very painful. Living in seclusion for years in Kunming, he was cautious and meticulous. Bringing up the two children of his younger brother, we all saw what kind of simple and frugal life he had. He had always lived in the small room which was separated off with some fencing, and besides one wooden bed, a stove, and a boiler for cooking by his door, he had nothing more in his home. Eating and reading he always sat on his rigid small bed. The only luxury he kept was to smoke a cigarette each day. To save money, he bought some tobacco leaves from the market and made the cigarette himself. We all knew how many steps there were in making a cheap cigarette because we had all helped Da Gu Die to make it. He would put some shredded tobacco on a piece of thin white paper and roll it into the shape of a cigarette and use some paste to stick the edges together; then his cigarette was done. After he had finished making it, he would pick up a cigarette to put into his pipe, and burn it, while he was lying down on his small bed and leaning against the wall to smoke; it was his most enjoyable time. Many years had passed. Under his care, his two nephews had grown up. Both had finished their middle school studies and had found a job so they could support themselves. Da Gu Die thought he would drift along until he retired, and then he would go back to Dali to spend the rest of his life. Unexpectedly, he met the Cultural Revolution. He was experiencing torment again, and he was close to 60 years old. In 1970, he was sent off to his hometown. He had to live in a low position right until the end of his life.

My older brother loved reading. While Da Gu Die lived in our back yard, he often talked with Ge Ge about ancient and modern history, sometimes even reciting poems and writing antithetical couplets together. Ge Ge admired the knowledge and culture of Da Gu

Da Jie's family in Kunming.

Die very much. He thought that Da Gu Die was intellectually proficient in history and had great learning. Such a principled and kind old man, could it be said that he didn't know that this period in his life and all the things happening around him were not normal? Of course, he knew. But at the time, he had no other choice than to exercise patience; he had learned to live by bowing and scraping throughout his life.

I felt sorry that I didn't have the opportunity to hear Da Gu Die's opinions about the Yan family and about the hard times he went through. By the time I decided to write this book and started to interview the old people who were still alive, Da Gu Die had left this world. Otherwise, there could have been much more precious content here.

During the Cultural Revolution, there were some very strange phenomena in our home. Because everyone had been called on to be part of the revolution, the whole country had suspended classes and stopped production. My older sisters who worked in another place knew that their identity was "the black puppy of the capitalist," so they didn't dare to join any kind of faction or organization but just came back home. And the three of us had no school to go to, so all the brothers and sisters including my two older brothers-in-law all stayed at home idly together. On the contrary, the unit Mama worked with was a very small neighborhood factory and didn't stop production. In our whole family, only Mama still went to work on time each day.

When my older sisters came home to take refuge during the Cultural Revolution, we seven brothers and sisters, and sometimes even my brothers-in-law and their children lived together in a room with a total area of less than 30 square meters. There were more than ten people eating and sleeping in this small room every day, it really was a scene of bustling and excitement. Each evening when bed time came, we had to put the table away and spread out some blankets on the floor in that small living room so that each person had a space to lie down. Two people now slept on Ge Ge's small bed, and the big bed where I used to sleep with Mama now sometimes had five people huddled together in it.

When the older sisters and their husbands were staying at home, armed conflict had started between the different factions throughout the country, and public transport had stopped. Even if they wanted to go back to their place of work, they could not do it. Because they were staying in Kunming, they could not get their food coupons and salaries, and having their young children live with them in this way made them feel very discouraged. They had a guilty conscience when they saw Mama as an old lady still go to work to make money and support the whole family. They often revealed their insecure feelings. Mama never felt it was not good; she was very, very happy; she was all smiles every day. She often said, "The outside world is so confused that our whole family can stay together peacefully is a blessing. I can see each of you every day; I think this is better than anything."

The seven brothers and sisters had not lived together with Mama since we were very little; this second time was during the early days of the disruptive Cultural Revolution for about seven months in total. Back then, the antagonistic factions of the Red Guards and other organizations had begun to use force; they had guns and attacked each other brutally. There was a period of time when the bullets often whistled "Shou, Shou," through the sky over our yard. No matter how confused and dirty the outside world was, our whole family could hide ourselves in that small room and enjoy some rare family happiness together with Mama.

By nightfall of each day, we would wait for Mama to get back home after work and cook dishes; then afterwards, we all sat around to eat dinner together, this was the happiest time for all of us.

It was also in those days every afternoon around 6:30, when I knew it was the time Mama would soon be home, I would often bring one or two of Da Jie or Er Jie's kids with me to meet Mama at the crossing of Qin Yun Street as I had done before. From when I was a little girl, I had stood there waiting for Mama, and now I brought her grandchildren to wait for her. The time and place had not changed, but with the lapse of time, what had changed was the number of people in our growing family, and I became taller and taller, but Mama had become more doddery every day.

Each time we walked to the crossing of Qin Yun Street, we turned our eyes to the right and fixed them on the end of Zheng Yi Road. We could not see Mama's small figure among the people bustling about on the street, however, we always spotted her familiar figure the moment she appeared. As soon as we saw Mama, we started to walk towards her. Within a few minutes we could see each other clearly. Usually for the last few meters, both sides would quicken their steps, almost running towards each other. As I burst out with, "Mom!" and her grandchildren chirped and called out, "Po Po!" (grandmother in the Chinese tone), we three generations would meet up laughing and joking. Mama would still use her old fashioned action, handing over the bag from her hand to me as was her habit and immediately picking up her grandchildren to give each of them a kiss. And then we all went home cheerfully, hand in hand together ……

As soon as Mama entered the door of our home, the whole family livened up in minutes. Mama strode into the kitchen, and within a few minutes the tangy good smell of the dishes she made would float into the air. At once our home was filled with warmth, and the family again enjoyed a pleasant time together.

"Put out the bowls and chopsticks for the meal; we will serve dinner," Mama cried out. No matter what food we had, just sitting together with Mama and eating the dishes she made meant we always enjoyed each meal so much. Mama still liked to take food from some of the dishes to put on the rice and poured a bit of juice from the dishes onto the little children's bowls as she had done for us when we were children.

In those days, there were more than 10 adults and 4 or 5 of my sisters' children who ate dinner together. Three generations, so many people huddled together over one table and another small table to have dinner. During the meal, the small room was filled with the hubbub of voices and bustled with activity. Since our room was way too small with the beds and simple furniture, the remaining space was very limited.

After dinner, we didn't want Mama to do anything else. Usually we would make a cup of hot tea for Mama so she could just drink tea and chat. The grandchildren would sit on Mama's lap, the whole family would talk cheerfully and with good humor, and sometimes the grandchildren would perform or sing a children's song. We all felt grateful for what Mama had done for us; we were all anxious to bring some happiness to Mama in the few hours she was home. Mama was surrounded by her children and grandchildren. She was satisfied. She often laughed heartily with us despite the fact that she already had a wrinkled face.

Ah, I do wish time could be turned back again so we could return to those years, to let that time of day come again and again! Our whole family crowded together, suffering together and happy together, and most importantly, we would be together with our darling Mama, not separated but spending the whole evening together with her.

Ah, there were so many moments which seemed so ordinary, but when I recall them now, they have become so precious.

Back then, the Cultural Revolution was unfolding in the whole nation like a raging fire. The leading article in the party newspaper told the people that "we would rather have the grass of socialism than to have the plants of capitalism." People followed Chairman Mao to make revolution everywhere. No one was engaged in production, and it caused the economy of China to be almost completely paralyzed. The Chinese people's lives had slipped to the edge of existence again. Often the rationed foodstuff, coal and all of the non-staple foods were not easy to buy; the shelves in the shop were empty. To buy food and what was needed for daily life, people often had to spend many hours queuing up and waiting. But sometimes, after many hours of waiting, it would be suddenly announced that things had sold out, so we would have to go and queue again the next day. There were a few months when there was nowhere to buy coal; this was the thing every family needed for cooking. How could we resolve this problem? Kunming people would go to the mountain on the outskirts of the city to fell trees for fuel, and they also started to dig up the silt at the bottom of Green Lake. At that time the bottom of the Green Lake was many meters deeper than before, and the silt was very difficult to burn. One day, we heard that there was a railway wagon full of coal arriving at the northern train station. My brothers and sisters and I, like the other citizens of Kunming, went out before day break pulling a borrowed cart to the gate of the northern train station and waited there. I remember our family team was led by my older brother-in-law. While we were walking on Qin Yun Street, his foot kicked a rust-eaten horseshoe. He was a Chinese teacher and said humorously, "Something will happen today, it is a lucky sign to kick a horseshoe. I am sure we will get some to take home." As expected, after waiting for four hours, we heard the sound of a siren, and the train with the coal pulled up at the station. Everyone swarmed towards the train and climbed up onto the freight car to start grabbing the coal. That day the northern train station in Kunming was totally out of control, hundreds of people were locked in tangled fights as people climbed up and down to get the coal. Our many hands provided great strength, and finally we managed to get some coal. After filling it up we pushed the cart home with boundless joy. When we got home and saw each other, we couldn't help laughing, because every one of us had inky black faces and hands. We were dirty and hungry and tired, but only our eyes were shining.

Under these circumstances, supporting our whole family was a tough job for Mama. There was one year when the only rationed food we could buy was wheat, which we needed to husk ourselves, and broad beans. Mama showed us how to take off the shells and grind the wheat into flour with a millstone. Afterwards, she taught us how to make wheaten food; we were not used to eating this and were unable to make it before because the main food for Kunming people was usually rice.

I still remember when Mama taught us to make dumplings. At first the most difficult thing was rolling the dumpling wrapper into a very thin round shape. We were unable to do it, so the next time we made the dumplings by ourselves, we used a rolling pin to roll the dough into a big sheet on the table and then used the edge of a glass to press out the round pieces, and used these to make the dumplings. We will never forget the best and tastiest dumplings Mama made. She used some wild shepherd's purse and a little minced meat mixed together as the stuffing and made each dumpling look very nice by pleating the edges. Mama taught us how to steam buckwheat cakes and corn cakes too. And she taught us how to cook a little rice together with some cabbage, radish, and pumpkin over a slow fire. But Mama's skills were not easy to learn. For example, when steaming the buckwheat cake, we often could not master the ratio of water and flour. When we poured them into the bamboo steamer, the liquid mixture would suddenly leak into the boiler, and as a result, we could not eat buckwheat cake but would drink the buckwheat soup.

It was also in those days that Mama started to make pickles for us to eat. In the summer season different kinds of vegetables came onto the market in a great quantity and at a cheap price, so Mama would buy some Chinese cabbage, eggplant, and green peppers and dry them in the sun. When she was home from work, she started to cut and chop, and then mix in a variety of seasonings. Finally, she would put them into some small jars. So, even in winter, we never lacked vegetables to eat with our rice. The pickles Mama made tasted very, very good. And she had several unique skills too, which made the pickles look very attractive and appealing to people's refined taste. For example, when she was making them, she would put in some slivers of fresh carrots. In this way, the pickled vegetables not only looked pleasing to the eye with their alternating red and green colors, but the sour and sweet flavors also created a very delightful taste. Then there were the Chinese chives. Nobody could imagine how she made them taste so good. They were very hot, but the grains of Pei Lan (a kind of Chinese vegetable) she put together with them were crisp, fragrant, and pleasant to taste, and the more you chewed them the tastier they became. Another pickle she made was eggplant mixed with rice flour. This also tasted very special. We didn't need any other dishes; we would have been happy to eat this with rice every day.

Back then, all of us had grown into adulthood, and we were at the age where we ate a lot of food. But it was also during those years that there was the greatest food shortage in China. I remember we always felt hungry and wanted to eat everything. Any food Mama put on the table would disappear immediately. At each meal all the rice in the bamboo steamer in our home would be quickly snatched with nothing left. When I think about this now, I think there was a reason; we were also unable to get any other snacks between meals. For the whole day from morning to night, we waited for two meals, so we always ate a lot of rice. Sometimes, in the afternoon at 4 or 5 o'clock, I felt very hungry. The only food I could have was still only rice. Then I would plead with Liu Jie who was cooking dinner to give me a half bowl of rice, and I would add some water and salt before I ate it. The best food I remember back then was rice rolled and shaped like a ball which Kunming people called "Fan Tuo." Of course, the most delicious of these were also made by Mama. She put a bit of rice into a frying pan, added a little lard and salt, ground the rice so it would stick together, then wrapped this soft rice into a piece of gauze in a round shape. When Mama gave it to us, she always said, "Be careful, it is very hot." We immediately put it into our mouths, not caring if it was hot or not. This food was nothing special, but for some reason we would think it was the best food back then. We wished we could have it every afternoon, but it was impossible. If one of us took one of these, it meant that when the whole family ate dinner together, we would be missing one bowl of rice, so we were too embarrassed to ask for it.

Under these difficult circumstances, nobody could believe that we all grew up without illness or personal misfortune. Now, as I remember this, I think it was the unique skills Mama had and the variety of pickles she made that gave us the extra nourishment our bodies needed for most of that period.

Nobody could compare with Mama's food-making abilities, whether she made a banquet or just different snacks and sweet refreshments; she was skilled at all of them. While she made stir-fry dishes, she was very fastidious. No matter the circumstances, all the dishes had to be colorful, fragrant, and tasty. For each dish she thought about what kind of seasoning she should use - an onion, two pieces of ginger, and these things she never omitted if she could help it. Therefore, whether it was a vegetable dish or a meat dish, they all had their distinctive, very delicious flavors. I remember I once ate Tang Yuan (stuffed dumplings made of glutinous rice flour and served in soup). The stuffing Mama filled this with was the chicken oil, sesame, minced peanut and brown sugar mixed together. Certainly this Tang Yuan tasted extremely good. Watching Mama making dishes or snacks was like looking at a work of art; the process and the results brought pleasure to both the eye and the mind.

During these later difficult years, Mama could preserve all the elegant habits she had developed in her rich family. For example, even if the room we lived in was very small and old, it was still clean and tidy. This was the first thing Mama taught us from our childhood. So despite the fact that the environment in which we lived was a worm-eaten compound occupied by many households, our home was always very clean. We had a few old glasses for drinking tea, and she made us wash them in salt water and put them, shining, on the tea tray. At each meal, before taking the food to the table, she always wiped the juice around the plate; she was never careless. When putting the dishes on the table, even if they were just very simple foods, she would take care to arrange them in pairs and groups, alternating the colors and matching them with the tableware. Mama indeed had a particular passion for an exquisite quality of life. Her favorite cake was a white, soft cake in a very petty round shape made by "Ji Qing Xiang," the most famous cake shop located in Ma Shi Kou in Kunming. Her favorite tea was jasmine tea which had a strong fragrance especially when the tea had been infused with jasmine; the most fragrant one was "three times infused tea." Often Mama didn't have the money to buy and enjoy such a high level product. She would buy some cheap tea and infuse it herself. She would buy one or two branches of Zhu Lan (a kind of cymbidium with a very strong fragrance) and use some thin cotton paper to wrap it up, and then put it into the bottom of a small tea pot with the tea. One week later her infused tea was done. She would make a cup of tea and hold it in both hands and enjoy it as much as before. If there were some distinguished guests coming to visit, like the mothers-in-law of my three older sisters, Mama would spend money to prepare this kind of tea and some pastries and sit together with them eating and talking. But, it was a great pity that in the latter half of Mama's life, the opportunity for her to enjoy this kind of life was very seldom.

This was because of the family's difficult financial situation from 1949 until Mama died, when the land of China went through a period of great material scarcity. The opportunities Mama had to display her skills were very few; the times when we had the nice food Mama made was limited. Mama hoped her children would keep on mastering this elegant demeanor, which was called "sitting has a sitting image, eating has an eating image," but these things were continually eroded and obliterated by the new thoughts of the new society. Gradually, this was also seen less and less in our family.

But even up until the present, when we 7 brothers and sisters meet together, we still believe that the dishes, the cakes, the pickles that Mama made were the most exquisite foods we ever had in our lives. Each day of Mama's life was always full of vitality; it was hard to find another who could compare with her among all of our relatives and friends. The moral excellence that she demonstrated in her speech and deportment exceeded time and space and left an indelible mark on us. Her influence was extraordinary in the lives of me and my brothers and sisters.

Once during the Cultural Revolution when all of us were together with Mama for the Chinese New Year, Mama made some special rice noodles for us, cooked according to the method of the Bai people of Dali. That day, as Mama's helper, it was the first time I had tasted this kind of delicious food. I participated in the whole cooking process, and it left a favorable impression in my mind.

Making the soup for pouring on the rice noodles was very complex, but when it was finished, that bowl of rice noodles was so delicious, it is difficult to use language to describe it. That day, each of us ate all the rice noodles, even the soup, and there was nothing left in the bowl. We all wanted to have more, but of course, it was impossible. After each of us had received one bowl, there was only a little soup and rice noodles left, Mama only had a few scraps in her bowl. It was the only time I had these special rice noodles in the 24 years I lived with her, and I will never forget it.

Another time also during the Chinese New Year, Mama made a rice cake for us; this was another traditional snack eaten by the Bai people.

After working busily for a few hours, she finally came in showing us a tray with a beautiful rice cake on it. This cake had a diameter of 30 cm and was 15 cm high, and separated into three layers with three colors; it was nicely decorated with tasty glazed fruit on the top and was made from a mixture of sticky and normal rice flour. Just like our grandfather many years ago, we all felt we did not want to eat it. We did not want to destroy it, so we all stared at it blankly. But the smell which floated through the air was so attractive; we all absolutely wanted to eat it, after all. This was the first time we had seen something like this! Mama said, "Cut it up, cut it into pieces, and eat it while it is warm!" when nobody touched it. She used a knife to divide it into 12 pieces, and we all got a piece of rice cake with three colors and some of the sweet things on the top. That year, to match the atmosphere with the eating of this unusual rice cake, we don't know from where, but Mama brought home some pine branches and spread them out on the floor of our small living room. As the green bed of pine needles was spread out, the small room was immediately full of their refreshing fragrance. We were all too impatient to wait, and immediately sat down on the soft pine branches. Later, as we held a plate with a piece of rice cake in our hands and sat down again, the feeling was wonderful. We felt sentimental and joyful, and we enjoyed the rice cake slowly, slowly. Although we only had a small piece, no one wanted to finish it quickly.

As Mama sat with us on the pine branches to eat the rice cake, she said humorously, "Long, long ago, in the ancient times, when we had Spring Festival each year, we always spread thick pine branches on the floor of our living room; it meant we welcomed the awakening of spring to our home. Today, I want all of you to experience it just once." Yes, we had heard something else from Mama about Chinese New year. Previously, when the festival came, she and Dad would also invite a team of dragon lantern dance performers to come and dance around the house. Finally, the host of the house would purposely stand on the second floor; he had a red bag with a cash gift in his hand and showed it from the window. At that moment, each member of the dragon lantern dance performing team, accompanied by cheerful drumbeats, would stand on one another's shoulders. The one who climbed the highest would wear the dragon's head while the rest of the team was hidden in the beautiful gown which formed the dragon's body. Suddenly this man would extend his hand and seize the red bag. This scene of bustling excitement always delighted all the people who were there, especially the children. It had become a special event at Spring Festival in our home.

But everything was now gone, and it had become history. All Mama could do was to let us 7 brothers and sisters have a small taste of the atmosphere of a real traditional Chinese New Year. During the Cultural Revolution, the alleyway where we lived, even the whole of Kunming city, was filled with sadness and violence. There must have been very few families who could spend their New Year like this.

It was because we had such a mother that in those years we were able to have a chance to taste these special foods one or two times. Even now, as I call it to mind again, it makes me feel incomparable warmth.

Mama, how could we forget you.

During the Cultural Revolution so she could support the whole family, Mama had borrowed some money from her colleague without telling anyone. Besides this, we didn't know that actually since the Cultural Revolution had begun, the job Mama had to do at her work was not frying dishes and selling the food. Every day when she got to the mess hall, the work she had to do was much harder than before; she had to wash all the vegetables, enough for a hundred people to eat, in cold water and cut up them. The reason she was made to do this type of coolie labor was because of her identity as the wife of a capitalist, so she had to accept this punishment and reconstruction. The red storm didn't neglect to hit her violently and mistreat her, such a frail, old woman. Mama went to work on time each day. She suffered these things by herself silently, and when she was back at home, her face was always full of smiles. One day, Mama was in too much pain to lift her right arm. We pulled back her sleeve to check and found out that her elbow joint and wrist were both seriously out of shape, she said, "I have to wash vegetables in cold water. I had to cut so many vegetables each day with this hand; when I lift them I am in pain. And I have to knead the dough for breakfast each day; I can only use my left hand to do it. Ai, I am old, I am useless." We all became aware that every day Mama entered the door of our home with a smile, but in her unit, what kind of laborious work did she have to do?

Mama could not continue to endure this "labor re-education," and the older brother and sisters wanted to go to the leader of her unit to plead for mercy for Mama, but Mama would not allow them to do it. She didn't think they would change their minds. Later, the movement throughout the nation went into the phase of "Criticize Lin Biao and criticize Confucius." When the attention of the Red Guards was on seizing power, the leader of her unit changed Mama's job. After more than ten years working together, they all knew that Mama had already transformed to become a real laborer in this society. And because she had to take care of so many children, they actually sympathized with her in her misfortune, but in the early days of the Cultural Revolution, nobody dared to violate the trend of the ultra-left. They had to go against their conscience, and do everything completely according to their demands.

Mama was getting older and older, and she was still toiling day and night for us. Her thin and small stature never stopped even for a day.

All the things she had done for us made all of us feel grateful in our minds. How could we repay Mama? Each of us brothers and sisters had different wishes.

First, let me tell you about Liu Jie's wishes. She saw how Mama loved to listen to the traditional opera, and since we could not have a radio at home, Mama often had no alternative but to sit close to the neighbor's window and eavesdrop. When Liu Jie was about 10 years old, she used her childish handwriting to write down her wishes on the wall above the head of her bed, "When I am grown up, I will buy a radio for Mama."

And Si Jie said, "Mama always feels embarrassed about her lack of money. When I have money, I will give Mama more and more."

Da Jie said, "After Mama retires, I will take Mama to Wen Shan and let her enjoy her later years there because she likes the peaceful scenery there."

Er Jie said, "When I have the financial ability, I will take Mama to Beijing because she has said more than once that she really wants to see what the palace the emperors lived in there look like."

My elder brother said, "I vow to surely help Mama to move out of this murky and moist room and move into a well-lit place."

My younger brother said, "I will buy something Mama likes to eat so she will gain some weight; Mama is too thin."

While they were carrying on these endless discussions, I smiled without saying a word. In my heart of hearts, I never thought there would be a day when I would separate from Mama. So my thought was, "I will take care of Mama forever; I will be with her every day."

On the first day of 1969, the day of Mama's birthday, late at night when Mama lay down on the bed, I moved closer to her and told Mama all the wishes of each of her children. As Mama listened, tears were running from her eyes and she said, "Mama doesn't want anything from any of you; you have such a filial devotion. Just knowing that you think of me is enough for me; even if I have to suffer until the day I die, it will be worth it." Each of us had our own simple desires, wishing we could repay Mama for her pains. We expected there would come a day when we could return and take care of Mama; we all looked forward to an opportunity when we could live happily and peacefully together with Mama. However, since we were living in those times, not one of even the most common wishes we had actually came true!

As the Cultural Revolution was still going deeper into society, Chairman Mao issued an order "to stress the revolution and to promote production," and people started to go back to their workplaces. My older sisters left Kunming and Mama to go back to their work units.

In the summer of 1970, Si Jie got married. Mama was very satisfied with this marriage because Si Jie's husband was the son of an old accountant who was Mama's colleague. It may be said, that the two elder people chose the marriage partner for their children, and the two youngsters fell in love at first sight, so everything happened in a rational way, and Mama was very happy. She talked it over with Mr. Zhou, a relative by marriage, and decided to handle this daughter's wedding herself.

Si Jie's wedding was held in the small yard where we lived, and Mama decided to make all the food for the 5 tables of the wedding feast herself. That day before day break, Mama was already up with her busy preparation. The whole yard was filled with joy. In the afternoon, the tables and chairs which had been borrowed from another family were put into the yard. The wedding tables would be set up in the two neighbors' rooms and in our room both inside and outside the yard.

At 6 o'clock, the bridegroom and bride were dressed up and presented to relatives and friends. When the guests were seated, Mama commanded all of us brothers and sister to take out the dishes one by one and put them on the table. Mama showed her ability that day; she made six delicate dishes and a soup for the wedding banquet in addition to the sweet food that she was good at - Bao Zi steamed with ham and sugar. When all the guests started to enjoy the food Mama had made and raised their glasses to congratulate the couple, Mama took off her apron and went into the back room to quickly dress and make up. Then she came back to the tables to propose a toast to the guests with a broad smile on her face. For many years, we hadn't heard her hearty and elated laughter which now filled the small yard once again, "Ha, Ha, Ha, I am so happy, I am so happy. Thank you, thank you for coming. Enjoy your foods, enjoy your foods."

From early morning until the end of the wedding banquet, Mama was busy all day long, but the whole time she never stopped laughing.

That day our family was harmonious and filled with pleasure, and it was also the day Mama was most joyful during the whole period of the Cultural Revolution.

After Si Jie got married, Mr. Zhou, the new relative by marriage, and Er Yi Ma would often come to our home and sit together with Mama to drink tea and chat or sometimes have a meal together. Mama looked as though she had ease of mind. In my memory, that year was the only year after Dad died that Mama had good moods, except for the period when she was running her Bao Zi shop.

After the wedding at the end of that same year, many units started to recruit workers and resume production. We three younger ones all had separate jobs after having been idle at home for more than three years. Liu Jie, although she didn't finish school, was assigned to the Kunming Shell-lac Factory and worked as a laboratory technician. I was sent to the countryside to receive re-education, but after half a year, I was recruited as a player in the performing arts propaganda team of the Yunnan Provincial Construction Company. And my younger brother was recruited as a worker in the Yunnan Baiyao Pharmaceutical Factory. We all found jobs, and this meant from then on, that each of us could at least earn some money to cram ourselves with food; we didn't need to completely depend on Mama's income to live.

That year we were all very excited. At last the time we had depended on Mama's support had finished. The heavy burden which had pressed on Mama's shoulders for years now could be laid down; Mama could relax for a little while.

When we three had just started to work, we moved into the dormitories in each of our units. After work every day, we had to take part in political studies till 9:30 in the evening. When we all moved away, our home suddenly became cold and cheerless, and Mama was not used to it. At that time, Er Jie's daughter Jing Jia still lived with Mama, and she went to the kindergarten in the day time and slept with Mama in the evening. Ge Ge went to work every day, and he often went home at night and ate dinner together with Mama.

Mama in 1969.

Mama still went to work continually. My work unit was just in the city of Kunming and not far from home, so I often went home to see Mama, especially on the weekends.

When I was back home, I still slept with Mama in the same bed. I discovered a small porcelain plate with some sweet-scented osmanthus flowers or jasmine on her bedside cupboard. Mama loved flowers very much, and she always liked to bring a bunch of flowers home in the holidays. In the summer season, there were people selling sweet-scented osmanthus flowers and jasmine at the market. This was the time she loved, and sometimes we could see she had two osmanthus flowers pinned to her chest. But it was a pity that there were many times she could only stand and look at the flowers and smell their fragrance. Since the money in her pocket was always very limited, she didn't dare to spend anything to buy flowers. I was so delighted that now Mama could buy some flowers for her home. In the atmosphere of this delicate fragrance before she went to sleep, Mama took up her *Dream of the Red Chamber* and started to read it again. She put on her reading glasses and dived into the book, often commenting that a certain section was written so wonderfully. She simply admired the imagination of Cao Xue Qing, the author of this book. Sometimes she would vividly and dramatically read a graceful sentence aloud. Another book Mama read with interest and talked about was *From Emperor to Citizen*, written in prison by Pu Yi, the last Emperor of China. Mama would hold this book in her hand, and look at the picture of this Chinese emperor who wore glasses with black frames. He wore a set of Mao's style clothes and his hairstyle was very drab. He was miserable and looked completely shabby. Mama sighed with deep emotion, "If an emperor can be changed in this way, is there anything, any person which cannot be changed? Oh, these are earth-shaking changes!"

Before I moved into the dormitory of my unit, I had been sleeping in the big bed with Mama for 18 years.

When I was a little girl, Mama always praised me as her "small stove and hot-water bag" because in the winter season I often went to bed early to warm up the quilt so that when Mama came to bed she would not feel the cold. I would often move to the other side of the bed and help her to scratch her back, and sometimes I tickled the bottom of her feet on purpose to provoke her laughter. When Mama was not feeling well, I would be a like a little nurse looking after her, bringing her medicine and water. The thing I could do for Mama that she enjoyed the most, was to give her a massage when she came home after work and lied down on the bed. I pounded her back, nipped her forehead, and massaged her temples and shoulders. After I had finished these, I would pick up both her hands and massage them. Each time I had finished all of these motions with my small, child hands, Mama always expressed her appreciation, "Ah, this is so comfortable; my Ling Ling is so good and gracious."

Sometimes when I came back home after work, I would still do the massage for Mama. I knew this was the thing she liked most.

In the early years of 1970, I had become a big girl with a full figure, and I was 1.68 meters tall. When I lowered my head down to Mama who was lying down resting with her eyes closed, looking carefully up and down her face, I would often ponder, Mama's face and her stature seemed familiar but strange. I often asked myself, "Is this our Mama who had always been so elegant, cultured and full of energy?"

No, not at all; she was not the same person at all. By then, Mama was just 50 years old, but her appearance was completely doddery. Her face already had many wrinkles. So much pain and anxiety had left two deep vertical lines engraved between her eyebrows; they could not be smoothed out any more. Her gracious facial features had disappeared; she had a sallow complexion and sparse hair. Her cheeks were sunken, and it made the front of her face protrude even more. Both her hands were covered in blue veins, and her joints were deformed. Her formerly tall stature had now become smaller and smaller; she looked like a child when she was lying down on the bed. And she always had cramps in her legs, and she coughed all the time. More than 15 years of the burden of responsibility had exhausted her body and mind.

The only thing that never changed was the neat habits Mama had kept throughout her life. No matter how old the clothes she wore, they were always clean. Every day her hair was combed smoothly. All her life, she always used the Chinese honey locust liquid she had made to wash her hair. It kept her hair black and bright, and when she was over 50 years old, she still had no white hair.

Mama was a person who loved to be clean; she enjoyed going to the bathhouse to take a bath. But in those years, it was not an easy thing for people to take a bath. Most of the time, they would heat up water and take a bath in a big wooden basin at home. When we were children, it was normal to only take a bath once one a month. Because we were so many children, we needed to heat up a lot of water, and Mama could not pay for all the firewood we would need. And back then even if you could afford 3 Jiao to take a bath somewhere, you could not take it whenever you wanted. In the whole of Kunming city there were only a few public bathhouses. No matter which one you went to, you had to be patient and queue up. Usually you would have to wait for several hours to take a bath. And when it was your turn, after you had bought the ticket and entered the bathhouse, your bathing time was limited; it was only half an hour.

I had some wages now so I went to the bathhouse to take a bath each week. I also wanted Mama to have more of these enjoyable times. Sometimes in the evening or on the weekend, I went to "Xiang Hai Bathhouse" in Nan Ping Street to queue up for Mama. An hour later Mama knew it would be her turn, so she would come carrying a bag with some clothes. Sometimes, when Mama entered the small room to take a bath, I would wait for her by the gate. Sometimes I would go and take a bath with her and help Mama by rubbing her back. Today, having half an hour to take a bath would be enough time. But I don't know why back then we all felt the pressure of time. Just when the big bathtub was full of water, and you had taken off your clothes and got in for only a few minutes, you would be told from outside the door to hurry up. The curtain would be lifted up by the attendant. First, she watched and if the bath was full you could not continue to run the water. Second, she reminded you ceaselessly, "Your time is over soon, hurry, hurry up!" In my memory, each experience of taking a bath was always a frantic rush. You had just come out of the water and stood on the floor and didn't even have your clothes on when another person had already entered and was waiting for you.

However, after taking a bath, your whole body was relaxed. Mama and I would walk home together hand in hand filled with happiness, the same feeling as of old. And I could always feel that taking a bath was very enjoyable and a great pleasure for Mama.

In the past Mama had loved to keep herself clean; now she could only preserve this habit a little bit. She always used a basin of warm water to wash her face and feet before going to bed. She took this very seriously; she also passed this habit on to all of her children. From when we were young, we all knew that if we did not clean our face and feet, we should not go to bed. Taking a bath in a standard tub with lots of hot water was now a very luxurious thing for all of us. So Mama always enjoyed this process very much. After taking a bath, she had a ruddy complexion and she changed into clean clothes from inside to out. When she got home, she sat at the mirror using some Vaseline to ceaselessly massage her face and her hands, and then she put some hair oil in her hair as she combed it. After Mama had finished this process, she looked fresh with energy. At that moment, she seemed much younger.

Mama's appearance was old, but while she was walking or doing other things, she was still dexterous. One day, after we had taken a bath and gone home together, I talked with Mama, "We all have jobs now, it would be better for you to retire early and stay home."

Mama shook her head and said one sentence to me, "I cannot have a rest; my mission is not finished."

What mission had Mama not finished? She didn't tell me. I could see there were still many things she was worried about in her heart. She needed to continue working; she knew the little income she had was still very important for the family.

She went to work every day as normal. Right now each member of the family was busy at their work, and the time for the whole family to meet together was less and less.

Among the 7 brothers and sisters, the oldest three had their own families and soon had children; they were financially struggling. The other four were not yet married, and except for Ge Ge who earned a salary of 35 yuan, we three had just started our jobs. Our salaries were each only about 20 yuan per month. This meager salary, after paying for food, left us with only a little pocket money. Sometimes we could buy some food or small things for Mama, but on the contrary, most of the time we still received some money from Mama. For example, I wanted to buy my first sweater after I had worked for more than one year. I saved my money for a long time, but it was still not enough, so Mama gave me 5 yuan and asked me to go buy it quickly. When I wore this yellow sweater and showed Mama, she was very glad and said, "Even Ling Ling has become a big girl and loves beauty; it is good, good!"

Mama didn't have any complaints; she was living peacefully.

During those days there were always some grandchildren who came to visit Mama. Jing Jia, the little girl who had come to live in Kunming since she was one year old, went to the kindergarten in the day time and in the evening she always was together with Mama. She had taken my place to sleep with Mama in the big bed. Later, Si Jie's children also often loved to come to the home of their grandmother and to spend some time with Mama, especially on the weekends and during their vacation.

The time of childhood has flowed away quietly and now these children have grown up and most of them have become parents. But in their hearts there is a strong affection they will never forget, the love their grandmother gave to them. This sweet and profound love is hidden deep in their hearts.

They all remembered how each Chinese New Year their grandmother would prepare a suit of new clothes for each of them. The needlework which was done with a mother's love was now passed on to the next generation with these six grandchildren. On the first day of each New Year, they cheerfully put on the new clothes their grandmother had made and stood before her. Some were tall, and some were short, and she would give each of them a little bit of "money as a lunar New Year gift." To surprise them, she would exchange her cash for brand-new coins or Jiao and put them on the table in order so each of the children would get a share. Although it was only a few Jiao which altogether was only worth around one Yuan, it brought a lot of pleasure to them. Just as in our childhood, they held the money in their hands and immediately left without a trace, going to buy something to eat or something just for fun. The delight of this small amount of "money given to children as a lunar New Year gift" by their grandmother left them with many nice stories which they still talk about today.

However, what she gave to the grandchildren then would not be worth mentioning today as it was only some children's clothes and the gift of some meager money. But in that year, it was enough to use up the whole of one or two months of Mama's salary. For a month after the New Year, Mama often only ate a few pickles with her rice because she didn't have any money to buy other dishes or anything else for her own use. Her clothing had become white after having been washed and washed for many years, and she didn't buy anything new. She said, "I am old; it doesn't matter what I wear. If my clothes are clean, that's all that matters." We could all see that Mama economized on what she ate, used, and wore in a way that would be unimaginable for most people.

Mama's thinking was the same as all the common people in China. None of them could have dreamt that after 1978 the political situation in China would change so greatly that the Chinese people would live a modern life without political pressure and with material abundance. All she was able to think about then was that all of her children would grow up into adulthood and hopefully also get married and have their own families. She said then her mission would be finished, and she could go and see our Dad. So this was the "mission" Mama had mentioned and wanted to complete.

Another time when I accompanied Mama to take a bath, I was rubbing her back when she suddenly told me about the desire she had kept in her mind for years.

While Mama was talking with me, she was so calm when she made mention of Dad; the yearning which she poured out and the expression in her eyes, none of these I could understand. Mama sitting in the bathtub was so thin and weak; her arms could not be called arms any more because they were only skin and bone. The breasts which fed me had all but disappeared, and on her chest were just two lines of flat ribs. When I was rubbing her back, I could see that she had a deformed spine. Looking at Mama's crooked and thin figure, looking at her haggard face full of wrinkles, I felt so sorrowful. To me, Dad was so strange, and I sometimes even had a grudge against him. Why was he so important in Mama's heart? And why did she still bear in her mind and constantly think of finishing the "mission" for him?

To be honest, I didn't like our father at all. During the time I was growing up, I had always admired those who had a father. I wished I could have been hand in hand with a father, that I could even once get some encouragement and love from a father, that I could shout, "Dad!"

But from the age of 4 years old, I had lost my Dad. I had never known what a father means to a daughter; my impression of my father became dimmer and dimmer despite the fact that so many people told me how my Dad loved me. The years of seeing the suffering Mama had to bear for her children alone caused me to look down upon Dad. I thought our Dad was a selfish person trying to escape reality; he didn't take responsibility for his children. The biggest problem was that, as a man and a husband, he let his wife down so much. He chose to give up, he chose to leave this world, leaving a woman of 38 years old to become a widow and bring up 7 children in horrible circumstances. Because of this I even looked on him as a cruel-hearted person.

But in the arduous years after Dad left Mama, we seven brothers and sisters never heard one discontented or complaining word about Dad from Mama. The one thing she regretted all the time was, "If I had gone out to find a job earlier to earn the money to send your Dad to the hospital, your Dad would not be dead. Ai, I always feel sorry about this, sorry to your Dad..." Dad would always be the best person in the world in her mind; the words she repeated unceasingly were, "Ai, a good man like your Dad, he was rare in this world! He should not have endured so much suffering." And so on.

She loved Dad with unswerving loyalty, and her love was so passionately devoted. My Dad was indeed fortunate to have found such a companion in Mama.

Often, when the whole family met together, Mama could not refrain from mentioning Dad. She would say, "If your Dad were still alive, how he would be delighted in seeing all of you brothers and sisters together." Sometimes, she would suddenly say, "Look, the eyes of your oldest sister are so like her Dad's, and Ling Ling's chin is also like her Dad's." Often, when she would get into reminiscing, it was difficult to divert her from it, and she would talk to herself aloud, "When your Dad was young, he loved playing tennis; he played the piano, and every day he was in Western dress and leather shoes, and there was always a great gathering of distinguished guests in our house. Oh, life was a dream!"

A widow's yearning words for her husband, the helpless words about her unchangeable fate, we could all understand. But Dad's actions in the prime of life, his feebleness in giving up, as we all grew up my brothers and sisters could understand this less and less. Sometimes we would express some censure about Dad, and when Mama heard this she always said, "You should not blame your Dad. He was an intellectual all his life, gentle and cultivated. His sense of self-respect was the most important thing to him. Without self-respect, it was indeed like peeling off his skin. He felt too ashamed to show his face. This society wanted him to become a person with no regard for his sensibility, to live a low life. It was too much for him, and he just couldn't bear it. It was pitiful; he had never experienced such suffering, and he was completely destroyed by this society. He only lived for 48 years, what a pity!"

Even though she only had a very short time with this almost perfect man in her mind, because of that short time, for the rest of her life from the age of 38, she had to face boundless pain and loneliness by herself. But because our Mama was a very traditional woman, she could not be completely concerned about it. By depending on her clinging loyalty, she could be calm and patient and wait for the day when she would go and see Dad. She believed that when she had finished her husband's last wish that he hadn't accomplished, the day would come. This was our Mama. Later, we heard some old people make a judgment of our Mama. They praised her as a typical woman who abided by "the three obediences and the four virtues" of the feudal tradition. Very few people today understand what "the three obediences and the four virtues" contain, and I was not clear about it either. Therefore, I looked up some related data and found out.

The "three obediences" are: to be obedient to the father before marriage, obedient to the husband after marriage, and obedient to the son after the death of the husband. The "four virtues" require a woman to keep a high level of morality, proper speech, a modest manner and diligent work. The specific demands were that a woman's morality must include loyalty and obedience. Her speech must be tactful and not impertinent. Her appearance must be sedate and unaffected, and her skill must be outstanding and capable.

Maybe nowadays we could not find such a woman in our modern society with this high standard. But I am sure that if we compare each standard with our Mama, she achieved all of them. She was indeed a rare and special woman! And we don't know how these concepts had taken root in her mind.

After Dad's death when Mama was isolated and cut off from help, and she started to believe in Buddhism. On the first and 15th day of each month, she went to the temple to burn joss sticks and worshipped Buddha trying to seek refuge. When I was a little girl, I often went with Mama to "Sheng Yin Temple" at Xiao Xi Men in Kunming to burn joss sticks. She believed that the human being has a soul; Dad was dead, but his soul was still alive. She could talk with him often, and if she prayed, Dad's soul would bless us from heaven. She thought she would meet Dad in heaven after she died. She also believed that human beings would have the next life. The life you had now and what you did would return to you in your next world. So if a person now had to endure misfortune, this was the retribution for evil they had done in a previous existence so you had no choice but to accept your fate. This point of view was really what gave Mama the spiritual strength for her life.

So, on the one hand she was yielded to her fate and meekly submitted to oppression, on the other hand she strongly required herself for the rest of her life to accumulate virtue and do good works and do as many good things as she could to carry her through firmly to the end. Her beliefs were a great spiritual motivator for her. Mama was kind and helpful to all the people she knew, and she was willing to help all those who needed help.

I remember that while I was living in the dormitory of my unit, I knew a young girl named Kai Le who lived with me. Kai Le came to visit me in my home, and while talking with her, Mama found out that the financial situation in Kai Le's family was very difficult. Her father was a military officer in the Kuomintang in the old society; now he was paralyzed and confined to his bed all the time. The four members of her family depended on her mother to make some handicrafts to keep the whole family alive. The next day, Mama asked me to take her to visit Kai Le's place, and she consoled Kai Le's mother. Afterward, she sent some handicrafts, which she brought back from her factory and normally processed at home in the evening, to Kai Le's home and let her mother do it. Very soon, her mother was able to make more income than before, and their life improved. In the small lane where we lived, if any family met trouble, Mama would always go to help them on her own initiative. Mama helped many of the neighbors when they had to prepare for a wedding or a funeral.

Mama paid attention to the relationships between people. The mother of our older brother-in-law lived alone in Chang Chun Road. At intervals, Mama would go to visit her and bring her a bag of cakes; she kept a very good relationship with this old lady. Our second brother-in-law was from Si Chuan province. His father once came to Kunming, and he was received with very warm hospitality by Mama. When he left Kunming, he was full of praise of Mama's conduct. Normally, Mama's kind manner was always liked by all the neighbors. There was a young girl who just got married and moved into our lane. She had a bad relationship with her mother-in-law and often came to our home to seek help. Many times after listening to her pouring out her troubles and giving her some consolation, Mama would accompany her back home and intercede for her with her mother-in-law, helping them to reconcile again. Mama's warm heart won her very good relations with people. In our small living room, if Mama was home, there was always some neighbor or guest sitting there. Even children four or five years old also liked to come to our home to play with us. Something that often happened was that when meal time came, there were some people who still had not left, so Mama would invite them to eat with us. Da Gu Die, who lived in the yard behind ours, often stayed behind to eat together with us. Some of the children who didn't want to go home were too short to reach the table, so when she served the meal, Mama would put a small square stool on the chair, so they could sit at the same level with us to eat. The gate of our home faced the lane and sometimes there were some beggars who went begging from door to door. They would pass their dirty bowl to our dining table, and Mama would never let a beggar leave empty. She not only gave food to them with smile, but she would also hand over a cup of warm water to them.

During the years when all foods were rationed and when we were financially struggling in our family, we didn't like these people coming to our home to scrounge our food. We could not understand Mama's behavior. Why would she rather share our food with others than let us eat more? We used practical jokes to prevent these "thick-skinned" people from coming to our home again. For example, in the evening before we went to the bed, Mama sometimes would make a little "night snack" for us to eat. The most precious food was boiled eggs with brown sugar.

At that moment, what we most hated and feared was that someone could come suddenly to our home and carve up our food even if it was only a spoonful. But like Da Gu Die who lived in the back yard and another relative called "Xiao Qi Shu," they not only came at our dinner time. Sometimes they also came in the evening and shared some of our food. We were afraid they were coming back, so when Mama started to cook food, we would put a small shoe on the top of the door of our room. If someone pushed the door, this shoe would drop on his head. One day when we were just holding a bowl in our hands, "Xiao Qi Shu" came, and this time he got a dirty shoe on his head. We laughed heartily, but then Mama carried the bowl that had a little food in it for her and immediately handed it over to "Xiao Qi Shu" as before, and said, "Come in, come in, those children were not nice." We really could not find any effective measure to deal with those people. Sometimes after they had left, we would have a dispute with Mama, asking why she had to do this.

Mama said, "If we all just have a bite of food less, all people can have a jolly time together; it is good." No matter how we argued against it, Mama's attitude laughed us out of court every time; she persisted in doing things her way.

But now it seems strange. Although we seven brothers and sisters each have a different characteristic of Mama's personality, each of us have learned to get along with people in the same way as Mama did. All our friends and relatives praise us for this. They think we are all like our Mama in this respect. We were taught by personal example as well as by verbal instruction by Mama; her words and deeds have influenced us so exquisitely that even we ourselves cannot explain how.

In the early part of 1970, Er Jie's family transferred to the Yunnan Mouding Copper Mine to work there. Er Jie worked in the clinic and her husband worked as a technician. This copper mine was located in the depths of the mountain, and the living and working conditions were very hard. Er Jie's family was living in a temporary shed. Once, Er Jie came to Kunming with the ambulance. Mama bought a bag of wheat flour and decided to go in this car and stay with them for a few days. In the evening after they had just arrived to the temporary shed, Mama washed her hands and started to leaven dough. The next morning, she got up early, boiled water, and made the Bao Zi she was so good at; later she steamed many of them. She asked Er Jie to go and invite all her fellow workers who lived around them to come and eat. Er Jie said all the people enjoyed the Bao Zi Mama made. On that mountain ridge for many years after that, many people at the Mouding Copper Mine still talked about the Bao Zi Mama made for them. They all said they would never forget the enthusiasm and generosity Mama shared with them. In those years, for someone to spend her own money, use rationed foods, and put in the time to make Bao Zi for people she had never met was such an amazing thing, and those common workers had never heard of or seen this in their lives. This happened after all of us children had a job, and the financial burden on her was just a little lighter. The characteristic of generosity in her nature appeared once again.

"Money can buy happiness; money has been used in a most worthy way." Mama would say as she always thought in this way. The needier the people were the more worthy they were, and the more happiness it brought to them. This was Mama's guiding principle.

Mama was such an amiable and easy-going person. Where ever she was there would be a harmonious and joyous atmosphere. When Mama was staying with Er Jie's family, on the weekend they showed a film in the open air in the mine. Mama sat on a small square stool and held one of her grandchildren on her lap to watch the film together with all the people. She was very excited and her cheerful laughter resounded everywhere.

"Doctor Yan, your Mama is so kind; she is so easy to get along with. We really wish she could live here all the time," the people living in the lonely mine always said to Er Jie.

Mama's beliefs also filled her with confidence in her children. Though the road of life was exceedingly difficult, she exerted herself and never gave up. She believed that "god helps those who help themselves" and "A good person will get a good reward." She saw her three older children living in an honest and upright way and having jobs and spouses and children. Other than this, she did not have excessive expectations. She hoped to use her strength to help us, the last four children, to get married and start our careers, and then she would be fully satisfied.

This was the goodness, the essence, and the original thinking of an old woman who had endured all kinds of hardships. Later, living in a well-balanced society, we needed to make sure Mama would see this day come. Because Mama had given so much to us, we should have made sure to reward her and make her wish come true. But while I am writing this, my finger cannot continue typing as my heart is ashamed. I feel greatly upset. Oh, time cannot be turned back and change that we were all unfair to Mama!

PAINFUL MEMORIES
(1970–1982)

The events that took place in our family at this time, I am hesitant to even mention and sad to write about. I don't know why something happened with us, the last four of Mama's children. One by one we unfortunately caused Mama so much anxiety that we made her hair go white and her heart break! One calamity after another forcefully pushed her into a hopeless and dry well! Our poor Mama should not have had such undeserved suffering! I have examined my conscience again and again, but I am unable to find out why she was forced to act in the leading role in this story which could not possibly be more miserable. Her heart that was already fed up with wounds was forced to once again suffer continual whipping and tearing, causing the last part of her life in this world to be so painful and miserable.

Oh, I really don't know why these inevitable things happened to Mama and her children. When I recall this phase of our history, I don't know how to narrate it. Tearing those wounds open again makes me really very sad.

Dear Mama, I beg you to give me a chance to repent; let me speak out all the words in my heart. Please forgive me! Even though bringing this out is so difficult.

Let me start by telling you about the first unpleasant thing that happened concerning Liu Jie.

In 1970 at Si Jie's wedding, Liu Jie was one of the waitresses helping Mama to serve the meal to the guests. Li Qi, one of Si Jie's classmates came to the wedding, and he fell in love with Liu Jie immediately when he first saw her. He started to woo Liu Jie fanatically. It was very natural that these two young people became completely lost in their love, and they would meet up almost every day after work.

The news that Liu Jie had a boyfriend spread fast. Mama and Ge Ge started to inquire about and check out their prospective son-in-law.

Because Mama in her mind had accepted the exhortation of "being obedient to her son after the death of her husband," whenever anything happened in our family she always consulted Ge Ge. At that time Ge Ge had a high position in his unit, and his speech and actions were definitely worthy of a man in this society. Mama had regarded her son as the head of the house for a long time and had set him up in the authoritarian position of "the eldest son who acts as a father" among his younger siblings. Without a doubt, the marriage of his younger sister had to get his approval first.

It was a great pity that after they had investigated him in many ways, Mama and Ge Ge came to the same conclusion. They didn't like this young man at all. They did not agree to Liu Jie continuing to have contact with Li Qi any more. They thought with one mind that this man was not a match for Liu Jie, and so it was impossible to allow them to keep a relationship.

Poor Liu Jie. Her first love caused her a great dilemma. She didn't know what she had done wrong. How would she stay near to the dearest people in her life, as well as her first lover with whom she was passionately in love? She had no idea what she should do. Her beautiful face always had an anxious expression and was often bathed in tears.

Mama and Ge Ge tried to persuade Liu Jie day and night continuously for many days, but nothing changed. Liu Jie was still meeting up with Li Qi as before.

One evening after 9 o'clock when I came home, I saw that Mama and Ge Ge were having a serious talk with Liu Jie again. Liu Jie had covered her face with her hands and was crying, and I could hear Ge Ge speaking

Ge Ge, Liu Jie (on the right) and me in 1964.

When Liu Jie was 20 years old.

to her furiously, "I have told you, and there is no room for discussion about this thing between you and this guy. If you dare to meet him again, you should not be surprised if I treat him in an uncivil way! I will do what I said!" Ge Ge was standing in the center of the room in a thundering rage. Mama let him angrily bawl at his younger sister. What I saw with my eyes was indeed the worst conflict that had ever happened in our family from when I was born. I was too frightened to take a breath.

In those days, I saw with my own eyes the kinds of unreasonable actions Mama and Ge Ge would take to stop this marriage. I could not understand why they intervened so harshly in Liu Jie's marriage. I felt sorry for Liu Jie, and when I saw her crying, I shed tears with her too. For more than one month, their attitudes were strong against her. This abnormal emotional behavior made the atmosphere in our home very depressing. Even when we all sat together to have a meal, nobody had a smile on their face. Mama and Ge Ge continued to watch what was going on with Liu Jie.

Their behavior back then and even now was not understood by many people. No one could understand the reason.

It was because the sixth child, my older sister, was really a very excellent girl. In Mama's and Ge Ge's view, for someone to qualify as a partner for such an excellent girl, they would be judged very harshly. They could not accept an average person like Li Qi!

Here, I need to write something to describe Liu Jie, the sixth child in our family.

Liu Jie had become a very special girl among us five sisters; she could be called a beautiful woman. When she was only 16 years old and studied at the chemical school, she was chosen as "the school beauty" by her classmates. When she was 20 years old, she was brighter and more radiant than average people; she was even called "the most beautiful flower in Kunming." When she walked along the street, she always had a strong appeal to people. People would turn their eyes toward her to take a look. And that was not all; she had just found a good job as a laboratory technician and wore a white long gown at her work unit which was in Kunming city. All of this made Mama and Ge Ge very proud of her.

Liu Jie was 4 years older than me. I remember she and I always had on old, shabby clothing. As we were growing up into big girls, we often wore the used clothes which our older sisters gave us. They were either too big for us or the style was totally not suitable for our age. As I have been writing this book, I have looked at many old pictures kept in our home. When I saw a picture of us two sisters and our older brother taken together in 1964, I could not help but burst into tears because that year, Liu Jie was a big girl close to 18 years old, but the clothing she had on was still so worn-out. The jacket she wore every day, all year round, had a torn neckband and wristbands.

However, nothing could hide her youthful awakening. She was growing particularly pretty, and from the inside to the outside her appearance was perfectly full and round. From here on, I think any words I could use to describe my older sister's features would seem pallid because from head to foot, from her facial features to her hair, teeth and complexion, nothing could be faulted. She was indeed a very, very beautiful girl just like a lotus out of the water with purity and dignity. And she had many skills that none of the other brothers and sisters could compete with. She was clever and capable, and she showed an ability to handle things way beyond her age even from when she was a little girl.

When Dad had just died of his illness and Mama depended on the sale of our family property to keep on living, one day Mama needed some money urgently, so she packed up some things and asked Liu Jie to go and sell them. There were two nice cheongsams and a pair of earrings of Mama's and two of Dad's hats. She was only 8 years old then. Mama simply told her about the price, and Liu Jie nodded her head and carried the cloth-wrappers and went out the door. When she saw me standing by the gate, she asked me to go with her.

She was carrying the cloth-wrappers in one of her hands and held me with her other hand and went towards the market. Ten minutes later, we were on Ru An Street where we could set up a stall and sell various goods. In the continuous flow of the crowd, she chose a busy place and opened the cloth-wrappers and put them on the ground, the two of us squatted in front of our things together, gazing at them blankly for fear of losing one.

For a while, people came to see our things and ask the price. I heard that the price Liu Jie told them was higher than Mama had told her. In the process of bargaining, her quick-witted and lovely face easily gained the love and admiration of the people, and very soon she had sold off all the things. Liu Jie counted the money, and it was much more than

Mama had told her; she was very happy. She put the money in the cloth-wrappers and bundled them up well, carrying them in her hand as we went home together.

Half way home, we passed by a booth that was selling stewed pine nuts on Wei Yuan Street. The smell was so good we were almost drooling at the mouth with greed as we stopped and stood there to take a look. Hesitating for only a few minutes, Liu Jie soliloquized, "It is fine if we use one Jiao to buy some pine nuts to eat; anyway, the money we got is much more than Mama said. Mama would not blame us." While she was speaking, she opened the cloth-wrappers and fished out one Jiao and bought 100 grams of stewed pine nuts. Immediately, our small trouser pockets were filled, we ate the pine nuts and arrived home cheerfully. Liu Jie gave the money to Mama and told her that we had used one Jiao to buy some pine nuts to taste, and while she was speaking, she took some pine nuts and asked Mama to have a taste of them too. Of course Mama didn't blame us at all; she was so glad to see that her daughter could handle things so well.

Liu Jie helped Mama to do many things. While Mama was running the Bao Zi shop, she was studying in the third grade at primary school. Each morning, the older siblings needed to help Mama with some physical labor, and because Di Di and I were too little to do those things, buying the meat for making the Bao Zi was her business. Every morning before day break, she always got up on time, put the money Mama had left on the table into her close-fitting pocket, and held a big basket in her hand to run to the queue in the Wei Yuan Street food market to buy meat and take it back home. There were some mornings I was awake early, and I followed her to go and buy the meat one or two times. Perhaps we were very short then, but in my impression, I felt that the basket in Liu Jie's hand was really big. Liu Jie would buy about 3 kilograms of meat and put it into the basket, which then became very heavy. I reached out one of my hands to try and help her share the weight a little. With the two of us carrying the basket and walking along a bit of road, Liu Jie thought that I walked too slowly, and it was better if she took it alone. I saw her put the basket on the ground, and then lean over to extend one of her arms into the handle of the basket which was high and about half her height. Then she used the other hand to quickly push herself up from the ground and lift the heavy basket onto her shoulder.

When she stood up and walked along the road, her slight figure was bent over all the time, she used all her strength to hold it up so she could get this heavy basket with the meat in it to our home. But this was what she had to do without eating anything each morning when she was only eight years old!

The booth that sold meat in Wei Yuan Street was not far from our home, only about a 10-minute walk. At 7 o'clock they started to sell the meat, and if there were not many people queuing there, it took half an hour for Liu Jie to get the meat. If there were many people queuing that day or if it was cold and rainy, she had to stand in the line and move along one step at a time. It was not an easy thing to do, but in that one year that Liu Jie was in charge of buying the meat, she never bungled matters. Maybe it was because she attracted the love of others, and because of her ingratiating way of speaking, the shopkeeper always cut the best piece of pork to sell to her. When she bought the meat, she picked up the basket and rushed home. Leaving the basket on the table, she quickly picked up her school bag and ran to school so she would not be late.

Every day when she was back from the market, she was always tired out, and her cheeks were glowing with beads of sweat, and the hair on her forehead was sticking together. When she passed by Mama's Bao Zi shop, she quickly grabbed a Bao Zi and told Mama, "The meat is on the table; I am going to school." Then running swiftly she disappeared. As soon as she got home after school, she helped Mama to cut meat, chop bamboo shoots, and stir the boiling sweetened bean paste. She was just a little girl but did everything so well.

It may be said that only she had completely inherited Mama's craft and all her kitchen skills, including the ability to make pickles and wheaten foods. When she was 17 or 18 years old, she learned the skills of crocheting and knitting to make a sweater. She did everything in a fine way. Back then, if there were some decorations spread out on the table at home, a special bedspread on the bed, white tablecloths with different patterns, some with the shapes of animals, such as a peacock displaying its fine tail feathers, it was Liu Jie who made it. Who knows how she could crochet them with just a crochet hook?

During the Cultural Revolution, Mama went to work every day, and all the housework was taken care of by Liu Jie. To prepare the meals for the whole family, Mama would sometimes leave her only 2 or 3 Jiao a day so Liu Jie could buy things to make the dishes. But Liu Jie could manage it well. She knew that the cooked red beans and bean curd were the cheapest foods back then, but she needed to go and queue for hours to buy it. She ordered me or Di Di to go and queue; this was the task we had to fulfill. For 8 Fen we could buy a bowl of cooked red beans and a bowl of red bean soup. Or if we spent 6 Fen we could buy a piece of bean curd to take home; everything else was her responsibility. She was always able to make sure all the people in the family ate well. I remember that she had had some inventions; one of which was praiseworthy. She used some Zhao Tong ketchup and cooked it with green peppers. (Zhao Tong is a small town which is well-known throughout Yunnan Province for making ketchup.) This was a most inexpensive but substantial dish. It was really a food for the poor with more spice and salt added, but we only needed a little. We ate it with rice, and then with a bowl of red bean and sour cabbage soup, our meal would be complete.

Liu Jie did not finish her study in the Chemical Technical School. During the first few months when classes were suspended, she would get about 2 Yuan of her living allowance from the school each month. The day she got the money was like a festival for us because she would always take me and Di Di to "Fu Hua Yuan" in Bao Shan Street to eat a bowl of rice noodles with stewed pork. Or at nightfall she would take a saucepan to go and spend 5 Jiao to buy a set of "over bridge noodles" (a famous kind of local food in Kunming). This food was special because of its soup; it was boiled with chicken and pork bones for hours. In the restaurant, a set of "over bridge noodles" was for one person to eat, but when Liu Jie brought one set of "over bridge noodles" home, she was able to make it enough for the whole family. All of us had one chance to taste this meat diet.

Whenever Mama was not at home because she went out to visit Da Jie and Er Jie, everything at home was well managed by Liu Jie.

Of the fixed food quantity we got each month, 30% consisted of kernels of corn and dried broad beans, a food grain other than wheat and rice. Many people didn't know how to process the dried broad beans to eat, but Liu Jie knew. She invented a method of roasting the dried broad beans which we all liked to eat very much. She used some salt and saccharin water to marinate the dried broad beans for 5 hours, and then she would fry them in hot sand, tossing them continuously. The beans exploded one by one, and after 20 minutes, finally they were crisp and soft with a creamy taste, a very delicious food. Every other week she would roast some of these beans and let us eat our fill. After eating this food, it would soon expand in our stomachs, and we could eat less rice. It was fine, and it achieved the purpose of economizing on our foodstuff. Seeing how we enjoyed this food so much, the young people in the neighborhood also wanted to learn how to roast these beans, but they were unable to master Liu Jie's techniques. Either the taste was not as good, or the sweet and salty were out of proportion, or the roasted beans were really "iron beans" where only a few exploded so were too hard to eat.

When I was teenager I didn't like to do housework, and Di Di was clumsy so could not do any housework either. But Liu Jie, to manage the affairs of the household well, made some regulations. Cooking for the whole family she could do by herself, but the other housework, such as going to queue to buy the bean produce, washing dishes, sweeping the floor, carrying water, tipping out the rubbish, each of us three had to undertake some of this equally every day. If we had not finished our duties, no one was allowed to go out to play. Washing the big things at home, such as the bedding, she took charge of, but each of us needed to wash our own clothing. She wrote down one week's arrangements and stuck it on the wall, and we all had to do these things. In this way each of us was trained to do housework, and this was useful to us for the rest of our lives. I remember my main duty each day was to sweep the home clean, to wash all of the glasses, as well as wiping the dust from all of the chairs and table. So, our small room, although it was old and dilapidated, was bright and clean and always tidy and orderly. And Liu Jie had always taken care of the cleaning and tidying up of Ge Ge's room and clothing. Liu Jie made sure his room was very neat and pleasing to the eyes. Back then I think it would have been difficult to find another nice room like this in the whole of An Ning lane. She used a crochet hook and thread and made many pretty pieces of crochet work and decorated different parts of Ge Ge's room with them; they were so beautiful. When my classmates came to visit me and saw this room, they certainly could not believe that in No. 7 An Ning lane in such a shabby yard with the strong atmosphere against feudalism, capitalism, and revisionism outside in the street, a small room like this actually existed in such a secluded alleyway.

Ge Ge had become used to the life of ease and comfort which Liu Jie offered him. He would find it hard to accept that his younger sister, who had served him carefully for more than ten years, could possibly leave his life and that his small room would no longer have this younger sister's touch. And that this sister, who was the closest to him and the most excellent younger sister in his mind, could choose to get married to a man whom he believed to be good-for-nothing. He felt a sense of responsibility, and he needed to come out boldly to make a decision for his younger sister who was still not well educated about the ways of the world. I think that these were the reasons he tried by every means possible to prevent Liu Jie's marriage. But because of the simple and crude means he used, the results were contrary to his wishes.

For many years, Mama often took home some odd jobs and asked us to do them together with her in the evening to help out with the family expenses. We would do jobs like stitching buttonholes and sewing buttons on the children's clothes Mama's factory made. Doing those things was not difficult but took time. While we were sitting together with Mama doing those jobs, we would talk and laugh; we all liked to do it. In the summer of 1967, Mama took home an odd job which was to make a hole in a small piece of fabric. The quantity was quite big, and it required us three siblings, who were idle at home, to do these jobs in a rush often by day and in the evening. I will never forget the experience we had in processing the labels; these odd jobs were very difficult to do, and even now when I think of it, my hand can still feel a dull pain.

At nightfall Mama would bring home a lot of small pieces of cotton cloth which filled a whole tricycle, unload them, and pile them up like a mountain that filled our living room. After dinner, Mama started to give us the processing instructions. We had to make a hole in the middle of the upper part of the small, white piece of fabric which had been cut into a 7 or 8 centimeter length. These small pieces of fabric would be hung on the goods and used as labels. In this way the factory made use of their waste materials to make money. The processing charge was very low, but the quantity required was big, so we could do this for many months. We could not be fussy if it meant we could earn some money. After we looked at the Mama's demonstration, we all thought it was an easy job and started to work at once. But after 10 minutes, we became aware that making a hole in this small piece of fabric was not easy at all.

We put a wooden stool in front of each of us adding a thick plank on top of it. Then we each sat on a low wooden stool, one hand holding a small Chong Zi (the Chinese name of this tool) that had a sharp round hole in the top made of steel and pressing the sharp side onto the middle of the fabric. With our other hand we held a hammer, aimed it at the Chong Zi, and hit down heavily. If it was hit accurately, the sharp edge of the Chong zi could cut through about 10 pieces of fabric. Then we would put the finished fabric aside and then get some new fabric and hit it to make the hole again. At the beginning, we thought this job was fun. While we were working, we were talking and laughing. But very soon, we had some trouble. The Chong Zi was very short and small; it was just a little higher than our fist. I don't know why, but as the other hand held the hammer, it would not often aim at the object, and the heavy blow sometimes would just hit the hand which held the Chong Zi on the part of our hand between the thumb and the index finger. When we hit that part of the hand, it was very painful even to the point of making us shed tears. As we worked for about 2 hours, Di Di and I were getting accidently hit over and over. We were aching and crying out, and we could not bear it any more, so we stopped. But we saw that Liu Jie kept on doing the job for hours. We had no alternative but to keep going. Liu Jie also sometimes hit her hand, but maybe because she was older than us, she was more focused and the times she hit herself were less than us.

One week after we had done this job, the part of our left hands between the thumb and index finger were all wounded and became black and blue. We had a temperature and it was too painful to touch. Sometimes it was too painful to sleep; we would hold our terribly hot left hand up high for the whole night. We were really unwilling to keep on doing this job and every day put on a long face. But we could see that Liu Jie was sitting there and continued to do this job in the day time and the evening, her head covered with big drops of perspiration. We had no choice but to sit there again morosely and keep on following her in doing this very hard job. If we hit ourselves, we would sigh in despair. If we carelessly hit ourselves again, we would cry out because it was really so painful that it reached into your hearts.

One day, Liu Jie gave us each a strip of cloth to twist around our hands as we held the Chong Zi before we started to work. In this way, even if we were unlucky enough to hit our hands, it would not injure our skin. It was much better than before. Another day, Liu Jie told us that the money we earned this month Mama said we could share it as our pocket money. We could do what we liked when we got the money. This was really great news, and it really motivated us. We all did this job for 6 hours that day and had no time to pay attention to the pain. One month later we finished all the processing of the labels, put them into the tricycle, and all three of us pushed the full tricycle to the factory. According to the calculation that making 3000 holes gained one Jiao, we received a total of 10 Yuan. This 10 Yuan, when I think of it now, was really soaked with our blood and tears. I don't know how many sad and painful tears dropped down on the stool in front of us, and each time we opened the piece of cloth which was twined around our hand it was bloodstained!

Mama did what she promised and let us share the money. She thought that we were working too hard. When Liu Jie got the money, as the person to handle the housekeeping, she decided not to share it all, she kept half of it for buying food. She took out 5 Yuan for us to share. Then she did more jobs and got 2 Yuan, and Di Di and I got 1.5 Yuan each. From this we could see that Liu Jie had a capacity for management.

To suddenly get so much pocket money made us extremely happy.

I remember holding my money in my hand and first going to the buffet on Qing Yun Street where I spent 1.2 Jiao and bought 100 grams of peanut brittle. This was the sweet I had been thinking about for years but had been unable to get. Afterwards, I rushed directly to a small shop where I could rent picture books which children like to read. I used 2 Jiao to rent many picture books. I sat there for the whole afternoon reading the books while I was eating the peanut brittle. What a wonderful day! With the money Di Di got, he bought something for fishing since he was very fond of fishing then. And Liu Jie spent all of her money and bought a pair of beautiful nylon socks to wear on her feet. Back then, nylon socks were new products which had just came onto the market. To have a pair of nylon socks with a pattern on them was something all girls dreamed of. With her love of beauty, Liu Jie was the first one to make her wish come true. She was also the first girl to have nylon socks among all the girls in the whole of An Lin Lane.

Later, we did this terrible job of processing the labels for many months. Each month when we sent them to the factory, except for the money we left to help out with the family expenses, we always had approximately 1 or 2 Yuan for pocket money. But the green and blue scars it left on our hands took about half a year to disappear after we had finished doing this work. So it was in our youthful years that we each experienced the hardships of life. Liu Jie was now a big girl of 20 years old, but she had never had any nice clothes. It was natural for all girls to love beauty, and in that year, she saved her meager income for a few months and made a carmine polyester shirt and bought a pair of new leather shoes for the first time in her life. Beautiful and lively all dressed up, Liu Jie was just like an angel from heaven who had come down to earth and attracted people's attention. There were so many people who admired this beautiful daughter; however, Liu Jie was a very traditional and dutiful person. She didn't have any social activities or hobbies. She would stay home all day doing needlecraft and taking care of the housekeeping. It may be said that she was a girl "hidden deep in the boudoir." Even though men felt she was beautiful, they knew there was no chance for them to woo her.

During the Cultural Revolution, Liu Jie, Di Di and I always stayed home together for more than three years. Time is fleeting, and now when I recall the past years, there are so many interesting things which well up in my mind.

Because we didn't have the money to buy a bus ticket, we would walk a 20 km round trip to Hai Geng near the Dian Chi Lake to play there. The girls in our yard or from the neighboring yards would sometimes go with us. Liu Jie would make some fried rice with egg and put it into a big mess tin for our lunch as we were leaving home. To walk to the place was no problem. While we were walking, we were talking and laughing, and everyone was filled with great delight. When we arrived at Hai Geng, we would take off our outer clothes and plunge happily into the clear water, and although we didn't have a swimsuit to pull on, no one laughed at us. We were swimming; we were laughing. Afterwards, we put on our outer clothes and trousers and lay down on the sandy beach to bask in the sun. We collected nice stones and ate fried rice there and waited for our underwear to dry in the sun. In the afternoon at about 4 or 5 o'clock, we started to walk back. On the way home we were thirsty and tired; the more we walked this 10 km long journey, the more difficult it was to take a step. At that moment, the thing we most longed for was to buy an iced-candy to eat. But we could not draw out 2 Fen from our pocket, so we finally dillydallied home. I was tired out and could not do anything except drink lots of water and lie down on the bed. Then it was always Liu Jie who would soon go to the kitchen and get busy cooking by herself, preparing the whole family's supper to be on the table on time.

In the summer during the rainy season, we heard there were mushrooms on the mountain behind The Golden Temple, so together with the girls in our yard, we got up before day break, carried a bamboo basket in our hand, and went up the mountain to pick mushrooms. The way there and back was about a 10-km tromp over hills and dales. Often when it was time to go back home at dusk, there were only a few small mushrooms unworthy of their name in our little basket. When we were back home, our stomachs rumbled with hunger again. We were exhausted and put these wild mushroom aside, not caring about them at all. It was still the same. Liu Jie would clean and cook the meals for us very quietly, and once again there was more delicious food on our supper table.

It may be said that Liu Jie was not only a good helper and little housekeeper for Mama; she was also the most intimate older sister and friend for Di Di and me during our childhood. And she deserved to be called the most loyal younger sister who was like a servant to Ge Ge. She was the most outstanding girl among all the girls in the area where we lived; she was indeed a princess like a crane standing amongst the chickens, lovely and kind.

I think anybody would get the impression that the sixth child of our family was indeed a special girl. So clever and capable, she had now grown up into such a beautiful and lively daughter. Mama's wish that she should have a perfect marriage was reasonable. And the extreme attitude Ge Ge showed then could be understood because he loved his younger sister so much. In the past this younger sister took perfect and minute care of his life, and he knew that his younger sister was a very nice girl. It would be a great blessing for any man to marry his younger sister. Ge Ge would be a great blessing for any man to marry his younger sister. Ge Ge cared a lot about what kind of person would get his younger sister, and he was preoccupied with Lie Jie's wedding. He thought that our family's financial condition was now better than before, so the marriage of this younger sister did not need to be inadequate; it should not be like her three older sisters who didn't even have a wedding. The marriage partner of this younger sister had to be an outstanding man, and she must have a big, nice wedding. Everything had to be worthy of this dazzling flower of the Yan family! He repeated his point of view again and again, "It cannot be random; it cannot be random. My younger sister is a beauty of beauties; her marriage will be a big event in our family. We have to be careful. I will take care of her affairs right to the end." He expected that his younger sister would have the best marriage and the happiest life in the world.

Yes, there was nothing wrong with their desires. They could not understand why Liu Jie insisted on continuing her relationship with Li Qi who was such a common person; he didn't even have a job then and had no professional skills.

I remember how Mama sighed in despair at this unsuitable marriage for Liu Jie. She and Ge Ge consistently believed that Liu Jie had not known this man for very long, and if they only brought some pressure to bear on her, Liu Jie would snap out of it. Therefore, almost every evening they talked with Liu Jie about this situation and exerted pressure on her time after time. But whatever they did, nothing happened. Liu Jie was still meeting this man secretly, and they were passionately in love.

One evening after 8 o'clock when I got home, I saw that a sharp conflict had occurred at home. Mama and Ge Ge were censuring and criticizing Li Qi. Ge Ge was roaring loudly and ceaselessly, "Make a clean break today, make a clean break today! This case needs to be settled today." Liu Jie was tearful. She was sitting in the living room beside the small ark with her head lowered and sobbing. I know it was difficult for her to make this decision.

No people could have imagined that in the same evening, Ge Ge had another action going on at the same time. At the same time that they had initiated their "joint attack" on Liu Jie, he had sent some people to the place where Liu Jie and Li Qi often had their date, and they gave Li Qi a sound beating. When these people came to report to him that they had now "settled with" this guy, I was wise to the fact that a great event would take place in our family.

As expected, the next day in the morning to everyone's surprise, Liu Jie left home and bade farewell to the family. From that day on, she never set her foot in our home. Ge Ge's extreme actions had resulted in a completely unthought-of outcome.

That evening when Liu Jie found out that Ge Ge had sent people to beat up Li Qi, she actually didn't sleep but cried for the whole night. The next morning when she went out the gate of our home, she didn't go to work but went to Li Qi's home. She felt very guilty when she saw Li Qi had been beaten up and injured for no reason, just for her. She felt she had let Li Qi down. Then, Li Qi who was young and filled with indignation and was not a man to be trifled with also called together some of his buddies and planned to settle the account with Yan Mao Qi that evening; they wanted revenge.

What would happen if they continued to fight? To prevent the situation from deteriorating, Liu Jie chose to stoop to a compromise. She implored Li Qi to give up his vindictive act, and she would get married to him no matter what. Since the family could not accept the man she loved, she said she would rather have this man and not the family. She lived up to her word, and from that day she decided she would never go home again. One month later, she and Li Qi hastily got married. She lived in another small room in another small lane. They had known each other for less than a year.

I could not remember how many people were extremely surprised by Liu Jie's act.

"It is often a really beautiful girl who has an unfortunate life! What a pity, what a pity!" the neighbors and friends and relatives bemoaned Liu Jie's fate continually. When the news spread, the whole family fell into depression, everyone was in pain.

This daughter hadn't listened to any advice, didn't even have a formal wedding. She had hastily dealt with such an important event in her life and had rashly gone to live with a man who she hardly knew.

"It is disgraceful; it is really most improper!" Mama was very disappointed, and she felt that Liu Jie's act had damaged her face and self-esteem too much. She didn't think Ge Ge had done anything wrong at all. She was depressed for a long time. She could never figure out why such a nice girl would humiliate herself like this. All of us brothers and sisters felt it was impossible to understand. Why had this dazzling hibiscus, which had risen out of the water of the Yan family, withered so quickly and completely?

Could the love between a man and a woman really make her so blind and confused to lose her common sense? Maybe it did because at that moment no one could understand what Liu Jie had done. Everyone thought that it was not worth it for Liu Jie to leave home for this man. And she didn't even have a wedding. What were her true thoughts? No one could figure it out.

Ge Ge may have had some regret about these serious unimaginable consequences once he knew Liu Jie was married because he went into his small room without saying a word for many days.

Liu Jie's girlhood bed where she slept in our home had always been a long table, and it was closely joined to the big bed where Mama and I slept. That morning before she left home she made her bed shipshape, and for a long time it was preserved this way. I still slept with Mama on the big bed, but we could not see Liu Jie's familiar and full-grown figure on the other bed beside ours any more. We could not get used to it right away; we often yearned for her in our hearts. Liu Jie had left home all of a sudden and now lived with another strange family. Were the people in this family kind or not, would they treat Liu Jie well? I can honestly say that when we thought about this, we all felt sad.

Certainly, the person who was the most grieved was Mama; this matter really hurt her. Looking at the empty bed, Mama cried many times. She spoke plainly, "She grew up, departed from me without saying a word. Everyone is more important than Mama!" The fact that Liu Jie had left her so easily and rashly made her consider the esteem her children had for her for the first time. She often sat together with Er Yi Ma and talked about this event again and again. She believed firmly and steadfastly that there was nothing wrong with the discipline she had subjected Liu Jie to.

Mama said, "By closing one's ears to the older people, you can suffer loss in a moment. The day when she feels regret will be too late."

Listening to Mama talking like this back then, I often prayed for Liu Jie. In my mind I hoped that Liu Jie was dashing ahead, with no regard for her safety to pursue a happiness which many people would admire. I hoped she would never have a day of regret. I also hoped that the man she regarded as more important than Mama, who was as a prince in her mind, would bring something even more precious into her world than Mama could give her. I expected that Liu Jie would be able to have a good life, at least that she would have a better and more comfortable home than she had in her girlhood.

Life still kept on going. In an instant, Liu Jie had left home for a few years. During those years, she had some connection with me, but the

372

estrangement between Mama, Ge Ge and her was never removed. She wasn't willing to adopt a conciliatory attitude with them.

Mama thought that even if she bore no ill will towards her daughter's marriage, she should wait for Liu Jie to feel sorry one day and come to her to make an apology. This was the side of Mama's personality which was eager that everything should be done in the right way. The problem was, Liu Jie was also a person who refused to take defeat lying down. Just because they had different opinions about the marriage issue, this mother and daughter who had gone through trials and tribulations together for more than 20 years had now severed all contact with each other.

"I was unfair to Mama in my life. I am a daughter with a guilty conscience. When I think of the words I wrote on the wall, I feel ashamed beyond words. I shouldn't have said I will buy a radio; I never bought anything for Mama, not even a candy!" Many years later, when all the brothers and sisters met together and whenever we talked about Mama, Liu Jie always said this.

This was the first unpleasant thing that happened in our family among the last four children and Mama. This was a sore spot for the whole family. For Mama, it was a dark spot that was difficult to blot out in her life's journey. Because the hardship she had experienced exceeded that of an ordinary person while she was nursing her children, to be a devoted mother deserted in this way was a heavy blow. It left a wound in Mama's heart too painful to touch. Before we became parents, we could not understand this hurt, today we understand it completely. But it is too late to change anything.

Since Mama lost a daughter who was as pretty as a flower, she then paid close attention to my marriage; she was so afraid that she would lose another daughter. I was more than 20 years old then, and it was time to consider marriage. Just like Liu Jie, I was growing up in a naturally graceful way too, and I was gifted in many ways. I was a solo player in one of the performing arts propaganda teams of the Yunnan Provincial Construction Company. (During the Cultural Revolution, every unit had their own performing arts propaganda team. The task of the team was to publicize the party's general and specific policies.)

Our Mama's sensitivity about her daughters getting married came from the sincerity of a mother's love. She hoped her daughters would be loved by decent and kind men, and she hoped her daughters would have quiet, smooth and steady, and harmonious homes. In those most distressing and difficult years, in the age of the ultra-left controlling the thoughts of the nation, there were certainly some parents who followed the rich and powerful. They wanted their daughters to marry a military officer, someone with power and wealth or a person whose family's class status was good (red) in order to change their own family's status. But the way Mama spoke, she looked down on such parents and daughters.

Our father was from the Bai people group, so all of us brothers and sisters were half Bai. We had five girls in our family, so when the film *The Five Jin Hua* came out, many people called us five girls "the five Jin Hua." (This was a very famous film about the story of five Bai girls and was produced in 1961 in China. The girls' last name was Jin Hua.) They thought that we were clever and had good looks which could be compared to the five Jin Hua girls in the film. Maybe because we had gone through so many hardships and tribulations or maybe because Mama taught us by her personal example as well as her verbal instruction and it had deeply influenced our personality that none of us five girls ever had a thought of wanting to climb the social ladder in order to have a better life. We all believed when we talked about marriage that love is the most important thing. Only if there was love between two people should they get married and live together.

The spouses that our three older sisters had chosen were ordinary intellectuals. The eldest brother-in-law was a teacher at the university.

The second brother-in-law was an engineer at a design institute, and the fourth brother-in-law was an engineer with a geological prospecting group. During that time of "knowledge is futility," they were people to whom society attached no importance. When the older sisters got married to them, none of these three older brothers-in-law had an illustrious position, and two of them worked in a different county, not Kunming. The common custom then was that the standard of a happy marriage was that they should have "three turning and one sound" item. A bicycle, watch, and sewing machine were the turning items, and a radio made the sound. When our three older sisters got married, none of them achieved this standard. But their spouses were decent, cultured people with professional skills, and they loved each other. Mama believed that was enough, and she accepted and respected their choices and sent her blessing and was passionately devoted to them. After the three older sisters got married, Mama regarded her three sons-in-law as her own sons and had a very good relationship with them for years with never any sign of disharmony. The three older brothers-in-law respected and liked their mother-in-law very much too; they were very close to Mama, sometimes even more than to their own mother.

Mama had not even had a chance to meet Liu Jie's husband face to face; her daughter had run away with him. This was certainly very unusual. So right now as Mama's youngest daughter, what kind of boyfriend would I choose and bring home to meet Mama?

In the family, almost everyone knew that I was the girl Mama loved the most dearly. Mama often said, "Among all of you brothers and sisters, Ling Ling and Mao Mao were the most pathetic children; they both didn't have even one good day in their lives." So, she always devoted much more of her motherly love to Di Di and me.

During the years when I was growing up in that small room and swaying in the midst of a raging storm, on the only big bed in our home, I had spent many memorable times with Mama.

From when I was a little girl, I had severe malnutrition. I was always sallow and emaciated with a big head and thin body and always looked pitiful. I was faced with death several times, but it was Mama's love and that she never abandoned me that saved my life. Until I was a teenager, my health was never good. I often got sick and had no color in my cheeks. My hemoglobin was very low due to serious anemia.

Mama could not take me to see the doctor, and she could also not buy any nutriments to give me. All she was able to give me was her love. I trusted in the love Mama gave to me, trusted in the expectation that Mama would be back home by dusk, and so I actually overcame serious illness many times. I slept with Mama under one quilt together with her, day after day. That was how I grew up. When I found a job, my health was still not good and I had a bony appearance. Mama heard that placenta powder could enrich the blood, so she bought one bottle of this medicine and insisted on giving me a spoon each day. Back then this was very expensive medicine. Mama said that before she was unable to buy any nutriments for me, but now she had to improve my health by any means. When I was in girlhood, I had serious dysmenorrhea. At the time of my period, Mama always cooked a bowl of brown sugar with egg and added some pepper and gave it to me to eat before sleeping. She also put some fried salt into a bag to put on my belly to alleviate my pain. I cannot tell of all the love Mama gave to me.

I remember that when I became a regular employee and had a 22 Yuan salary per month, I always heard Mama cough in the night. After I got my salary each month, I always bought one kilogram of honey for Mama and asked her to take some every day. I hoped it would help her to reduce the phlegm and relieve her cough. But she begrudged herself and as long as I was at home, she always made a cup of honey water for me, asking me to drink it. I told her, "This is what I bought for you; I don't want to drink it."

But she would say, "If you do not drink it, Mama will not drink it either. I want you to take some honey; this will make me happy."

Mama loved me so much in this way. Even when I was 20 years old, each Chinese New Year Mama would still make a new dress for me herself, just like in my childhood. When she saw me wear it, she was delighted. In 1971, the whole family had a photo taken together. I was sitting beside Mama, and the dress I wore that day was one Mama made for me that year in the Spring Festival. In the Spring Festival of 1972, I was away performing and didn't have a holiday at home. On New Year's Eve that year, Mama cooked a chicken as before for the whole family for dinner. That day, Mama cut the leg off the chicken and kept it for me. To prevent it from going putrid, she steamed it two times a day, in this way she preserved the chicken leg for 5 days until I came back home. Then she watched me eat it and laughed happily.

My working times were not stable since I had performance activities; I was often out and away from home for about 10 days or half a month. Sometimes, when I came back home in the day time, Mama was not home. I would wash and dress up and go to Mama's factory to see her and give her a surprise. This was really a very joyful thing for Mama. In her workshop, Mama often took me to see her colleagues; she was proud to introduce me to each of them:

"This is my youngest girl." Back then, there were many people who thought that I looked like the leading actor Ke Xiang who was in one of the Revolutionary Model Dramas called "The Cuckoo Mountain." (In the 10 years of the Cultural Revolution, there were only 8 dramas performed on the stages throughout the nation. They were called the Revolutionary Model Dramas. *The Cuckoo Mountain* was one of those.) When Mama's colleagues heard that "Ke Xiang" was coming, they all gathered around to look at me; Mama was very delighted. People saw that Mama's youngest daughter had grown up. She looked slim and graceful, and her colleagues would say to Mama, "Ah, this is so nice, so nice. Your hard time is over."

With Mama's hand in my hand, we would walk back home together, and I knew Mama was very proud. On the way home, when people looked at me attentively because of the player's demeanor I had then, Mama had a satisfied look on her face. When we were going through An Ning lane, Mama nodded and greeted the neighbors and looked so happy. Then, Mama looked quite old in her appearance; walking together with me with my tall stature, she was increasingly emaciated, short, and small. However, the image of Mama in my mind was always the same. The feeling Mama gave me was always warm no matter whether the seas changed into mulberry fields or the mulberry fields into seas. In my mind, she always had black hair and was never old. She was gracious, elegant, and outstanding. Each time my hand was in Mama's hand and we were walking together, I always felt unrivaled happiness, just like in my childhood.

The relationship between Mama and me was very, very intimate. I also knew clearly that Mama loved me so, so much. Would Mama's hard times really be over soon? Wasn't it me who had been telling Mama that I was willing to be with her every day and that I was willing to take care of her for the whole of my life and that my marriage would satisfy her?

Why does a child have to grow up? Why does she have to become an adult and get married and have a family of her own and be apart from her beloved Mama? Even now, I don't know how to narrate all the things that happened with me and Mama. Why could I not possess the man I loved and not lose my loving Mama at the same time!?

While Mama was still in pain from the loss of her daughter, I rubbed salt into her wound, leaving her continuously aching and bleeding. Where was my conscience? In Mama's mind, I was such a lovely and docile daughter. Why was I now also blinded by love? Would I rather give up my own affectionate Mama and go and live with another man, and was this man really worth my love? Does love, which is really so selfish, have to hurt someone, even my most darling Mama? Well then, what is the meaning of love?

I have examined my conscience again and again. Readers may be guessing that my marriage was also not normal and hurt Mama very much. It was true. The man I loved and married in the wonderful days of my youth was a "Rightist" with a very low social position at the time, and he was 15 years older than me. His name was Gao Lin An and was a teacher at the Yunnan Arts Institute.

The harm my marriage brought to Mama went way beyond that of Liu Jie's marriage in that very year. This marriage brought to Mama not only sorrow and disappointment, but also endless fear and restlessness.

What kind of person was a "Rightist?" Here I think I need to relate another very cruel and inhumane part of China's history since there were innumerable people of insight in China who experienced personal misfortune from this political movement.

From the establishment of the People's Republic of China to the present day is about 60 years. In the course of socialist history before the "setting wrong things right" in 1978, landlords, rich peasants, counterrevolutionaries, evildoers and rightists were the five kinds of people who were regarded as the object of the proletarian dictatorship. A few of these people are still alive today. These people still remember what they suffered from 30 years of inhumane politics, treatment that destroyed their spirits. They suffered political persecution even unto death, and a few people like Gao Lin An and I, experienced this horrible life for years and are still alive today. It is unbearable to look back at the painful past, but it cannot be brushed away like a cloud blown by the wind either. So, despite the unpleasantness of recalling this life, I would still like to record and narrate the facts here.

In the early days when Mao controlled the country, the red political power classified four kinds of people: landlords, rich peasants, counterrevolutionaries and evildoers who had committed criminal offenses as the enemies of the proletariat. After "The Anti-Rightist Movement," people who were classified as "rightist" instantly also fell into the enemy class. Together with the four kinds of people above, they were now in the process of accepting socialist reconstruction. "No random speaking and movement is allowed, only be well-disciplined." This is one of the slogans we could see everywhere during Mao's time in China. The kinfolk of these people experienced trouble too and had to endure social discrimination.

From 1950, Mao Ze Dong implemented a series of radical political movements to achieve socialism and to consolidate the dictatorship of the proletariat in the whole nation. These movements left the masses living in dire poverty. People were disquieted and on tenterhooks, but the deterrent force of red political power forced people to keep their resentment to themselves, choking with silent fury.

In April of 1957, the party newspaper the *People's Daily* suddenly came out with a leading article calling on people throughout the country to use the "loudly sound out, give out, argument and banner (Da Zi Bao)" to make criticism of the Party, to help improve the working style of the Party, and to come against bureaucracy and sectarianism. It especially welcomed the intellectuals to offer their constructive suggestions and opinions to the Party. After hearing the instructions of the Party, the intellectual public was overwhelmed by this unexpected favor. The Communist Party would re-administer the country all over again. The

Communist Party trusted in us so much, and our country could be changed. One by one they stated their views frankly and proposed their opinions to the Party. The teachers and students of the university where there were many intellectuals responded to the call of Party even more enthusiastically. Those young students were about 20 years old; they were artless, simple, and candid and had an exaggerated opinion of their abilities. Everything from the administration of the school to different aspects of life in society, they gave their opinions and ideas directly and sincerely to the Party Branch or their Party classmates. Gao Lin An was one of those young people.

It was reported back then that more than 10,000 items of advice, recommendations, and suggestions were drawn from different provinces and provided to the Party Central Committee. But only a few days later, another leading article saying that "things have changed" appeared vividly in each large newspaper. The leading article quoted some criticisms and suggestions of public figures that had been offered to the Party and said: "This is a savaging onslaught of the bourgeois rightists towards the party. But then, the Party Central Committee had expected this in advance. This movement was precisely the plan of the Party Central Committee to "attract snakes out of the hole," and in order to "win by striking only after the enemy had struck." The leading article referred to Chairman Mao's words:

> "Evil people of all descriptions must come out of their cage
> so we can annihilate them. Poisonous grass must be allowed to
> come up in the land so we can easily cut it out."

The Communist Party drew the net in to give some people a hard time. This was a simply totally unexpected event for thousands upon thousands of patriotic people. To use such a trick to damage the intellectual was so terrible; the whole event was colored by conspiracy. According to the book *The Beginning and End of the Anti-Rightist Movement* reported that at the time they discussed how to treat those people who had recommended suggestions to the Party. The Party Central Committee even in the top level of leadership had a dispute. After all this had implicated a country's political credibility and was a moral issue. But at the meeting of the Party Central Committee, Mao Ze Dong, this number one leader of the Communist Party of China, laughed heartily and said, "Just call it an open trick." Mao Ze Dong had settled it with a final word; the tragedy was now inevitable.

According to the official statistics in 1978 when they tried to redress the mistreated rightists, in May of 1958 when The Anti-Right Movement was declared, there were 550,000 people who were classified as "Rightist" throughout the nation. Most of them were the core members and outstanding people of the arts, education, scientific and technological circles as well as the democratic parties. They included many preeminent people amongst the university students. They were doing nothing more than responding to the call of the Party Central Committee and telling the truth, but they immediately fell into a hell on earth. All of them were finished and became the object of the proletarian dictatorship and were reduced to the enemy of people. People who had been labeled a "Rightist" were immediately reduced to a lower rank and salary or had the payment of their salary stopped but retained their office, were discharged from public employment, were reformed like criminals through labor, were sent out to the border area or countryside, put in prison, and so on. People with the innocent heart of a child had offered their penetrating judgments to the Party, but the result was just the opposite; they all met with a miserable end. When they realized they had been completely fooled, it was already too late; they could but cry without tears. Most of the young people who had been labeled rightists were in this state of mind. Both then and now, political critics domestically and overseas consider there is no precedent in human contemporary history for such a purging movement of the intelligentsia.

A famous writer Mr. Cong Wei Xi was also innocently classified as a Rightist, and from being a young and promising writer, fell into hell on earth. He wrote about the cruel persecution he experienced during those times in several books. In his book *Tend Towards Chaos*, he described practically the whole story of The Anti-Right Movement when he was forced to leave Beijing as a Rightist at 22 years old and sent away under escort to be reformed through 20 years of labor on a farm. I opened the book and hadn't read the details but had just barely seen the pictures of the writer from a young age to 1979 when the rightist had been redressed and the sorrow and desolation deep in his eyes, and I started to suffer pain in my heart. It was so similar to Gao Lin An's experience! As I read this book, I felt indebted as if I had received it in person. I don't know how many times I cried sad tears. Another well-known writer Cheng Zhong Shi wrote *The White Deer Plain* (the writer and the book are both very famous in China), and after reading through this book, he came out with the following impressions:

> *"This is thoroughly frightening reading… even though I have read many world class masterpieces, while I am reading this I often have to close my eyes and am often left breathless."*

This is just a small picture of the bloody persecution the rightists have suffered in China.

In 1956, when Gao Lin An went to Beijing to study at the Central Art Academy, he was full of zest. He entertained lofty ideals and was open in his thinking and speaking. While he was talking with his roommates or classmates, he expressed some of his own opinions about the Russian political situation, Stalin, and Tian An Men in the capital city of Beijing. After "The Anti-Rightist Movement" had started, the words he had spoken were written down on a banner and "exposed" by two progressive classmates. At the criticism meeting in his class where the Party cadre asked him why he would publish such freedom of speech, he adopted an indifferent attitude and repeated his opinions again, "To my way of thinking, Stalin is rude; he is lucky I didn't describe him as brutal. Before I came to Tian An Men, I felt it was an amazing building, but now I really feel it is nothing extraordinary; it is just the palace of the feudal emperor. I am not interested in it." He never realized that this was a serious political movement. What he thought in his mind, and what he said was all the same. His frank speech was immediately criticized and corrected firmly by his classmates. One Party student pointed at his head and disapproved with an irritated voice, "The portrait of chairman Mao hangs in the gate tower of Tian An Men, and you dare to say Tian An Men is the palace of the feudal emperor; you are an ultra-reactionary!" However, Gao Lin An didn't learn a lesson from it. One day, he listened to a classmate making a speech and weeping bitterly he said, "By looking at these chairs and desks in the classroom, I am aware how much attention the party and chairman Mao have paid to us." After the meeting, he talked about it with another classmate saying, "If there are no chairs and desks in the classroom, how could we have our class? The government should provide the chairs and desks for students." On the second day, he was "impeached" again for what he said, and he received another criticism by his classmates. In August of 1958, the school came into the last phase of separating the rightists. The summer vacation was even delayed. All the teachers and students didn't attend class every day but attended meetings. They were ordered to seize "the rightists hiding in the revolution team." Everyone was overcautious in their speech and behavior. They were so afraid of this terrible label being put on their own heads because of any carelessness. But Gao Lin An could not manage his mouth well, and he made another mistake. While he was eating with a close classmate, he poked fun at it and said, "The summer vacation is delayed; it seems they have to ferret out and stop some Rightists. Come, come, and seize me." It never occurred to him that this time he had to pay a disastrous price for what he said because what he said did happen. Unfortunately his name was on the last list of "The Bourgeoisie Rightists" published by the Central Art Academy! Reputedly, because the school could not fill its rightist quota, he and Yuan Yun Sheng, the two most excellent students of the Central Arts Institute at the time, were "selected from" all the students over and over again and finally were unjustly pinned with the label of "Rightist." That year, the Central Art Academy of Beijing had less than 400 people, but there were 59 teachers and students separated as "Rightists"!

"It is unforeseen; it is too unexpected." At that moment, although he regretted it, he was surprised and hated himself for doing it, but it was too late to change anything.

Just because he had said the above words, some very ordinary free speech which seems like nothing now, in the summer of 1958, the fate of Gao Lin An suddenly made a 180-degree turn, and in a day, his status had become the enemy of the proletarian dictatorship. From that time, he started 20 years where his life was an inhumane nightmare. When he received the piece of paper which was the "rehabilitation notice of the Rightist" from the Central Art Academy in 1979, he was already 42 years old; 20 years of his youth had been spent to no purpose living in the state of being "inferior to others." As I use the words "one piece of paper" here, all sorts of feelings well up in my mind. In the land of China, when a person suffered undeserved political persecution and was trampled on for 20 years, it was something on a grand scale and done publicly and without restraint. But at the end, the person merely received one piece of paper; the event was over, nothing else. There was not even a public meeting to declare it!

By way of punishment, Gao Lin An graduated in 1960, he was sent to Kunming in Yunnan Province. In this small city where he was a stranger in a strange land, he was assigned to be a teacher in the Yunnan Art Institute. During the following years, he lived in the status of "no random speaking and moving is allowed, just be well-disciplined." This "inferior to others" life was to go even further than the experience Mr. Cong Wei Xi had in his reform through labor on the farm because the people on the farm all had the same status. But when a Rightist lived amongst the common crowd, he was a special race of person and could be extremely discriminated against by anyone. He was a lowlife whom everyone could censure, could denounce, and could even beat up and scold arbitrarily; he had lost all social position.

I wish I could enumerate some facts to explain how as a "Rightist" he suffered from all kinds of inhumane discrimination and damage during those 20 years, but when my mind starts to think of those things, the tears too quickly fill my eyes. I don't know if I can write about those painful past events.

When Gao Lin An came to the Yunnan Art Institute in the year the school was just established, he was the first graduate from the Central Art Academy of Beijing. The school arranged for him to teach pencil sketch lessons for many classes, and his superior artistic talent was warmly received by the students. The first year that he stepped onto the platform in the classroom, he was really full of enthusiasm and wanted to show his best and teach each class well. He tried to use this way to atone for his crime, to let people know that he was not in any way wanting to "oppose the Communist Party or oppose socialism." He tried his best to rebuild himself, striving to get "rid of the label of rightist" as soon as he could and become an ordinary person in society. So, no matter how many classes they arranged for him to teach, he never complained. But, the leaders of the school, especially the two leftist leaders, had engraved on their minds that Gao Lin An was a "Rightist" in his file. They were not going to allow him to just have a normal life at all. He wore a white shirt and black western style clothes as he taught in the classroom; while he was teaching a pencil sketch lesson, wholly absorbed in his demonstration, suddenly, one of the leaders rushed into the classroom and burst out towards Gao Lin An in front of all the students, "Gao Lin An, stop drawing, you go and do hard labor now. You go and unload coal from the vehicle in the front of the mess hall right now!" At the beginning, even all the students who watched this person questioningly felt that treating a teacher with this kind of attitude was going too far. And Gao himself did not stop right away and didn't stand up at once but continued with his drawing. The person who had come in would not wait. He gruffly took the pencil from Gao Lin An's hand and threw it on the ground, and ordered, "I asked you to go, and you should go; didn't you hear? Hurry up! Stand up." He had no choice but to rise and follow the man to the truck, and climb up, start unloading the coal from the truck one piece at a time. This labor took several hours to do. The time came for serving the meal and hundreds of teachers and students came into the mess hall in succession. They were surprised and puzzled to see that this young handsome teacher who had just come from the Central Art Academy was moving coal alone, streaming with sweat. His white shirt was filthy, soaked with sweat. His face was covered with coal dust. The leftist leader thought an opportunity had arisen and he pointed at Gao Lin An, speaking loudly and solemnly to everybody, "A Rightist, this guy is a Rightist, everyone must be clear. He needs to accept reform through labor. From now on any dirty job, any hard work, just call him to do it. You all know now, ok!?" People talked at great length, and their expressions showed all kinds of strange feelings. When he was only 24 years old just setting foot in a new starting point in his life, the admiration and esteem a young person was supposed to have had changed into rebuke and censure. At the very start, he thought this kind of unfair treatment might be temporary since it was all because he had said some wrong words? If this was what you had to experience to reform yourself and turn into a renewed person, you should take it in silence. He never thought that the punishment waiting for him would never stop. This invisible cap on his head, no matter how well he behaved himself, could never be removed. Moreover, as one political movement unfolded after another, this invisible cap on his head became more and more heavy, pressing down on him and almost suffocating him to death.

Back then since the Yunnan Art Institute was the only higher art school in the southwest of China, there were often some foreign guests from Burma and Vietnam who came for a visit. Whenever this happened, he was not allowed to go out but had to stay in his bedchamber. If he was having a class, he was asked to leave the classroom and stand outside somewhere and was watched by someone, not even allowed to gaze around. When he had first registered in the school, he was able to live together with the other young teachers in a dormitory, but later he was asked to move into a storehouse which stored the odds and ends at the school. In the end the place which was arranged for him to live in was not a room, but one corner of the place where coal and firewood was stored for the mess hall. When the Cultural Revolution started, he was forced to move into this place. It was an angled small room of less than 2 square meters by the stairs on the first floor of the library. I don't know how to describe this narrow space. This was the place where mops and brooms were kept and you could not stand up in it but only sit. If you were lying down with your head inside, your feet would be outside the room. Even receiving such disparagement and humiliation before the flock of good looking young people who were studying arts there, they thought was not enough. He was ordered to clean the men's and women's toilets in the school for two years. As the political movement deepened during the Cultural Revolution, he often had to wear a black board with both his hands twisted and tied up and be accused and criticized at meetings to which he would be escorted by two people. Because the former wound was not able to heal, when he was tied up with rope again, it caused injury to both his arms and the front of the chest where they were bundled. The injured skin could not recover smoothly but formed scars on his skin, and even now they are still on his body. Once, he had half his head shaved by the red guards before a big crowd and was sent away to be paraded through the streets under escort. They used red oil paint to paint the half of his head which had no hair. With the mad sound of their laughter and playing, the oil paint dripped down his neck and face. One of his eyes was complete covered with the oil paint, but he was not allowed to wipe it. In this way with one eye watching the road, he was paraded on the street for two hours. Another terrible suffering he experienced happened during the Cultural Revolution and lasted for many months. Every morning at 6 o'clock when the music of "The East is Red" was heard, he had to hang the black board around his neck and kneel on the ground of the playground right in front of Chairman Mao's portrait to "ask for morning instructions" from Mao. Even on rainy days, he had to kneel there. The black board was very heavy, and the rebels purposely used very thin iron wire to hang the board. After enduring the weight of it on his neck time after time for months, the iron wire sunk into his skin, and the back of his neck was badly mutilated for a long time leaving a scar. Over a period of 20 years of re-education, he was sent to a farm time after time far away from Kunming to receive labor reform. In those 20 years, his status was that of a formally authorized teacher at the school, but for much more than 2/3 of the time, he had to clean the campus, clean the toilet, feed the pigs, pasture the cattle, plant crops, be a bricklayer and storekeeper, and do other various physical labor.

This "Rightist" status caused him to lose all basic human rights. All his letters had to be read through by the security section of the school before they arrived in his hand. Even letters from his mother needed to be checked; there was no exception. Year after year, as he accepted this endless punishment without feeling, living in a circumstance which bored him to death, he was once again unwilling to be lonesome and took up his brush to paint quietly. Painting was still a habit he found hard to part with, especially when he had just come to Yunnan from Beijing. He found that the local conditions and customs in the border area were so colorful, like a dreamland, and he was unable to control the impulse of his heart and wanted to paint. Well this was the thing "the Leftists" who had neither learning nor skill hated to see the most. If you still wanted to paint proved that you were yearning for culture; you wanted to show you were a useful person. This was enough to make sure you were still "resisting" rebuilding. Your paintings were nothing; you could paint, and we can damage them easily! So, some oil paintings that he had produced full of enthusiasm were inevitably destroyed by fire. One big sized oil painting which he had painted elaborately, they took away when it was just finished and used it as a board and nailed it onto one side of a packing bag, putting it into the storehouse and using it for holding tools. Seeing how his paintings met with catastrophe like this, in his pain he destroyed two paintings he had just finished, cutting them into pieces by himself. Once he painted an oil painting of three A Xi people group girls waking in the sun. Back then, even the students from the dance department who saw this painting, praised it and said it was "very beautiful, filled with lingering charm." But soon the "sweep black painting movement" came, and he knew that this painting was unable to escape doom, and unwilling to let another person destroy it, he could not help but break it down himself again. That day he looked at the painting for a long time and grudgingly put his hand to it. I was in his room and I saw the sad expression on his face. I told him to cut the parts of the head up and use a piece newspaper to wrap it. Afterwards I took it and hid it in my dormitory for a long time.

While I am enumerating some of the humiliation and persecution he experienced, piece by piece of the bloody picture appears before my eyes once again making my heart tremble and grieve even now because most of the events I have seen or experienced together with him. Whether in the past or the present, I always sympathized with him in his misfortune, and I am full of compassion for the unfair treatment he had.

A young person and a student of college just because he used some free speech, just because he expressed some true thoughts to a classmate which didn't cause any harm to anyone or to any situation, a nationwide political movement made him be "impeached and his disclosure exposed" by somebody. The informer performed a meritorious service; the speaker became a guilty person. Where is the righteousness and conscience of this society? Even if he had said some wrong words, did he need to pay such a high price for it? Did he need to accept such brutal punishment for 20 years? Mao Ze Dong initiated the "Anti-rightist Movement" in person. Mao Ze Dong said himself that the theory of a proletarian dictatorship he put into force in China he had developed from Marxist-Leninist thinking. He did what he wished without restraint and unscrupulously and roughly trampled on humanity. Seeing the kind of persecution Gao Lin An endured for 20 years, doesn't it surely mean that Mao's brutality would make people's hair stand on end?

And he was only one person amongst thousands of students from An Hui province who wanted to enter art school and matriculated at the Central Art Academy in Beijing. While he was studying at the academy, his achievements were always excellent; he was regarded as a "gifted scholar" by his teachers and classmates. When he started to teach at the Yunnan Art Institute, he not only taught rigorously and seriously in the classroom, but also showed his talent at portrait drawing. He could draw the outline of a lifelike portrait in a few minutes and could also quickly draw a portrait as a cartoon in an exaggerated way. His special talent in painting was immediately loved and esteemed by the students. Soon, he was admired and adored by young people from the society who loved art. A young person named Li Wei lived in our back yard when he was studying violin at the Art Institute. He also adored Gao's talent very much.

One day in 1967, it was Li Wei who took Gao Lin An to No. 7 An Ning Lane where they talked together volubly, writing poetry, and painting. A few days later, Li Wei took him to our home and introduced him to my older brother, and he praised Gao as an "unusual painter." When an artist came to our house, and we heard that he could draw a portrait to perfection, we all asked him to draw a portrait for each of us to keep as a souvenir. The portraits he drew for Liu Jie and me were done in a pencil sketch, and he painted an oil painting for Ge Ge. Back then, it was the first time we had been in touch with art. We didn't know anything about art; we only knew that the portraits he painted looked exactly like the person. When a potted daffodil Mama had planted was blossoming nicely, Mama asked him to paint this flower. We all gathered around him to watch, and in about two hours, a brightly colored potted daffodil appeared on the canvas in front of everyone. We all valued his art work very much; we stuck our portraits on the wall at our bedside. The oil painting of the daffodil was framed by Ge Ge and hung in his small room. In those days, Gao Lin An wore a black western style suit and rode a bicycle to our yard. From his dress and temperament, I could feel that he was a little different from the young people in our society; he looked like a person with high aspirations. Ge Ge welcomed this new friend, and very soon they were together drinking and chatting. Sometimes they went together on an outing. When I was just 16 years old, I saw him. I just greeted him with a smile, even though we had not formally spoken to each other.

In the spring of 1968, an art group called "Sing the Praises of the Red Sun" gave a public notice of a vacancy for a singing player in Kunming. They wanted to rehearse Chairman Mao's poems and to open a performance in the theatre in Kunming. I had loved singing since I was a child, and now I was encouraged by some good friends to go for the audition. After several first tries and a retrial, I was chosen as a member of the soprano part of the chorus. When I went to register, I was told that all the members of the art group had to live in the Yunnan Art Institute to rehearse for three months. While we were rehearsing there, we needed to take strict vocal music training with a music teacher from the art institute. It was a rare chance to learn, and we didn't need to pay and could get the training from a professional music teacher from a top art institution. I felt very lucky and packed some very simple bags and went to the Yunnan Art Institute.

I don't know if this was the so-called "will of Heaven" because during those three months when I lived on the campus in the small area of Ma Yuan village, I saw another side of the life of the artist who with a laudable tolerant spirit had taken up a brush to paint in our home. He looked extremely lonely and was subjected to endless bullying and humiliation. The fate of this person provoked sympathy and mercy in my heart. At that time the relationship between us changed.

One day when I had just moved into the art institute, I suddenly saw him in the mess hall, and because he was someone I knew, I thought I should greet him, so I nodded to him with smile. I don't know why he looked at me in surprise, but it seemed as though he purposely pretended not to know me. Another day, when we brushed past each other, he didn't say a word but handed over a piece of scrap paper to me. I didn't understand. I walked to a place without people and opened the scrap, and on it he had written, "All the people here are very bad; you should not come here; you hurry up and go back to your home." I didn't understand what he meant by this note. I didn't know why I couldn't come to this place, so I didn't pay serious attention to this matter. But then, I soon got to know.

Many days later I saw him standing alone in the garden of the campus cutting branches as a line of shrubs was pruned evenly by him. I wondered at what I had seen. Wasn't he a teacher in the art institute? Why was he doing this kind of work? On another day I saw him holding a broom and walking to the women's toilet, asking loudly at the gate, "Is there anybody in there? It's the time for cleaning." I wondered what his status really was. He was too young to be a capitalist "roader" or one of the evil people of all descriptions who were exposed for publicly criticizing and denouncing society. What mistake had he made to cause him to have to accept this punishment of hard labor? I kept my eyes open and observed him. I found out that he was unable to attend any of the ordinary recreation and sports activities which the young teachers of the school did. For example, each afternoon around 5 o'clock after we finished rehearsing, we often played table tennis or basketball with the students and teachers together. At that moment at a distance, he was laboring alone. When people went to the mess hall to eat, laughing and joking, he also stopped working and came to get his meal, but he never talked with anybody else. He carried a big porcelain enamel bowl in his hand, and after he got his meal, he walked back to the place where he lived. One day, I walked closer to the place where he lived and looked at it carefully; it was not a dormitory but a big storehouse where wood, plaster figures, and other sundries were piled up. Everything I saw made me very sad.

One nightfall, I saw Gao Lin An standing by a water tap and drinking cold water. Looking at him more, I felt that his hair was different from his normal style. I walked toward him, and gradually I saw that he looked pale. He was black and green around his eyes, and there were some wounds on his face and hands. I was shocked. After he drank the water, I saw him arching his back with his hand pressed on the wall, slowly walking with a limp back to the big storehouse where he lived.

It seemed he has been injured, something bad must have happened to him. I worried about him all the time; I could not even eat dinner. In the evening I quietly walked into the big room where he lived. I found him lying in the corner on a shakedown on the ground. When I walked closer to his bed and squatted down next to him, I saw his eyes were filled with pain. I saw that his hair had been cut, some short and some long. I saw blood on his shirt which was on the ground bedside him. My tears now flowed naturally. I asked him, "Why did they beat you? Is there anything I can do to help you?"

"I, I have told you that you should not stay here; you won't listen to me," he looked at me and this answer was not what I had asked. I wanted to make sure about what had happened to him, but I saw he was too weak, too pitiful, and didn't want to speak any more. At that moment, I thought he didn't need to explain anything to me. My instinct told me that this was a matter of life and death, and he needed help. I started to look after him to the best of my ability; the relationship with him started like this.

Later I found out that two days before I saw him, he had twice encountered a sudden and violent beating, and he nearly died. The only reason was that he and his friend Ni Zheng Da had gone together to a hill in the western suburbs to paint a landscape painting. That day they both planned to sketch a landscape; they brought an easel, and slowly climbed up the peak in the suburbs. They chose a view and started to sketch. They never expected that to paint a landscape painting on this wild, open mountain would cause such big trouble for them. When they had just drawn some lines and hadn't started to paint any colors yet, they saw a team of people who were wearing "The Artillery" on their sleeves and holding guns in their hands walking towards them. These people were rebels from the Smelting Factory there. They asked why the two of them were painting there. Their answer was that there was no reason, the landscape was just beautiful. They didn't know that this piece of land now belonged to the rebels of "The Artillery," and this territory was under their control. They continued to ask some questions like what faction of the rebels are you from? They answered, "None of them." Who would have thought that this answer would make them very unhappy? Because back then, the two big rebel factions in Kunming had run into circumstances which made them as incompatible as fire and water, and they would kill each other without blinking an eye. Since they were there to paint raised doubts, and those people believed that Gao and his friend were from the opposing "8.23" faction sent there to help them draw a topographical map. They took Gao and his friend to their headquarters at the bottom of the hill and told them that they would send some people to their units to find out if they had told the truth. One hour later, the person sent to do the research came back by bicycle. He proved that Ni Zheng Da was a common person and released him on the spot. But according to the information they got, Gao Lin An was a Rightist from the Yunnan Art Institute. That such a "class enemy" dared to go and paint in their domain meant that they decided to teach him a lesson. They brought ropes and tied him up and wanted to send him to the art institute like this. Gao Lin An resisted them and said, "I was there for less than half an hour. I did nothing but paint; on what basis do you tie me up?" This offended them and made them angry, and they struck and kicked him. After the beating, they cut his hair in a mess and hung a black board on his chest with "The Rightist Gao Lin An" written on it and sent him away under escort from Hei Lin Pu to parade him through the streets to the art institute. When they arrived there, rebel workers reported the case, and the people from the two rebel factions were very angry. They thought that Gao Lin An made their reputation look bad, and they made thorough detailed inquiries about why he had gone there to paint. He explained it and said that he really didn't know he was not allowed to go there, but to their surprise, he repeated the words which made him seem ignorant of the times.

"I was there just to paint for less than half an hour; what law have I broken?" He asked for big trouble for himself.

"How dare you be so stubborn and reluctant to admit your mistakes; how dare you reply so defiantly?" "Do you still think of painting, to hell with it!?" "You, a Rightist, were nearly mistaken as a member of our factions; are you qualified? Do you want to court death?! Beat him!"

They rushed at him and started to strike him violently. Among those people there were teachers and students. Although they were "the unusually lucky people" who were studying and teaching arts, when they wreaked their brutality which was aroused by the great revolution, they were even more savage than the working class. Some of them not only beat him with their hands, but also used crabsticks and brooms and even took off their leather belts to lash his head and face. That day, if the leader of the factions of "The Artillery" had not shouted for them to stop, Gao Lin An would already have been dead. Because he had previously received a thrashing in the morning and hadn't had any food and water and was sent away under escort and paraded through the streets, when he encountered another savage act, he was suddenly bleeding from the nose and mouth, falling into a swoon on the ground and fainting. He was pulled into the place where he lived by some people who threw him onto the ground and walked away. Hence, nobody was concerned about his life or death. He was in a stupor and slept on the bed for two days. He felt very thirsty, and he tried to stand up and walk to the water faucet outside by his room to drink, and then by chance I saw him! This was surely God's will that while Gao was in a most dangerous and disastrous moment, God let me appear before him.

The pocket money Mama gave to me was only 3 or 4 Jiao for a week, so I could not buy much of anything for him. Something I sent him at first was a bottle of Yunnan Bai Yao (a famous medicine for relieving pain and traumatic injury) and two eggs which I stole from home. He had suffered great bodily harm and even his watch was broken. Not only was every part of his face bleeding, but he had also injured the bones of his leg. One month later, he still could not walk normally. Later, I learned his urine had blood in it for a long time. I think even his kidneys were injured. During this period, I was right there in the Art Institute, and it provided me the chance to do many things for him. I helped him to buy medicine and to get boiled water. I sent food to him secretly and so on. I wished he would recover soon, but I didn't have money to buy any good food for him. I saved some food coupons from my limited supply and gave them to him. I hoped he could go out to the small restaurant by the school to have a bowl of noodles. Because he was weak and sleeping on his bed for so many days, he could not eat at all the rough meal I got from the mess hall for him.

Even though his social status was so inferior, it didn't influence my sincerity towards him. He said that what I gave him was the only time in this cool-blooded world that he received pure love and care from a girl in the 10 years since he had been classified as a "Rightist" when he was 22 years old. He himself could not believe there was such a simple person in the world. Afterwards, in a letter he wrote to me, he said that from then on he felt he had been seized by a "bright lamp in his life of suffering."

Three months later, I left the Art Institute and started to perform all over. Then, I was sent to the countryside to receive re-education as were all of the young students back then. Afterwards, I was hired as a solo player in the performing arts propaganda team of Yunnan Province Construction Company. Gao was sent to the farm and departed from Kunming just as he recovered his health. For more than 2 years, we didn't see each other. But something which no-one believed could happen did happen. When we met again, our relationship slowly began to develop.

The relationship between Gao Lin An and me grew from a friendship into love. Getting married and becoming a family took 8 years. I never let him go, and thinking about it now, perhaps it came from not having a father's love since my childhood.

As I was growing up, I didn't fully understand about the love that was in my mind and the longing deep in my heart for a mature, strong love of my own. So, even though the unit I worked with, the performing arts propaganda team, was a place where many nice young boys and girls gathered, I never had favor with any males the same age as me. I had no luck in love with young people.

Though I was living in an age where culture was nonexistent, I was discontented with my lot and had some higher and more beautiful things stirring deep inside my soul. I had disdain for common people satisfied with their common life. In order to have a different life in the future from others, I grasped every chance to equip myself, to fill up the lack that I felt from not receiving a higher education at the university. I had joined the performing arts propaganda team as a solo player, and in people's eyes it was an extraordinary role, but I just used the position as a means for living. When a book named "English 900" suddenly appeared in the shop window of the Kunming foreign language bookstore, I and some young people, who like me were discontented with their lot, went together to find an English teacher and started to study English during our hours off after work. Meanwhile, we were looking for all the literary masterpieces from China and foreign countries which we could discover. We exchanged books to read. Some books were hand-written copies which had been handed down secretly to a few scholars; we sought by every possible means to read them. Afterwards we would meet together to talk about the book. Once we even borrowed the book "The Count of Monte Cristo" written by Dumas the French writer. We were only allowed to have it for one week. It was impossible to pass around such a thick book for perusal, so my friends all agreed to let me read it through and then I narrated the contents to them each evening. At the same time while we were studying English, we learned some English songs. We were playing guitar and singing, and our hearts which had dried up seemed to receive some irrigation. One evening with a bright moon in the sky, we covertly locked up the windows and door and respectfully listened together to one symphony by Beethoven.

That evening, to avoid trouble, we met together and listened to the musical works of this remarkable talent from many ages ago in a small room by an open swimming pool. Our English teacher told us that we should wear our nice clothes and come; he said he wanted us to listen to "holy music." We were all sitting together quietly when the teacher took an old long-play record out of his bag which he had stored, covered with dust, under his bed for years since the beginning of The Cultural Revolution. He put it on the phonograph; all was quiet, and then a heart rending movement resounded to the skies. From the beginning to the end, while we were listening, we were burning with righteous indignation. When it was finished, we found out that it was *The Ninth Symphony* of Beethoven. We were amazed that such wonderful and beautiful things existed in the world, so extremely different from the revolutionary songs from when we were born and the songs of Chairman

Mao, and the 8 revolutionary model dramas which were playing everywhere then. I believe that all of us were really captivated by those "bourgeoisie things". When the music had stopped, we actually could not speak a word for a long time.

I want to thank God. I think it was He who guided me to get to know these people at that time. When I was just entering society, it was a real influence on my spiritual life; it made me feel dignified as if I lived in another world. Sometimes, we forgot the ugly society around us, and we were intoxicated to our heart's content in our own world. It made me different from the young girls and boys of my arts team in some ways. To them, I was a person aloof from politics and material pursuits. Yes, while I was alone by myself, I don't know how many times, I was intoxicated with the romantic love and the stories of a noble life described in the books I read. I was filled with marvelous thoughts and wonderful dreams about love and my future life. Recalling those times now, I still think it was indeed the best time in my whole life, though it was very short!

Once again God arranged for me to meet Gao. One evening in the fall, I left home to buy something in Nan Ping Street. While I was walking through An Ning Lane and turned a corner, I met Gao Lin An again. He had just come from Nan Ping Street to turn onto An Ning Lane on his bicycle. There was a bike parking station near the road crossing, he wanted to park his bicycle there and go shopping in a nearby bookstore. Back then he was in charge of the reference room at the school. If I had left home a few minutes later, or if he had come to the place a few minutes earlier, we may have missed meeting each other. But without any person between us, we two meet together. Face to face with each other a few seconds later, suddenly, he put one of his hands on my left shoulder and said the word, "Beautiful!" I felt embarrassed and blushed and lowered my head. But I soon raised my head and gave him a sweet smile.

"You haven't changed at all, except you are more beautiful." He looked at me dumbfounded, and immediately I felt the strong love in his eyes. In the setting sun, we were standing on the street very quietly as if we had stopped breathing. I have to be honest; he was the first male in the world to touch me. I don't know why, but when he patted my shoulder with his hand it made me feel very warm. Praising me, loving me in this way, really touched a sensitive nerve in my heart of hearts. I felt this was the love I was thirsting for; it was deep and kind. And he said that day, the smile I showed him also touched him so much, such a bright and sincere smile he hadn't seen for a long time. He was sure I was not corrupted by this dirty world. I hadn't become slick and sly; I was still as clear as crystal; I was still "Xiao Ling". (Xiao Ling was my pet name; Xiao in English is "little.") In his mind I was the girl he was seeking. So, after he went back to his dormitory in the evening, he didn't sleep for the whole night but wrote a love letter nine pages long and sent it to me. How could I resist all those enthusiastic and burning hot words? In the evening we made our first appointment. When I walked out the gate at my work unit and saw him waiting for me under a street lamp, neither of us spoke but immediately embraced tightly. We started to go out on frequent dates; we were really passionately in love. My work unit was close to the Da Guan River; there was an arched bridge there, and under the bridge became the place where we met secretly. He told me about his family and all of the things he had experienced in his life, including how he was classified as a "Rightist," and how his current situation had gone from bad to worse.

He said, "It doesn't matter, I am used to it. The only thing I still want to do is to paint." Not long after that, he took me to two places where he often met some friends from the society. One place was called the "Artist Salon" by those young people who were keen on fine art and who met together there after work. It was located in a small lane off Wei Yuan Street in Mr. Ni's house. There were many red camellias blossoming in the yard, and many paintings and drawings hung up on the wall in a small room. Some of Gao's small oil paintings had been put up in a prominent place by his friends. I could see they all esteemed Gao very much; he was surrounded by the sincerity of all the young people. Another place was by the Green Lake; it was the home of Mr. Zhou Shan Pu who was of the Na Xi nationality and was a famous scholar. Mr. Zhou had been sent out of Kunming and transferred to Lijiang to do manual labor for labor re-education. Mrs. Zhou wore white sleeve covers and swept the street every day. But their son "A Ba" loved painting and calligraphy. In their home there were always some friends who were keen on literature and fine art who met together. Gao also received a most warm welcome from them. All of those friends knew that Gao was fond of drinking and had a great capacity for liquor. So, if he appeared at these two places, a bottle of alcoholic liquor and some simple food would soon be put on the table. Most of the time it was only a cup of liquor and was only offered to him. They listened to him talk volubly with great respect. They listened to him talk about Michelangelo, Delacroix, Repin and Surikov (two famous oil painters of Russia), and listened to his opinion about what was beautiful and ugly. Other times he didn't talk about art, so they listened to him talk about UFOs and other civilizations in the universe which he believed existed.....he seemed to be a cultural authority in these two places. They also liked to stand behind him to watch and emulate his painting. So, these two places had become where Gao temporarily performed his "portrait painting," painting the portraits of many of the relatives of those friends. Some portraits he painted were very nice; they have preserved them until now. When Gao took his girlfriend to meet them, they all showed great interest in me.

These two places were full of sentiment and the atmosphere of the art world. They lived in harmony there. It was so different from outside where civilization was being atrociously destroyed and people were killing each other in revenge; it was a sharp contrast. The scene of them coming together to paint, to talk about fine art, to appreciate literature, this was coincidentally the life I was yearning for in my mind. I really liked to go to these two places with him. These two places became a refuge for Gao Lin An during the Cultural Revolution and also became the storage house for the few oil paintings he created in that special period. But, the friends in these two places also suffered much grief and blame because of him. In the later period of the Cultural Revolution, the school wanted to search for his art works, and these two families were checked many times by the security section of the school.

One evening, before we were about to part, Gao Lin An suddenly handed me two thick books; it was the world masterpiece *John Christopher* written by the famous French writer Romain Rolland. He told me I should read the books carefully and I must tell him what I think about the books after I had finished reading. I read the books in tears. I don't know why, but in the course of reading the books, I sometimes linked Gao Lin An and the leading character in the novel together. In some parts I even thought it was like a description of the life of Gao Lin An. When someone has a very special talent and, at the same time, has been endowed with an extraordinary character, he seems "unusual" or "eccentric" in some respects. They always seem to detest the world and its ways and are incompatible with real life. In fact, they could not understand the reality of this world, and the real world could not understand them either. Living alongside the common people, they were really like lonely ghosts wandering in the air.

At that moment, I realized clearly that Gao was using this to figure out my intentions, to see if I was able to go along with him, to go through the whole of his unlucky life together with him. Then in another letter he wrote, "The life of the artist is always painful, but they leave the most beautiful things to the world."

404

As I had the opportunity to enter the inner world of the artist through this book and as I had more contact with Gao Lin An, I believe I understood art, as well as life, more profoundly. Then I made a decision. I would love Gao Lin An forever. I wanted to be with him and go through all of this arduous and tortuous life with him. I thought he must have love in his life, and he should have a family. His life should not in any way be like Christopher, who repeatedly suffered disappointment in love and spent a lonely life in the world. I told myself that even if no one in the world loved him, I would. Then I even examined myself seriously once more and, wishing I could be more perfect, I was willing to dedicate myself to him completely!

We were secretly in love with each other; neither of our units knew, nor did my family. The Proletarian Cultural Revolution was still greatly expanding. Gao was still under surveillance from the art institute, and his punishment was elevated, but he told me, "I can suffer any difficulty now; if I only think of seeing you again, nothing can baffle me." Each time when we parted, he habitually put both his hands on my shoulders and asked me to smile for him.

"Xiao Ling, your beautiful smile gives me the most comfort in my lonely life. I am struggling in the ocean, and the only thread of light I can see is you…" When he was sent out of Kunming to a farm to take up rough labor reform once again, he would send me letters full of his emotional thoughts. Although I had told him "I love you!" innumerable times, he was still afraid that since we were often separated, another person may have a chance to step in and take me away from him. He knew that the path of our love would not be smooth.

In the summer of 1973, Mama and Ge Ge finally found out that we were in love. One day, Mama saw me sitting on the back of Gao Lin An's bike. She saw that both my hands were around his waist and we were talking intimately together.

Mama could not accept this fact at all; she was shocked and panic-stricken and could not sleep for many days. One night, she talked with me until 5 o'clock in the morning. She was very sad, and as she spoke she was crying. Her voice was hoarse. She used every means to persuade me saying, "You must deviate from this terrible person as soon as possible; you really should not jump into this fiery pit."

Now that another one of his younger sisters was a traitor and had become involved with such a person, Ge Ge flew into a rage. He hated this "devil" intensely, and he even vowed that he would expose Gao to mortal danger. Ge Ge's intervention with me went even further than what he had done to Liu Jie. But I dared to argue with him, not just cry. Once, I even sneered that Ge Ge was vulgar and that he was ignorant of what true love was.

During those years the whole nation was ruled by "The Gang of Four." (For the 10 years of The Cultural Revolution, the leadership of the Party Central Committee in China was controlled by four people, one was Mao's wife. They were called The Gang of Four after the Cultural Revolution.) For a family like ours, life was hopeless. Every day we were treading on thin ice, so why would I want to jump into a deeper abyss? And inevitably if I married such a notorious person, it would have a political implication for and affect all of my brothers and sisters. The landlord, the rich peasant, the counterrevolutionary, the evildoer, and the rightist - everybody was so afraid to be associated with those five types of people. If one of them was identified with any of us, it would stain all the members of my family; everyone would become black upon black, and it would be difficult to keep a foothold for ourselves in society. Why was I obstinately sticking to a wrong course? Was I, as Mama had described Liu Jie then, "possessed"? I really don't know.

Our love story did seem to go beyond our wildest dreams. Even as Mama and Ge Ge discovered us, we had already made a pledge to love each other to the end of this life and never separate. It was impossible for anyone to break us up.

However, Mama was the closest person to me. She and I had been deeply attached to each other for more than 20 years, and I could not stand to hurt her. I did not want to heartlessly leave her as Liu Jie had done, so I told Mama I would not get married to this man right away, but I was unwilling to seek any other man for a husband. I asked her to forgive me. Mama looked at me, shook her head, and sighed, "Oh, Ling Ling, you are too foolish. You could absolutely have a better life!"

One day, Mama had a talk with me again. She held my hand and asked me to raise my head to look at her. As our eyes met, she said, "You tell Mama - do you think I would hurt you?"

"No," I immediately shook my head as I answered.

Mama looked at me and told me that she was not cruel-hearted or selfish, but she wanted me to get married to a person that she liked. She tried to analyze the situation practically and realistically. Even if we did not pay attention to the political situation, the age and the personality of this man did not match mine at all. If I married him, I would not have any happiness in my life. Because an artist was always subject to changing moods, being his friend would be fine, but we should not live together. Mama told me that she hoped her youngest daughter would have a stable family, and a husband who knew how to take care of his wife. She even referred to a word from a foreign film to scare me saying, "If heaven wants to punish a woman, she will get married to an artist." She advised me earnestly and asked me to leave this man. Mama spoke to me with deep love, "Listen to Mama just once. Mama really hopes you have a good life. Mama knows your personality. Mama actually doesn't want you to have an unfortunate life!"

That evening, Mama and I both had tears covering our face. I told myself that perhaps she was right; perhaps I had found a wrong marriage partner, and perhaps I should absolutely leave this man. On one hand, I begrudged being separated from Mama, but on the other hand, I couldn't leave this man who needed my love and care so much. This man was in some ways like my elder and in other ways like my lover. He was alone in Kunming with no one to care for him, and I was deeply concerned. I was too difficult to sever our relationship. For many years, I didn't want to cut off my relationship with my family, but I also didn't want to break off my relationship with Gao. But it was impossible to keep both relationships in my life as they were.

One Sunday Mama stayed at home, but I left home early to go to meet Gao Lin An by the Dian Ci Lake. He was painting a seascape there; I sat beside him to watch him. We parted under the lights. I got home around 7 pm. When I entered the room, it was silent. I walked to the small kitchen at the back and in the twilight at sunset, I saw Mama sitting on a small stool by the hearth and cleaning the boilers. There was some plant ash in front of her. She held a handful of grass and was cleaning a dark boiler, and two boilers were beside her. In those years, every family used coal for cooking; all of the boilers were smoked and became pitch black. Mama was wholly absorbed with her cleaning and didn't know there was someone coming.

I was leaning on the doorframe of the kitchen staring at Mama blankly. I was suddenly so moved my tears almost poured out. My eyes clapped on Mama's sparse hair hanging down covering her thin face. She was mechanically moving her hand, preoccupied with this petty thing as if she had forgotten the whole world. At that moment, Mama was no longer strong like the great Tai Mountain, but she seemed just like an ant, an ant who didn't know how to stop for a rest. She only knew how to work hard, too busy to stop, with not even time to look at the sky. My eyes were moist as I squatted down by Mama. I felt a little self-accusation for I had forgotten her again this weekend and left her at home alone. I faced her and called out, "Ma." Mama abruptly pulled her thoughts away from her work.

She spoke to me excitedly, "The whole day I have been home alone; you have finally came back. Mama has prepared some food you like; we can eat together." She stopped her work to rise and wash her hands and to cook. I helped Mama to finish the cleaning job. After a while Mama and I started to eat together. Mama put some of each of the dishes into my bowl ceaselessly, and she ate only a little. She looked over at me eating and smiled without saying any words. It made me feel even more sad. During the past several years, I had never taken a boyfriend home. Mama naturally knew who I had met for the whole day when I was out, but she didn't want to say anything more. Maybe she had already anticipated that another of her daughters would leave her soon. She had a limited time to share with me right now, and she was content with her lot.

After eating, Mama told me, "You help Mama to stew some medicine. I don't feel very well today. I went to see the doctor and got some Chinese medicine." I opened the package and poured the herbal medicine into a pot, added some water, and put it on the stove to decoct. While I was stirring the herbal medicine, looking at the steam rise, all at once I was full of mercy for Mama and tears started to drip down. In those years, Mama had become weaker, and she often had a cough. She often went to see the Chinese doctor, and then decocted the herbal medicine by herself. She was never concerned about the condition of her health in front of her children. My impression was that Mama had never even once had to lie down on the bed or let others serve her. Anything she was able to do herself, she would never ask for help with. She was unwilling to bother anyone, including her children. In the evening, when we were coming back home, we were accustomed to seeing Mama decoct the herbal medicine and keep watch by the stove herself. And today, I could have been home and gone to see the doctor with her this once. She had no excessive requirements, no complaints either. But all the children could so easily forget their Mama. That day I told myself I should spend more time with Mama later on.

In the still of the night, I lay down with Mama on the bed, and I specially narrated a film to Mama. It was called "Flower Girl" from North Korea and was a popular show in each cinema in Kunming then. This was a "super crying film," the people who went to watch the film could not help but cry. I suggested Mama also should go to watch this film, but she said, "I don't want to watch it. It is enough that I cry for myself. I don't think there are any other people who have a life more miserable than ours in the world." It was true; when we uttered a stifled cry of agony in the cinema, it was because the girl's fate resonated with us, and we felt as if the life shown in the film was just like the life we were having.

One day, Ge Ge brought a girl home to come and eat dinner. After the girl left, Mama and Ge Ge were together excitedly talking about the girl. So Ge Ge was also in love. He had known the girl for a period of time, and the day he took her to our home it was to let Mama look her over. After only a short time, Mama immediately liked the girl. Mama praised the girl ceaselessly, and she was radiant with joy and said, "Good, good, she looks fine. You invite her to come again tomorrow." I felt joyful myself. Mama's life may have changed; she would have more joy. After all, Ge Ge's marriage was the most important event in Mama's mind, as well as for our family.

Ge Ge's girlfriend Xiao Kun was not tall and had a round face. She was a shop employee in the sales department of the Kunming Medical Company. The reason Mama liked Xiao Kun, I think, was because of Xiao Kun's personality. She was the kind of person who had a good relationship with others, very amiable. According to her experience and personality, she believed that whether a woman was doing a great thing or not was not important, but if a woman could create harmony she was a good woman. Mama liked a girl who had good intentions toward others. She often said to us that she wished we could be such a person, "even-tempered and good humored." Her eldest son's wife, her first daughter-in-law, had a gentle and kind character; she thought this was an essential quality. Mama believed that with those qualifications Xiao Kun would live in harmony with Ge Ge's brothers and sisters like one of the family. After that Xiao Kun was invited by Mama to come to eat dinner with us often. She came with a smile on her face, and she left with a smile on her face too, not saying too much. The more Mama examined her, the more she liked this girl.

In those days, whenever Mama and Ge Ge met together, they were always talking about Xiao Kun. Mama inquired about Xiao Kun's favorite food. Then she started cooking it for her, hoping that Xiao Kun would come to eat dinner at our home every day. She observed that their love was progressing with happiness and gaiety, and she said with satisfaction, "I can set my heart at rest; that our family can take in a girl like this must be our reward for the virtues of our ancestors." Back then, none of us children approved of what Mama was saying, in our eyes. Xiao Kun was too common to be a match to our older brother who was "tall, great and complete," and in our minds Xiao Kun seemed too feeble for him in many ways. But Ge Ge was a nice young man with filial piety, so when he picked a partner in marriage, he first thought of who Mama would approve of. Compared to him, Liu Jie and I were really "possessed, and going astray"; we were indeed "beyond redemption."

In the evenings after 11pm, Mama and I would be going to bed, but Ge Ge was still not home. Mama would put a chair behind the door; then she leaned against the bed and read a book as she waited for Ge Ge to come back. Half asleep, she would hear someone push the door and the chair would make a sound; it was Ge Ge coming. As long as the light by her bed was still bright, Ge Ge always immediately walked to the small room where we were living and stood in front of Mama. He would light up a cigarette and hand it over to Mama. Then they would talk in whispers. Most of the time, they were talking about Xiao Kun, her family, her habits, even talking about what color clothes suited her the best. After smoking one cigarette, Ge Ge left Mama's room, and they both went to their dreams feeling satisfied.

I remember one night after Ge Ge came home, he didn't talk about Xiao Kun with Mama but handed over two boxes of imported medicine to Mama. Although Mama didn't know the foreign language, she put on her reading glasses immediately and held these two boxes, looking at them again and again. Ge Ge told Mama this was the best foreign medicine in the world, made in Romania, and it promised longevity. It was called "H3". He turned around and got a cup of hot water and gave it to Mama telling her, "You take one now."

Mama was so touched. She took a pill from the nice medicine box, put it in her mouth and swallowed it happily. I knew this was the most expensive gift Mama had ever received from her children. Previously, Da Jie and Er Jie had brought some medicine to Mama, but they were just some special local products from Wen Shan Three Seven. At that moment, when her son presented such a rare medicine to her hoping to prolong her life, his filial piety was indeed priceless. That night, I had been sleeping on the bed with my back towards them, but I heard all the conversation between them although Mama didn't know it. The evening of the second day, when I got home, she showed me two boxes, and delightedly told me, "I only took it two times, and I feel full of energy today; this medicine is so good. Your older brother is a dutiful son."

Yes, Mama was very proud of her oldest son. After making great efforts in those years, Ge Ge showed his talent in many ways and stood out conspicuously. Then he was transferred from his unit to the Kunming Medical Company and took the secretarial position of the revolution committee in the Medical Company. Because he held this post, he had the chance to bring the imported medicine to Mama.

But the problem with me was not settled, it still was an anxious load on Mama and Ge Ge's mind. Sometimes, when Ge Ge came back home at midnight, the conversation between them was not in the room where Mama and I lived but in Ge Ge's room. I knew they were talking about my issue. Since I hadn't married this "bad" person, they thought they could still prevent this marriage from happening. Some days, when I got up in the morning, I could see a letter Ge Ge had written to me on the table. In this letter he enumerated a variety of Gao Lin An's wrongs. He described Gao Lin An as a brutal wolf who wanted to catch me like a lamb and not set me free. He was full of resentment and dissatisfaction.

He said, "If I didn't care about such a very serious matter, I would not be your older brother." Even though as a result of his intervention, our family had lost one girl, right now he still thought that the matter with me was very serious, and he must deal with it. Because he was involved in political circles and was an administrative staff member in his unit now, he was clear about the status of a Rightist - what it meant for him, for our family and for me, such a young girl.

Lately, both our units found out that Gao and I were in love. To obstruct the relationship between us, I was becoming "the object of help" for the Communist Youth League in my unit, and various "helpful" activities were directed towards with me. No one could understand why I would take a fancy to such an old person who had such bad luck. The secretary of the League branch in my unit talked with me once more. As a political cadre, he certainly knew what my prospects would be if I married a Rightist. He was a kind person and said to me, "If you already know the result, and you still pursue it regardless of the consequences, what kind of person are you? You are stupid. I sincerely want to help you." I know at the time, I was indeed obstinately sticking to a wrong course, because there was no advice that could change my mind. The Art Institute also knew that Gao Lin An, a Rightist, had a young, nice girl who loved him. They treated him even more severely; the best measure to stop us having contact was to send him to the farm, making him leave Kunming for months.

During those times, Ge Ge continued to make use of all the ways and means he could think of to persuade or educate me to leave Gao Lin An. Once, he even asked one of his friends who held power then and worked in "The Revolution Committee" to get Gao Lin An's personal files from the security section of the Art Institute and showed me his "crimes" in order to rebuke me. Some of those documents were the "thought reports" and the confessions written by Gao Lin An. Poor Gao; in the past years, he had criticized himself again and again so many times. He had worn every kind of profane label on his head. But the majority of the files preserved in the security section were letters of accusation. The contents of those letters of accusation left me dumb-founded. There were several impeachment files which reported that Gao Lin An often used a big cylinder to look directly at the sky. They were suspicious that he was contacting the foreign enemy's broadcasting station abroad with this tool. I knew the big cylinder they mentioned, and it was an astronomical telescope his father gave him as a gift. He liked astronomy; sometimes he used this instrument to observe the sky. While he worked in the Art Institute in the past for more than ten years, there were so many colleagues and students who wrote these letters of accusation about him and reported him for so many "crimes." He couldn't have known earlier that his every speech and action was under surveillance by people. When they finished talking with me, they thought I would be afraid and would leave this person who "was guilty of the most heinous crimes" at once.

On the contrary, I was more sympathetic with him in his misfortune. I felt deeply pained about his living under such terrible stress all the time. I didn't answer them with words but cried endlessly for hours.

At the end of 1974, seven of us classmates who studied English together were accused by "the red bound feet" of the street neighborhood committee. (The old ladies who worked in the street neighborhood committee were called "the red bound feet" by the people since they were from red families and had bound their feet. And those old ladies were always doing bad things.) We were locked up in the Kunming city militia headquarters for examination for 11 days. They asked us one by one to talk behind each other's backs and expose each other; we were forced to report what we had been doing while we were studying English together. They said they had found out that our English teacher was also a Rightist. Because there were two Rightists who were in contact with this place, they thought that we young people may have possibly been "corrupted and roped in" by these two bad people and had become the new counter-revolutionaries. They thought this place could be turned into a black "Petofi club" (Petofi Sandor was a famous poet from Hungary. In 1956, he set up a club against the political persecution of Khrushchev who was the general secretary of the Communist Soviet Union.) They said this was now a chance to help and educate us and change our thinking. After this mental suffering, each person had a bad record on their personal file in the security section of the unit. All the young people were afraid of this, and our English class was forced to disband. My formerly close friends did not contact me after this happened, and I started to realize the serious consequences of being in touch with a Rightist.

In April of 1975, the whole of Kunming city was on the alert because there was a delegation of foreign military officers who were visiting Kunming on the 12th of April. This was the first time Kunming city had received a foreign delegation. In preparing all the details for welcoming this delegation, one month before they were coming, the Kunming public security bureau had issued many prohibitions. All units and individuals were informed that on the day nobody was allowed to go to the department stores since the delegation would go to visit there. The people in the department store who would be shopping on the day were people selected carefully from the song and dance ensemble and the university. They were the sort of people who could be trusted politically and would also look refined and wear pretty clothes. From nine in the morning to four in the afternoon, the kind of people who could walk around and which street they could appear on had been arranged carefully by the government. The delegation arrived on schedule; the city government also completed their reception duties satisfactorily. But on the second day after they left, the Kunming public security bureau sent a "public notice" to all the units in Kunming that said they had received a report from the "revolutionary masses" saying that Gao Lin An had planned to try and meet those foreigners to complain and call for a redress for himself. Once this case was checked and approved, the public security bureau would punish this audacious rightist severely. With no excuse, he was sent out of Kunming secretly under escort by the militia in full battle array to be examined in the afternoon of that day.

The "public notice" enumerated the time and place Gao Lin An had arranged to approach the foreigners, and it was exactly the time we two had met together somewhere. So, after I listened to this public notice at the meeting of my unit, I realized immediately he was framed. After the meeting, I rode my bicycle to his place, he was not there and the door was locked. The second morning, I went to the public security bureau to appeal for him. When the officer asked me what my relationship was with Gao, I told them, "I am his girlfriend; we have known each other for many years, and we are going to get married soon."

I knew this matter was serious, that this accusation would condemn him to prison. I worried about him so much; I hoped I could see him right away. This information was fed back to the security department of my unit at once. A whole employee meeting was held in the afternoon, the party secretary spoke loudly at the meeting:

"It is a misfortune that there is one person in our unit who has associated with this criminal wanted by the law. She went to the public security bureau and admitted she is the girlfriend of this guy. Oh, she could have a good future, but she doesn't want to. Unfortunately she volunteered to gang up with a Rightist. I can tell you all she is just sitting here."

People started to talk about me; the people in the know scorned me with their eyes. The party secretary continued, "We hope this young girl doesn't refuse to come to her senses! There's still time now to break with this Rightist, to make a clear distinction with him."

The meeting was over, the young people from the performing arts propaganda team, with whom I had previously been together laughing and joking, now no longer wanted to walk together with me. I could not adapt to this in a short time. On the second day because of my personality, I still wanted to greet others with a smile, but I was rebuffed repeatedly. People were all standoffish to me. At that moment, I realized that in their eyes, I had become a proletarian enemy. I was a member of "the landlord, the rich peasant, the counterrevolutionary, the evildoer, the rightist." I had become an unusual human being; all the people were afraid to touch me.

However, and maybe this was the power of love, none of the things which happened influenced my thinking and actions. Though I was lonely and without any help, in my mind the person I missed and paid close attention to was still Gao Lin An.

More than two months passed filled with worrying and misgivings. One day, I suddenly received a letter. My name and address were written on the envelope in a poor hand. I ripped open the letter; it was a short letter Gao Lin An had written on a piece of a cigarette case. He had asked a buffalo boy to help him send it to me. There was a map he had drawn on the paper to tell me where he was. He told me he may not be able to come back to Kunming. The act of malicious persecution this time was to separate us completely. On this piece of cigarette case, he expressed the strong feelings he had for me. With thickly dotted writing, he wrote: "I tear my chest and lift up my voice: why can I not have love? Xiao Ling, I am waiting for your coming. I want to hold you tightly in my arms, to kiss you."

I read through this letter written on a dirty cigarette case with tears covering my face. And I carefully looked at the place he had described. It was Xiao Duo Gu village in Xundian County in Yunnan which was about 120 km from Kunming. I quickly made a decision that I would go and visit him immediately. But my situation then was that the unit and our family could follow me, so I must keep this action secret. I did something just like an underground worker in a film. I went to a friend called "Lao Ba" who was the most trusted by Gao Lin An and asked him to go to the train station to help me to buy a ticket to Tian Sheng Qiao Stop in Xun Dian. We made an appointment to meet around the corner from the train station the next morning. I wore a straw hat as a sign, we pretended not to know each other, to make sure there were no people watching us, and he handed over the ticket to me without saying a word. I quickly walked into the waiting room at the train station, and stepped onto a train which went to Xundian. After more than four hours later, I got off at the Tian Sheng Qiao Stop according to the prompts on his map. I carried a big bag with many things I had bought for him and started to walk up the mountain path by the route he had drawn on the map. After walking for about 7 km, finally, I arrived at the Junior high School of the Yunnan Agricultural College which was now no longer in use and had now become a place to lock up those "monsters and demons—forces of evil people of all descriptions" from the universities of Kunming city to be reformed through labor and to be investigated. (During the Cultural Revolution, people who were ferreted out from their units and were condemned as worthless were called "Ox-headed devils and serpent gods." The room where those people lived was called a "cowshed.")

I met Gao Lin An in the depths of the mountains in Xundian county far from Kunming although it was only for a few hours, and we were under surveillance by a member of the workers propaganda team and a militia holding a gun from when I arrived there until I left. But it urged me to make a final decision. (From 1972 Mao sent the workers propaganda team to every university to be the leaders there. The member of the team was a worker of working-class parentage from the factory.)

That afternoon, when I walked to the top of the mountain, when I saw one cowshed after another there, I knew Gao Lin An must be in one of these rooms. The rooms they lived in were very simple and crude, just made with some wood blocks. The door was made from wooden twigs; you could see in from the outside, it was really like a cowshed for animals. I quickly searched one room after another; I hoped we could have a little time to meet by ourselves before they discovered us. I finally found him, but, when I pushed open his door, he just stood up from his bed. We hadn't yet opened our mouths to speak when we were immediately encircled all round by people. A strange little girl had appeared on the top of the mountain, and there were people who had already been paying attention to me for a long time. We could not talk a word by ourselves; people were always watching us. They interrogated me severely: how had I found out about this place? I remained silent, didn't answer them. Gao Lin An disregarded those people watching us, he held me tightly in his arms, saying over and over, "I was sure you were coming, that you must be coming."

In the evening, he brought a small box and gave it to me; he said there was a gift in it for me since my 24th birthday was coming soon. In the public eye, I opened the box because everything between Gao and I had to be checked by them. I really didn't expect that he would give me such a precious gift. There were 24 small animals in different shapes he had made himself. He had carved each one from some tree branches which were the only raw materials he could find in the depths of the mountain. While I was looking at those lovely animals, he watched me and asked me, "Do you like them?" He put both his hands on my shoulders as before. His expression was like a father who was very fond of a daughter.

I looked at him, nodded, and burst into tears. Perhaps the leader of the workers propaganda team was touched by the sincere emotion he had seen from us. On the second day in the morning, when we implored him to allow Gao Lin An to take me to the train station, at first he would not allow it, but finally, to our surprise, he agreed. We ran swiftly on the mountain path. We had this little time without people watching us after we had been apart for several months - how precious it was! We were hand in hand as we were walking hurriedly; at the same time, we were stopping to embrace, wishing earnestly that time would stop. But we had to walk quickly because there was only one train that passed through this stop, and I could not miss it. At 11:30 the train pulled up to the platform. I set my foot onto the small train and the moment our hands were separated through the window, we were both crying. Afterwards, for over four hours, I sat on the train, and I cried all the way. That evening when I came back to Kunming, I made a decision. I will get married to Gao Lin An at once! I wanted to be together with him to bear all of his trials and tribulations even if we had to stay in the depths of that mountain or even if he was framed and sent to prison. I planned to go and meet him again as soon as possible.

I went to Xundian a second time, and got to the place where Gao Lin An was locked up and being investigated. I persisted and stayed for two days there. I wanted to experience his life there. That evening I arranged to sleep in the clinic with the woman doctor. In the early morning at 6 o'clock the next day, I got up. Because I knew it was the time Gao Lin An had to carry water, I wanted to carry water together with him. Gao Lin An had told me that when he was on the farm, the intensity of the labor for him was always stronger than for others. By way of added punishment, every day before day break, while other people were still in a deep sleep, he had to get up and take a pair of pails and go down to the foot of a hill to get water from a springhead, and carry water to

Gao Lin An made this sketch after I visited him in the farm
(He wrote: "Xiao Ling came to the farm in Xun Dian in 1975").

the mess hall on the top of the hill many times, until he had filled the cistern and there was enough water for the cooking needs of all the people for a day. After this hard work, he could have his breakfast. He always had some mashed noodles left over by the people. Then, he had to start laboring with the other people by 8 am. As I expected, I saw he was already carrying the water to the foot of the hill by himself. I took a pair of pails and walked to him, starting to carry water with him. When we had gone up and down about 7 or 8 times, the cistern was almost filled. Around 7:30, the people from the worker propaganda team, army representatives, the people from the security section, and the other people being investigated there, whose ideological problem was "not as serious" as Gao's, had all woken up. They all were standing on the hill and had seen the scene of the two of us carrying water, climbing the steps, one in the front of the other one. I don't know if some people were moved by seeing Gao Lin An and I set down the pails and squat together to eat the mashed noodles that they had left by the door of the mess hall, but some of them came to stand around us. I could feel that their attitude had changed. They were not as malevolent as before. One leader from the workers propaganda came to me and said, "You are indeed not normal; you are willing to suffer hardship with him."

After breakfast, Gao Lin An and I went together to drive 13 buffalos up into the mountain. During that time the examination had produced no result yet, so apart from having to continue to write his self-criticism, during the day his job was to put the buffalos out to pasture. He still wore a white shirt under his old western-style black clothes, and a pair of leather shoes, but one of his trouser legs was long and the other was short, and the bottom of his trousers were stained with slurry. On his head he had a big straw hat like one which the local peasants wore. He had a dark complexion, carried a big basket made from thin bamboo strips on his back with an umbrella, a lunchbox and a water bottle in

422

it. He held a whip in his hand for driving the buffalos. Looking at his appearance, I felt very sad. As we walked shoulder to shoulder, I found out that his body would tremble uncontrollably at intervals, it was not normal. I asked him why he had this symptom. He said, "The period of time in this place is fearful; the first month after I was sent here under escort, I had to answer so many inexplicable questions every day. And each evening I had to accept accusations and was denounced at the meetings as I was asked to justify myself. If I had nothing to say, I was criticized as 'not having been touched in my soul.' The meetings always lasted until 10pm, but at sleep time I was not allowed to turn off the light, and there was a person watching holding a gun. I really didn't know that this great misfortune would come, my nerves were stretched so tight. One night when I was sleeping, I suddenly started to tremble like this. If I continue to go on like this, one day I will be mentally deranged," he said crestfallen.

I was grieved, walking beside him crying. We drove the herd of buffalos to a sloping field and stopped there; the buffalos started to silently eat the grass. We chose a big umbrage and sat under the shade of the tree. We were surrounded by mountains which stretched as far as the eye could see, a sweet and intoxicating scent, which only existed in the wild, filled the air. At that moment it was as if we were hidden from this world and had come to a fictitious land of peace. Gao Lin An held me in his arms, embraced me tightly. After a while he muttered to himself, "How nice, the blue sky, the white clouds, and my beloved girl." I gave him free rein, letting him enjoy this rare sweetness for this very short time. I held my breath and let him hold me close. Suddenly, he raised my head, looked into my eyes, and said, "Xiao Ling, I am so afraid I will lose you. Without you, I don't think I could keep living in this world. Tell me now you will not leave me."

I looked at him, answering him resolutely and decisively, "No, it will never happen. I will love only you for the rest of my life." Soon, I moved my lips to his ear and stealthily added, "We are going to get married at once, we will be together every day."

"Ah! Are you sure!? ......" he shouted out.

O, had those buffalos heard my quiet words? Together they loudly cried out as if they wanted to give us their blessing. And the birds in the forest were also "chirping" calling out without end, as though they were playing a special love sonata for us.

Actually, these were the only congratulations Gao Lin An and I received from this world.

In the middle of September, after 5 months of checking, based on lack of evidence, the case of "wanting to be close to the foreigners" was finally put to an end, and Gao Lin An came back to Kunming. We decided to get married at once. To do everything legally, we hoped we could first get a marriage license. But when we went to the sub-district office to get a marriage certificate, we needed to provide a written testimony from both our units which said that we had agreed to marry. It was not difficult for me to get the paper from my unit, but Gao Lin An spent one week, even showing the constitution of the People's Republic of China to the person in charge of his unit. It was not easy but he finally got the paper. On the 23rd of September, we went to the sub-district office and secretly got the marriage certificate.

I wrote a short letter to Mama that said: "Please forgive me, Mama. I still want to be with this man." From then on I departed from the one person who loved me the most selflessly. I had certainly never thought that this was the way I would unexpectedly bid farewell to Mama.

Just in the afternoon of that day, I carried my simple baggage on my bicycle and moved into Gao Lin An's dormitory. No congratulations from any friends and relatives, no wedding either. In this way, we started our own "new life." Back then, I did not complain, and I had no regrets. I believed that if we only had love, no matter how hard the life in front of us, we could go through it together.

His empty and small room didn't even have a double bed. We didn't have any furniture either. The first day when we were together to prepare our first meal, I found out that we only had one bowl in our room. It was a big enamel bowl that Gao Lin An used for getting food from the mess hall each day. I took this bowl and went to the mess hall to get our meal; it was rice on the bottom and another dish on the top. We ate our dinner together face to face, taking a bite in turns. We didn't feel uncomfortable; we laughed as we ate.

On the 30th of September, it was announced that there would be two days off for National Day. We suddenly came up with a daring idea. Why not leave Kunming for Shanghai? Because Gao's family lived in the middle of China closer to Shanghai, we could have a honeymoon. We pooled our money together and bought two "hard seat" tickets to Shanghai. This daring and romantic decision made us extremely excited. Of course, we didn't tell this information to anybody. We didn't ask for leave from our units either. Our marriage was not only opposed by my family, both our units had also created all sorts of obstacles, so we had no way to obtain approval for leave. We quietly got on a train and left Kunming for Shanghai.

After a trip of three nights and two days on a hard seat, we arrived in Shanghai. We stayed one day with Gao's uncle in Shanghai, then transferred to another train and took 10 hours to get to Ben Pu in An Hui province where his mother lived. We stayed there for two days and got on another train to go and visit his father in Ji Nan where he worked and stayed another two days. Then we returned to Kunming by the same route. Most of our time was actually spent on the train, but for our whole lives we would always remember every detail of the trip, remembering what we had experienced in those 12 days forever. After visiting Gao's family on this trip, I got to know that his father Gao Xue Qin was also an unfortunate rightist, who had formerly been the president of the Shan Dong Provincial College of Medicine. He lived in difficult circumstances too. And his mother lived with his younger brother in Ben Pu. Because her family had two rightists, it meant her life was in a situation which was inferior to others. Therefore, even though her eldest son had taken the daughter-in-law into their home, they didn't hold a feast or any celebration activities to welcome the bride. But on this journey, some things happened which were totally unexpected and which brought us some pleasant surprises during our trip.

When I was in Kunming, there were many people who thought that I looked like the leading actor Ke Xiang in the revolutionary drama "The Azalea Mountain." On this trip, since I was the bride, I dressed up better than normal, and I was always together with a man who had the demeanor of an artist, so even more people believed I was that leading actor. In Shanghai, Benpu, and Jinan as I walked on the street, people would chase after me to look, and some people even asked us directly, "Where are you performing 'The Azalea Mountain' this evening?" It was interesting and something we never thought would happen. Though we felt a little annoyed, it actually brought us some unexpected fun. By our appearance, who would have believed that we were both just the objects of the proletarian dictatorship in this society!

In those 12 days, we really enjoyed as much as possible each minute that nobody knew "what kind of people" we were. There were no eyes keeping watch on us; we were really at liberty like two birds that had flown out of the cage! But the happiness was very short-lived when the train stopped at Kunming station and we got off. Our hearts were heavy at once. We knew the gate of the dark prison had opened for us again. In order to live, we had to be back at the unit where we worked. We knew

The wedding picture Gao Lin An and me took in Shanghai in October, 1975.

what punishment was waiting for us. As expected, from the second day we were back at each of our units, we both paid a high price for the 12 days of our romantic journey. For about a month we had to accept criticism and write self-criticism. Gao Lin An was not allowed to stay in Kunming and was sent to the farm again. It always happened like this if the Leftists thought that he had made any mistake in their eyes, he was sent to the farm. They always believed that physical labor was a magic weapon to punish and reform people.

Our marriage really began in an unusual way; our love story had temporarily spread around the campus and community. Our friends certainly believed that we were a couple who had hit it off perfectly, and yet there were more people who could not understand. When we were walking together on the campus, I heard some people pointing at me and saying, "Look, look, she is the girl who got married to the rightist."

"If this man was not a Rightist, maybe he could not have got married to such a young and beautiful girl. This girl sympathized with him in his misfortune, and that is why she married him." Some people would talk like this.

Some leftists in his department always made him suffer and one secretary, named "Zhao" from the representatives of the army, refused to accept it as final. (From 1975, Mao had sent an army team to the university too. They, together with the workers propaganda team, managed all the affairs in each department.) Whenever they saw us together, they were always full of hate, jealous and indignation. One day, without knocking, they kicked our door in and rushed in, they looked around, finally picking up Gao's painting which he had just finished and was still on the easel and said, "You got married, and started to paint again. You think that one day you could be free from persecution, you are dreaming! We can break this painting right now." They threw the painting heavily on the ground and were foul-mouthed in our room. Before they left they said, "Anyone who comes to visit from now on must go to Teacher Li next door to register, don't forget what you are."

Where we lived then was a very old multi-storied building. The rooms were side by side and separated by one wall between each family. All the families set up a stove at their door and cooked in the middle of the passageway. The family who lived opposite and next door and occupied two rooms was a man named Teacher Zhang and his wife Teacher Li. They were from red families; they were always the favorites with the department in power. Teacher Li had a glib tongue, and she was carrying on intimately with the leaders of the workers propaganda team from the Gejiu tin ore mine. Those people often came to her home to drink and eat, and this family was really a trusted core member of the Party. So that day, when those people ordered me to go to her home to register my visitors I didn't take it to heart then. On the one hand, I thought the people who came to visit us were only a few; on the other hand, I saw that this young teacher was always dressed up fashionably and the sound of music could be heard from her home, so I thought she could not be a very "left" person who would make people suffer.

But, one day later, the mother-in-law of this family drew me aside and told me something in my ear which astounded me. She told me that her daughter-in-law had placed us under surveillance each day. She also told her to keep watch on our family too. If any people came to our room, she must remember to report to her. Any conversations between Gao Lin An and me were also listened to. The old lady told me that the wall of the room was not sound proof; whatever you talked about could be heard by everyone. We should be careful what we said from now on. This old lady was about 60 years old. She was provided for in her old age by her son and came from the countryside. She finally told me, "I have watched your behavior each day and thought, 'how could you be an evil person?' I decided to tell you this. My daughter-in-law is actually not kind."

Afterwards she took care of me, even selling me some eggs, which the hen she had raised had laid. I was very appreciative of her warning and always had a good relationship with her. But from then on we had to be watchful and "beware of eavesdroppers" everywhere and every day. In the early days of 1978, the old building we lived in had been condemned as unsafe, so the school built a new dormitory. Each family in succession moved into the new apartments. But we could not to get a key to a new apartment, only our family still lived in the old building. Gao Lin An went to talk with the leaders from different levels in the school many times, the three members of our family finally moved into our "new apartment." It was one of the darkest, smallest apartments, under the gable, into which nobody was willing to move, it was only 18 square meters in size. This really was the life we had together with the "high-ranking intellectuals" after we got married. Because Gao Lin An told me about the kind of suffering he had experienced, I knew there would be more humiliations waiting for me in the future.

Despite this marriage facing so many barriers from the beginning and seeming unusual in some ways, since I choose this myself, I vowed in my heart that I would not go and seek help from anyone else, and I would not bring any harmful political suffering on any of my relatives. From the day I started to live with Gao Lin An, I broke off all relationships with my family members. I also initially stopped contact with most of the friends I had before I got married, to keep them from embarrassment. Only the old friends from Wei Yuan Street and the Green Lake loyally held onto their friendship with us. Those uncommon friends wanted to give their blessing to us. When we came back from Shanghai, they knew that we didn't even have a bed. Li Zhi Heng could do some woodwork, so he made a double bed and two small cabinets for us in the yard of the Ni family who lived in Wei Yuan Street. They painted the furniture, and sent it to our room by tricycle, and our room started to look a little bit like a home.

Although Mama was already prepared for any contingency regarding my marriage, when the day really came, she still found it difficult to endure the suffering of losing another treasured daughter. During the two days off for National Day, she sat on her bed alone the whole time. She smoked ceaselessly, and wept, "What evil have I done. I have a hard lot. Why should my daughter also have a hard lot? Ling Ling, you thought you could evade solving the problem by walking away. You do not understand your Mama's heart. From now on I will be in a state of anxiety for you for the rest of my life!" she looked up at heaven and lamented, weeping in grief.

I knew I had hurt Mama so much. Er Yi Ma came to me one day; she told me that just one month after I left home, Mama immediately looked a lot older. She did not speak too much, but her heart was in pain.

Er Yi Ma said to me, "Ling Ling, you know how your mom loves you; her heart aches to see you suffering. You got married to such a person;

you were muddled. It was not easy for your Mama to bring you all up. To be stained with the repute of 'Rightist' means you will suffer an unrighted wrong, and your mom will suffer wrong too. It was so unfair that you and your older sister Liu Jie treated your mom in this way." I remained silent. At that moment, I did not realize the deep harm my behavior would cause Mama. I tried to defend myself. Weren't Ge Ge and Di Di beside Mama; they still could bring happiness to Mama.

Her three older daughters were not in Kunming, and her two younger daughters at her side both had shameful marriages. It was really intolerable for Mama, and she had lost face completely with all the people who knew her. At the very least, the people would think that her daughters did not respect her at all. Was this the repayment she should get for the travail of her whole of life? She really could not understand why all of these things would happen to her.

I have to say, this was the second unfortunate event that happened in our family and was caused by me. That year was the fourth year after Liu Jie had left home. Mama didn't have anyone with whom she could vent her grievances. In those days it was only when she met with Er Yi Ma that Mama could pour out her woes.

Whenever she mentioned me, she would not only complain, the tears would well up in her eyes, "My poor Ling Ling, she suffered together with me from her childhood; oh, I wish she was not grown up. What kind of life will she have in the future? It will be lowly, inferior to others in society! Everyone will bully and humiliate her. I feel distressed that this nice girl of mine will not experience wellbeing!" She blamed it all on Gao Lin An and said, "I will never forgive Gao Lin An. This guy, he is a devil. It was him, he snatched away my younger daughter, and forcibly pulled her into a big fiery pit."

Poor Mama, she had love mingled with hate. Mama was so worried and anxious about me, she was completely aware of the social reality I would face.

The small room we lived in when we just got married was in a location where there were dormitories of many schools in Kunming. There was a railway which went through that area, and a small lake called "Lotus Lake" was located not far from there. During the Cultural Revolution, the events of family which had been ruined often happened by the railway and the lake. Mr. Li Guang Tian, the principal of Yunnan University was the first to commit suicide by drowning himself in "Lotus Lake", and there were many successive incidents among "The Rightists" and "The Counterrevolutionaries" from the colleges of people drowning in the lake or dropping to the track to commit suicide. I had seen and heard those terrible incidents myself. Since as a girl I got to know a Rightist and had married him when I was 24 years old and had made a family with him and had experienced the inconstancy of human relationships which I experienced after my marriage in the years I lived together with him, I thoroughly understood the life of the "Rightist" group. In the big family of socialism, there were no words to describe clearly how the title of "Rightist" ruined a person's mentality and health. It was really, really so cruel and fierce. And that accumulated 20-year wound left a fearful shadow. It made you go into hiding throughout your life, and you could never extricate yourself from it.

Back then, Mama's state of anxiety about me was natural. And I was unwilling to bring any trouble on my family. Though we were living in the same city, I persisted in not contacting any of my family even though I was thinking of Mama in my heart every day.

Not long after we were back from Shanghai, I found out I was pregnant. Though we didn't know what kind of life we were going to have and had an uncertain future, we still wanted to give birth to this child. We believed that this baby was the quintessence of our love; it was a precious gift God had given to us. In the gestation period, my body's reaction to the pregnancy was very serious. I really wished I could eat something Mama had made, but I dared not go to the place which was my home before, and I held on firmly despite the extreme rumbling of an empty stomach. When I was close to giving birth, I prepared clothing for the baby. I wished I could get a blessing from Mama. I knew that when my older sisters gave birth to a child, Mama was always busy early on working on the sewing machine, preparing many things for the new baby and sending them to the older sisters. But I only had myself to welcome this baby when it was born. Late one night the birth pangs started suddenly, I was aware that the baby was coming; I carried some cloth-wrappers in my hand and sat on the backseat of Gao Lin An's bicycle, and we hurriedly went to the hospital.

For many hours in the pre-delivery room, I lay down on the bed, moaning and groaning piteously. I was aching all over, I cried out like a child when I had been sick, "Mama, Mama, it is too painful, I can't bear it, you come, you come and save me!" However, Mama could not hear the call from her daughter.

After the baby was born, I was weak and lay down on the bed, my eyes brimming with tears, and as I looked admiringly at the other women in the same room, I saw they had so many friends and relatives who came to visit them. I swallowed as I saw that they were complacently drinking chicken soup. I dared not to have any extravagant hopes that I would have some chicken soup. I was only wishing that even one or two people would come and stand beside my bed just to take a look at my son. But my bedside was cold and cheerless each day; no one came to visit me. The morning after my delivery, the only nutriment I had was a bowl of rice noodles Gao Lin An had bought from the snack bar at the gate of the hospital.

As I left the hospital, I carried my baby home as a first-time mother, and I was out of my wits. Nobody came to teach me how to clean or how to breast-feed the baby. I was certain nobody would come to take care of me in my confinement either. I so longed that my relatives and my friends would come to our small room to have a jolly time with us, that someone would come to see this baby who was just born, would come to give me and the baby a few words of greeting. Naturally, we seldom had people come to visit us. Liu Jie carried her daughter on her back and came to see us sometimes, but she had to go to work every day, so she could not spend more time with me.

Every day I struggled to get up from my bed, take care of the baby and do all of the housework, and go down stairs to clean the diapers under the tap water at the campus. I continued to eat the food we got from the mess hall. I hadn't have even one day when I could eat some nourishing food to build up my health or receive some special care as a nursing mother was supposed to. I persisted by myself to breast-feed the baby and took all of the housework in hand, and when my baby completed the first month of his life, I was exhausted. My hemoglobin fell to 5.6, and I fainted twice. I was holding on firmly despite extreme pain but frequently bursting out weeping because I had realized that Mama's prophecy, "An artist can never be a good husband" was true. Gao Lin An could not do any housework. He also could not give me any special care and consideration. And, when our baby was not yet three months old, he was sent to the farm again. The cold-bloodedness of the outside world and the grim reality of life caused my emotions to become lost in pessimism and disappointment. I remember there was a power cut one evening, and there was only a candle which gave out a faint light in our small room. That day my son seemed to catch a cold; he would not fall asleep and was crying and fidgety. I held him in my arms, while I rocked him. I was crying out involuntarily, and we cried together for hours until both of us had shouted ourselves hoarse.

How I wished there were some people who could stretch out their hands to give us some help, even if they only came to me to give me a few words filled with warmth and encouragement. No, no one came. I was living in isolation and cut off from help all by myself for a long time.

But nobody could be blamed. Neither my Mama nor any of my relations and friends did anything wrong. I grieved because of the cruel times that had taken the life out of humanity; it had produced so many obstacles and estrangements between people and had broken up so many peaceful families. It also meant that we, a daughter and mother, who had formerly depended on each other for survival, could not see each other even though we lived in such a small city and were not far from each other.

Life kept on going depressingly. I didn't know about Mama's life. I didn't know if she had forgiven me. And I, in the process of nursing a child alone, when it had just started, was more clearly realizing the hardship Mama had suffered for us. I could not help imagining over and over again, how Mama could have done all of those things because she had brought up not only one child, but seven!

Only when you are nursing your own child do you realize the loving-kindness your parents have given you. I missed Mama very much.

Before, Mama, Liu Jie, Di Di and I lived together in a small room, but now her daughters had left her and only Di Di still stayed with Mama, and Ge Ge still had his own room.

Di Di worked in shifts, if he went to the night shift he would sleep at home in the day time. He still did not speak much. What he could give

Mama to show his love for her was to buy one or two better cigarettes for her when he got his wage. Then he would sit with Mama without speaking and smoke a cigarette and have a cup of hot tea together with her.

I don't know what Ge Ge's reaction was when he knew I had made my final choice. I don't know what resentment Ge Ge had in his mind about his second sister daring to violate his authority and do such a daring thing. I only had his words engraved on my mind, "If you dare to marry this Rightist, you can get away! Get away as far as possible! You will never again enter our home!"

Then, I exhorted myself that it was best not to admit that I was his younger sister, so I would be sure not to interfere with the growth of his official career. I also understood that the other brother and sisters might have their own difficulties in having contact with me. I told myself since I had made the choice, I had to go on this difficult path alone.

Ge Ge was very busy every day; he had more and more friends. There were different friends of his who came to meet, to drink, to eat together in our home. The leaders of the "8.23" rebel faction which he joined in his business circle had become the honored guests of our family.

Ge Ge by nature loved revelry; he loved to be the center of attention. Mama didn't know what Ge Ge was busy doing from morning to night every day out in society. She only knew that there were so many people who came to visit her son. This son must be a promising youth, and she was very willing to busily run around after him. She cooked different dishes and offered them on the table, so Ge Ge and his friends could enjoy meals together. As long as Ge Ge and his friends were happy, she had no complaints. When they finished eating and started to talk loudly, Mama took the remains of the meal to the kitchen; she washed up all the cups and dishes, and cleaned up alone, her thin figure running around in circles. Mama looked like Ge Ge's maidservant then. The older sisters advised Mama, she did not need to serve Ge Ge like this, but Mama never thought like them.

"He is my son, is there were anything wrong with loving my son? I am willing to do anything for him," Mama often answered them. Of course, at that time, Ge Ge's girlfriend Xiao Kun also often came home. She talked and ate with Mama together, and it made Mama feel her life had some hope. The girl friend Ge Ge had chosen absolutely coincided

Ge Ge and Xiao Kun in 1975.

with Mama's wishes. I think, when Liu Jie and I left the family, she must have comforted Mama in some way with the hurt Mama had from her two daughters' marriage issues. I don't know exactly what Mama thought at the time. I guess, the memory of the unkind things her two daughters did to her gradually faded. Her attitude was to pay close attention to Ge Ge since she had started to talk about his wedding with him. She was planning that the wedding date would come soon, and she was looking forward to having her beloved grandchild, the person who could carry on the Yan family name, as soon as possible.

Who would know what a great misfortune would unexpectedly come!

On the 20th of December in 1975, Mama left home to go to work as normal and Di Di was sleeping at home since he had a night shift the evening before. By noon, Ge Ge was handcuffed and taken under escort by some policemen who came into our home after they had confirmed that this was where Yan Mao Qi lived. They started to search, rummaging through chests and cupboards, mainly in the small room where Ge Ge lived by himself. They searched everything in it even the wooden floorboards were pried open and checked. Afterwards, they put the radio, gramophone records, all of his writings, and three of his diaries, everything they had found in his room into a big box. Then they took him away from the home under escort.

To search somebody's house without a search warrant and confiscate his property, back then, was not unusual at all. Timid Di Di was overcome with fear. He did not dare to ask them anything; he just watched them swagger off. At nightfall, when Mama came home after work, she saw that the whole house was in disorder. She trembled with fear about what had happened. She asked Di Di to go with her to the police station to inquire about it. The answer they got almost scared Mama out of her wits. They told her, "Your son Yan Mao Qi has committed a counterrevolutionary crime. He is in custody and in detention for questioning, and today we went, acting under orders, to search for evidence of this crime in his home." The policeman told Mama severely that Yan Mao Qi was exposed by somebody; he often had counterrevolutionary meetings with his friends at home, and together they spread and read reactionary newspapers and periodicals and listened to an enemy broadcasting station. The public security office believed this was a counterrevolutionary organization who had tried in vain to overturn the proletariat Cultural Revolution. At that moment, all people involved in this lawsuit had been arrested and were under detention.

This information was just like a lightning bolt. Then and there, Mama clearly knew the serious consequences of this accusation. When she was back at home, she could not sleep for the whole night. Thinking it over again and again, the next morning, she told Di Di calmly, "Your older brother was certainly framed; he was treated unjustly. I will go and appeal for him.

Mama was perfectly calm and collected, even to this day Si Jie finds it hard to believe. Si Jie said that evening when she came back home she found out that an incident had happened. She was very afraid then. Her child was so little, and she had no idea how to help Mama. The only means she could think of was to persuade Mama to go and ask leave from her unit and depart Kunming and go to Cheng Gong with her. She knew that because such a great event had happened in our home, Mama would be treated inhumanely in her unit. She had to go somewhere and stay away from trouble. But Mama didn't agree to go with Si Jie and said, "I am going to the public security office tomorrow, I cannot leave him alone, I have to appeal for him, and I have to help him. Even if I only have a thread of hope, I will not give up."

At the beginning of the Cultural Revolution, Ge Ge was just 20 years old. He was full of vigor and vitality. He loved writing as a hobby, and his style of writing was not bad. His talent was put to new uses with the Da Zi Bao and the overwhelming arguments, opinions and debates which they expressed, and he also joined a faction of his unit. Just like all the youth, he didn't know the real purpose Mao Ze Dong had in starting up the Cultural Revolution. He also threw himself into this revolution which was without precedent in history. He thought that because he was born in a "black" family, by taking part in this revolutionary activity, maybe he could prove by his showing off that he was willing to cast off his old self and make a complete break with his bourgeois family. And then perhaps there would be a day when he could be accepted and put into an important position in society. Ge Ge was sure that he was a person born to do great things. He wanted an opportunity to show his special talent. Before the Cultural Revolution, there was scarcely any possibility and he always had to bow and scrape, and he drifted along aimlessly in his unit. Then he believed that opportunity was coming, and he would fully show his promise in every possible way. But, many years passed, and he felt very disappointed because whatever he did, his position was still to run errands. He saw there were so many people who were stupid and clumsy and with limited ability, and because they were from a "red' family, they were promoted incessantly and put in very important positions. And he himself, because he was born into a bad family, no matter how hard he worked and showed that he was a person of exceptional ability, he was never put into an important position but just kept as an ordinary administration officer, suspicious of others, and on guard against any unexpected event. All of this made him feel very oppressed. While he was growing up, he started to think deeply and started to have some of his own opinions about the Cultural Revolution.

There were some close friends of Ge Ge's who often came to our home. They were from the same faction. When they met together, it was hard to avoid talking about the political situation at the time and to pass on some materials to each other and read some publications and discuss some hearsay. Perhaps they had some complaints and dissatisfaction with the authorities. That was all, nothing more. Mama was living in this home every day, and she had never seen these young people having a meeting there or doing any "counterrevolutionary activities" as the policeman had said.

Our brave Mama really started an appeals course to go to Ge Ge's rescue. She went to all the levels of the police office time after time, and she reported the truth of the situation to the different police officers time and again. However, it was the time of "Red terror" in the nation, and all Mama received were hardhearted looks and words which struck back at her. Sometimes she even got a rude rebuke and slander. There was never even one time when they listened to her patiently or showed her any sympathy. Some policemen even roared at her ferociously, "Shut up! While we were listening to what you said, we knew you could be counted as a counterrevolutionary too. We clearly know the political situation of your family, but because you are too old, we cannot arrest you. It is best if you go home to stay there and be obedient!"

Ge Ge had been in captivity for several months, and nobody knew where he was. Mama lost all contact with him. Si Jie said that in those days, she didn't know if Mama was making a deliberate gesture of calmness, or if she was really not afraid of it. She could feel that Mama was not flustered at all. Mama believed wholehearted that the final conclusion of the judicial office must be a lack of evidence, so, her son would be back home safely one day. For so many years she had stood up to all the tests, having experienced varied political movements, the willful arrest of a person, and then letting them out after a few days. These kinds of things she had seen so much.

She still went to work every day, but in her mind she was expecting to hear something from Ge Ge. She asked Si Jie ceaselessly to inquire about how the case was going. She told all the relatives and neighbors, "My oldest son didn't do anything to violate the law. I am certain he will come out soon."

She often went to see Xiao Kun at the doorway of the shop where she worked. If it was only herself there, she walked up to her and talked with her for a little while. She told Xiao Kun not to be afraid; Yan Mao Qi would be home soon after a short time of checking. She invited Xiao Kun to come and eat at home as before. Xiao Kun was in low spirits, her boyfriend had become a "counterrevolutionary," and she was trembling with fear. Just having to face the leader and her colleagues every day filled her with fear and trepidation. How could she dare to come to our home again? While she was talking with Mama, she shed endless tears and could not say a word. Mama understood her difficulty; she sympathized with this youthful girl and the trial she was facing now. Each time she parted from Xiao Kun, she walked home crying, and she looked at the sky and prayed, "O, God! If you do not pity me, pity this girl. She is only 20 years old! I beg you, I beg you to bless my son and let him come back home safely!" She didn't know what else she could do to help Ge Ge take a turn for the better and come out of danger. If it could help her son come out, she was even willing to kneel down on the street.

In those days she and Di Di were living in the small room. They parted from each other in the morning, met each other at nightfall in the small room, and ate dinner together. They lived a forlorn life which seemed bland but suffered all kinds of torments in their hearts.

Who was to know that this disaster was not yet finished. To everyone's surprise, the most frightful calamity in the world silently befell the mother and son who were dependent on each other for survival.

One evening, after Mama and Di Di had eaten dinner together, Di Di told Mama that there was no sugar left in the bottle at home, so Mama took the sugar ration ticket in her hand and went to buy sugar in a shop by the corner of the alleyway. She bought half a kg sugar, picked it up and walked home. Altogether it took less than 10 minutes. When she returned home with the sugar in a small bag in her hand, she found out that Di Di was already asleep on his bed. She thought maybe her young son was not feeling well, so she walked closer to look at him.

"Ai Ya!" she cry out loudly, the sugar spilled on the ground. She saw an empty DDVP bottle on the bedside table; her son was foaming at the mouth. Her youngest son was committing suicide!

Oh, I cannot keep writing, I am trembling, shaking in my heart, shaking in my hands …… I cannot imagine that anyone in the world would have strong enough nerves to endure such a shock! An old lady full of sadness and worry, now saw for herself that another of her sons

442

was killing himself before her eyes. My god, this was something which absolutely should not happen!

Mama's mind must have gone blank then; she was scared and almost fainted, but, in only a few seconds, Mama, the most unique Mama in the world, held Di Di in her arms, and called out loudly, "Mao Mao, Mao Mao, my son, tell Mama what has happened to you, why have you chosen to do this, you cannot die in front of Mama! No, you can't!" Her tears welling up like a fountain, she continued to call out, "Mao Mao! Mao Mao! You wake up, Mama is calling you!"

In Mama's embrace, with Mama's crying, Di Di opened his eyes, he stared at Mama, two lines of tears silently running onto his face, the corners of his mouth twitched, and he made a sound, "Mama! I..." the words didn't come out, he was foaming at the mouth and fell into a coma.

"My god! You hold on, Mao Mao, Mama will go and ask someone to take you to the hospital."

Mama laid Di Di down, she ran unsteadily to the end of our lane to a family she trusted. She knocked on their door, exerting all her strength. When they opened the door, she was already not firm on her feet, she was trembling all over, "It's bad, it's bad; I beg you to help me take my son to the hospital! He has committed suicide," tears covered her face as she piteously and shakily begged for help.

Two kind men from this family hastily followed Mama home, put Di Di on a bicycle, and rushed to the hospital.

Mama, our Mama, this old lady close to 60 years old, followed the bicycle, running after them.

Once, two times, three times, she was unable to control her legs and feet and went down on her knees in weakness and limped along the street. She picked herself up and followed the bicycle in the front, running, running like someone insane, her face bathed in tears, her mouth calling out loudly, "God, you pity me, you show your mercy to my son! You save his life! You cannot take his life when I don't know why; Help, Help!" The pedestrians on the street didn't know what had happened. They were looking at this old lady with her hair disheveled and terrified. They saw her running and crying out in misery.

"Mao Mao, you cannot leave before Mama, you must tell Mama why you want to die, you must hold on!"

Seeing the gate of the hospital, Mama was shouting herself hoarse, "Doctor, Doctor, help, help! I beg you hurry up and save my youngest son's life!"

God listened to Mama's praying, intervened in the fight for death, and Di Di was saved! The doctor said that if you were only a few minutes later, the hospital would not have been able to save him! When the news came from the emergency room that her youngest son was out of danger, both of Mama's legs felt like jelly, and she shakily lay down on the floor of the hospital. Mama was almost utterly defeated by this terrible experience, this second calamity which happened so suddenly. That evening she herself lay down on the sickbed in the first aid room of the hospital.

People all knew that Di Di was a kind and honest person. Why did he want to kill himself so suddenly?

When Di Di was born, the whole family was living in the most depressed situation. When he came into the world, there was none of the joy the family had before. Even though he was only the second boy in this family, he never had any special attention. The family had already lost the ability to give him any special attention. Sometimes we even thought he was a burden and that he should not have come into our family. Mama often said that Di Di was a child who never had even one good day in his life. It was true. When he was born, Dad was suffering from a serious illness and kept to his bed; he could not even carry Di Di in his arms.

Di Di was the least blessed child amongst all of us. Since the first day he existed, Mama cried bitterly, sighing with deep feeling that he was not coming at the right time. During the period he was conceived, Mama was feeling very depressed all the time. He was born in a small dilapidated and dank room and was wrapped in tattered clothing. Mama always carried him on her back. He cried on Mama's back and slept on Mama's back. He grew up day after day in the depressed atmosphere of our home. His life was filled with poverty and hunger from when he was born. Because he suffered from malnutrition, he was unusually thin and weak. He was always a reticent boy with tattered clothes, slow in his responses, and very pitiable amongst us seven brothers and sisters. Of all the brothers and sisters, only his personality was introverted, very much like our Dad. He was over two years old when he started to walk, staggering unsteadily, and he started speaking even later. While he was studying at the primary school, his results were not good either. We were both at the same school, and the teacher and classmates could not believe that we were brother and sister. We were very different in our personality and appearance.

From my impression, the way Mama loved him was also different from the other brother and sisters. Mama treated him as a grandmother treats a grandson. When she spoke to him, she was always advising him with earnest and patient words.

As time went on, we had all gradually grown up. All six of us children were physically and mentally healthy and soon entered society. But as an adult, Di Di was distant and quiet in character. He was timid and taciturn and unwilling to talk to strangers. When the Cultural Revolution began, he was unable to finish his primary school and had a job when he was only 16 years old. Since he didn't have any special skills and had a low education, he was the only one of us to undertake a laboring position. He was different from us in many ways, and he was nothing like his older brother. Di Di had none of the overbearing and haughty personality of Ge Ge. His personality was timid and humble. He was the opposite of his older brother. But all the relatives and friends, as well as we brothers and sisters, admitted that Di Di was a very loyal and kind person.

Di Di and I grew up together. When I was in the third grade, Di Di also went to study in the same primary school with me. When, the other siblings were studying in the middle school, they had their lunch at the school. Mama worked in the mess hall, and she could not come back home to cook for us. The two of us learned to look after ourselves when we were very little children. We had an arrangement that whoever got home early would be the first to make a fire and start to cook lunch. But, I often cooked for Di Di because he was too little to cook, and sometimes I disliked and discouraged him from butting in. I felt he was clumsy.

One day I got home very late because I had to do something at school. When I entered the yard, I saw Di Di sitting on the doorstep of our home. There was blood on his face, and his mouth and nose were black and blue. I asked him immediately what had happened with him. Di Di wouldn't tell me what had happened at first but pointed to the rice and a bowl of potatoes he had cooked on the table, and said to me, "I have cooked food for you; you eat it. I won't eat today."

I certainly would not eat by myself; I continued to make detailed inquiries about what had happened to him. When he started talking to me face to face, I suddenly saw that one of his teeth was gone. I was startled, and I shook his shoulder and asked him loudly what was wrong. He was crying and told me, "I fell down from the second floor stairs in the classroom building, my tooth was broken!" he did not finish speaking.

I was scared and burst into tears. What's to be done? I used my cuff to wipe his tears, and told him, "You wait for me here. I am going to call Mama." I turned around and ran to Mama's work place.

While I was running I was crying, and when I got to the mess hall, I was out of breath. It was the lunch time, and there were many people queued up by the window, Mama was selling rice there. I rushed to the front, and at a distance from the window I spoke to Mama loudly:

"Mama, go home quickly. Xiao Mao has tumbled, and his teeth are broken. Go, hurry up!" I could see there was surprise on Mama's face, but while she was listening to me, she continued to sell rice to the people at the window and didn't speak a word to me.

I pressed her again, eyes brimming with tears and asked her to go home with me at once, but Mama said to me calmly, "You go home first, when I finish my job I will come."

At that moment I could not understand why Mama was so cold and detached when she talked to me, and further more I could not understand why, when Mama heard her youngest son had an accident, she was so aloof and indifferent. I looked at Mama, and I was sure she would not go home together with me, so I had no choice but to leave the place and run back home. On the way home, I was crying loudly all the same. Entering the gate, I saw that Di Di was still sitting on doorstep. His eyes were full of fear and his face had become more swollen, but I could not get Mama to come home. I didn't know what I should do and could not help bursting into tears. I was crying, Di Di was also crying as he followed me. We cried for about an hour like this; it was not easy until Mama finally came back home.

Mama didn't send Di Di to the hospital at once as I had expected to put his tooth back in. Di Di had been holding a small part of his tooth in his hand the whole time. When I was 10 years old, I believed childishly, if we only went to the hospital, the doctor would put his broken tooth back together. That day, Mama just used some clean water to wash his face and teeth, and applied some gentian violet to the affected part. With that, she asked how this had happened to him. When she found out that it happened because Di Di was naughty and didn't walk down the stairs after the class but went down on the handrail, lost his balance, and hit his chin on the ground causing this calamity, she gave Di Di a scolding. Then she asked us to hurry up and eat lunch and go to school. I was not happy that Di Di was being treated like this.

I begged Mama again to take him to the hospital, Mama said, "They cannot do anything to help. This is a new tooth which has just grown, and the root cannot be pulled out. The doctor cannot put the broken part together. I don't have money to take him to the hospital either."

That day Di Di and I were not in the mood to eat; we only had a little food and went to school again with long faces.

Each lunchtime, the dish Di Di and I ate with our rice was potato. When we came home after the class, we made a fire and put the boiler on to heat the rice first, then we would use a knife to pare two potatoes, and cut them into threads, then cook them in some oil and salt. We were too young, and still did not have the skill to cut the potatoes into threads so they were often just some long narrow piece, and sometimes we carelessly cut our fingers. But, that day, at only 7 years old, Di Di had not only cut the potato and cooked it with his small hands; he had also heated the rice, and prepared a meal for me. He endured his pain to make this meal for me; it was a meal I will never forget. The potatoes he had put in the bowl were as thick as chopsticks and not nicely cooked. They were blackened but full of Di Di's honesty and kindness. That meal I had when I was 10 years old became the meal which touched me the most in my life. Often after that when I was cutting or eating potatoes, this would come to my mind.

Many years after this happened, poor Di Di only had half a tooth, so he disliked talking with people or laughing and he became even more diffident and self-abasing. He was always extremely lonely.

When Di Di was studying in the sixth grade in primary school, the Cultural Revolution had started, and all schools had suspended classes. Liu Jie, Di Di and I stayed together idly at home. I remember, during this time, we often went out to meet our classmates, but he never went out. He raised doves in our yard. Later, he loved fishing, and he often went to fish alone, leaving home in the morning and coming back in the evening. His demeanor was quiet like that of an old man. This was Di Di's behavior and personality.

Ge Ge was too severe with him, so, he always kept his distance from Ge Ge. We never saw him talking together with Ge Ge about anything or drinking and eating together. Because of his position in the family, Ge Ge treated Di Di, who was 8 years younger than him, like a severe father would with his child. Di Di was humble and had self-knowledge. He knew he was not clever, so he put himself in the lowest position. It was always like this. The person he most relied on was Mama; second was Si Jie who treated him well. He was also unsociable when he was together with Liu Jie and me since we were described as having "a glib tongue" by people. He never seemed to trust strangers, and he liked to live a solitary existence without seeking company.

When he was 16 years old, he had a job working as a locksmith.

That year Mama took him to see the dentist who inserted half a metallic front tooth for him. Mama asked Liu and I to take Di Di to register at his factory. That day, as we were pushing a bicycle which held Di Di's small parcel and were about to leave home, Mama told Di Di again and again, "Setting foot in this inclement society, my heart is at rest about your other brother and sisters, but I am not at peace about you,

Mao Mao, because you are too naïve and vulnerable; Mao Mao, if you meet any trouble, you come home to tell me, do you hear?"

Mama was really full of anxiety and worry about her youngest son because she clearly knew Di Di's weakness. "Ai, my poor son, all alone, modest and cowardly. I don't know what kind of bullying and humiliation he will be subjected to. Thinking of him, I cannot set my heart at rest." Mama sent her youngest son off at the gate with tears in her eyes.

Now with what happened with Ge Ge, all us were involved in this trouble. Each person was interrogated at the public security bureau. Da Jie and Er Jie's family were not living in Kunming, but they were interrogated too. A special group was sent from the public security bureau to go to the place where they were to examine the case. During this time, Si Jie's husband had just transferred his job from Dali to Cheng Gong. Their work unit was not far from Kunming, and he often came to visit Mama's home together with Si Jie. They certainly became the main target of examination, and they were interrogated many times. When Si Jie recalls those days, she still has a lingering fear even up to the present. She said that those policemen who handled the case looked thoroughly ferocious. Her baby was less than 2 years old then, and each time she was interrogated, she had to carry the baby in her arms. Many times the baby was too scared to cry because of the attitude and devilish look of those people. Later, whenever he saw anyone wearing a police uniform, he would be afraid and cry in fear. But the interrogation was not finished, when those people came again, she had no choice but to put her baby in her bosom and nurse him to gag his crying.

Because Di Di and Ge Ge were living under the same roof, and he was a single man too, they considered there was a great possibility that Di Di had participated in this "counterrevolutionary group." He naturally became the main suspect of the public security bureau. They continued to go to the factory where Di Di worked to call him and take him from his worksite to the security section to be interrogated. It always lasted a few hours each time, and their attitude was very ferocious.

Poor Di Di was used to being alone. He was 8 years younger than his older brother, both of them had very different characters, and he never did anything together with Ge Ge, didn't even know any of Ge Ge's friends either. He really knew nothing about what Ge Ge and his friends talked about and read or their activities. So, when these people came to ask him questions, what he said to them the most was, "I don't know anything about my older brother's business." Since he was not good at expressing himself, after he had finished speaking he would look up at the ceiling and keep silent. It provoked them to anger as they thought he was refusing to cooperate with them, and in order to antagonize him, they started to use some vicious words to irritate him and make him say something more.

For a few weeks in succession, he was called in to be interrogated by some policeman; the news had already spread amongst the people in the factory, and each time he talked with them, their attitude was very strong. He was so afraid to see them, and he was close to a nervous breakdown. He didn't know how long this kind of life would last and, when he was back home, he never told Mama what had happened in the factory. He didn't want Mama to worry about him. He was just more silent with knitted brows.

That day, he was interrogated violently for the whole afternoon, and finally they trapped him into making a confession. They tricked him saying, "We heard about the little bamboo pole which held the antenna on your roof; it was you who climbed up on the roof and installed it there. Why have you never talked about this matter? Do you know that this means you have helped your older brother to install a special antenna for receiving radio signals from the enemy broadcasting station?"

My god, Di Di was aware that he was involved in Ge Ge's case. He explained to them hurriedly that because he is short and his weight is light, one day he was asked by Ge Ge to climb up on the roof and install the little bamboo pole. Ge Ge had a radio, but he really didn't know the content of what Ge Ge listened to. He even assured them, "I would never touch anything of my older brother's; for several years I never entered my older brother's room."

They couldn't trust in what he said and said to him severely, "How dare you still say that you don't know anything about your older brother's business? You have been forced to tell the truth bit by bit. If you dare to say you don't know once more, we could arrest you and send you under escort to the public security bureau to be checked there. Until then maybe you should say that you know everything!" Those people stood up, leaving the room saying, "You think it over carefully; we are coming back tomorrow!"

That day on the way back home, he was laden with anxieties. The more he thought about it, the more fear he felt, "Maybe they will come to arrest me tomorrow and take me away in the public eye. What would the people from the factory think of me? If I hide in my home and don't go to work tomorrow, they may come home to arrest me. Perhaps they will come and search our room and confiscate our things again. What kind of place is the public security bureau? What kind of life would I have if I am put in the prison?"

"It is too terrible!" he thought it over and over; he had no one to talk it over with. He wanted to tell Mama, but he found it difficult to bring the matter up. He felt terribly dizzy with fear, and he thought he had no way to escape, so he decided to choose to die.

On his way home, he walked into a drug-store and bought a bottle of DDVP with high toxicity. He went home calmly and ate dinner with

Mama like any normal day. He sent Mama away upon some pretext, sat on his small bed, and took the top off the bottle of poison.

While he was determined to leave this world, in his heart the person he was still reluctant to part with was his loving mother. He walked up to Mama's bed, facing the pillow Mama slept on every day and said, "Mama, I am unwilling to leave you, but I have no other way to go. They will come and arrest me tomorrow, and I am so afraid of it! You forgive me." For the last time, he looked round this silent small room where he was born, had grown up, and experienced trials and tribulations with Mama for 22 years. Shedding mournful tears, he shouted, "Mama, Mama, I am so sorry I am leaving, I am leaving." He drank the whole bottle of poison in one gulp and lay down on his small board bed.

In the years after Di Di had taken the job, his behavior in the factory was obvious to all. He was good at his technology and his morals were good. Nobody could believe that he would do anything wrong. That an honest worker was forced to take his own life shocked everyone and the news soon spread through the whole factory. The leader of the factory, who had a conscience, appeared personally at the public security bureau to be a guarantor for Di Di. They had to agree not to continue to come and interrogate Di Di and let him off for a while.

But the matter of the suicide for Mama and Di Di became a dark shadow for the whole of their lives. Living under this dark shadow both of them suffered all kinds of torments in their bodies and minds from then on.

Mama stayed on her sickbed for a long time. Although she was not completely broken down by this event, she was too weak to continue working in her factory. It was almost the time for her to retire, so she went through the procedure of retirement and stayed home. We all understood why Mama was able to hold out. On the one hand, the trouble with her older son was not finished, she would never fall down.

On the other hand, the current situation of her youngest son meant she could never leave him alone.

"God, you help me; you allow me to keep on living. These two sons of mine, their lives are hanging by a thread. You cannot, you cannot take my life away right now! I beg you, I beg you!" Mama often looked at the sky and cried out.

"This is too miserable; it is too brutal. Dear sister, god would never treat you like this, you will not die, and your two sons also will not die, never. God! You open your eyes to look at her, you help my young sister!" At that moment, the only person who was present with Mama every day was Er Yi Ma. She felt she was unable to actually do anything to help Mama to extricate herself from the predicament; she just cried and shouted together with Mama.

Di Di had his intestines and stomach cleaned out, and he got home that day and soon recovered his health. But the psychological damage did not heal so easily. After this event, he was even more reticent; sometimes he didn't speak at all for a few days, and he sat on his bed for a long time. After resting for a period of time, one day he suddenly told Mama that he could not face his colleagues and relatives. He was unwilling to go back to the factory and work there anymore; he only wanted to stay home with Mama every day like he was now.

"What you are saying?" Mama looked at him extremely surprised; this was really terrible news. At that moment, Di Di had not yet recovered from this trauma, and Mama didn't want to blame him too much. She didn't say a word. But, in Mama's heart, from then on it was impossible for her to have any more peace. In some ways, there was a striking similarity between Di Di and our father. When they met any difficulties and obstacles from outside, the only port of refuge they could think of was Mama. In this world, the only person in their lives they trusted was Mama. Only this woman could bring them a sense of security. When they escaped to a place of no return, even if they died, they wanted to die beside this woman.

Mama understood that if Di Di was going to stay downhearted like this, even if he was alive, his whole life was finished. This fearful idea oppressed Mama; her black hair gradually went white. Many nights, she lay awake all night. In the day time she looked haggard, and had a mournful countenance.

"What's to be done? If this youngest son is living like this, is it any different to death? My god!" she sometimes cried as if she was in a trance. She was always worried about his son.

In the mornings, Di Di got up. After he had washed and dressed, he went to the kitchen and cooked breakfast and put the food on the table. He timidly asked Mama to eat together and no matter what day, if Mama did not come to eat, he sat silently and waited for Mama. He would not touch the food by himself. Seeing that this son apparently hadn't grown up, only a mother could feel with kindness how alone her son was. How he was still attached to his mother and needed her help. Mama regained her senses and she told herself, "No! Be sure I cannot fall down; this child needs me, and I will be the mother of this child forever. I must save this child! In this world only I can support this child and lift him up!"

In those days, Mama dragged her weak and sick body and struggled to get up on time every morning. She put on an act of behaving as if nothing had happened, and talked with Di Di ceaselessly. Sometimes she asked Di Di to go shopping with her. In the market, she chose Di Di's favorite food to bring home. In the small kitchen, she purposely allowed Di Di to be her helper, cooking a meal together. While the two of them were sitting together to eat, Mama always forced herself to have a smiling countenance, "Now you don't need go and work in shifts, this is a rare chance for us two, mother and son, to sit and eat together every day. You eat a little more, gain some weight, and Mama will be happy." She picked from some dishes and put them ceaselessly into Di Di's bowl.

Some days, she saw that Di Di's emotions were unstable again. He would lie down on the bed and not get up. Mama squatted beside Di Di's bed and held his hand and spoke to him softly, "Mao Mao, Mama knows you don't like the people outside. Get up and be with Mama for a little while, is it ok?" When her son got up, she put his favorites on the table for breakfast within a minute. Whenever there was a chance, she told her son again and again, "Mao Mao, you listen to Mama speak to you. You didn't do anything wrong, you are too honest, too kind."

She spoke to Di Di, "Your actions prove that you are a person with a conscience. It is better to be like a shattered vessel of jade than an unbroken piece of pottery. You were not even afraid of death. Nobody would look down on you."

"The people who want to obtain confessions by compulsion are the ones who are utterly without a conscience. It was they who committed a crime; they did you wrong, forcing you to try and take your own life. You didn't make any mistakes. You see, they are not coming to you to trouble you now. They are in the wrong."

"This thing has already completely passed. You are a man, and you must face your future bravely. The trouble with your older brother is not finished. Would you like Mama to be in a state of anxiety and to worry about you both separately?"

One evening when they were sitting together silently drinking tea, Mama looked at Di Di with deep love, she told Di Di, "Mama is always together with you. You don't need to be afraid of anything!"

"Yes, Mama is always together with me; I don't need to be afraid of anything!" Of all the things Mama said, this word reassured Di Di. "Even if there were all bad people in the world, if there was injustice, if none of them treated me fairly, didn't I still have Mama? I don't need to be afraid of anything!" That evening with the comfort from Mama, Di Di cried his heart out for a long time like a little baby.

Er Yi Ma was the one who saw how Di Di was growing up. She was always full of pity and love for this youngest child of both families; if this world would not let even such an honest and kind person off, it was really not allowing people to live. She also came to persuade Di Di time after time, one day she even said to Di Di, "Mao Mao, if you really want to die, your Mama and I, we will both die with you together."

During those times, Si Jie was worried about Di Di and Mama, and after her work, she often carried her baby, who still needed to be breastfed, on her back and rode her bicycle on the 20 km journey home to see them. The next morning before daybreak, she would carry the baby on her back and ride her bicycle for 20 km again to go to work. She was heavyhearted and worried about Di Di's situation too, and she often talked with Di Di patiently. She said, "Mama only has 30 Yuan for her pension, if you are idle at home, letting Mama support you, have you even thought about the kind of life you will have with her? Mama is old, she is so worried about your older brother, and we should not add any more trouble to her. Mao Mao, you cannot give up and be hopeless; you must stand up by yourself!"

With the comfort and advice of two mothers and his older sister, Di Di seemed to start thinking deeply about what course he should follow. Di Di had a guilty conscience about always living with Mama every day. Mama's appearance had told him how heavy the anxiety was which she endured in her heart and how mournful her eyes were. But he was still hesitant, not daring to take his next step. Mama was taking great pains to wait for him to take the load off his mind, just as in the past.

One night, under a dim light, Mama set the table, and the two of them were sitting face to face and started to eat dinner together. While Mama picked out some dishes, which were favorites of Di Di, and put them into his bowl, she looked at him with deep love and asked him to eat a little more. Di Di suddenly seemed to wake up to reality, and he eventually opened his mouth and spoke to Mama, "I've come around to the idea now. I should go to work anyhow, Mama, because I want you to be alive for several more years."

"Oh, Mao Mao, thank you!" mother and son both put down their bowls and embraced each other closely, choked with sobs.

Up to the present day, many neighbors, even Di Di's colleagues in the factory, still remember the scene that day when Mama accompanied Di Di to the factory.

That morning Mama held the hand of her youngest son firmly; they walked slowly from home to the Yunnan Bai Yao pharmaceutical factory together. When they entered the leaders' office, Mama spoke to them, "I am an old woman of 60 years, and I can guarantee that my son will not do any bad thing. I beg you to show your mercy, to treat him well. He is only 22 years old; I beg you to be lenient; please take him in. My life will not last much longer. I brought him in person to hand him to you today. I thank you, all of you. Thank you!"

Tears covered Mama's face, and she made three deep bows to the leaders there. Such a couple, a mother and son of suffering, such a sincere speech, wouldn't it touch a person even if they

Di Di in Yangshuo, Guanxi Province.

458

only had a little conscience? There were some female cadres, who even shed pitiful tears. They went together to Mama and Di Di and embraced them. One old leader in the factory held Mama's hand and talked with Di Di:

"Yes, we trust in what your Mama is saying; you are unable to do any bad thing. As long as you feel you are fine, you are welcome to come to work from tomorrow."

One of the experienced workers, who had taken on Di Di as his apprentice since he was 16 years old and entered the factory on the first day, heard the news and came. He patted Di Di's shoulder and said, "Come back to work, come back to work, you have nothing to be afraid of, how could you be a bad person? Later, if there are any people who come to make trouble for you, I will be beside you. Can you set your heart at rest now?" Simple and honest Di Di nodded continuously to them. Mama thanked them again and again.

Early on the morning of the next day, after being idle at home for over two months, Di Di put on his uniform and walked out the door as he used to do toward the factory. Mama looked at the view of his back yet still did not rest assuredly. She followed behind Di Di quietly. After a half hour of walking when she saw Di Di step into the gate of the factory, she went back in a hurry. She felt as though a load had been taken off her mind, and she walked directly to Er Yi Ma's place. She told her older sister what she had seen this morning, and as she was telling her, she shed tears.

"My youngest son was lost and found again! I am so happy! You

Di Di is a honest and kind person.

come to my place this evening. I will cook some of his favorite dishes, and we will eat dinner together with him to congratulate him." Mama wiped her tears and hurried on to the food market. By nightfall, the meal was ready and set on the table. She and Er Yi Ma were sitting together and waiting by the table. Seeing Di Di enter the door of his home, both the older women stood up, "Mao Mao, Mao Mao, you are coming; how was today?" they asked him with one voice, and Di Di was touched. He told these two old women that all of the leaders and colleagues were nice to him today. Some of the older masters had talked with him, and they cared for him very much. At lunch time, they sat together with him as if nothing had happened.

"It is so good! We feel relieved; we feel relieved," both the old women said with one voice again. The three of them sat down and had the most reassuring meal they'd had for over two months.

So, when Di Di saw that the righteous leaders and colleagues at the factory didn't discriminate against him and that he had ceaseless encouragement and deep love from his two mothers, he returned to work, and returned to society, even though he was still reticent.

From then on, Di Di grew up more and more. Later he had a family. His wife is virtuous and capable, and they have a son who is handsome and spirited. We were surprised to find out that when he was into his middle age, he looked very much like our dad with his smart features and easy manner. We had only seen our father mainly in pictures since we had very little contact with him, but he was an unforgettable Dad, and now it seemed he had revealed his character and appearance in Di Di, and it meant we could see him often, isn't it amazing?

When Ge Ge had his incident, Liu Jie and I were living in our own small rooms, and we were not in the know about the case. After the event, it was a former neighbor we knew who told us the news.

To be honest, due to the marriage issues where Ge Ge showed his uncompromising attitude towards us and the excessive actions he had taken with our boyfriends, it caused Liu Jie and I to break our ties with the family completely. It caused discord between Mama and us until we severed relations. For many years, Liu Jie and I had a grudge against Ge Ge. So, when he was arrested and was confronted with this calamity and sent to prison, we were not sympathetic with him in his misfortune at all. Instead we thought he was destined to come to this grief. Back then, when the public security bureau sent policemen to us to enquire about his case, we even gloated over his misfortune, "It is indeed retribution; good will be rewarded with good, and evil with evil. Now he also finally has such an outcome. If he had been locked up in prison earlier it would have been better." We spoke those evil-minded words.

We didn't know what cruel-hearted people we had become. Living in an abnormal society, our naturally kind personalities had been corrupted and become rusty and deformed. In spite of all the trials and tribulations, we had experienced together under one roof as we were growing up together, we brothers and sisters went as far as to be full of hostility and would even prefer the proletarian dictatorship so we could vent our hatred. We were really in a state of utmost confusion and were "indeed utterly conscienceless." This Mama had said she could not forgive us, Ge Ge's two younger sisters.

Many years have passed. We and Ge Ge have certainly already restored good relations from when he just came out of prison until now. But, now that I have brought up the past again, I want to earnestly request Mama and Ge Ge to forgive the childishness and ignorance we had at the time and to forgive the resentment we had against him then. If we were also faced with our child choosing a spouse, we would have completely understood the attention Mama and Ge Ge paid to us then. I want to take this opportunity to tell Mama and Ge Ge, we have the same precious blood in our bodies; how could our conscience have died out completely? We need no more than to obtain clemency from you, though our request for forgiveness is coming from us after so many years.

Liu Jie and I didn't know anything about the matter of Di Di's suicide attempt then. We heard about it in 1982 when all the brothers and sisters were meeting together again. People together talked about the many things which happened after we had left home. It was too late for me to repent. I felt so much regret that I didn't go to visit Mama and give her a little comfort when there were so many adversities that happened to her. Actually, there was one chance, but I missed it…..

That was a day in September in 1977. My son Deng Deng was a little boy over one year old, and he was just able to walk. When I saw the scene of an old lady playing with her grandson in the campus, I admired them very much. I conceived an idea, and I wished Mama could see Deng Deng just once. I thought, if only Mama could see this lovely grandson, perhaps she would pardon me for my disobedience, and we could resume the deep affection between mother and daughter which we had before.

In the afternoon that weekend, I changed Deng Deng into some nice clothes, sat him on the front of my bike, and rode to the crossing of the road close to the home I had lived in for more than 20 years. I pushed my bike and walked into An Ning Lane, and uneasily went to the gate of my home. I popped my head in and looked about, but unfortunately the door was locked. I had no choice but to turn my bike around and slowly exit the lane. But, I didn't walk away right off; I stood at the crossing of Qing Yun Street for a long time. I had an expectation in my mind. Maybe Mama had gone to the food market, in a little while she would appear somewhere by herself as I had seen her do so many times when I was a little girl. I gazed blankly at the crossing of the lane. I thought if only Mama appeared I would take her grandson and together go towards her and call to her loudly, "Mama ……"

With a thirsty longing in my mind, I wished I could hold Mama's hand again and chat cheerfully with her. I even started to teach my son to call out, "Po Po" (grandmother in the Chinese tone), time after time.

We were waiting and looking at the crossing of the lane. It was a pity, this moment did not come. While we were there we did not see Mama's figure appear. It was getting dark; unhappily I had to take my son back to my small room.

Later, my husband was often sent to the farm far away from Kunming. I needed to go to work to take care of the baby, and my job then was not as a singer in the performing arts propaganda team. I was appointed to be a factory worker in the same company. My life was shaky and unstable, and I often felt very depressed. Sometime I had to carry my son on my back to go to the farm to visit my husband. I didn't think of going to look for Mama again.

Deep in my heart I always believed that Mama was alive and healthy. I wished for there to be a day in the future, when everything would change for the better, and it would not be too late to go and see Mama.

Dear Mama, where were you that day?

I censured and bitterly hated myself once again. Why didn't I go to the ice-cold room to visit Mama again in the four years after that, to give her a bit of comfort, or even if only to talk with her, to console her heart which had suffered enough from hurt. I knew that the attitude I treated Mama with was so unfair. That I wiped Mama from my memory was really a lifelong regret for me, and when I think back on it now, I still feel ashamed beyond words. Examining the whole of my life, I didn't do anyone a disservice, but I really let Mama, who endured all kinds of hardships, down! My personality from then on was not completely whole, and it has left a regret for the whole of my life which I have been unable to remedy. It has become a pain in my heart forever. The guilt and mental suffering may always accompany me for the rest of my life.

The event of Di Di's attempted suicide was the third hit Mama got from her children.

The trouble with Ge Ge, for Mama, was virtually as disastrous as being drowned. Because of the position this son had in Mama's heart, nobody could fill it!

After Di Di started to go to work again, the thing Mama paid attention to every day was Ge Ge's case. She went to the different government offices to enquire; they didn't tell her anything about what was going on. One day, two policemen gave her a lecture and said, "All you think of each day is to reverse the verdict for your son; you keep on saying he is innocent. Now you are so anxious to know where he is because you want to go to give him some secret information, to unify your statements. You go home, behave yourself!" They repeated some words which had been spoken at home, and Mama realized that their home was under surveillance.

Who was doing this dirty deal? By observing carefully, she found out that the family Gong who lived opposite us had been bought over by the public security bureau, and they were serving in this role now. It was terrible; there was a mean ear at the wall! From then on, if she wanted to say anything about Ge Ge to Si Jie and Di Di, they would go to the small kitchen at the back, or do the best to lower their voices, so only they could hear the words.

A long time passed, and they never heard anything about Ge Ge, and Mama felt she was almost going mad. She often sat on her bed and lay awake all night till day break. Si Jie finally found out that Ge Ge was locked up in the Xi Shan detention house in the western suburb of Kunming. One weekend, Si Jie rode on her bike, then took the ferryboat, climbed the mountain, and finally got to the place. She wanted to know the progress of the case from Ge Ge directly. Since they had been unable to determine the nature of this case and make a judgment for such a long time, maybe it was going in a better direction. She wanted to see Ge Ge for herself so she could tell Mama the concrete facts. That afternoon, after innumerable registrations and checks, Si Jie went in to the "reception room". When she saw Ge Ge, she immediately cancelled her original idea because different from the other suspects, Ge Ge had on fetters and handcuffs. He walked out under escort by four policemen. Seeing that Ge Ge's figure looked very emaciated, and his ankles were drenched with blood, Si Jie felt so sad, and tears ran down her face.

"Oh, how did you get like this? Mama misses you so much; she wants to know about the processing of the case. She is looking forward to seeing you soon; she thinks you will get out safely…" Si Jie could not keep talking.

Ge Ge talked with Si Jie calmly, "I cannot get out at all. I ask you to take care of Mama; don't tell Mama I am locked up here. You don't need to come to see me again, and if you have time, go and appeal to the higher authorities for help. Appeal to them to redress the wrong that has been done to me, I…"

"You are far too reckless. Take him away!" Ge Ge had not finished talking. It was interrupted by a policeman who looked like an officer. Ge Ge wanted to say something more to Si Jie, but he was forcibly pushed out the door. Si Jie stayed there crying, unwilling to leave the room. A kind policeman saw it and told Si Jie some information about this case. Since the first day that Ge Ge was arrested, he had not admitted his guilt. He had argued strongly on sound grounds all the time. During every stage of the trial, no matter what means they used, he never pleaded guilty. So, he was regarded as an offender "with an abominable attitude, who put up a desperate struggle," and they subjected him to discipline which was getting more severe day after day. At the latest interrogation, he replied defiantly to the judge. By way of punishment, his penalty was increased and he was put in fetters. He had to have them on even when he was sleeping at night. He told Si Jie that this case had already been examined and approved; the written judgment would come out soon.

"It is impossible that Yan Mao Qi will be set free with a verdict of 'not guilty' since he has stubbornly clung to his wrong position; the only option is that he will be sentenced for a capital felony," he told Si Jie seriously.

At that time, it had been close to one year since Ge Ge and his friends were arrested, and they were kept apart to be interrogated. Finally, the main evidence used to condemn them was a newspaper known as the *Xin Dao Daily*. This was one of the newspapers sold in Hong Kong every day. A friend of Ge Ge's who worked in the Kunming TV station then didn't know where he got this newspaper. After he had read it, one day he brought it to Ge Ge's place and let all the people there read it through because it was a newspaper from overseas, and they had never read it before. The friend of Ge Ge's didn't take the newspaper back. Ge Ge used it to cover his leather shoes, and put it under his bed. When they came to search his room, they found it and took it to the public security bureau. Because such a newspaper then had become the evidence of "have maintained illicit relations with a foreign country," no matter how they tried to explain it, they could not make it clear.

This newspaper, which came from a capitalist society, had been found in a bourgeois family showing that "the black puppy certainly is seething with hatred against socialism." And Ge Ge had some diaries where he had written a few opinions about the authorities. Ge Ge and his friends who often came to meet together in our home, five people from the same faction, finally, were all formally determined to have the nature of a "counterrevolutionary criminal gang"!

It was related to the political background then. It was not only these few young men, but there were many comrades in arms from the same faction who had "fought" together for about 10 years, and who at the time had been labeled as innocent. But now right away, they became "counterrevolutionaries who wanted to attempt to usurp the proletarian dictatorship," and were sent to prison. This was a lesson paid for with blood by those rebels after they had followed Mao Ze Dong and the Cultural Revolution for 10 years. Prisons everywhere throughout the nation were suddenly packed.

From when the Cultural Revolution started, Mao Ze Dong aroused the consciousness of all the people in the nation to action and participation in it. Year after year, the factories had stopped production, the schools had suspended classes, and the normal way of life was upset. People could not do what they should be doing, and all of them were forced to become involved in this "unprecedented" political movement. They were either actively or passively taking different roles. In this utterly chaotic situation, Mao Ze Dong had given himself the air of a "great commander," leading the people from the bottom to the top to "sweep away all the monsters and demons." (During the Cultural Revolution, all sorts of bad characters, class enemies, bad elements, monsters and demons – referred to the forces of evil people of all descriptions.) The people who wanted to save themselves from damage changed sides in this war with each other. Not only was this battle between colleagues and classmates, it was even between husband and wife; father and son also fell out and became personal enemies and attacked each other. Many people were full of hatred, were jealous and suspicious, and took precautions. It was not enough; Mao Ze Dong smilingly issued an uncivilized call, saying "Fighting the people gives me joy without end!" The rebels from different factions had learned nothing except how to manipulate and give somebody else a hard time; everyone had mastered this with great proficiency. In the end, everyone said they were "safeguarding the revolutionary line of Chairman Mao," but there was only one faction who could come to power. Every political force really went to the last stage of an open war between factions. Unfortunately, the faction Ge Ge had joined could not come to power. The one which held power treated them as the enemy and made them suffer to the death by whatever means, and many people became prisoners in an instant. This circumstance made no difference to the whole nation. Mao Ze Dong personally initiated the Cultural Revolution. It caused thousands upon thousands of Chinese people, who were hoodwinked for a moment and participated in it, to finally become the objects who were buried with the dead in the political struggle of Mao Ze Dong. The victims of this movement, the numerous people and families who were involved it, far exceeded those of all previous political movements since the beginning of history in China.

Before Ge Ge, such a common person, met with this misfortune, there were victims of the Cultural Revolution in the land of China who were top leaders who had struggled to seize the state power together with Mao Ze Dong and were called his intimate comrades in arms, such as Liu Shao Qi the vice-chairman of China, Peng De Huai the minister of the Ministry of National Defense, and some of the top leaders of the communist Party of China, who had died a tragic death in prison long ago. The numbers of high level leaders from different provinces who had all formerly followed Mao's line of thought and then struggled against it and suffered cruel injury and death, were innumerable. Furthermore, lots and lots of intellectuals and countless young and ignorant Red Guards had been twisted around Mao's finger but not realizing themselves that they were spending their youth and life at such a cost. This was indeed a Cultural Revolution without precedent in history. During just the first year in which it began, in different cities of China, there were tens of thousands of outstanding people from the cultural circles who could not bear the physically injury and mentally affects and took their own lives themselves. The Cultural Revolution not only caused countless people to die an unnatural death, the worst thing was, that Mao Ze Dong in person used 10 years to educate a generation of Chinese how to hate and how to break faith with each other. Dignity, individuality, freedom, sentiment, faith, sincerity, civility, as well as sympathy and mercy, those qualities which are treasured the most by human beings, were all destroyed by the Cultural Revolution. So, the terrible Cultural Revolution was summarized as "an unheard of calamity in human history" by the later generations.

Our family had gone through all kinds of hardships and difficulties but finally could not escape from the disaster of the Cultural Revolution. Because Ge Ge met with misfortune, our long-suffering Mama was innocently driven to a road of ruin.

The day that Si Jie got to know Ge Ge's information, on the way home, she was so afraid and disappointed. She was conscious that for about one year, Mama had had a gleam of hope in her mind - that one day her oldest son would come home safely and tell her personally.

Si Jie wished she could say, "Mama, it's nothing, it was only a mistake." But now, the most terrible thing would happen soon. What's to be done? She was so worried that Mama would be unable to endure it. The only thing she could do was to ask Mama to leave Kunming and to go to Cheng Gong where she would be less informed and could avoid this for a while. In the evening while they were eating dinner together, she acted as if nothing happened and invited Mama to go to Cheng Gong for a rest for a few days. Mama firmly disagreed with her. She insisted that she would like to stay home in An Ning lane; she said she could cook for her youngest son there, but everyone knew she was waiting for the news from her oldest son every day.

On January 31, 1978, a notice written with red characters on a big piece of white paper, the court verdict from the Kunming Intermediate People's Court, appeared in the streets and lanes of the whole city of

Kunming, and terribly, the names and photos of the people who were pronounced guilty were also on this notice. By this everyone knew that at 10 o'clock in the morning of that day, there would be a judgment meeting held in Kunming's Tuo Dong gymnasium, and 10,000 people would participate in it. Afterwards, those prisoners would be forcibly bound, put on a truck, and taken under escort with the roar of tweeters to be paraded through the streets. After passing through all the main streets of Kunming, they would be sent to prison to finally serve their sentences. This form of public display had arisen to "terrorize the class enemy with military force" and had started at the beginning of the Cultural Revolution. It happened often on the streets. People faced the fearful with no fear, and its fearfulness disappeared.

At around 9 o'clock in the morning, Mama went out to go shopping in the fresh market in Wei Yuan Street as she was used to doing. As she was walking to the street crossing, she saw many people looking at a new notice which had just been stuck up on the wall. She understood that there were some people to be sentenced that day and walked closer to take a look.

"Oh!" her oldest son's name was in the foremost place!

"The prime culprit of the counterrevolutionary group, Yan Mao Qi, refused to confess a crime and was sentenced to 15 years' imprisonment."

15 years! Everything before Mama's eyes suddenly became dark, the sky and earth were spinning around.

I cannot image what feelings Mama had then, and I was ignorant of how she got home alone. But, at around 11 o'clock, she had on her best clothing, and appeared on Nan Ping Street at the crossing with An Ning lane. She leaned against a wall and stood there silently. As she stood there, certainly, it was totally different from those crowds who were waiting and watching the bustling scene, but Mama had her purpose. According to her resolute and steadfast personality, she waited there wanting to see for herself her son whom she hadn't seen for more than a year, and she also wished that her son could see her. She hoped their eyes would meet for a moment and that in that instant she and her son would both find the courage to support them to keep on living.

At noon that day, on Nan Ping Street, amongst the huge crowds of people, Mama looked haggard. The piercing roar of the tweeters shouted out again and again, "Long Live the Proletariat Cultural Revolution!" "The class enemy will not surrender, we must make him die out!"

From a far distance she saw that there were 5 trucks coming together with 20 culprits who were condemned that day. Just on the first truck, she could clearly see her lifeblood—the most important person in her life, in broad daylight suffering and allowing himself to be trampled on. Ge Ge was trussed up tightly and standing on the truck under escort, both his arms were turned back forcibly by two policemen, and he had a black wooden board hung in front of his chest, which had written on it: "The Counterrevolutionary Yan Mao Qi." There was three XXX in red on his name. While the truck was slowly driving closer to the crossing where Mama was standing, she saw that her son was struggling, exerting his utmost strength, time after time. Stubbornly raising his head and looking around, but time after time, his head was pushed down heavily by the two policemen who held both his arms, so he could not see the crowds who were standing on the pavement. All he could see were the wheels of the truck......

When the truck arrived at the crossing of An Ning Lane, Ge Ge once more suddenly raised his head again, his eyes looking around. After the event he told us that before he entered the gloomy doors of the prison, he also wanted to see his most beloved dear ones in the world, to see his Mama…..; however, the time for his eyes to look around was really too short, only a few seconds, in the disorderly crowds, he couldn't catch the vision of his mother at all. But, Mama, who was concealed in the crowds, rose up on her heels, and she did see her son clearly, the son she hadn't seen for over a year. She saw him, she saw that her beloved son had been suffering and was disfigured beyond recognition…,

Oh! The tears in my eyes blur my line of sight. Once again, I am unable to continue to write, this, this is really too, too cruel!

I don't know if there is any other mother in the world who could endure such a heavy hitting! I don't know, while Mama was mixed together with those people who had experienced so many different political movements, if their human nature had become completely apathetic, and whether they saw the act of homicide as a game. As a mother, what kind of feeling must she have had at that moment when she saw her dearly loved son trussed up and under escort on a truck. I certainly don't dare to imagine how she walked back home alone in the public view of the neighbors to the sound of their sternly cool and unfeeling words.

That evening at around 7pm, Si Jie came home after work from Cheng Gong and pushed open the door. It was pitch-dark at home, and she called out, "Mama?" She saw that there was the shadow of a human figure moving gently by the small stove. She found out that Mama was sitting there transfixed with fear. Si Jie understood right away that Mama already knew about what happened to Ge Ge. Just now while she was on the way home, she had also seen that eye-catching notice. She leaned close and sat beside Mama giving Mama a sidelong glance with a dull look in her eyes. In her heart, she was full of misery and sorrow. She held Mama's hands and burst into tears. She said at that moment Mama looked so tiny and weak. She was so painful and helpless.

Just like the faint spark in the stove beside her, it seems she was about to die out…

Mother and daughter both sat face to face, temporarily without words, quietly interdependent on each other next to the faint stove, letting their tears run silently.

After a while it was Mama who broke the silence, "You go to the police station and ask where he is. I will go to the prison to see my son!" Si Jie looked at Mama in amazement. Then she heard Mama sigh deeply and say mournfully, "Oh! 15 years, I am afraid I will not be alive till the day he comes out!"

Her aged and miserable cry suddenly filled the dark sky over An Ning lane. However, that evening her tears were already used up because she had been crying for the whole afternoon by herself. At that moment she just could not control herself and cried piteously, hoarse and exhausted, "Why, who can tell me why? God! My family is completely ruined!"

"My son, why do you have to suffer such persecution? They have sent you into the prison; it will hound me to my death."

"I cannot live any longer, where you are, my son? Mama wants to see you…"

Mama was under the pressure of this tremendous calamity, she was unable to extricate herself.

That day, Di Di had worked in the factory in the daytime, and he also got home after 7pm. Later on, Er Yi Ma came. Facing such a terrible calamity, as the family members of a counterrevolutionary, they could only close the door and windows and cry at home together.

The darkest time in the Yan family once again tumbled down in the small room of No.7 An Ning lane. The atrocity of the Cultural Revolution would finally push our Mama into a bottomless chasm! That year Mama was 60 years old. It had been 22 years after she had lost her husband, and now unexpectedly, she was faced with losing her beloved son! How could she endure such a tragedy, how?

In the following few days, Mama could not live as normal. With knitted brows, her thoughts and feelings were completely wrapped up in this terrible matter. One night at midnight, Di Di slept on his small bed opposite Mama's bed. Suddenly he was woken up by a cry of fear; it was the sound of Mama in a dream. Di Di rolled out of bed and stood at Mama's bed. In the darkness, he could faintly see that both her hands were swaying in the air, as if she wanted to hold something back. He stretched his hand out to turn on the reading lamp, and heard Mama cry out, "Don't arrest me, don't arrest me! I didn't do anything wrong, all the year round I was only thinking of my 7 children, nothing more. Ai Ya, it is true, it is true. You release me, release me!"

Di Di held Mama's hands and said to her, "Mama, Mama, nobody came to arrest you." He was crying and shaking her.

"Yes, they were here, they were here to arrest me just now; they had handcuffs in their hands," Mama opened her eyes wide and was still badly shaken. She was crouched into a small ball, trembling and with cold sweat covering her face and her head. Di Di got a cup of water with some sugar and he helped Mama up to drink it. Throughout the night he turned on all the lights and sat beside Mama on her bed until her emotions gradually calmed down. During those days, with the terrible trauma Mama was going through, she was always hallucinating. She always felt there was somebody who wanted to arrest her.

Mama this is too pitiful, so Si Jie firmly took Mama to Chong Gong, but after only two days there, she wanted to come back to Kunming. She asked them to inquire quickly about which prison Ge Ge was in. She wanted to go and look for him.

That day was the seventh day after Ge Ge was put in prison. In the Yunnan Provincial Second Prison, which was especially used to lock up political offenders, while Ge Ge was doing physical labor, he was told there was a relative who had come to visit him; he could stop laboring for half an hour. Ge Ge wondered who would come to visit him in the prison; he would have thought that at best Mama may have sent Si Jie or Si Jie's husband to come, to talk some things over. In order not to add to the family member's burden, he hurriedly ran back to the prison house, changed into his best clothes, and then went to the reception room of the prison.

He could scarcely believe it. Glancing at the people, it was actually his Mama. He saw Mama was wearing clean clothes, and although both her eyes were full of tears, she forced herself to have a smile on her face as she appeared in his line of vision. Furthermore something which Ge Ge could never have imagined, that day, standing next to Mama, were Si Jie and his girlfriend Xiao Kun.

All sorts of feelings welled up in everyone's hearts. They sat on both sides of a simple table; there were two prison policemen standing beside them. This was the first time the family had met together after two years since Ge Ge was locked up for investigation. Before they started to talk, they were all choked with sobs.

"Listen, the meeting time is only ten minutes." The word from the policeman woke everyone up.

Mama was so afraid to waste any minute, she threw out her hands right away and held Ge Ge's hands firmly in both her fists, pulling them closer to each other. Mama, still was Mama, she started to speak first. As she cried out, "Lao Wu," ("Wu" in Chinese is five, Lao Wu is the fifth child in the Chinese tongue). Ge Ge lifted his head to look at Mama as if he had been wronged, like he used to when he was a child, and yelled out to her, "Mama, Mama! ......"

Mama looked at her son with deep love, and spoke to him calmly, "Stop crying, and you listen to Mama carefully." Ge Ge held back his tears and nodded at her. Mama started to speak loudly in the prison, this place she had never been in before, "You listen to what I am telling you. This case is a case of injustice, and one day sooner or later, it must be exonerated and redressed. Mama has read through your court verdict many times. "Active counterrevolutionary, refusing to confess a crime' - this accusation punished by 15 years' imprisonment is really unjust! If you have violated the law, they can write it out; if they cannot write it out, it means you haven't violated the law. You didn't do anything wrong, why do you have to confess? I came here today because I just want to tell you that Mama will appeal against this legal decision by any means. You must be firm and persistent and stay well. You don't need to worry about me; you can set your mind at rest. Mama will keep her life going, and I am waiting for the day you will get out of prison ......"

Ge Ge could not restrain his sad tears. He wanted to fix his eyes on Mama, to listen to her speak carefully, but, his tears were running continually, once more covering his line of sight. "From a boy to a man, I have never cried like this before Mama. For two years I had experienced misfortune and inhumane treatment. It was the hardest time I have had in my life, yet I was never feeble, never shed tears! Today, what's wrong with me?"

"Mama, Mama...," he was whimpering and could not speak any words. However, he could not waste time. He wiped his tears, looked at his Mama who was weary with suffering, and nodded his head continually. At the last moment, he said, "Mama, I will keep living bravely. I will continue to lodge an appeal. I know I didn't do anything wrong. You see, your son hasn't been destroyed by them. I am sure I will get out soon. But, I don't want you to come to this place again. Mama, you have to agree with me that you will never come here, all right?"

In Mama's later years, there were so many tragedies which had happened in her home that it meant she could not even have a day of peace. In prison, Ge Ge had plenty of time to think deeply about it, and he felt very sorry for Mama. He told Si Jie seriously, she should not let Mama come to visit him in the future.

Facing his girlfriend who had come here unexpectedly, the girl who originally would be his bride, Ge Ge felt ashamed beyond words. He didn't know what he should say to her. From the moment she saw Ge Ge, Xiao Kun had been crying the whole time. Right now, she realized the last two minutes was the time for her and her beloved, but, apart from crying and crying, she could not say anything. Ge Ge looked at this poor girl, looked at her face full of dread and tears, and he really didn't know what he should say. He simply stared at her blankly and shook his head painfully and continually, not able to say a word. Yes, in his heart of hearts, he still hoped to be with this girl, but in the situation he was in now, how could he ask a girl who was just 20 years old to wait for him outside the prison? He didn't know how many years he would be there; maybe it would indeed be 15 years. After a while, he said to Xiao Kun calmly, "I am so grateful that you dared to come and visit me, a counterrevolutionary. But you should not come to this place again; since you work in our unit, it will influence your situation. From today, forget me."

"Ok, you all go home. I am so happy I could see you all today." Ge Ge told them rationally. The three kind women were aware the time for parting had come; they were all crying again. Ge Ge was looking at them, sighing, hanging his head. He felt very uneasy. Mama fished out a towel to wipe her tears, and she put a bag on the table; there were many things she had brought for Ge Ge from home.

The policeman who was beside them, and opened the bag to check it. Ge Ge saw the stuff Mama had brought for him filling the table. There were fruit drops, the crisp pork which was his favorite food, toothpaste, toothbrush, underwear, a white shirt, and other commodities. When they finished the check and handed those things over to Ge Ge, Mama said to him, "Take a fruit drop, take a fruit drop, I want to see you take one." Ge Ge obediently took one candy and put it into his mouth.

"Wa, why is this candy so sweet?" he immediately became aware that he had never tasted in his past 30 years. While he was swallowing, he looked smilingly at Mama, and he didn't know how to express his gratitude. In the last two years before his case was judged, except when he was brought to trial, he was regarded as a "major political suspect." Ge Ge actually had been put in a dungeon by himself where it was too dark to see his hand in front of his face. Because he never admitted his guilt and had several altercations with the judicial police, he had suffered corporal punishment and worn fetters for 8 months. Every day his food was clear soup, with some cabbage and noodles. The iron chains rubbed his wrists and caused the wounds on both his legs to become infected and fester. For a long time he had endured inhumane physical and mental suffering. He had already forgotten what the flavor of a sweet was. Today as he tasted the candy Mama had brought him, what he experienced, naturally, was a sweetness which entered the depths of his heart, because, besides the sweetness of this small candy, he also tasted the love of those dear ones who had brought it for him.

"Mama, thank you!" he held Mama's hands, looked at Mama as he said those words. At that moment, he had already vowed to himself in his heart, even if only for his Mama, he had to keep living courageously. He must get through this deep and secluded valley of death in his life's journey; he must get to the end. Because he had a mother waiting for him outside the prison!

Meeting with Ge Ge at that time released some pressure of Mama's pain. When Ge Ge showed that he could face danger fearlessly and calmly, Mama was very happy.

"He is still my son who has a lofty and unyielding character," Mama sighed with feeling in her heart! Good, he hadn't collapsed at all, he was still living self-confidently and strongly; though from his appearance, Ge Ge looked a bit emaciated and had a haggard face.

The 10 minutes was over; it was time to part, and Mama loudly left words with Ge Ge, "Good, set your mind at rest, don't be upset, be brave! Mama is waiting for you!" The words Mama spoke there, which inspired awe as she upheld justice, attracted the other prisoners and their relatives beside them who were weeping and sniffling as they moved their heads to look at her.

Back then, nobody knew what direction China would tend towards. To exonerate a "counterrevolutionary" was almost like talking about a story from "The Arabian Nights." That Mama went so far as to have the courage to speak such words before the prison police in the machine of the proletarian dictatorship was really hard for people to believe. Afterwards, when Ge Ge came out of the prison, the chief policeman there sighed with emotion and said, "Your mother is really a woman with courage and insight; she could be called a heroine."

I believed Mama's purpose in going to the prison in person to see Ge Ge and ask him to take a candy in front of her, and saying those words to Ge Ge was to pass some information to Ge Ge – That the love from your mother is unconditional, selfless and fearless! As she had saved her younger son's life one year before, Mama also wanted her oldest son to know that in this world, even if everything has turned against you, even if everyone has left you, your mother will be the person you can depend on forever; she will be your hope. No matter what has happened, there is still one thing you can always have - the love from your Mama! It is as rain and dew, as a sweet spring, which flows from your mother. If this love was the only thing that existed in the world, you would never be forced down a blind alley because you still have your Mama!

What Mama had promised and what she showed Ge Ge by her actions was that from then on, the love she had for him would never end, except at the end of the world.

The second day after she had visited Ge Ge, Mama went to the department store, bought two writing pads 100 pages thick, put on her glasses, and started to write appeal letters. With a great number of Chinese characters, it took her about a week, and it was finished. She folded them neatly and with great care, and put them in an envelope. She went to the post office herself, and sent out the letters to the Kunming city, Yunnan provincial, and even the different levels of the court and judicial departments in the whole nation.

One day, it was the visiting day for prisoners. Mama asked Er Yi Ma to come with her; both old ladies held something in the hands as they went to the prison to visit Ge Ge again. That day, when Ge Ge heard there were two ladies who had come to visit him, he guessed immediately they were Mama and Er Yi Ma. He hurried back to the dorm, and changed into another suit. This was special clothing which was pressed under his pillow, and worn only when relatives came to visit. Then he went to meet them. When he saw that both the old ladies were travel-worn and had such kind faces, he could not bear to berate them for coming to this place again; he just talked to them calmly, "You see, I am fine, I am fine here."

"This is not like being in detention. Every day we just do some physical labor; we are not beaten or scolded." He tried to reassure the old ladies, wanting to set their hearts at rest.

Mama carefully looked him up and down, nodded her head and spoke to him, "Good, you look good. I have come here today because I just want to tell you personally that I have finished writing all the appeal materials and have sent them out. I have sent them to the different levels of the judicial departments, and now we are waiting together for the good news. I must help you to get out of here." Hearing what Mama said, Ge Ge was very touched, and tears welled up in his eyes again.

"Mama, thank you, I…," He stared at Mama blankly; he felt tongue-tied, and could not say anything else to Mama.

"Er Yi Ma, I thank you too. Thank you so much for accompanying my Mama and walking such a long way to come and see me." Ge Ge turned around and nodded to thank Er Yi Ma.

"Lao Wu, you don't need to thank me. In the whole world there is only one person you should thank, that is your Mama! You should always remember your Mama's loving-kindness. I do hope you will get out earlier; then you could repay your debt of gratitude to your Mama! Only I know the difficult life she is having every day!" Er Yi Ma burst into tears. Mama's face was also covered in tears.

"No matter how difficult things are, for Mama's sake, you must bear it. Don't confront their toughness with toughness back to them. To avoid more suffering you must be willing to comply with this, ok?" Mama urged Ge Ge again and again, as though she was exhorting a little child.

"Yes, I promise you, I promise you." Ge Ge answered Mama obediently.

That day, Ge Ge found out that, as well as candy, Mama had brought him a big bottle of pork cooked in soy sauce. As she gave Ge Ge those things, she instructed him, "This is to eat with rice; every day you put some in your rice when you have your meal." Ge Ge knew that in order to cook such a big bottle of pork for him, not only Mama, but Si Jie and Di Di would not eat any pork for a month because back then, each person only had a ration of 200 grams of pork per month. But this time, it was Mama who had brought it to him in person, and it wouldn't work if he didn't take it. Ge Ge had no choice but to accept this bottle of pork. He implored Mama that she should not come to visit him again. Also she should not send any food to him, but she should pay attention to her health. Mama told him, "I am old; never mind me. Mama is worried about your health. You must take care of yourself. You still have a long life. You must remember Mama will never leave you."

His face full of tears, Ge Ge told Mama, "Yes, I will take care of myself, Mama; you must also take care of yourself. Now go on home."

Visiting time was over, and they watched Ge Ge turn around and walked towards the prison house.

"Ai Ya, you come back, what's happened to your feet?" Mama shouted out. Because Ge Ge had been injured by a rolling stone while working on the construction site two days before, he now still walked with a limp.

He told Mama, "It doesn't matter, in a few days it will be fine." No, Mama insisted that Ge Ge take off his shoes to let her check. Ge Ge took off the shoes, and Mama squatted down and looked carefully and told Ge Ge what he must pay attention to and how he should be careful. She finally left the prison with Er Yi Ma. The next month on the day for visiting prisoners, Si Jie brought a pair of military leather shoes for Ge Ge, and a piece of paper where Mama had written:

"Dear son, when you go to work, you must put on these leather shoes, so your feet will not be injured again. Be sure to remember! Signed: Your Mama, Ruo Bi."

"Mama…" he held this pair of shoes, and two lines of warm tears streamed down his face. He knew this pair of shoes would have cost half of Mama's retirement pay!

It is said that a man should not cry easily, but Ge Ge said, each time he met with Mama, each time when he saw the things Mama sent to him, he would lose control and tears would roll down. Except for when he was busy laboring and could take his mind off it, the person he mostly thought about was his Mama. Sitting on the cement floor of the prison house, he often could not refrain from tears. He said that the times he cried the most in his whole life was the period he was in the prison. And the main reason for his tears was when he thought of Mama's deep maternal love!

"Mama, my loving mother, how can I repay you?" he would say in the prison house behind the high wall. Ge Ge often held the iron railings and heaved a deep sigh towards the sky; he was filled with deep sorrow.

On the other side of the high wall, the spiritual prop which supported Mama to keep living each day was the hope she had in redressing her son's injustice and helping her son to get out of prison as soon as possible. When she sent out the letters of appeal she would count which day the letter would arrive at the collection offices, and how many days it would take before she would receive a letter in reply. She looked forward to this obsessively; she always stayed home at the time she thought the mail carrier would come. However, two months passed, and she didn't receive one reply. She continued to write, continued to send out, and anxiously longed to hear from them. Half a year had passed, and the letters she sent out repeatedly were like stones dropped into the sea. She never received even a single word even if only to tell her that they had refused to accept this case. She didn't give up, and she told Si Jie and Di Di, "There are too

The last appeal letter mama wrote to the judicial office in 1979.

many people locked up in prison, too many cases; perhaps they cannot try our case right away. We must be faithful. If anyone has a sense of justice and they read the materials I have written, I believe they will deal with the case at once. There will be a day when we will receive the message that they have accepted it and will start to hear the case. Once they start we have hope." Her belief propped her up. She went to the department store and bought thick pages of writing paper again, and unyieldingly, she put on her glasses and kept writing ceaselessly and then went to the post office to send out the letters once again.

Once, when Si Jie went to the prison to visit Ge Ge, she passed him a little piece of paper on which Mama had written some words, "My dear son, if there is anything Mama can do for you, no matter how hard, Mama will try my best to do it for you. Signed: Your mother, Ruo Bi."

"If there is anything Mama can do for you, no matter how hard, Mama will try my best to do it for you." Mama felt that because of her tenacity and willpower, the matter of redressing the injustice for her son, which she had been working on for so long, must have a response. While Ge Ge served over two years in prison, she wrote about a hundred appeal letters with over a million Chinese characters (back then there were no copy machines) and sent them to all the levels of the public security department in different cities in China, but it did not move anybody. No office wrote back. She looked forward to hearing from them with eager expectation and longing. She waited until her hair became white, but she heard nothing. As the relative of a counterrevolutionary, she had to accept the reality which was simply that she was inferior to others.

At the Qing Yun Street residential sub-district office, which was called the Qing Yun Street residential revolutionary committee, there was an old, fat woman whose family name was Wan. She was the vice-director of the residential revolution committee and was worthy of the name of a fanatical follower of Mao Zedong's well-known saying: "to see the people struggle gives me endless joy!" She was a malicious person. Every day she wore red sleeve covers on her arms and walked up and down each small lane, carefully investigating any "new cases of class struggle" amongst the families, which she then reported to the residential revolutionary committee and settled with the people. The residents of that area who lived under her watch every day were filled with indignation and had a grudge against her, but nobody dared to offend her. They privately called her "vigorous teeth." (Note: "vigorous" in Chinese is Wan, which is the same pronunciation as her family name.) At that moment, how could she let Mama off? On just the second day after Ge Ge was judged, she held a special street residents' meeting and came to give notice to Mama herself that she must be present at the meeting. When all the family representatives from the area were sitting in the yard ready for the meeting, it was clear that Mama was just sitting in front of her, but she still loudly called the roll and asked:

"Is Su Rio Bi who lives at No. 7 An Ning lane here?" After Mama answered her, she started to speak clearly and at length:

"Today, you are called here to this meeting because there is an important thing we need to announce. Our residential revolutionary committee is not safe. There is a family whose daughter got married to a Rightist, and that's not all. Now, their son is an active counterrevolutionary and has been sentenced to 15 years imprisonment. The written judgment from the court has just been put up outside. Everyone must pay attention to this family; the class struggle is very complex in our area!"

All the people knew who she was talking about. They were all looking at Mama and were whispering to each other. Mama certainly did not dare to argue; she hung her head low and silently suffered the humiliation of this "vigorous teeth." For several years after that, this woman with "red bound feet" never forgot that Su Ruo Bi, this "class enemy," lived at No. 7 An Ning lane. If there were any social activities, she always came to our home in person and told Mama she should stay home and was not allowed to go out. Whenever an important political activity like National Day came, usually, there were some slogans and watchwords stuck on the walls of the streets and lanes to display the state's force. The red slogan had words like: "Long live the dictatorship of the proletariat!" "The class enemy has not surrendered - we must make him die out!" "A stern notice to the landlord, the rich peasant, the counterrevolutionary, the evildoer, the rightist: No random speaking and moving is allowed, just be well-disciplined!" "The day that the broad masses of the people are delighted is the day when the counterrevolutionary is devastated!"

At those times she would especially stick those slogans on the wall of the small lane outside our yard, so when Mama walked out of the gate she would be confronted by them. Our poor Mama was totally helpless, and there was no way out of this incomparably humiliating situation she was living in.

One day, when she was eating dinner with Si Jie and Di Di, Mama spoke to them pessimistically, "My eyes are blind, and I cannot continue to write. Lao Wu's case looks hopeless." Si Jie and Di Di were depressed too; they could not say anything to console Mama as an atmosphere of disappointment overshadowed them. They often saw Mama sitting blankly; she always shed lonely, sorrowful tears, which rolled mournfully down the face which had been through so many misfortunes of life.

Mama was old and she certainly didn't know that, in the land of China, there were millions upon millions of people like Ge Ge who, because of this factional struggle, had been sent to the prison. If one day the political situation completely changed, the central and city governments could not deal with every single case. Those victims of the political movement they would have to stay in prison unjustly.

Mama looked to the government, looked to the law to uphold justice to help her rescue her son. She had really used all of her strength. She tried and tried, but it was useless. Nothing had happened. She was disappointed and felt she had lost all hope.

"My dear son, Mama could not save you. What could Mama still do for you!?" she beat her breast and stamped her feet in deep sorrow. One day in the evening, when Si Jie was lying down with Mama on the big bed, Mama suddenly said to her, "Lao Si, I have some things I want to tell you." (Lao Si meant No. 4 child)

"Mama, you say it," Si Jie looked at Mama.

"After I die, you promise Mama that you will still go to visit Lao Wu," the tears were dripping from her eyes. "I don't think I can live much longer; my one request is that you do this for me."

"Mama, I can promise you. But, you are not allowed to say these words; we all want you to live well. Mama, we all know it is not easy, it is too hard for you," Si Jie found it difficult to cover up the grief in her heart. She cried bitterly together with Mama and could not say any more words. She thought about it for a while and then she said, "Mama, how about you go to Da Jie's place for a period of time. I will send a telegram to Da Jie and ask her to meet you at the bus station."

Mama interrupted Si Jie's train of thought strongly, "No, you must not arrange this for me. I am not going anywhere." Si Jie understood Mama's feelings; her oldest son was locked up in the prison in Kunming, and she would absolutely not depart from Kunming, not even one step. She didn't continue to write appeal letters, and now the whole thought in Mama's mind was to think about what kinds of things she should send to her son on the date she could go to visit him each month.

No matter whether it was in the past or in the present, people were always deeply touched by what they saw or heard about all the things she had done for Ge Ge while he was in prison in those final years of Mama's life. I have to say, our Mama was indeed a rare mother in this world.

Her retirement pay was only 32 Yuan per month, and she would spend more than 2/3 on her son. The first time she sent some fruit drops to

Ge Ge and she saw how joyful her son was when he tasted them, she believed that sending fruit drops was better than white sugar. The fruit drops were easy to take, and he could bring some with him when he went to work or have them any time of day. After making her decision, each month she used the whole of the family's sugar ration ticket to buy the fruit drops, and nobody could have one, including herself. Together with the other things she bought for Ge Ge, on the 15th of each month, the date for visiting the prisoners, she or Si Jie would take them him.

Mama tried whatever means to make life easier for Ge Ge in prison. As well as sending candy and some commodities to Ge Ge every month, she also bought the ration of meat back home, and cut it into small pieces, added some eggs and wheat powder, and fried up some soft pork or cooked some pork in soy sauce, then put it in a big bottle and sent it to Ge Ge. She thought these two kinds of meat could be stored for one or two weeks, and Ge Ge could have some each day for nutrition. She was worried about Ge Ge's health and afraid that if Ge Ge ate the poor food in prison year after year, when he got out, his health would be bad, and it would be too late to restore it. Ge Ge told Si Jie who often visited him again and again, to pass the word to Mama that she should not send those foods to him; she should eat those nutriments herself. But, Si Jie knew clearly that Mama loved her son, and she was determined to do it. Nobody could dissuade her in any way. If she did not send the things she prepared to Ge Ge each month, she would feel uneasy, so, the best thing was to obey and to send the things she prepared to Ge Ge on time. When on the 15th of each month she had just sent the things and come back home, Si Jie could see that Mama had started to prepare the things for next month to send to Ge Ge.

In order to let her son know he was still loved by his family, she not only visited Ge Ge often herself, she also sometimes took her grandchildren with her to visit their uncle. When Da Jie and Er Jie's family came to Kunming, she asked them to go and look up their brother in the prison. She told them, "We are one family; you must look after him. I am too old to walk such a long way to the prison; I hope that you can go on my behalf to visit him." Everyone knew that each time after Mama had visited Ge Ge, she always shed sad tears for the whole day and had a sleepless night. They didn't want Mama to go to that place anymore. Therefore, when they came to Kunming, they always submitted to Mama and went to visit Ge Ge in the prison on her behalf.

The suffering went on. Could she do anything more to encourage Ge Ge, to help him face his difficulties with strength? Mama was really racking her brains. One day, she actually asked Ge Ge's girlfriend Xiao Kun to take a photo with her, and she sent it to Ge Ge when Si Jie went to visit him again in the prison. Ge Ge was very surprised and touched. It made him feel conflicted emotions. On the one hand he certainly hoped that these two women in the photo were really waiting for him outside because those two women were indeed the dearest people he had in the world! But on the other hand, when he looked at the photo, Mama was getting older and older and Xiao Kun looked so delicate. Wordless pain and sentiment immediately sprang up in his mind as he knew his case was making no progress, and he would not get out of prison soon. It was impossible to expect these two women to wait for a man in prison for 15 years! On that day, when he knew it was Mama who had asked Xiao Kun to take this photo together and send it to him, he could not sleep for the whole night. He looked at the photo again and again, his heart was uneasy, "Ah, these two women, I have let you down. I am too indebted to you. God, tell me what I can do, what I can do for them?" While he was looking at the photo, he could not help bursting into tears. He shook the iron fence of the prison, once again crying into the air.

How had Mama asked Xiao Kun to take the photo together with her?

It was at noon. Mama brought two Bao Zi and went to the place opposite the shop where Xiao Kun worked and waited there quietly. After Ge Ge was sent into the prison, she often went there to wait for

Xiao Kun to look in on her. If the family ate chicken, she would save the best parts of the chicken and send them to her. That day, she saw that Xiao Kun was off duty and walked out of the shop. As she walked to a quiet and secluded place, Mama stealthily came up behind her and called her name. Xiao Kun turned her head; Mama said to her smilingly, "I am bringing you two Bao Zi. They are still warm; you must eat them." As she said it she handed over the Bao Zi to Xiao Kun. Xiao Kun was moved by Mama's sincerity.

"Thank you so much, I feel sorry that you are always sending some food to me, you don't always need to come and look in on me." To make Mama happy, she took the Bao Zi from her hand and started to eat them.

Mama looked at her; once again she had a broad smile on her face as she talked with her, "Today, may I ask you to do me a favor?"

"Yes, What can I do for you? Please tell me," Xiao Kun asked readily.

"I wish you would go and take a photo with me." Xiao Kun didn't ask why but said, "Fine."

She followed Mama and went to a photo studio on Jin Bi Road and took the special photo. On this photo, at first glance you can see that Mama has dressed herself up elaborately. Her hair is shiny, and she changed her clothes and wore a woolen cloth jacket which she did not normally wear. But the bleak and distressed appearance and expression in her eyes could not be covered up. Both her eyes were sunken, she had dark rings around her eyes, her eyes had lost their luster and looked straight ahead, and the corners of her mouth were closed tight, but she forced herself to smile. Xiao Kun was 8 years younger than Ge Ge. When they took the photo, she was only 22 years old, and she should have had an innocent and lively look, but in this photo, the expression in her eyes clearly showed she was frightened and panic-stricken. Her head was bent towards Mama; she also forced herself to smile for the photo.

Taking such a photo at such a moment, they actually both knew what the purpose was. They had a unspoken understanding. Their hearts were bleeding, but they tried their best to put on a smiling face. This small photo was full of the deep love and virtue of these two women! It was this photo which then became a treasure for Ge Ge in the prison. From the day in July of 1978 he received it, he put it in the

The photo mama and Xiao Kun took together and sent to the prison.

pocket of his underclothes; it stayed with him in the prison day and night.

Every day he could taste the deep love of his mother. What could he do to repay her, even if it only brought her a bit of comfort? Ge Ge racked his brains to come up with an idea. One day, when Mama and Er Yi Ma went to visit him in the prison again, he suddenly handed over 20 Yuan to Mama.

"Where did you get this money?" Mama was surprised and asked him.

"This is money I have saved for a long time and I want to give it to you, Mama." Ge Ge hurriedly explained. When prisoners were sent to prison to serve their sentence, they all had to do different jobs each day; each prisoner received 3 Yuan per month as a reward. Many people would spend this 3 Yuan totally on the day they got it, buying something to eat or use. Ge Ge only used a little money to buy writing paper and a pen for writing the appeal materials. He begrudged using even one Fen of the rest of the money and carefully saved it for more than a year and finally saved the 20 Yuan. He knew, at present, this might be the only means he had to express his love to his dearest mother. As he put these folded one Yuan and two Yuan notes into Mama's hand, she immediately felt her son's total devotion, and scalding tears poured from her dim eyes.

When Ge Ge was in his prime age.

"Mama appreciates your kindness, but I don't want the money. You should buy something to eat, you need nutrition." She pushed the money back into Ge Ge's hand.

"No, Mama, you must take it. I could not find anything else to give to you." Ge Ge implored Mama. They both took their stand and pushed the money to and fro; finally, Mama put the money into the pocket of her underclothes.

Er Yi Ma witnessed what happened there, when she walked out of the prison with Mama, she said to her, "Ai, San Mei, your son is a dutiful son, he knows how to respect you, it is so good." That day, Mama was intoxicated with a spirit of joy.

In the evening, when the whole family ate dinner together, Mama put the money on the table, she told Si Jie and Di Di about her son's devotion once again, "It is amazing, he was still thinking of me even while he was in the prison. I am content with my lot, I am so happy. You give me some ideas, I will use this money to buy something special for him and send it to him next month." At that time, Mama used the 20 Yuan and bought many special things and asked Si Jie to send them to Ge Ge. She didn't spend even one Fen on herself. In those days, she had nowhere to turn for help, no choice but to seek help from the gods in heaven; she often turned her face to the sky and piteously entreated over and over again with tears covering her face:

"Gods, if you want to punish me, you can add all the retribution to me. I beg you let my son get out of that terrible place. I implore for your mercy, let him get out safely while I still have breath! Gods, I don't have any other means to do anything. I come to you; show your sympathy to me; pity me!" She also went to the temple devoutly time after time, burning joss sticks and prostrating herself before the image of Buddha, and throwing herself at the Bodhisattva to pray for a long time. She prayed the gods could help her.

Each year on the Tomb-Sweeping Day, she still remembered to go with concern and visit Dad's grave. For her, in her darkness, the only place she could go to implore, go to sob, was the grave of her husband. Then only Si Jie and Di Di could accompany her to go and visit Dad's

grave. For over 20 years, they saw with their own eyes how Mama was loyal to Dad. Each time before she went to the grave she always prepared articles of tribute and changed into neat clothes. During the years she was living under stress, her health was going from bad to worse, and mountain climbing was too hard for her, but, even if she had to lean on a stick, she still went to Dad's grave each year. As she used to do, she lay on

Mama placed all hopes on her eldest son.

Dad's grave and loudly told him all the things which had happened at home. Her hoarse voice and deplorable crying always lasted for several hours under the sky of the desolate Mian Shan mountain, "Why is there no end to my hard time, Ze Gao. I cannot bear it! You help me, you help me!"

"I cannot live any longer, I will come to see you, but, I haven't fulfilled the task you left for me. Lao Wu is in the prison, and I would die with a grievance. I could not close my eyes when I die! What can I do; I cannot help your oldest son, and his future is still unknown! My god, you tell me what I did wrong in those years. Why do I have to accept such cruel suffering!?"

"All the ancestors of the Yan family, you show your power; rescue my son from the prison! I pray to heaven, but it doesn't answer me. I beg the Buddha, but it doesn't work. I have nowhere to go - you pity me, pity me! I am unable to keep up my efforts!" After a few hours of weeping in grief, Mama was mentally and physically exhausted and not firm on her feet when she walked down the mountain. She needed support from the hands of Si Jie and Di Di.

"Mama was indeed living in hell on earth!" Si Jie said. In the final years of Mama's life, she yearned day and night for her son. She expected that one day her son would suddenly get out of the prison and come back to her side.

During those times in Beijing, in October of 1976 after Mao Ze Dong passed away, the Political Bureau of the Central Committee of the Communist Party of China arrested the "Gang of Four" including Mao's wife Jiang Qing, Wan Hong Wen, Zhang Chun Qiao, and Yao Wen Yuan and declared the Proletariat Cultural Revolution had completely finished. That day we could say was the day the Chinese people really obtained liberation. The people of the whole nation had suffered 10 years of hard times. Every family was wild with joy; they all went out into the street with festive singing and dancing. People raised their glasses and drank their fill, celebrating that the nightmare was over. At that moment all the people rushed to purchase alcohol in the shops, and all the alcohol sold out in one day. But, several years later, from the top to the bottom, China was still ruled according to "the existing guidelines" which Chairman Mao had formulated to handle affairs. The ultra-Left course and policy which had lasted about thirty years didn't change, and political life for the Chinese people was still moving in the same lethargic orbit as before. Nobody knew what the next step for China would be. The Chinese people raised their heads and waited as they looked forward to see if the light was really coming.

Two years passed, in December of 1978, the Central Committee of the Communist Party of China held the Third Plenary Session of the Eleventh Central Committee in Beijing, and the tribulation of the Chinese people had finally come to an end. Because on the 22nd of December, on the day the congress was over, the extra of the *People's Daily* used red colored print to publish in full the communiqué of the Third Plenary Session of the Eleventh Central Committee. This communiqué let the people of the whole country read the great news which they had never dared to think about for years. The communiqué said:

> "This plenary session was firm in criticizing the erroneous guideline of "two all", and decided to bring forward the end of the use of the slogan of "take class struggle as the guiding principle", deciding to finish the mass movement on a nationwide scale, and to transfer the focal point of the work of the Communist Party to the construction of the modernization of socialism and putting into practice the policy of reformation and opening. We put forward the mission of strengthening social democracy and the perfecting of the socialist legal system, and

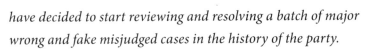

have decided to start reviewing and resolving a batch of major
wrong and fake misjudged cases in the history of the party.

   The Communist Party of China will be formed with the second
generation central leadership group with Deng Xiao Ping as
the key figure, to guide the Chinese people everywhere to come
into the new period of construction of the modernization of
socialism."

(Note: "Two all" is the abbreviation of the following sentence: "All the policies Chairman Mao made, we have to uphold firmly. All Chairman Mao's instructions, we have to consistently follow." This was the guiding principle of Hua Guo Feng the Chairman of China after Mao's death. He put it forward and carried it out from 1976-1978.)

Television was not common then in China, and on the street, each family had a communiqué in their hands. All the people were striving to be the first and feared lagging behind because the communiqué had a bearing on the destiny of all the people, so they read it carefully word for word.

That year Mama was 61 years old. As she read this communiqué she also, like hundreds of millions of people in the land of China, could scarcely believe her eyes. According to the words written down, it was not only the Cultural Revolution that was finished, but her 30 year nightmare also over completely! Would this terrible political movement never happen in China in the future? According to this, could the Chinese people have another kind of life? The most important thing was, according to the words written in the communiqué......

"Ai Ya, my son will be saved!?" Mama was delighted beyond measure; she said to anyone she happened to meet. "You see, the central leading body of the Party will review and resolve the wrong and misjudged cases. Great, it is great. My son has a hope; he will come out of prison."

One day when Er Jie came to Kunming to visit, mama not only shared her optimistic expectation that her son would get out from the prison soon but she also talked about me. She said, "The Party center certainly will handle the matter of the Rightist too. I do hope Gao Lin An can take away the label of Rightist. Xiao Ling and her child could then raise their heads and lead a normal life in society. Ai, I pray for it, pray it will happen as soon as possible. How many times I saw Ling Ling so miserable; she should not suffer disaster like this." While she was speaking, her emotions were overwhelmed with sorrow. Er Jie told me that Mama had been concerned about me all the time, but because Ge Ge's matter was such an urgent distress, she cannot give her attention on me.

On January 15th, 1979, she put the communiqué in her handbag, and together with one of Ge Ge friends who was called Lao Qiu, she went to the Yunnan Province Second Prison to visit Ge Ge once again. This time as she went to visit her son in the prison, she held something in her hand. It was a vacuum flask; she held it in her hand with great care the whole way. Ge Ge had already read through this communiqué in the prison, and he was in high spirits. That day when he was told that his mother had come to visit him again, he hurriedly ran back to the dormitory and changed his clothes, putting on the clean white shirt and gray trousers which had been pressed under his pillow for a month. After he changed his clothes, he immediately looked vigorous and energetic. He combed his hair, and walked to the reception room quickly.

"Mama, my day of freedom will be soon," he said excitedly when he saw her.

"Yes, soon, it is soon. Mama is waiting for the day to come when I will come to the prison to welcome you back home." As she was starting to talk, she was crying. While she was weeping, she handed the vacuum flask to Ge Ge.

"Open it and look at it; see what I have brought for you." After the policeman had checked it, the vacuum flask was passed into Ge Ge's hand. Nobody could have imagined what was in the vacuum flask which Mama had carried carefully the whole way.

"Mama, how did you get this!?" Ge Ge cried in surprise when he opened the lid. For this moment of celebration Mama had brought to Ge Ge a cup of ice cream, one of her son's great favorites.

Eating ice cream was a very luxurious thing back then. Five Jiao could buy a small cup. The big cup of ice cream Mama had brought for Ge Ge cost at least 2 Yuan. That day Mama insisted on doing it, and she went to Beijing Restaurant on Xiang Yun Street and bought it because this was the restaurant which made the best cold drinks and snacks in Kunming. Back then, no one could understand why a mother would want to send such a cup of ice cream to a person in prison. "Eat, you eat it now, so it will not melt completely," Mama said to Ge Ge who still stared at the ice cream blankly. Ge Ge focused on Mama, and he knew, at that moment, the best way to comfort Mama was to do as he was told. So he picked up the vacuum flask and started to eat the ice cream. While he was eating, he glanced at Mama, his eyes full of tears. And Mama smiled from beginning to end as she watched Ge Ge eat the ice cream, her head to one side, not saying a word. She fixed her eyes on Ge Ge and looked as if she was intoxicated with self-satisfaction.

This beautiful picture from real life made Ge Ge's friend Lao Qiu sigh with deep feeling, "Ah, this everlasting love between you and your mother, it was really a rare thing in the world! Everyone admired this." He knew that the hearts of both the mother and the son, at that moment, had lit up with the hope that they would meet at home before long. As a friend, he was indeed eagerly looking forward to seeing this day come as early as possible, and he told Ge Ge, "Old fellow, for your Mama's sake, straighten up! Victory is in sight!"

"Yes, for my Mama, I will hold on right to the end until I get out." Ge Ge answered his friend loudly with his gaze fixed on Mama's eyes.

Life in the prison was very hard; one day seemed like a year. And since Ge Ge had ceaselessly appealed his case, not admitting his guilt, he was regarded as refusing to accept rehabilitation, and he had suffered many terrible penalties and harassment in the prison. But, whenever people went to visit him in the prison, he never mentioned any of these painful experiences to them, he always forced himself to have a good attitude. Especially when he met with Mama, he always greeted her with a smile. He knew this was the only thing he could do to console his mother. She was so old and ailing just like a candle flickering in the wind. But now that the ice and snow were finally starting to thaw, he would stride out of the prison and go home soon.

He said, "I will try my best to render service to repay my mother's kindness; I will be with her every day at home." That day, Ge Ge was extremely excited as he was thinking of these things with great feeling, and he talked much less than normal with Mama. After he had eaten all the ice cream, Ge Ge licked his lips clean and said to Mama, smiling, "Mama, you don't need to come and see me here again. Next time, we will be together eating ice cream at home."

"Yes, Yes! Mama is waiting for your good news. Mama will get your room ready for you; I am waiting for you to come back home." For the first time, Mama showed a smile in prison and calmly waved goodbye to Ge Ge. In both of their hearts, the firm faith that they would meet again in the small room of An Ning Lane very soon had become the most eager expectation in their hearts. It certainly had also become the spiritual prop to help them to live well from this time on.

They lived to count the days and waited for the day to come with sheer focus. However, the thing they were expecting did not happen for a long time. Ge Ge could not come out of prison right away because there were too, too many wrong and misjudged cases during the Cultural

Revolution. From the cadres of higher rank to the common masses, the cases of innocent people locked up in prison, put under surveillance, and killed had indeed piled up like a mountain. Just in the Yunnan Provincial Second Prison where Ge Ge was, there were 3,500 political prisoners who were sentenced to over 15 years imprisonment! Because the rank of cadre took priority with the cases, when the time came for Ge Ge's case, it was already August of 1982. By then he had been in prison for a full 7 years! And our Mama had already passed away 3 years earlier, suffering from this heinous wrong and dying in her grief. She eventually could not wait for the day that Ge Ge got out of prison! The desire she had wished for that she could spend one year, one month, even one day with her beloved son living together peacefully would never come true!

One day in August of 1982, Ge Ge was called to go to the office of the prison. There were some people from the public security organization sitting there who told him, "After deliberating we have decided about your case. The original case was judged with too harsh a sentence, we will now change the original sentence to three years imprisonment and release you ahead of schedule. You have exceeded the term of imprisonment, today you can leave here." At 3 o'clock that day, Ge Ge walked out of the gate of the Yunnan Provincial Second Prison.

"Mama, I came out!" Ge Ge burst out into the air when he walked out of the prison gate.

"Mama, Mama, did you heard me? I have finally received my freedom." He was shouting out as if he was crazy.

Wearing the white shirt Mama had sent to him, with a shabby military bag on his arm, he made great strides towards the city. As he was walking closer and closer to the gate of his home, he could not control his emotions, he was trembling and tears covered his face, "Mama, dear Mama, why could you not wait for me to come back? Mama, Mama, where can I find you?" It was on that day that he formed the plan in his heart to file a lawsuit against his imprisonment and not stop until it was resolved.

"Not for three years, not even for only one day, should I have been put into prison!" he vowed. And for himself and for Mama, he would certainly get justice.

After 7 long years he again entered No.7 An Ning Lane, stepping through the threshold of his own home, and Ge Ge could not help bursting into tears. He saw that the display in his small room was as before, neat and clean. He knew that the last time after Mama had visited him in prison, she had fixed it up to welcome her son home. Walking into the small room where Mama had lived for most of her life, the old and shabby big bed where Mama had slept for over 20 years still in the same place, grayish white bedding, grayish white pillow which were just as in the past, but, where was the most familiar, the most intimate figure?

"Mama, Mama, I am coming back, where are you!?" Ge Ge threw himself on Mama's bed and cried out involuntarily. Suddenly, Ge Ge saw a very big plastic bag beside Mama's bed filled with many candy papers of various colors.

"What are these? Why are they here?" Si Jie told him that they were the wrapping paper from the fruit drops Mama had sent to him in the last few years. Since she was not allowed to take the candy papers into the prison, each month, when Mama used the family's whole ration of sugar tickets and brought the fruit drops back home, she would sit at the table, and peel off the wrapping paper from each candy one after another. They accumulated month by month, until there was such a large bag full of colorful papers. Si Jie told Ge Ge that Mama begrudged throwing away those candy wrapping papers and would say, "Whenever I see these papers, I know Lao Wu has some candy to eat in the prison, and he knows he has a mother who is thinking of him every day on the outside."

Ge Ge was very shocked by those words, he again experienced the deep love and concentrated attention Mama wanted to give him, "Ah,

Mama, Mama, my dearest mother, why did you not give me a chance to repay you!" Ge Ge raised a cry again and again. He was overwhelmed with sorrow. At that moment he understood completely why Mama insisted on sending some candy to him every month. It was because she wanted to use the only sweet thing she could find in the world to give to her son, to moisten her son's heart when it was in great pain. She didn't send sugar, but sent the fruit drops to the prison. It was clear that she wanted her son to take one each day, to take his mind off the hard days and nights in the prison.

Yes, in the prison where he was heavily guarded, in each day of lost freedom, when Ge Ge saw those beautiful candies, it was as if he saw Mama's soulful eyes every day. When he put the small candies into his mouth one by one and swallowed a tiny bit of sweet syrup, letting them go into his body, he tasted the sweetness and happiness of Mama's presence with him. It was this sweetness and happiness which piled up day by day and formed great strength, sustaining him at all times and supporting him to live undefeated in that hopeless situation until the day he finally came out the prison. Today, he wished he could hold his Mama's hands and pour out his heart, to reveal his innermost feelings in a steady flow to her. But there was no Mama, only the empty house; who could he pour out to?

"My dear Mama, you said that you were waiting for me to come back!?......"

"Mama, Mama, I am so sorry to you. The debt of gratitude I owe you, I can never repay you!"

"Mama, Mama, you have gone too early. You died so miserably!" That day, Ge Ge cried in grief in Mama's room for a long time. He went down on his knees by Mama's bed for the whole night!

That year, Ge Ge was 36 years old, and as Mama's eldest son, he had so many wishes to render service and repay his Mama. At that moment, all his wishes had vanished completely like soap bubbles, and this caused Ge Ge lifelong regret.

When Ge Ge came out of the prison, his girlfriend Xiao Kun soon came to him because she had waited for him all along. Everyone knew that when China was enveloped by the Red terror, of the people who came out of prison, only very few were fortunate enough to have a "yellow handkerchief" to call on.

(Note: There was a Japanese film which was called "The Happy Yellow Handkerchief" which was very popular in China. It was a story about a girl waiting for her boyfriend to come home after he was sent to prison. The famous words in the film during the time they were apart were when the girl told the man, "When you come out of prison, if you see a yellow handkerchief on the roof of my home, it means that I am still waiting for you.")

Ge Ge was one of these lucky people. Wasn't it a miracle? And this Mama had prepared entirely for Ge Ge by herself. My sister-in-law Xiao Kun told me, "It was because of your Mama, your Mama was so kind to me. When I thought of her, I felt I should not leave your older brother alone. I was not willing to make your Mama feel sad. I told her I would wait for him until he came out. What I promised your Mama, I am doing now."

Mama's deep and true love touched the conscience and won the sympathy of Xiao Kun. It enabled her to withstand the rumors and slanders in society, the loneliness and the cold shoulders of others, and sincerely wait for a political prisoner for seven long years. It meant Ge Ge could reunite with his girlfriend when he came out of prison and have a warm family very soon.

Writing here, I want to tell Mama to comfort her. Dear Mama, by your great blessing to Ge Ge, he came out of prison in the year of 1982 when the spring breeze was blowing in China. Lying in prison for seven years, he wasn't defeated by his unjust fate. When he came out, he was still a true man, and his body and mind were still healthy. Although he only had 5 Jiao with him, with the help of his brother and sisters, he started an undertaking. His first job was to ride a tricycle and sell soft drinks. He only could earn one Yuan a day. But, relying on his own efforts, very soon, in just one year, he got married and started his career. Later, he had a lovely daughter, and his career went very well.

For over 20 years after he came out of prison, Ge Ge has done one thing for you as well as for himself at all times. He wanted to redress and exonerate the grievances of the counterrevolution group in those years.

Time has passed and the situation has changed. Even the other people concerned with this case have already gradually faded from memory. They have made the best use of their time enjoying as much as they can, the rare and calm life in the land of China, not to concerning themselves with the past. But only Ge Ge still appealed courageously for truth, for righteousness, also for you, dear Mama. To persist for many years in doing one thing without flinching would be impossible. But he did. Mama, Ge Ge was doing this thing for you because he knew you really wanted to see it before your death.

Relying on this faith, Ge Ge worked with perseverance and went to court. If we count the date from his arrested, the time he spent on this case was 30 years! At last, on the 8th July of 2004, he received a "retrial decision" from the Yunnan Provincial Higher People's Court, which informed him: the case is turned into a retrial procedure. Waiting for another half a year, on the 31st of January in 2005, at 10 o'clock in the morning, in the re-examination court in the new building, the stately Yunnan Provincial Higher People's Court, the judge declared to the court:

"The case of Yan Mao Qi's counter-revolution is a framed-up, wrong case. I recall the original sentence, and he is acquitted." That day he received the final adjudication to redress and exonerate the grievance

504

of his case from the Yunnan Provincial Higher People's Court. This righteous piece of paper came really too, too late. It took 30 years!

What Ge Ge got in his hand was only a piece of paper, nothing else. He didn't get any economic compensation or even one word of "sorry" from any person of the government office. But, the final adjudication Ge Ge received was the greatest, most successful thing that Ge Ge had done for himself and for his Mama in the whole of his life. Because this was the final victory for a warrior and his mother who struggle and achieved, its value indeed is beyond measure! That day, Ge Ge said, he didn't have any special excited feelings; he only felt "the sky is very blue." Of course, for him and his mother, this day was the day which really dispelled the clouds and they could see the sun; they were restored to justice!

People often use "like father, like son" to describe those people whose features or personality was very much like their father. But in our family we could use "like mother, like son" to describe Ge Ge, because he is just like you, Mama.

That day, when Ge Ge held the final adjudication in his hand, the first person he thought about was Mama. Coming out of the court, he rushed to Mama's grave at once. He read through the whole righteous adjudication to Mama, even when it became late. He told Mama word by word, "Mama, my unjust case has finally been redressed and exonerated of all grievances. The day you wished to see has come Mama, and we were successful in the end."

"Mama, I was able to do all of these things, because I have you, I have you, such a firm and steadfast mother!"

Dear Mama, what you have given to us, not only the life, but also the confidence and support which was a massive rock that we could rely on in our life's journey. Upholding justice, undaunted by repeated setbacks, good character - all mothers in the world should endow on their children, and we really did get these from our Mama. The events of history did not allow us to receive a high level of education, but if asked where our wisdom and knowledge came from, we would say with one voice: it came from our Mama. We all believed the person who influenced us the most in our life was our Mama.

People often say, "A father's love is as a mountain, a mother's love is as the sea." But I want to say here, our Mama is the sea and also a mountain. When I recall the love Mama has given us, what she taught by personal example as well as verbal instruction, and think of the all things she has done for us, time after time, I feel it is amazing and unimaginable. Mama was such a small and weak woman. When she had a noble and rich life, she was not self-important or arrogant, when she had a poor and hard life, she did not feel inferior or despise herself. She always kept the same attitude and standard throughout her life; where did she store such huge energy throughout her life? Where did she store such huge energy? She simply was a fountain of love and strength which had an inexhaustible supply and always available for use!

MAMA'S FINAL YEARS
(1978–1979)

There are still some things I haven't finished relating about the final years of Mama's life, so let me continue to talk about them here.

After Ge Ge was sent to prison, Mama's social status changed to being the relation of a counterrevolutionary. One of her daughters had married a Rightist as well, so she became a person who had lost all social position and was despised and insulted by everyone in the community. She was treated with disdain by the neighborhood committee and her unit. Her every move and every action was watched, and she was under surveillance and reported on by the Gong family from the "proletariat" in the same yard. All of these things, she could bear silently. But thinking of her son with affection and worrying about her son in her heart, this was the calamity which incessantly oppressed her, causing her to lose her appetite for food and toss about in bed.

Da Jie and Er Jie could not come home on leave for a long time because they were busy with their jobs and had their children to look after; they seldom came to look in on Mama. Si Jie still worked in Cheng Gong; she also had two kids, so it was only on weekends that she could come and see Mama. When Jing Jia started her primary school studies, Er Jie took her back to the family. So the people who lived in the small room at No.7 An Ning lane, were Mama and Di Di - just the two of them. Di Di worked in shifts around the clock; sometimes he was home in the day time, sometimes in the night time. He understood that Mama was vexed in her heart, but he was always sparing with words, unable to say anything to comfort Mama. Yet, what he could do was to put all of his salary into Mama's hand each month and let Mama use it to manage the lives of two people. He knew that the meager pension Mama got she used for Ge Ge. If he worked in the day time, after work he never went anywhere; he always came home at once to be company for Mama. The two of them sat together to eat dinner, not speaking much, but they both treasured the time very much…. you pick out some dish and put it into my bowl, I pick out some dish and put it into your bowl….without saying a word but still communicating the affection between mother and son to each other. After dinner, one had a cigarette in their hand, lit by the other. They had a cup of tea, sitting together again quietly till late at night when they each went to bed. Mama was conscious that Di Di was timid and overcautious, so to protect him from thinking about Ge Ge's event again, she never allowed Di Di to go to the prison which was such a terrible place. On the 15th of each month when it was the day to go to the prison to visit Ge Ge, it was always Si Jie who undertook it.

During that period, the old woman "sister Ding" from the countryside would still come to visit Mama occasionally. This kind old woman was then over 70 years old. She was hunchbacked, all her teeth were gone, and she walked slowly. But if she came to our home to see Mama, she was sure to wear her best clothes and was sure to carry some of the best crops she had gathered from her field. By Mama's expression and looking at the cold and cheerless scene in our home, she was aware that there were some unlucky things which had happened in our family. Where were all the children?

But she never asked any questions. She only came to Mama for company and sat with her a little while and brought something she could give to Mama. That was all, and she was satisfied. She always came to look in on Mama one or two times a year. At the end of 1978, Mama did not see her for a long time. Mama thought maybe she was sick, or she could not walk the long journey to come to her. One day, Mama carried a bag of cake, first taking the bus to the east station, then walking about two hours to get to "sister Ding's" house. As expected, "sister Ding" was suffering from a serious illness; she had been keeping to her bed for months. As Mama was standing before her bed, both of them knew this might be the last time they would meet in their lifetime. The two old women didn't speak any words but held hands and cried together. Two months later, this kind old woman died in her home.

This was another legendary old sister who, like Er Yi Ma, connected with Mama's life. Afterwards I found out about some of the experiences of "sister Ding's" life. Earlier, her husband had died when she was 40 years old. She was also a chaste woman, and she remained a widow and brought up her daughter by herself and stayed celibate until her death. She never received an education, but she was such an honest and simple person. Without using any sweet words, she just used her unadorned actions to express her love to Mama and understood her state of mind and her tribulations. She was indeed a very good person, how I yearn for her!

In the final years of Mama's life, the people who often came to chat with Mama before or came to drop by and scrounge and eat, suddenly were much less. At No.7 An Ning Lane the visitors were few and far between. Since people were practical, they all knew at that moment that it was better to keep a certain distance from this family and not ask for trouble. The person who often came to sit beside Mama, to keep her company and talk with her a while, or to eat a meal with her, was only her sworn sister, Er Yi Ma. Back then, Er Yi Ma was retired, and for more convenient contact with Mama, she even found a small room in No.14 An Ning lane and moved into it. She met Mama almost every day.

I don't know why, but Er Yi Ma did not escape the cruel torment of life. Since she had the job in the pickle factory, she went to work laboriously there each day; she never dared to be absent any day, only wanting to get the 30 Yuan pay at the end of the month to support her whole family. Both of her hands were soaked in the pickles every day, the strenuous manual labor and moist working conditions destroyed her noble appearance and health rapidly. When she was just 50 years old, all her hair had already become totally white and her face has covered with thickly dotted wrinkles.

More than 10 years had passed, and just like Mama she had brought up her two sons into manhood, and they each had a job. She thought she could relax a little, but her older son was rather troublesome to her. This son looked handsome, and every day he wore a dark blue work uniform and carried a lunch box in his hand as he went to work; he always had a refined and courteous manner. Like the children in our family, Er Yi Ma could not supply tuition for him to study in the university, so after he finished high school, he found a job in the Kunming Nan Ba Chemical Plant and started to support himself. But, since the class status of his family was not good, from the first day he entered the plant, he was appointed to burn the boiler. Although he was capable, he could never be promoted, so he did the job of burning the boiler for over 10 years, The salary was very low and the intensity of labor was very high. After work every day, he was pitch-black from head to foot and even his hair was full of coal cinder. He felt he had gloomy prospects so he started to drown his sorrows in alcohol. Bit by bit he became too fond of drink, and finally it was unmanageable. Every day, the most enjoyable thing for him was excessive drinking. He could drink a whole bottle of liquor each time, and he used all of his salary for buying liquor each month. He became immersed in alcohol to numb himself. When Er Yi Ma came back home, she always saw the same scene every day. Er Yi Ma was gentle and soft and was never able to rebuke her son. As she looked at her son's behavior, she was only able to cry. She cried in front of her son, when she came to Mama to pour out her troubles, she could also only cry. Many times, Mama went to Er Yi Ma's place and talked with her son. Many times Mama and Er Yi Ma together held the hands of this son to patiently persuade him. He nodded his head and promised with a smile, but on the second day he would drink as before. Faced with the two old women who, with good intentions, urged him time and again, he once revealed his thoughts, "You don't need to persuade me at all; I am already incorrigible. I have been weary of my life for a long time. When I am drunk, I can forget reality. You let me drink, let me drink until I die."

"Oh, it is such a pity, he is so young. How could we save his life?" the two old women sighed with feeling but felt quite helpless, and could only watch him sink into vice. One day, a terrible thing finally happened. The oldest son of Er Yi Ma died of alcoholism. The doctor said his liver had been totally destroyed by the infused alcohol. It happened in 1976, he was then only 38 years old.

In those days, Er Yi Ma cried for days and nights. Mama was sad too, and they shed tears together. At the bitter end, it was these two old women who sent this young man to the mountain to be buried.

In those years, both families had misfortune again and again with one heart break following another. At that moment, the reason for Er Yi Ma to keep on living was her second son – the docile Du who was 8 years younger than his brother but a very sensible child. He had shown a natural gift for painting since he was a little boy, and several times he entered himself in an art examination but was not selected because he came from a black family. He gave up his art dream and went to a primary school to work as a teacher when he was 20 years old. He was refined in manner, had a cultured style of conversation, and he always gained the praise of our Mama. When he saw his mother suffering because her rebellious son had treated her so badly, he vowed to himself he would be very devoted to his mother so she could spend her later remaining years in peace. All the neighbors could see how this son took care of Er Yi Ma so attentively and adequately, almost like a girl. Even the way he talked with her was gentle and soft. In those times of adversity, this mother and son were admired by everyone. But when Er Yi Ma made mention of this son, she always shed tears saying, "I am sorry for him because he is looking after me, such a lonely and old woman. No girl can have a date with him, and it is impossible for him to get married either. Girls will look down on him." Yes, many years later Du and Er Yi Ma were living together in a small room of 10 square meters. Two single beds and one small table filled the room. They cooked on the step next to their door; they lived a simple and frugal life. Du was over 30 years old, but he still didn't have a girlfriend. He was very willing to live with his mother in this way, and they depended on each other for survival. Then and there, this honest and tolerant son was indeed the greatest blessing that God gave Er Yi Ma in this world. Er Yi Ma was closely related to and mutually dependent on Mama until the end. The second year after Mama died, she followed her younger sister and passed away from this world.

When our Si Shen was still living far away in Dali, she was also in her old age. The greatest blessing for her was her five children who always lived together in Dali with her. Nevertheless, the class status of their family caused them to suffer from unfair treatment too. None of her children received a high education, and each of them had to find a job and support themselves when they were very young. The third daughter of their family started to undertake a job as a woodworker when she was 16 years old, a job which usually only a strong man could handle.

I remember that Si Shen took her to Kunming in 1973. When she talked about this daughter with Mama, Si Shen started to shed sad tears, "The younger generation of the Yan family is now doing sweaty backbreaking labor. I often feel distressed, but how can I help her? To keep life going I have no option other than to let her continue to do it." Si Shen and Si Shu were university graduates, but their five children could never use their talents in the small town of Dali. They had to accept their fate and live a humiliating existence for years. At the end of the 1980s, without political stress, each of them finally cut a striking figure, and obtained well-deserved regard in society. I admire Si Shen's family because all the children showed their devotion to their mother, and Si

Shen had a peaceful life in her later years. Si Shen lived to be 87 years old and died from an unknown cause.

What sustained Mama to live firmly and persistently was waiting for her son to come back home; she waited for that with all her heart.

But from the day she had sent the ice scream to Ge Ge, day after day went past without any indication or information that Ge Ge would come out of prison. She was living with gritted teeth, anxiously looking forward with sheer desperation, expecting the day to come. But it would not come for a long time and too late for Mama!

Half a year had gone by, and Mama had become aware that this thing was not as simple as she thought. Ge Ge would not come back home within a short time, and she was in low spirits again. Si Jie often saw that Mama would not speak a word for hours; her eyes were brimming with tears. As she slept with Mama on the same bed at night, she often heard Mama coughing fiercely throughout the whole night unable to sleep. Sometimes, after she took some Chinese traditional medicine, her cough would ease a little, but Mama didn't have surplus money to buy medicine very often.

In those days, if she could not go to visit Ge Ge personally, Si Jie visited him, and she would bring back a small piece of paper from the prison. It was the receipt Ge Ge had signed after receiving the things the family sent to him. On the paper there was only Ge Ge's signature, nothing else, he was not allowed to write any other words on it by the prison. But, each time Mama got this paper in her hands, she always looked at it over and over. She wished there could be something more on it. This small piece of paper with Ge Ge's signature held together the endless lovesickness and hope between the mother and son for a long time. It almost became the spiritual prop to keep Mama alive.

During that period of time Mama was living in very poor circumstances. All of the non-staple foodstuffs were rationed, and she begrudged eating them, saving them and sending them all to Ge Ge.

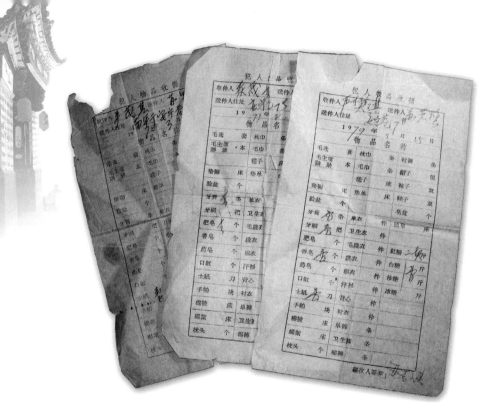

Some of the "Prisoner Receipts" Ge Ge signed after receiving things from mama.

She was also excessively anxious, and her health got worse and worse. Mama's body was lighter and lighter. She walked more and more slowly, and the sound of her voice was more and more gentle. She was simply so feeble she could fall down. Her physical and mental health and her economic situation all added to her extreme misery. The three older sisters could not bear to see Mama live like this; at intervals they would "deceive" Mama into going to their place to stay a while. But as long as she was away from Kunming, she would be distracted and restless because she always kept thinking about her son in prison. They had no choice but to send her back to the small room in An Ning lane.

Mama told them, "Let me, one person, be in a state of anxiety. I don't want you seeing my mood each day and feel bad with me. You send me home." Mama was this kind of person. She shared her happiness with others, but she kept all her suffering to herself. Throughout her life she liked to say, "A person should be Sheng Su." "Sheng Su" is in the Kunming dialect, and it means: you must be careful and strict with yourself; you should not bring any trouble to others. Mama was indeed a "Sheng Su" person for the whole of her life. She never expected to get anything from others. She was unwilling to add any trouble to others either. In her mind, her life was giving and commitment forever without receiving.

In the summer vacation of 1979, Er Jie sent her 12 year old son Bi Cheng to come and live with Mama for a month. Before she left, she handed over 5 Yuan to Mama. It was a month's cost of living for Be Cheng. Be Cheng remembered very clearly that even such a little money, Mama didn't receive it at once, and she told Er Jie, "If you feel embarrassed, you don't need to leave any money with me. I will take care of his life very well each day. You just set your heart at rest." She took the grandchild in for a month. He was growing up and his appetite was quite big, so it meant Mama would have to pay out much more, but his impoverished Po Po (grandmother) never refused. Mama was such a person. She always made allowances for others' difficulties, earnestly wishing she could share some of the load for others. With her children, she certainly wanted to share even more.

Da Jie and Si Jie's children often spent their vacation time with Po Po too. When they recall the times they lived together with Po Po, they felt very close to her, and they regretted that those nice times were too short. But, though it was short, many happy memories were still engraved on their minds forever and became the most indelible memories of their childhood:

"The dishes Po Po made, that was the most delicious food in the world."

"Every Spring Festival, Po Po would make a set of new clothes for me."

"The money Po Po prepared for us as a lunar New Year gift, she always changed them into new ones."

"Po Po often asked me to tell her something about our kindergarten and asked me to sing a song to her."

"I loved to sleep with Po Po ; Po Po would tell me an interesting story."

"Po Po always carried me in her arms and gave me a kiss and told me she loved me."

"I think with longing of Po Po; Po Po was the very best person in the world."

When the grandchildren were grown up, they often said these things with one voice.

I knew when Mama was with her grandchildren and enjoying the family happiness together was the happiest time for her. It would reduce some of the suffering in her heart. Therefore, I want to thank God, thank God that in the final years of Mama's life, he gave her those true earthly feelings that nobody could take away from her. Let her taste a little warmth and comfort in the boundless night of darkness and hopelessness. The small hands and childish smiles of her grandchildren must have wiped the tears off Mama's heart and brought her relaxation for a short while.

Jin Jia lived together with Po Po for about 7 years, the longest time with Mama amongst all of the grandchildren. During the time she lived together with Po Po, she and Po Po had established extremely deep feelings for each other. When she was 5 years old, I once asked her a question,

"Jin Jia, who is the person you like the most in the world?"

She immediately answered me without the least hesitation, "I like my Po Po the most." Afterwards, she soon said the following words, "When I am grown up, Po Po will become a child, and I will take care of Po Po very well." Her rich imagination and her simple words set off roars of laughter from us then, but, today, while I am writing these words down, I feel a lump in my throat; tears are forced from my eyes.....

Here and now, just like Jin Jia, I do wish Mama could really become a little child to give me an opportunity to take care of her very well!

However, the people who are the most passionate and self-giving in the world are called mamas and the people who are the most careless or easily selfish are the mamas' children. The way we treat our own mama doesn't show family devotion, only spending a little time to go and visit a few times a year. We brothers and sisters once said what presents each one of us would give to our Mama when we were grown up, but actually no one fulfilled their promise!

When I had just started to experience the hardship of being a mother, I needed to go to work and take care of a child by myself. I was busy each day. Mama had faded from my memory, or, I believed stupidly that Mama would never pass away quietly; she would be alive for ever...

On schedule, the summer of 1979 came; September was the season each year when a large number of fruit and vegetables came onto the market. As normal, Mama cleaned some of the pots which she used to put pickles in and dried them in the sun. She went to the fresh market at intervals, bought some low-priced chili, green vegetables, and eggplant and took them home, dried them in the sun, and prepared to make different tasty pickles. Now, she was waiting for the end of month to get her pension. She would then go to buy some aniseed and other condiments and buy some rice wine, then cut and mix these vegetable together and put them into the pots. Each year, these pots were full of different pickles Mama made herself and sent to her daughters who were not with her.

On the 19th of September, it was a sunny day. Mama went to the public bathroom and took a bath, and went to the barbershop and had a haircut. She changed into clean clothes inside and out, and with her hair cut short, she looked fresh and energetic. At about 3 o'clock, she came back home. She washed all her clothes she had just taken off and put them on the clothesline. After 4, she carried a hand basket in her hand and went to the fresh market in Wei Yuan Street again.

It was the beginning of autumn; it was the season Kunming people could eat wild mushrooms. The dealer from the mountain brought various fresh mushrooms and laid them on the ground to sell. All at once, Mama saw Gan Ba Jun. It was the one of the wild mushrooms which was a great favorite of hers. She hesitated a while, then she fished out 1 Yuan and bought 200 grams and bought two more vegetables. She carried the basket and went home. When she came home, she sat at the table and started to clean the Gan Ba Jun carefully. (Gan Ba in Chinese is beef jerky; Jun in Chinese is mushroom.)

Gan Ba Jun is rare among the wild mushrooms. Its shape is not like the common mushroom but looks like a small piece of black salted beef jerky, so it got this name from the people. I knew from when I was a little girl, this was Mama's great favorite dish. But Gan Ba Jun was the most expensive of all the wild mushrooms on the market, so Mama could not easily get it. And Gan Ba Jun was also difficult to clean because while it was growing, it was mixed up with some couch grass and mud. Before washing it, these must be picked out first.

I have helped Mama clean Gan Ba Jun in my childhood; I know it was not easy. After tearing them into thin pieces we would wash them time after time, if all the mud and sand were not cleaned away, they would not taste very nice when you ate them. But, it was worth going through this process. When the cleaned Gan Ba Jun was cooked together with some green pepper and garlic, it was really the tastiest food in the world. And the Gan Ba Jun Mama cooked was even more special because Mama's recipe was different from others. When she cooked Gan Ba Jun, she would add some chives, and sometimes some threads of ham. So it was not just the taste that was good, but while she was cooking it, the smell of the Gan Ba Jun would float in the air. When it was put on the table, it had several alternating colors. When you saw it you would immediately want to taste it, when you put some into your mouth, it was so delicious, simply one of life's great enjoyments.

That day, Si Jie's second son Xiao Rui was with Mama. It was also the first time in 1979 that Mama had bought Gan Ba Jun, so she was very excited. After she had cooked the Gan Ba Jun, she cooked another vegetable and a soup with bean curd. The grandmother and grandson together put the rice and dishes on the table, and set out three sets of bowls and chopsticks, they sat beside the table, and silently waited for Di Di to come home after work.

At 6:30, Di Di came home on time. The first words Mama said to him were:

"Today we have something tasty. I bought some Gan Ba Jun; come on, let's eat dinner." Mama lifted the plates which covered the dishes and filled three bowls with rice. They sat together around the table, and started to eat. They all first put their chopsticks into the Gan Ba Jun and ate the dinner together cheerfully.

It had been a long time since they had eaten such a good dish, and the three of them enjoyed the meal very much. Mama finished her first bowl of rice, and then she asked Di Di to give her a little more. When she held the bowl up, it seemed she felt as if something was wrong with her. She closed her eyes for a few seconds; then, suddenly, her head fell heavily onto the table.

"Mama!" "Po Po!" Di Di and her grandson didn't know what had happened to Mama. They were temporarily at a loss. They quickly carried Mama to her bed.

"Mama, Mama, what's wrong with you?" Di Di shook Mama and asked her loudly. He saw that Mama had closed both her eyes as if she had fallen into a coma. She could not speak, but her hands and feet were shaking. Di Di realized Mama was in imminent danger, but he didn't know what he should do. In this emergency all he could think of was to quickly go for Er Jie who was a doctor. He asked his nephew Xiao Rui to look after Po Po, as he speedily rushed to Er Jie's home on his bicycle. Because Er Jie's husband had been transferred to Kunming with his work, the whole family had just moved into the dormitory of the Kunming Engineering College where the brother-in-law had started his new post six months earlier. Back then no one in Kunming had a telephone in their home.

Going there and back, by the time Er Jie and Di Di had ridden their bicycles back to An Ning lane, it was already one hour later.

Before they entered the door, they heard the sad and shrill crying of the nephew Xiao Rui. Putting their bicycles aside, they quickly ran to Mama's bed. They saw that Mama's complexion was purple; she was short of breath and trembling all over.

"Mama, Mama, I am here," as Er Jie shouted to Mama, she held Mama's hand and took her pulse. When Mama heard the sound of Er Jie's voice, she opened her eyes and glanced at her, and both her hands firmly took hold of Er Jie's hands. While she was still slightly conscious, it seemed that she realized that her daughter who had the skill and knowledge of a doctor had come to save her life.

After checking Mama's pulse and looking at her eyes, Er Jie was aware that Mama was at her last gasp, so she decided to send Mama to the hospital for emergency treatment.

They borrowed a ladder from a neighbor, spread a quilt on it, asked Er Yi Ma's son to help, and then they used this simple method to hurriedly carry Mama to the nearby Kun Hua hospital. Her grandson followed them, running and crying ......,

When they arrived at the hospital, the doctor immediately gave Mama oxygen and started urgent resuscitation. At that moment, Mama calmed down for a while, and her breathing was smooth and steady. She had a normal complexion and looked as if she had fallen asleep. Everyone thought Mama could be saved. But it was only a little while, and she

"Mama, don't get excited, please be quiet, we are all beside you. If you have something to tell us, wait a moment and say it slowly." Tears covered Er Jie's face as she held Mama's hands and was close to Mama's face as she gently comforted her. But it didn't work; she saw that Mama was more and more agitated. It seemed she could no longer control her emotions, and she was crying for help, and wanted to say something. A few minutes later, she held both her hands up high again, and opened her eyes, she tried her best to sit up, but she couldn't do it. Suddenly, both her hands came down heavily, her head fell to one side, and she left the world peacefully.

I use the word "peacefully" to describe Mama's expression when she passed away because when I saw Mama the next morning, she gave me that impression. Tears and mourning would be no more, tribulation had passed. She had been relieved of all of the heavy loads and shackles. Having departed from this world, she looked really peaceful in a way that had never showed on her face during her life. It makes me believe that at that moment, Mama had flown into heaven; she was meeting Dad, whom she had yearned for day and night, and there they were hand in hand…

That morning when I heard the information about Mama's death, I cried and ran to Mama in the hospital, but she already slept on the ice-cold cement table in the mortuary.

As I fixed my gaze on Mama's face, which I hadn't seen for four years, my tears suddenly stopped …..

I could not believe my eyes, because Mama's appearance filled me with wonder: the face which was always covered with wrinkles and showed how she had experienced the many vicissitudes of life, at that moment was actually so smooth and sedate. Her forehead, which previously had perennial knitted brows, had unfolded, and her young features had appeared again. Both her eyes were naturally closed and her skin was softer than normal. The corners of her mouth had opened a little bit as if she was still breathing. Her hair was glossy, her clothing was neat and clean, and both her hands were across her chest.

I felt as if Mama were taking a nap in her clothing and had lain down silently on her bed just like any normal day at noon 20 years ago. Back then, when Mama came back home, she was very tired and would tell me, "Ling Ling, I am going to take a nap; wake me up in half an hour."

"Ok, Mama you go to sleep quickly." Whenever Mama slept, no one was allowed to make a sound; I wanted Mama to get a good rest for a little while. I would watch the clock carefully, not wanting to wake Mama up one minute early. But today, today I could not wait, I stretched out my hands to shake Mama's body as in the past. I wanted Mama to wake up.

"Mama, get up!" as my hands touched Mama and started to shake her as I had 20 years ago when I wanted to wake her up, I immediately found out that Mama was already ice-cold from head to foot. She could not hear my shouts any more, she could not sit up any more either.

"Mama, Mama, you rise up!"

"Mama, what's wrong with you. Mama, what's wrong with you!?"

"Mama, you answer me, you answer me!"

"Mama, why do you not speak, Mama, Mama, you speak; you open your eyes to see. It's Ling Ling here, I have come to see you, Mama, you; rise up!" I shook Mama with all my strength, crying and shouting madly at her…

"It's too late, Ling Ling, you didn't come to see Mama until today, it's too late!" without words, Mama's face told me clearly that this was her answer.

"Mama! I was wrong, I was wrong; you get up and listen to me! Please give me a chance, give me a chance, god, my god!" No matter how I beat my breast and stamped my feet in deep sorrow. Mama was still silent. She would never again hear my deep regret and my crying out. It was too late, too late. It was irreversible. Mama had utterly disappeared from my life in this way! Oh, why didn't I come to Mama until today! I was overwhelmed with sorrow... I cannot forgive myself...

Liu Jie came to see Mama too; she didn't have an opportunity to buy a radio or any other things for Mama because Mama didn't need to listen to the radio or need anything anymore. In Liu Jie's heart, she would regret this for her whole life.

When Si Jie heard this sad news, she ran home from Cheng Gong, she could not see Mama for the last time. She dared not believe that Mama had left her in this way; she sprang on Mama and said to her, "Mama, someone just gave me a few eggs; I was going to send them to you tomorrow; why did you not wait for me to come back? Mama!"

"Zu Ming, you and your children should eat those eggs; Mama feels grateful for your care and love," Mama would certainly say this to Si Jie.

Si Jie was very devoted, especially after Ge Ge's incident. To alleviate Mama's suffering she disregarded the political pressure and persisted in visiting Ge Ge in the prison, bringing great comfort to Mama. In the final years of Mama's life, Mama was fortunate to have such a daughter beside her.

Da Jie was teaching, so an urgent telegram was delivered to her in the classroom. As she opened it up she felt if she had been struck by a thunderbolt, and she could not control herself right away, "God, my poor Mama!" She could not help bursting into tears in front of all her students.

When she came to Kunming, grieving all the way, she pushed the door open, calling out to her Mama loudly. But in front of her was a black coffin. Mama, the person she missed every day had already passed away two days ago.

Ge Ge was told the sad news while he was doing physical labor.

"O, god, why did you let my Mama die in a situation where she had lost all her hope! .... my god!" he felt like the sky and earth were spinning round; he became ice-cold from head to foot. He insisted on going home to send Mama off. After a whole day of examination and approval, Ge Ge became the first prisoner who was approved to go out for the funeral of a parent from the Yunnan Provincial Second Prison. He was escorted by two policemen; they sat together in a police wagon and drove from the prison to the city. He was first taken to An Ning lane, where he rushed to the small room where Mama used to live and threw himself on his knees; he called out with his face on the small bed as if he was mad, "Mama, Mama, I am coming to see you, where are you, where are you?"

The simple and crude small bed was empty. The familiar figure of his loving mother had already vanished from this small home. He could never see her again, and he shed sad tears and could not control himself, "Mama, Mama, you promised me you would wait for me to come back!"

"Mama, my dear Mama, you didn't give me a chance to repay you. You didn't even give me a day!" The front of his clothes was soaked with tears.

He begged to go to the hospital to see Mama for the final time, so the police wagon drove to Kun Hua Hospital. When he stepped out of the police wagon, he was told that he was only allowed to stay with Mama for 10 minutes, and there were two policemen standing beside him. This terrible farewell ceremony deeply shocked everyone, including the staff in charge of the mortuary; there was a tense atmosphere in that place. The thousands of words he had wanted to pour out to Mama in the prison after being apart from her for four years, at that moment, Mama could not hear them anymore.

No, it is not necessary to say anything now. So Ge Ge stood silently mourning beside Mama, staring at Mama blankly, not saying any words, as he fixed his eyes on Mama for 10 minutes, until the tears dropped and wet the ground before him and obscured his line of sight. When the policeman urged him to leave, he fished out a white handkerchief from his pocket and covered Mama's face with it.

"Mama, your tribulation was too grave. You go; it is better you leave this extremely evil world," Ge Ge told Mama silently.

Oh, all of this was just as Mama predicted. She could not wait, could not wait for the day Ge Ge would come out of prison! This world could not tolerate this mother and son being interdependent, and it forced them step by step to finally be cruelly separated into two worlds.

"Mama, I can't even attend your funeral, please forgive me. I request you to take care of all Mama's funeral affairs," Ge Ge said those words to all of us there as the policeman forced him to go into the police wagon. When the police wagon drove out of the gate of the mortuary, Ge Ge was aware that this was the last time he would see his Mama. The most miserable sad and shrill crying in the world shook the skies and the land, "Mama, Mama, Ah, Mama......!" Ge Ge cried the whole way from the hospital to the prison.

The third day after Mama died, we her children and some of Mama's grandchildren went to a mountain and buried Mama. Based on what Mama had said before her death, she was not cremated, but put into a rough coffin. She was buried on a hillock looking towards the pines around Hei Long Tan located in the northern suburbs of Kunming on the 21st of September in 1979.

"Mama, have you really left the children you loved and gone to a far place?"

"Mama, Mama, where are you now?" the days after Mama had just passed away, I faced the sky and inquired ceaselessly. I wished I could get an answer from Mama.

I knew this world had done so much harm to Mama; it was not worthwhile for her to continue staying in this place.

But, at the last moment when her life was about to finish, she lifted both her hands and looked towards the sky time after time, struggling, and crying out, what did she want to say. I really want to know Mama's last desire. I have thought deeply about this every day.

Maybe my pure-hearted plea had touched Mama; one night Mama suddenly appeared in my dream. We two were sitting together shoulder to shoulder; she stroked my head as she used to do and asked me, "Ling Ling, do you really want to know the last words Mama wanted to say?"

I took hold of Mama's hands firmly, and nodded to her and said, "Yes, Mama, please tell me."

Mama cried out involuntarily with heartache upon heartache, "Mama is still worried about each of you!" as she was crying, as she raised up her hands, as if she was helpless, she kept facing the sky and soliloquized, saying the following words, "God, may you let me see my oldest daughter Zu Yin again, I didn't see her for about a year, I miss her so much!"

"Lao Er, my Zu Hui, you just came back to Kunming, you have three children, and Mama wished to help you settle down. Mama was unwilling to leave you!"

"Lao Si, Zu Ming, Mama thanks you for your care these years. The family needs you to take care of them in the coming days; your younger brother needs you to go to visit him. Mama requests you to do this for me!"

"Mao Qi, my dear son, when you were sent to the prison, I knew I could not live longer. Mama only wishes I could have lived two years longer, that I could send something to you once more. Mama feels so sorry for you. Mama promised to appeal for you, but it had no outcome. What day will you be out of prison? Your case of injustice is not settled. I indeed cannot close my eyes when I die. I have everlasting regret! Dear son, Mama wanted to see you one final time, you come soon!"

"Lao Liu, you thought that Mama didn't miss you and disliked you? You are wrong, you are such a clever and tricky girl, how could Mama dislike you? You should understand why Mama intervened in your marriage. It was because Mama loves you so much because Mama wished for you to have a nice family!"

"Ling Ling, Mama's youngest daughter, you slept with Mama in a bed, you grew up and suffered together with Mama each day, and Mama dreamed of you many times. There was a devil in the world which forcedly broke us up, a bitter mother and daughter. Mama was aware that you were living under stress, and Mama was always worried about you. Mama wished to see you, to see your son, but it was impossible…"

"Xiao Mao, my honest and kind son, you are the one person Mama was most anxious about! You don't even have a girlfriend, you will be alone by yourself from now on; how will you keep on with your life!? My youngest son …"

Mama was crying and shouting ceaselessly like the scene that Er Jie had described to me of the few minutes before Mama died. She struggled to hold both her hands high towards the sky. Mama continued to speak to me, "That day, in the final minutes when I struggled to sit up, I hoped that I could hold all of you, my seven children in my arms. Before I left this world, the thing I wanted the most, it was that god would give me a final chance, to let me stroke each of my children with my own hands …

"But my children, why are you living far apart from each other, why are you not beside Mama! Mama could not see you all!" Mama sobbed her heart out once more.

I sprang on Mama and held her emaciated body tightly in my arms, and cried out loudly just like her, "Mama, I am going to call all of the brothers and sisters to come back, you wait here," I told Mama.

"Oh, Mama has been waiting for this moment for so many decades, how are you able to do it? Mama cannot wait any more!" Mama looked up at the sky and shook her head as she answered me. After pausing for a little while, Mama continued to say to me, "Ling Ling, you must tell all of your brothers and sisters that without Mama, you should look after each other because this world is vicious, the family must stay united!

"Mama is going to see your Dad, my dear children; no matter how you have treated Mama, Mama will never bear grudges against you. Mama loves all of you forever!"

She finished all the words a mother should say to exhort her children before she went on a long journey. Now Mama seemed she would start on her way, so she kissed my head and broke loose from my hands, suddenly flying towards the sky.

"Mama, Mama, wait, don't go, wait a moment," I stretched out and wanted to hold Mama. I was crying out and rolled out of bed. I was aware that what I had heard and seen was a dream. I awoke from the dream, my pillow wet with tears.

"Mama, Mama, in this world from now on, will I really never have you in my life? No, No, I am not willing to let you go!" Just like in my childhood, I was so afraid and helpless and dark without my Mama. I could not suppress the sadness in my heart. I cried broken-hearted for the whole night. I really could not dare to believe that, in the days to come, in this world, I would no longer have Mama!? The thread of sunshine which had given me warmth for 28 years, would it really disappear forever, would it never exist again? I really didn't like my life without Mama!

That night, as the chill and solitude like a fierce wind enclosed me all round, I glanced right and left and felt so isolated and helpless. Once more, just like when Mama was not with me in my childhood, I cried out involuntarily again and again, "Mama, Mama, you come back, you come back!"

Mama had finished her tragic life of 62 years. She answered her curtain call peacefully and withdrew from the stage which was full of noise and clamor.

Mama toiled day and night for the whole of her life, but the only wealth she left after she died was 2.6 Yuan in the pocket of her underclothes.

The night after Mama passed away, lightning accompanied peals of thunder, and heavy rain fell from the sky. It fell for hours. Er Jie and Di Di didn't come back to No.7 An Ning lane from the hospital until 2 o'clock in the morning. And in the small room which had witnessed 26 years of Mama's suffering life, they cried broken-heartedly for the whole rest of the night.

Er Jie said, "That whole night it rained hard; even the heavens were weeping for our pitiful Mama!"

But I don't think so. I believed, that day, heaven was welcoming our Mama in a special way, welcoming the hero mother returning from earth to heaven.

Mama, you have experienced so much tribulation, you are so tired; you really need rest.

Er Yi Ma, who had become the sworn older sister of Mama, was deeply grieved by Mama's passing. And she only lived less than half a year after Mama died, also departing from the world which had treated her so unfairly. This loyal, intimate friend, who was interdependent with Mama for over 20 years, on her deathbed had one request. She wished to be buried beside her younger sister. Her son satisfied her desire and buried her beside Mama's grave in Hei Long Tan.

In 1985, we brothers and sisters moved Dad's ashes from Mian Shan to Hei Long Tan, and buried our parents together in one grave. We built a new grave for them and set up a gravestone at the front. From then to the present, the two of them have silently rested in peace on a green hill which is surrounded by a pine forest. We all go to visit the grave on Tomb-sweeping Day each year, because when we go there, we have a chance to call out "Mama" once more and to tell her all the things which have happened with us.

There is a famous Jewish proverb: "God cannot spare time from his main work to attend to each person, so he created mothers." I lift up my head and look at heaven and give thanks with a grateful heart. I thank God that he created such a perfect mother and chose to give her to us seven brothers and sisters. During the years when we depended on each other for survival together with Mama, she gave us warmth, and brought sunshine to us in the spring, summer, autumn, and winter of our lives. Our mother's love was just like nectar to moisten our hearts, like drinking sweet spring water in the desert, giving each of us wings, so we were able to go through the wilderness and desert of our life's journey step by step until today. The great love Mama gave to us was the most precious gift we have ever had in this world. Yes, because we had such a mother, each of our lives was rich and colorful. We indeed could be called the happiest people.

Dear Mama,

You are a unique masterpiece of God. You are extremely loved by me forever! I am looking forward to meeting you again in heaven.

POSTSCRIPT

The process of writing this book was much harder than I could have imagined. When I had to open up the memories covered with dust and once more face that time long past, it was really like uncovering a scar, the pain of again opening a wound. Only I know how difficult the feelings of pain I have had to bear. Why did the Yan family have to experience such heavy suffering? Why was the life that we and our Mama experienced so miserable? So many times, I have immersed myself into this sorrow and found it difficult to pull myself out. For days and nights I felt overcome and dizzy, whether sitting or standing. Tears accompanied me from the beginning to the end of writing the book.

But it was the process of writing this book which has given me an opportunity to write down "Mama" - this affectionate word - thousands of times, and at the same time, while I was writing these words, I could call out "Mama" as much as I liked. For 30 years I hadn't called out the name "Mama" time after time like this. When I called her, I was excited as well as grieved. Sometimes, I felt that I was not writing but having a heart to heart talk with her; it was like Mama was sitting beside me. I could feel her breath and see her tears. So I have to say, this writing has given me a rare experience of happiness and has made me so cheerful. My mother's love that I hadn't experienced for a long time was like happy lightning; it touched me profoundly over and over. Sometimes I really could not refrain from trembling. I have had three years that were like being together with my dearest Mama. This has been another of the warmest times in my life.

It is hard to believe that the time is going so fast. It has been 30 years since Mama passed away. Our small household of the Yan family, Mama's seven children, has already gradually increased into a big family with 46 family members. In 1996, Da Jie and her husband retired and moved back to Kunming after they had worked hard in the education sector in the small town of Wen Shan for 40 years. Since then, our whole family often sees each other and reunites in Kunming. During these 30 years, all of our family members - Mama's children, grandchildren and great-grandchildren, as well as the hundreds of millions of people in the land of China, are experiencing a gratifying change in our homeland. We finally have had some of the good life we never dared to think about 30 years ago. Such a life, for many Chinese who didn't experience the life of the past, may not be satisfying, but because we contrast the present with the past, we know that those 30 years compared to the recent 30 years were extremely different.

However, the biggest regret in our hearts as we sigh with feeling that our Mama passed away too early, is that she could not experience such good times even for only a few days. If Mama didn't have to be anxious for the basic necessities of life, if Mama didn't have to sleep in that small dark room with a leaking roof any longer, if Mama's nerves, which were stretched tight and filled with alarm for years, could relax a little... The biggest wish for all of us was for Mama, who loved jolly times, to have been with all of her children and grandchildren, reunited to enjoy meals together, to talk together, and to laugh together in harmony...

We all know this was what Mama would have liked the most. These are not extravagant things but are what any mother in the world would enjoy. Before the end of her life, why didn't she have the right to enjoy this for even one day!?

Ge Ge has had a secret regret throughout his life because he did not have a chance to serve and repay his loving mother.

Mama worried about me. Her heart could not relax until she eventually died. At the end of November 1979, we received the "redressing the Rightist notice" for Gao Lin An from the Central Arts Academy in Beijing, but because it was a few months late, we could not let Mama know this news. It was such a pity and has made me sigh deeply throughout my whole life.

Over the past 30 years, I always think of Mama, and it has never weakened with the passage of time. I cannot explain why, but as I get older, my love for her is growing stronger and stronger. So many times I dream of Mama when I am sleeping. I think of Mama when I see certain scenery, I understand Mama when I read certain stories describing a mother's love, and I connect with Mama in my mind when I set eyes on a certain woman who is suffering persistently and dauntlessly. Mama's lovely voice and happy countenance, all the things Mama has done for us seven children, each detail, causes me to think about this deeply.

One autumn afternoon last year at a chrysanthemum show in Da Guan Park, I saw a kindly old lady who was slowly enjoying the sight of the chrysanthemums. She was surrounded by her children and grandchildren. She was short and small but was particular about her dress and looked very tasteful. Among the brilliant purples and reds of the flowering shrubs, the old lady was smiling. Sometimes she lowered her head and concentrated her attention on a flower; sometimes she put her nose close to a flower to smell as if she wanted to inhale the fragrance of the flower into her heart. The old lady's manner, the old lady's behavior looked like our mama who loved flowers so much. I stared at the sight before my eyes. I don't know why tears fell quietly from my eyes. At that moment, my biggest impulse was to rush to her and hold her closely in my arms and call loudly, "Mama!"

"If only the wild goose is still alive, the young wild geese would feel happy; if only the parent is still alive, the children would feel happy..." This is part of a verse in an old folk song. People who still have parents maybe cannot completely understand the meaning of "happy" in that verse. But for me, losing my father at four years old and having lost my Mama for a long time now, I immediately sigh with deep feeling at the meaning. I always admire those people who can be interdependent with their parents for a long time. Without Mama, my happiness is much less. Now Mama is only a person hidden deep in my heart.

I know I have a shallow knowledge and small talent and a clumsy style of writing, and I should not overestimate my strength to write a book. But I also know my mother was so insignificant and lowly, who would naturally be forgotten by people and history if I don't share her life with the world.

I want to sincerely thank Mrs. Liu Yi Jie, the chief editor of China International Culture Publishing (HK). It was she who gave me her affirmation and encouragement when she had just read through the first draft of this book. With her deep love and care, this book finally could be formally published.

"It withers and falls and becomes mud, ground into dust, it is still as sweet-smelling as before." The flower Mama loved the most in her life was the plum blossom. Lu You wrote down this sentence in his poem "Praise of the Plum Blossom." I think it summarizes the whole of my Mama's life, short but uncommon. (Lu You (1125-1210), a famous poet in the South Song Dynasty of China.)

Many years have flowed away, and Mama has not been beside me for a long time, but her quiet elegant sweet smell still fills the air? I can still feel that I am together with her every day. Since her sweet smell is just as before, her sweet smell will last forever.

Yan Ling Ling - Mama's youngest daughter
First draft September 2006
Revised September 2009
English translation first draft July 2011 and revised February 2012 and again July 2012